China's Economy:

Theory and Practice

中国当代经济理论与实践

张建武　邱依婷　宋晖　唐静　主编

中国社会科学出版社

图书在版编目（CIP）数据

中国当代经济理论与实践：China's Economy: Theory and Practice:
英文/张建武等主编. —北京：中国社会科学出版社，2021.12
ISBN 978-7-5203-8915-0

Ⅰ.①中… Ⅱ.①张… Ⅲ.①中国经济－研究－英文 Ⅳ.①F12

中国版本图书馆CIP数据核字（2021）第163198号

出 版 人	赵剑英
责任编辑	王 衡
责任校对	朱妍洁
责任印制	王 超
出 版	中国社会科学出版社
社 址	北京鼓楼西大街甲158号
邮 编	100720
网 址	http://www.csspw.cn
发 行 部	010-84083685
门 市 部	010-84029450
经 销	新华书店及其他书店
印 刷	北京明恒达印务有限公司
装 订	廊坊市广阳区广增装订厂
版 次	2021年12月第1版
印 次	2021年12月第1次印刷
开 本	710×1000 1/16
印 张	30
字 数	468千字
定 价	158.00元

本书主要作者

张建武　　邱依婷　　宋　晖　　唐　静　　杨　宇
官华平　　姜　巍　　李翠兰　　Danish　　吴周恒
刘　琳　　刘　芹　　张晶晶　　唐　凯　　田云华

Preface

China's Contemporary Economy: Theory and Practice comprehensively introduces various aspects of China's Economy, concentrating on describing the primary institution reforms and industry development of China's economy since the reform and opening-up. The book generally presents theories and practices since the reform and opening-up in separate part. The book combines various types of macroeconomic and market-oriented economic theories such as Marxist Political Economy, Socialist Market Economy, Government and Market. According to the previous theories, the book set out from China's Industrialization, further introducing Reform and Development of Chinese Enterprises, Rural Vitalization and Poverty Alleviation, The Opening-up of China under Economic Globalization and so on, which are related to actual practices in the process of China's economy development. The book simultaneously concerns on the balance between historical practices and theories conducted in the past decades since the reform and opening-up and expected actions towards a sustainable China's future economy, covering the global economy. ***China's Contemporary Economy: Theory and Practice*** take a global approach to the combination of theories and practices based on the entire history of China's economy development, uniquely putting forward many methodologies like the formulas of calculating the currency and the amount of surplus value.

The first chapter is written by **Huaping Guan**. This chapter introduces the significant proportions of Marxian Economy theories and divides it into three different stages. The initial argument is the development and renewal of Marxian Economy theories. Specifically, it gives detailed description of Marx's Theory of Surplus Value. This chapter sketches the basic principles of Marxist political economy and its practical experiences in China, using numerous numbers of concrete examples. The author of the second chapter is **Wei Jiang**, particularly explaining the developing progress of China's industrialization. In this chapter, you can get involved in the knowledge of historical development of China's Industry and the evolutionary orientation in China's future industrialization. This chapter also delves into sketching the three driving forces of economic development in China's industrialization. In the third chapter, **Cuilan Li** demonstrates each key point and its influence during every phase of the transition from planned economy to market economy. This chapter additionally analyzes how real estate market reform, along with the reform of monetary market, synthetically affects China's economy. It also highlights the complete course which western enterprise system attempted to integrate into the socialist market economy, leading to a innovatively modern enterprise system. The fourth chapter is written by **Danish**. In this chapter, he provides three aspects about urbanization. He offers an overview of Chinese urbanization and the benefits, accompanied by the issues about emerging challenges (costs) of Chinese urbanization. The conflict between current urbanization progress and emerging challenges can be studied in the third part of this chapter when Danish concentrate on introducing new urbanization policies and remaining challenges. The author of fifth chapter is **Yu Yang & Yiting Qiu**. This chapter specifically promotes an understanding of rural revitalization and poverty alleviation, containing a brief overview of poverty alleviation in rural areas. It touches China's rural policy and rural agriculture subsidy with several prominent tools complied in real-life cases. This chapter also introduce current regulations and institution about land in different using. A particular focus is on rural industry, education and environment protection in this chapter. In the sixth chapter, **Zhouheng Wu** raises a introduction about macroeconomic performance and policy. In this chapter, it provides description of Chinese macroeconomic performance in different history stages, Chinese current monetary system, and Chinese current fiscal policy system. In the seventh chapter, **Hui Song** has intended to introduce the optimizing doing-business environment in China. In this chapter, the overview of doing-business environment in the world about new problem and corresponding solutions is discussed. Both new stage of China's urban doing-business environment as well as business environment and entrepreneur's willing are combined to analyze. In the eighth chapter, **Zhouheng Wu**, the author of this chapter, concerning about the China's economic transformation towards a substantial future, makes an abstract about the rapid growth of China's economy since 1970s .This chapter also contains the factors restricting the rapid increase of China's economy, the problem and corresponding solutions. It also offer the advantages and traits about high-quality economic development, defining China is putting more weight on the quality of economic growth. Based on the previous introduction, author further discuss about the future restructuring measures on the current economic structure to achieve longer-term sustainability in economic development. As for the nineth chapter, **Qin Liu** tries to address the global economic governances. In this part, it set out to introduce the supervision to international trades between the United Nations and World Trade Organization. It additionally arranges to argue about the possible questions and corresponding solutions in international supervision, the direction and orientation model of reform in global economic governance. It also suggests the functions of financial systems, leading to the guidance about methods to control the financial risks in a reasonable range. The tenth chapter is written by **Lin Liu**, about the employment and income distribution in China. In the next three chapters, they are written by **Jingjing Zhang, Kai Tang, Yunhua Tian** in turn. All of them minutely accomplish their studies and make a cooperation to enrich the whole book, providing more relevant research achievements in the final of the book.

Contents

Chapter 1

Basic Principles of Marxist Political Economy

Marx and Engels use dialectical materialism and historical materialism to establish a theoretical system that clarifies the laws governing the production, distribution, exchange, and consumption of material materials at all development stages of human society. Marx believes that the economic foundation determines the superstructure; the development of productive forces will promote the evolution of production relations, and the production relations will also affect the productive forces.

Marx adhered to the theory of labor value. He discovered the duality of labor contained in the duality of commodities: specific labor creates use value, and abstract labor forms value, making the nature of value scientifically explained. Marx discovered that the value created by the capitalist using the labor force of the hired laborer over the value of the labor force itself was the true source of "surplus value", and founded the "surplus value theory", which laid the cornerstone of Marx's economic theory.

Marx comprehensively examined the reproduction of total social capital, and divided social products into two types of production materials and consumption materials in physical form, and divided them into three parts: constant capital, variable capital, and surplus value. Based on this, in the above, the conditions for the realization of simple reproduction of capitalism and the expansion of reproduction of capitalism are analyzed, and the profound contradictions in the realization of capitalist value and surplus value are clarified. Marx analyzed the entire process of the capitalist economic movement from essence to phenomenon, clarified the process of value conversion into production price and surplus value into profit and average profit, and further clarified the surplus value in industrial capitalists, commercial capitalists, borrowing capitalists and division between landowners. Through a comprehensive analysis of the economic structure and economic movements, Marx proves the inevitable economic crisis and came to the following conclusion: the contradiction between the concentration of the means of production and the socialization of labor must reach an incompatible with its system. At this point, labor and management faces sharp confrontation.

The Communist Party of China led the people of all ethnic groups in the country to victory in the New Democratic Revolution and the establishment of People's Republic of China. Under the guidance of Marxism, great socialist construction has been carried out. Under the strong leadership of generations of leaders, we have concluded a socialist way with Chinese characteristics that suits China's national conditions and achieved great success in economic and social construction. China has become the world's second-largest economy and the largest trader of goods. At the same time, 5G communications, high-speed railway systems and other high-tech innovation capabilities have led the world. China has entered a new era. It will be guided by Xi Jinping's thoughts on socialism with Chinese characteristics in the new era and adhere to the five development concepts; continue to closely integrate the basic principles of Marxism with Chinese practice, carry out theoretical and practical innovations, and create a more brilliant socialist construction cause.

1.1 Overview of Marxist Political Economy

1.1.1 Production of Material Information

The production of material information is the basis for the survival and development of human society. The production of material data refers to the process in which laborers use labor data to process labor objects according to their intended purpose, and change the shape or nature of labor objects to make it suitable for people's needs. The production of material data must have three basic elements: labor of the worker, labor data, and labor object. ① Labor of the worker: A person with labor capacity and labor experience has a purposeful activity in the production process. Among them, labor refers to the labor capacity of a person; labor refers to a person with labor capacity; labor refers to the exertion of a person's labor capacity. ② Labor data: All material data that people use to transmit their mental and physical labor to the labor object, mainly referring to production tools. It also includes all other means of production except labor objects and production tools, such as buildings and roads. ③ Labor object: the object of labor processing. The means of labor and the objects of labor are called means of production, which are indispensable material conditions for people to engage in production. Only by combining with the means of production, workers can produce and create material wealth. Objective factors for the production of material information. Whether it is a primitive society with very low productivity or a modern society with relatively developed productivity, people's labor process must have these three basic elements. Without any of these elements, production cannot be carried out. In addition to the two basic elements of labor and means of production, factors such as management and science and technology also play an important role in the production process.

(1) Two Aspects of Production Methods

In the process of producing material data, people must obtain all types of material data they need from the natural world and have a relationship with the natural world, thereby forming social productivity. The production of material information is not the isolated production of a single person. The collective nature of human production activities determines that people must also have relationships with each other in the production process, thereby forming a social production relationship. The material production of any society includes both productivity and production relations.

Ⅰ Productivity

People's ability to conquer nature, transform nature, and produce material materials reflects the relationship between man and nature.

1. Measurement: Labor productivity, that is, the number of products produced during per unit time.

2. The composition of productivity. Includes human factors and physical factors: workers' labor and means of production. The laborer is the main body of the production process and the leading factor in productivity. Laborers create production tools, use and improve production tools, and increase the efficiency of production tools. The physical factor refers to the means of production. Among the means of production, production tools play the most important role. Advanced production tools can reduce human labor intensity and save time. It is the most important indicator

of the development level and development status of social productivity. It is also the main symbol of dividing the economic era. Human society has gone through four economic times. Hunting and gathering economy (hereinafter referred to as "harvesting economy") (stone tools), agricultural economy (ironware), industrial economy (mechanization), and information economy (PC). Science and technology also played an important role in the development of productive forces. Science and technology are systematic experiences summarized by people from production practices and scientific experiments. Marx believes that "science and technology are also included in productivity". Deng Xiaoping proposed that "science and technology are the primary productive forces". Science and technology will penetrate the means of production and labor capacity, improve people's ability to transform and conquer nature, improve and perfect production tools, improve labor skills, increase labor productivity, and make the same amount Even fewer workers can produce larger quantities and higher quality products in the same amount of time. It can be considered:

$$\text{Productivity} = (\text{workers} + \text{labor data} + \text{labor objects}) \times \text{science and technology} \qquad (1.1)$$

II Production relationship

Production relationship: The relationship between people during the production process. There are two levels of production relations: narrow and broad. The narrow production relationship refers to the relationship that occurs in the direct process of acquiring natural resources and processing. Such as the relationship between managers and workers in the enterprise. Generalized production relationship, the relationship formed from the process of obtaining natural resources to the final consumption of products produced by these resources. In the absence of money, people often obtain relevant products through distribution first, and then obtain the products they need to consume through exchange. This production relationship, which includes production, distribution, and consumption relations, is a generalized production relationship. The research object of political economy is the production relations in a broad sense including the production relations in a narrow sense. Production relations are the most basic relations in human social relations.

(2) The Relationship between Production Relations and Productivity

Productivity determines production relations, and production relations affect productivity. When the production relationship meets the needs of the development of the productive forces, it can promote the development of the productive forces, otherwise it will hinder the development of the productive forces. At this time, the production relations will change to adapt to the development and changes of the productive forces. Whether the relationship between people in a company is harmonious can promote or inhibit productivity.

(3) The Relationship between Economic Foundation and Superstructure

The economic foundation is the sum of production relations, that is, the sum of people's production, distribution, and consumption relations constitutes the economic foundation of society. The superstructure is a political, legal system and social ideology built on the economic foundation and adapted to the economic foundation. The economic foundation determines the superstructure. The superstructure acts on the economic foundation. The superstructure serves the economic foundation. When the superstructure adapts to the economic foundation, it promotes social progress, otherwise it hinders social progress.

Marx summarized the rules of the development of human society as the process of continuous development and evolution of the social structure composed of productivity-production relations (economic foundation) superstructure. In this process, productivity is the most active and revolutionary factor. It is the determining force, and the determining role of productivity is transmitted to the superstructure through the production relationship. At the same time, the superstructure's reaction to the production relationship affects the development of productivity through the reaction of the production relationship to the productivity. It is generally believed that the research object of political economy is towards undestanding of production relations and its development law. But it is not an independent study of production relations, but research of production relations and their development laws in the process of contradictions between productivity and production relations, economic foundation and superstructure.

1.1.2 Economic Attributes of Goods and Labor

(1) Two Factors of a Commodity: Use Value and Value

Use value: the usefulness of the commodity, that is, the attribute that the commodity can meet people's certain needs. The nature of use value: First, the use value of a commodity is determined by its natural attributes (not subject to human thought and will), and is determined by the physical, chemical, biological, and other attributes of the item. Various articles have different natural attributes, can meet people's different needs, and have different use values. For example, food can meet people's needs for nutrients, houses can meet people's needs for shelter from the wind or rain, and machines can meet people's needs for production activities. Books can meet people's spiritual and cultural needs. Second, it must be the use value of labor products. For example, the use value of sunlight in the natural world can only be the use value of general items. Use value is not unique to a commodity, but any commodity must have use value. Third, the use value of a commodity is produced for people other than the producer, not for the producer's own consumption needs. Commodities must be exchanged to transfer use value to those who need it in society. Use value is the material bearer of exchange value. Fourth, the use value of commodities reflects the relationship between man and nature, and does not change with changes in social production relations. For example, wheat, whether produced by serfs or hired workers, has a use value that meets human nutritional needs, and it will not be different. In other words, the use value of goods does not reflect a particular social production relationship.

Exchange value: Once the items with use value enter the market for exchange, they have exchange value. The exchange value is first expressed as a quantitative relationship or proportion in which one use value is exchanged with another use value. For example, a farmer exchanges 20 kg of millet for another farmer's 8-foot cloth, and the 8-foot cloth is the exchange value of 20 kg of millet.

Value: Why is the exchange value of 20 pounds of Xiaomi equal to 8 feet of cloth or a hoe? What determines the exchange ratio between different commodities? Marx believes that the production of commodities consumes a certain amount of human brainpower and physical strength. Such mental and physical expenditures are ordinary human labor with no difference. This labor is homogeneous and can be compared in quantity. General human labor condensed in commodities is value. As long as labor is added and water is processed into mineral water, it has value and can be exchanged with other commodities. Different commodities contain different values. The values are qualitatively the same. Only the difference in quantity can be compared with each other in terms of quantity. The reason why commodities with different use values can be exchanged with each other in a certain proportion is precisely because they have condensed as much human labor.

The nature of value: First, value is the social attribute of goods. It embodies the social relationship of exchange of labor among commodity producers. Second, the value is realized after the goods are sold.

The relationship between value and exchange value: The value of a commodity is inherently abstract and cannot be manifested by itself. Performance can only be achieved by swapping with another commodity. Exchange value is the external concrete manifestation. Value is the basis of exchange value, and exchange value is just a manifestation of value.

The relationship between value and use value: Commodities are opposites of value and use value. Unity is indispensable. Use value is the material bearer of value. There is no value without use value, and it will not be a commodity, such as waste products that appear in the production process. Although it consumes labor, it has no use value and cannot be used for exchange, so it cannot be a commodity. There is use value but no value can not become a commodity, such as air sunlight, is not a product of human labor, does not have value, so it is not a commodity; there are also some things that are both labor products and use value, but not for exchange but What is used for own consumption is still not a commodity. Therefore, it must have both use value and value as a commodity. Opposition is manifested in not being able to possess at the same time. A party as a commodity exchange cannot obtain both the value of the commodity and the value of the commodity at the same time. To realize the value of the commodity, it is necessary to surrender the value of the commodity. The key to this contradiction is the smooth exchange of goods.

(2) Duality of Labor-Specific Labor and Abstract Labor

Specific labor: Different commodities have different forms of labor to produce them. For example, the production of bread requires the labor of a baker. They use tools such as ovens to process raw materials such as flour to produce bread. In order to produce goods that meet various needs, people have to carry out various specific forms of labor. Labor performed under specific forms is called concrete labor. Specific labor creates the use value of commodities.

Specific labor is not the sole source of the use value or material wealth it produces. Only when specific labor is combined with natural material can it create use value. Without land minerals and other natural materials, specific labor cannot create any use value. Therefore, the British scholar William said that "labor is the father of wealth and land is the mother of wealth". Land here refers broadly to natural matter. Therefore, specific labor reflects the natural attributes of labor, reflects the relationship between man and nature, and is an eternal condition for the existence and development of human society.

Abstract labor: Although the labor for the production of various commodities differs in specific forms, they all consume human mental and physical labor. This kind of indiscriminate general human labor aside from the specific form of labor is abstract labor. Abstract labor forms value, concrete labor production and use value, and abstract labor production value. Different specific labors are qualitatively different and therefore cannot be quantitatively compared. Abstract labor condensed in different commodities is qualitatively the same, only quantitative difference. The reason why various commodities with different use values can be compared and exchanged with each other is because they are all condensed with abstract labor and have value. Specific labor and natural materials together constitute the source of use value. Abstract labor is the sole source of value. Abstract labor, as a value entity, is condensed in commodities and cannot be seen or touched, and can only be manifested in the process of commodity exchange. It reflects the social relationship between people and is the social attribute of labor.

The duality of labor determines two factors of the commodity: specific labor creates the use value of the commodity, and abstract labor forms the value of the commodity. The doctrine of the duality of labor was first discovered by Marx, who himself saw it as "a hub for understanding political economy."

(3) The Value of the Commodity

Individual working hours and socially necessary working hours. The value of various commodities is qualitatively the same, and they are all general human labor condensed in the commodity. The magnitude of the value of the commodity is determined by the general human labor condensed in the commodity. The measure of the amount of labor is labor time, and the amount of value is measured by the labor time it takes to produce a commodity. Some people are more skilled in producing the same kind of goods, some are less skilled, some use more advanced tools, and some have less advanced supply equipment. The labor time consumed by various producers varies. Individual labor time, labor time (*t*) required by a single commodity producer to produce a unit of merchandise. Socially necessary labor time, the value of a commodity is determined by the average of the individual labor hours of the various producers who produce the commodity. This average is called the socially necessary labor time, and the average labor time for all commodity producers to produce units of goods. (*T*) Calculation

formula $T = \dfrac{\sum q_i t_i}{\sum q_i}$: (i = A, B, C ...)

Table 1-1 Calculation formula of average working time

Production conditions	Product quantity (weight)	t	Calculation (weighted average)	T
A	80	8		
B	30	4	$T = \dfrac{80\times8+30\times4+10\times2}{80+30+10} = \dfrac{780}{120} = 6.5$	6.5
C	10	2		

The socially necessary labor time is strictly defined as the time required to produce a certain use value under the average production proficiency and labor intensity of the society under the normal production conditions of the existing society.

The so-called normal production conditions in the existing society refer to the current level of technology and equipment that has been reached in the production of most products in a certain production sector. If the annual production of cotton yarn in the whole society is 1 million pieces, of which 800,000 pieces are produced by textile machines, and only 200,000 pieces are produced by hand spinning wheels, then the use of spinning machines is the existing social normality of the cotton spinning sector. Production conditions.

Under the normal production conditions of the society, each worker who produces the same commodity has different labor proficiency and labor intensity. In the same working time, skilled labor and high-intensity labor can create more value than unskilled labor and low-intensity labor. The amount of value is directly proportional to the necessary labor time of the society.

Socially necessary working hours are essential for commodity producers. If the individual labor time of the unit of production of the commodity producer is higher than the socially necessary labor time, the excess labor cost will not be recognized by the society, and it will not be compensated. It will be at a disadvantage in market competition, and will lose money or even lose money, bankruptcy. If the individual labor time of a unit of goods produced by a commodity producer is lower than the socially necessary labor time, and the commodity producer still sells his goods according to the value determined by the socially necessary labor time, he will be in a favorable position in the competition and can get more gains. Therefore, the necessary labor time in society stimulates the producers to improve their technology, increase labor productivity, and promote the development of social productivity, which plays a very important role in the development of the commodity economy.

(4) Changes in the Value of Commodities

Definition of labor productivity: the number of products produced per unit of time or the time it takes to produce a unit of product. The value of a commodity is determined by the socially necessary labor time to produce it. However, the socially necessary labor time is not fixed but changes with changes in labor productivity. Therefore, investigating the law of changes in the value of commodities is mainly examining the relationship between the value of commodities and labor productivity. Labor productivity can be expressed by the number of products produced per unit of labor time. It is expressed by the formula: labor productivity = product volume / labor time. Determinants of labor productivity: the skill level of the workers, the level of science and technology, the socially integrated form of the production process (division and collaboration, organizational management), the quality of the means of production, and the quality of natural conditions, etc..

The relationship between the value of unit commodities and social labor productivity. Labor productivity is the productivity of workers. It includes social labor productivity and individual labor productivity. Social labor productivity refers to the labor efficiency of all laborers in a production sector in the same period to produce the same labor product; individual labor productivity refers to the labor efficiency of individual labor producers to produce a product. Labor productivity is directly proportional to the amount of value in use of goods and inversely proportional to the amount of value of units of goods. The value of a unit commodity is directly proportional to the socially necessary labor time for producing the commodity, proportional to the complexity of labor, and inversely proportional to the labor productivity of the society.

1.1.3 The Essence, Function and Circulation Law of Money

(1) The Generation Process of Currency

The development of commodity value forms has gone through four stages of development: simple or accidental value forms; total and expanded value forms; general value forms; and monetary forms. Money is the product of the development of commodity production and commodity exchange to a certain stage, and is the inevitable result of the inherent contradiction development of commodities. After the emergence of money, it played the role of a general equivalent, and the value of all commodities was expressed in money. The contradiction between the intrinsic use value and value of a commodity is externalized into the opposition of commodities and currency.

(2) The Function of Money

The function of money is determined by the nature of money, and it is a concrete manifestation of the nature of money. In a developed commodity economy, money has five functions.

First, the value scale is the primary function of money. The so-called value scale is to measure and express the value of all other commodities with money as the scale. Second, the means of currency circulation is to serve as a medium for commodity exchange. Third,in the circulation of goods, after the goods owner sells the goods in exchange for money, he no longer buys other goods, but saves the money. At this time, the money in his hands becomes the storage currency, which is the function of money as a storage means. Fourth, the purchase and sale of goods were initially paid in cash. With the development of commodity circulation, the phenomenon of deferred payment on credit purchase and sale of credit appeared. After a certain period of time after the purchase of the goods, the arrears were paid. At this time, the currency performed the function of payment means. As a means of payment, currency was originally used to pay off debts, and later it was used to pay rent, interest, and wages. Fifth, the function of the world currency is the function of currencies that go beyond national borders and perform general equivalents in the world market.

(3) The Law of Currency Circulation

The law that determines the amount of money required for circulation in a certain period of time is the law of currency circulation. The content of this law is the amount of money as a means of circulation, which depends on three factors: (1) the number of commodities to be circulated; (2) the price level of commodities; (3) the velocity of currency circulation. The product of the first two items is the total price of the product. The amount of money required in circulation is directly proportional to the total price of the commodity, and inversely proportional to the speed of currency circulation, expressed by the formula:

$$\text{Money Needed} = \frac{\text{Total Commodity Price}}{\text{Currency Circulation Speed}}$$
(average number of circulations of the saem unit of currency)

$$(1.2)$$

1.1.4 Law of Surplus Value

(1) Conversion of Money into Capital

Ⅰ The total capital formula and its contradictions

The currency circulation formula for commodities is:

W (commodity)-G (currency)-W (commodity)

That is, commodity producers sell the goods they produce, exchange them for currencies, and then use these currencies to buy the goods they need.

The capital circulation formula is:

G (currency)-W (commodity)-G (currency)

That is to say, the capital purchases a specific commodity with a certain amount of currency, and then sells the commodity and exchanges it back for currency. The capital circulation formula G—W—G′ reflects the common characteristics of various capital movements such as industrial capital, commercial capital, and borrowed capital. It is applicable to all forms of capital, and is therefore the general formula for capital. The contradiction of the general formula. The general formula of capital contradicts the law of value in form. Because according to the requirements of the law of value, commodity exchange must follow the principle of equivalent exchange, and value multiplication does not occur in circulation. However, the total capital formula shows that after two phases of trading, the value of currency has increased in circulation.

First of all, value multiplication does not occur in currencies in the G-W stage, because currency is used as a means of circulation and a means of payment here only to realize the value of the goods it purchases. Secondly, the increase in value cannot occur at the W-G stage, because the sale of goods can only change the value from the form of goods to the form of money, without changing the amount of value. In the end, value multiplication must occur on commodities in the G-W stage. The owner of the money must purchase a special kind of commodity, which has a special use value. Through its use, it can create value, and it can create greater value than its own value. This particular commodity is labor. Therefore, labor becomes a commodity, which is the prerequisite for the conversion of money into capital.

II Buying and selling of labor

The labor force is a person's ability to work, which is the sum of physical and mental strength in a living human body. In any society, labor is the basic element of social production. However, it became a commodity only under certain historical conditions.

First, there are two basic conditions for labor to become a commodity: the laborer must be personally free, have the right to control his own labor force, and be able to sell it as a commodity; you have nothing, you have to live by selling labor. These two basic conditions were formed during the long-term development of history.

Second, the value and use value of labor goods. The value of labor goods is determined by the socially necessary labor time to produce and reproduce labor. Since the labor force exists in the living body, its production and reproduction is to maintain, restore and continue the physical and mental strength of the laborers, which requires the consumption of certain means of living. Therefore, the time required to produce labor can be converted into the time required to produce these means of living. It includes three parts: the value of the means of living necessary for the worker himself to reproduce his labor force; the value of the means of living necessary for the worker to raise his children to continue the supply of labor; labor education and training expenses are used to train labor required for capitalist reproduction.

(2) Sources of Surplus Value

I Capitalist labor process and value multiplication process

Value appreciation process. We first analyze the capitalist production process as a process of value formation. Suppose that the capitalist asks the worker to produce 10 kg of cotton yarn, which consumes 10 kg of cotton and costs 10 yuan. The value of worn equipment and other labor materials is 2 yuan. The value of the daily labor is 3 yuan. The worker can be created in 6 hours of labor. It takes 6 hours of labor to produce 10 kg of cotton yarn. When the worker spins 10 kg of cotton into cotton yarn after 6 hours of labor, the material form of cotton changes, and the original use value no longer exists. However, its value has not disappeared. Instead, it has been transferred to the new product cotton yarn and becomes part of the value of cotton yarn. Similarly, the value of worn parts of labor materials such as machinery and equipment is also transferred to cotton yarn. This transfer is achieved by the specific labor of the worker. While workers produce cotton yarn with specific labor, they also spend a certain amount of abstract labor, which condenses to form new value in the commodity. 6 hours of labor created a new value of 3 yuan. In this way, the value of 10 pounds of cotton yarn is equal to the value of the transfer of production materials of 12 yuan, plus the newly created value of 3 yuan, for a total of 15 yuan. This is equal to the value paid by capitalists to purchase means of production and labor. This result is meaningless to the capitalist. In order to realize the purpose of capital value increase, the capitalist will inevitably change the value formation process into a value increase process.

When the capitalist buys a worker's labor for one day, he/she obtains the right to use the labor for one day. Although workers work 6 hours a day, they can produce labor value. However, in order to produce surplus value, capitalists must extend the working hours of workers to more than 6 hours. Assume that the capitalists let the workers work 12 hours a day, then the workers will produce 20 kg of cotton yarn and consume 20 kg of cotton, valued at 20 yuan; the wear of machinery and equipment will also double, and the value will be 4 yuan; In the production process, the specific labor transfer value of the workers is 24 yuan, and 12 hours of abstract labor creates a new value of 6 yuan. As a result, the value of 20 kg of cotton yarn is 30 yuan in total, and the capitalist's prepaid value is 24 yuan in the value of the means of production and 27 yuan in the value of labor 3 yuan. The difference between the two is 3 yuan. It can be seen that the production of surplus value is due to the capitalist extending the labor time of the worker to more than the time required to compensate the value of the labor force, so that the value created by the worker exceeds the value of his labor force and realizes value multiplication. Through the above analysis, the contradiction of the total capital formula is finally resolved.

II Constant capital and variable capital

Capital is always divided into two parts, one in the form of means of production and the other in the form of labor. They perform different functions in the process of value multiplication. According to their different roles in the production of surplus value, they are divided into constant capital and variable capital.

First, the part of capital that exists in the form of means of production is consumed in the production process, the form of use value changes, it is processed into a new product, and its value is transferred to the new product. This transfer does not change the amount of value, but the old value of the means of production is reproduced in the new product, so it is called constant capital (c).

Second, the value of the part of capital in the form of labor will not be transferred to new products in the production process. Because the value of labor paid by capitalists was consumed by workers to purchase means of subsistence. This part of the value is reproduced by workers in the production process. The use of labor not only regenerates the value of labor, but also produces surplus value, which changes the original capital value and realizes multiplication, so it is called variable capital (v).

(3) Production Method of Surplus Value

I Surplus value rate

The value of commodities under capitalist conditions consists of three components: the old value transferred as the means of production of constant capital, which is represented by c; the part of the new value that compensates for variable capital, is represented by v; Residual value part, expressed in m.

Since surplus value is the result of changes in variable capital, to show the degree of capitalist exploitation of workers. Constant capital must be removed, and only the proportional relationship between surplus value and variable capital must be examined. The ratio of surplus value to variable capital is the rate of surplus value. Using m' to represent the rate of surplus value, then $m' = m / v$.

Since the variable capital is produced by the worker during the necessary labor time, and the surplus value is produced by the worker during the remaining labor time, the rate of surplus value can also be expressed in this form, that is m' = surplus labor time / necessary labor time. The rate of surplus value is closely related to the amount of surplus value obtained by capitalists. The amount of surplus value depends on two factors, one is the level of the surplus value rate, and the other is the total amount of variable capital. Using M as the amount of surplus value, the formula for calculating the amount of surplus value is:

$$M = m/v \times V = m' \times V$$

Therefore, there are two ways for capitalists to increase the amount of surplus value: one is to increase the total amount of variable capital and hire more workers; the other is to increase the rate of surplus value and squeeze more surplus value from each worker. Because the increase in the total amount of variable capital is limited by the amount of capital within a certain period of time, increasing the rate of surplus value has become the main way for capitalists to increase the amount of surplus value.

Ⅱ Absolute surplus value production

Absolute surplus value production refers to a method of extending the surplus labor time and increasing surplus value by absolutely extending the working day under the condition that the necessary labor time is unchanged. The surplus value produced as a result of the absolute extension of the working day is called absolute surplus value. In addition, the surplus value produced by individual enterprises due to increased labor intensity also belongs to absolute surplus value.

Ⅲ Relative surplus value production

Relative surplus value production is to increase the production of surplus value by changing the ratio of necessary labor time and surplus labor time in the working day. Under the condition that the working day is constant, the surplus value produced by shortening the necessary labor time and correspondingly extending the remaining labor time is called relative surplus value.

IV The relationship between absolute surplus value and relative surplus value

First, the two are essentially the same. Regardless of whether the workday is extended or labor productivity is increased, the result is an increase in workers' surplus labor time, an increase in the degree of exploitation of workers, and an increase in the amount of surplus value.

Second, absolute surplus value production is the general basis of capitalist exploitation and the starting point for relative surplus value production, because surplus value can only be generated if the working day is extended above the necessary labor time. At the same time, only on the premise that the working day is divided into necessary working time and surpluse working time, they can further shorten necessary labor time, extend surplus labor time, and produce relative surplus value.

Third, the two methods of producing surplus value play different roles at different stages of the development of capitalism. In the early days of capitalism, capitalists exploited workers primarily by means of absolute surplus-value production. With the development of capitalism and the advancement of science and technology, especially after the emergence of the large machine industry, relative surplus value production has gradually become the main method for capitalists to increase the degree of exploitation.

Fourth, the law of surplus value is the basic economic law of capitalism. Its content is that the purpose and motivation of capitalist production is to pursue as much surplus value as possible. The means to achieve this goal is to continuously expand and strengthen the exploitation of wage labor.

Reasons shows as follows. The law of surplus value determines the essence of capitalist production; the law of surplus value determines all major aspects and processes of the development of capitalist production; the law of surplus value determines the whole process of the emergence, development and destruction of capitalist mode of production.

1.1.5 Capital Accumulation and Its Historical Trend

(1) Capitalist Reproduction and Capital Accumulation

Ⅰ Simple reproduction of capitalism

The simple reproduction of capitalism means that the capitalist uses all the surplus value exploited for personal consumption, and reproduction is only repeated on the original scale. Assume that the production cycle is one year. The capital paid by the capitalist at the beginning of the year is 10,000 yuan, of which the constant capital is 8,000 yuan and the variable capital is 2,000 yuan. Assuming that the residual value rate is 100%, the value of the product after the end of the year-end production process is: $8000c + 2000v + 2000m = 12000$. The residual value of 2,000 yuan is used for capitalist personal consumption. In this way, the capital invested in production and the value of the products produced in the next year are still the same as in the previous year. Production is repeated on the original scale. This is simply capitalist reproduction.

Ⅱ Capitalism expands reproduction

The characteristic of capitalist reproduction is the expansion of reproduction. The expansion of capitalist reproduction means that the capitalist does not use all surplus value for personal consumption, but converts part of the surplus value into new capital for purchasing additional means of production and labor, so that production is repeated on the basis of expansion. The conversion of surplus value into capital, or capitalization of surplus value, is called capital accumulation. This shows that surplus value is the source of capital accumulation, and capital accumulation is an important source of expanding reproduction.

Ⅲ The essence of capital accumulation

Capital accumulation is transformed from surplus value, and surplus value created by the capitalist's free possession of workers is transformed by the law of ownership of the production of goods. Under the conditions of production of goods, the producers of goods are all owners of goods with equal rights. Only by surrendering their own goods can they own the goods of others. They can only exchange equivalently. No one can possess others' goods without compensation labor. This is the law of ownership in the production of goods. In a capitalist society, the capitalist, by virtue of his possession of the means of production, occupies the surplus labor of the workers free of charge; on this basis, he further unceasingly occupies more surplus labor for free, which is the law of capitalist occupation.

(2) Increase in Organic Composition of Capital and Relative Overpopulation

I Organic composition of capital and its changing trend

The composition of capital can be examined from two aspects. From the perspective of value, capital is composed of a certain amount of constant capital and variable capital, and they maintain a certain proportional relationship. This ratio of constant capital to variable capital is called the value composition of capital. From a material point of view, capital is composed of a certain amount of means of production and labor, and they also maintain a certain proportional relationship. Generally speaking, this certain proportional relationship depends on the level of production technology, that is, the higher the level of technology, the greater the number of means of production used by each worker; otherwise, the less. This kind of proportional relationship between the means of production and labor determined by the level of production technology is called the technological composition of capital. There is a close relationship between the value composition of capital and the technical composition of capital. Generally speaking. The technological composition of capital determines the value composition of capital, and changes in technological composition will cause changes in value composition. The change in value composition usually reflects the change in technology composition. Marx called the organic value composition of capital, which is determined by the technical composition of capital and reflects changes in technological composition. Usually expressed as $c: v$.

With the continuous progress of science and technology and the development of the capitalist economy, especially after the emergence of the large machine industry, the organic composition of capital has continued to increase. This is because capitalists are personified capital. In order to squeeze more surplus value and defeat their opponents in the competition, they must do everything possible to adopt new technologies, update machinery and equipment, and promote labor productivity. At the same time, capital accumulation has increased capital, provided favorable conditions for capitalists to adopt advanced technologies, updated machinery and equipment, and strengthen division of labor and cooperation, thereby promoting the improvement of labor productivity. This will inevitably make the capital technology composition continue to increase, and consequently the capital organic composition. Therefore, the continuous improvement of the organic composition of capital is an inevitable trend in the development of capitalism.

Ⅱ Relative overpopulation

Reduced demand. With the continuous increase of the organic composition of capital, as capital accumulation continues to grow, the most serious impact on the fate of the proletariat is the creation of a relative surplus population. This is because, under the condition that the organic composition of capital increases, the increase in total capital means an absolute increase in the variable capital component. However, as the constant capital portion of the total capital is increasing, the variable capital portion is showing a relatively decreasing trend. Of course, the demand for capital for labor will be relatively reduced. Moveover, under the condition that the original investment is unchanged, due to the use of new technologies and new machinery and equipment, capital no longer needs to hire so many workers. As a result, there was a phenomenon that some "excessive" workers were fired, that is, "machines crowded out workers", and the amount of capital needed for workers was definitely reduced.

Supply increases. First, due to the continuous advancement of production technology and the widespread use of machines, many operations have become simpler, and the physical requirements of workers have also been reduced, resulting in a large number of women and children flooding into the factory. Second, the development of capitalism prompts the rapid differentiation of small producers, the bankruptcy of a large number of peasants and craftsmen, and the joining of the labor force. Third, the fierce competition of capitalism has brought some small and medium capitalists into bankruptcy. They need to find another job, and many of them are forced to become hired laborers.

It can be seen that under the capitalist system, with the continuous growth of capital accumulation and the continuous improvement of the organic composition of capital, two opposing trends occur: on the one hand, the demand for capital's labor force is relatively, or even absolutely, reduced On the other hand, the supply of labor is increasing rapidly. Consequently trends, a large number of workers will inevitably be unemployed, thus forming a demographic phenomenon unique to the capitalist system, that is, a relatively surplus population.

1.1.6 Capital Circulation and Turnover and Social Capital Reproduction

(1) Capital Cycle

Three stages of industrial capital cycle and three functional forms. Capital increases value in a continuous circular movement, and the only capital that can increase value is industrial capital. Industrial capital refers to the capital of all production sectors operating in a capitalist manner, and it includes the capital of various material production sectors such as industry, agriculture, and construction. The cyclical movement of industrial capital has to go through three stages of purchase, production, and sales, which are connected to these three stages, and in turn take three functional forms: currency capital, production capital, and commodity capital.

First, the purchase phase. It is the industrial capitalist that uses the qualifications of a purchaser of goods to use monetary capital to buy goods such as means of production and labor as factors of production. Let be If G is the currency, W the commodity, A the labor force, and Pm is the means of production, then the purchase stage can be expressed asfollows:

$$G\text{——}W < \begin{matrix} Pm \\ A \end{matrix} \tag{1.3}$$

Second, the production stage. At this stage, industrial capitalists use the qualifications of capitalist commodity producers to use the purchased labor and means of production for production. After the production process, labor is consumed, raw materials are processed, machinery and equipment are worn out, and commodities containing surplus value are produced. Compared with the original product, the value of the product at this time is not only different in the form of use value, but also the value is increased. Therefore, the second stage of the capital cycle is the stage in which production capital is transformed into commodity capital. If the production process is represented by P, the interruption of the circulation process is indicated by the dashed line, and W' represents a commodity containing surplus value, then the production stage can be expressed by the following formula:

$$w \bigg\langle \begin{array}{c} Pm \\ A \end{array} \cdots P \cdots w' \qquad\qquad (1.4)$$

Third, the sales stage. At this stage, the capitalist sells the produced goods to the market and sells them back for money. At this time, capital returned to the original form of money. However, this currency is different from the original prepaid currency and has changed in quantity. In addition to the original prepaid currency, it has brought a new increase, that is, surplus value. In this way, commodity capital is transformed into increased monetary capital. Formulated as:

$$W' \text{——} G' \qquad\qquad (1.5)$$

$G' = G + g$, where G is the value of prepaid capital and g is the realized surplus value.

The industrial capital cycle is the process of starting from one form, going through three stages in turn, transforming three functional forms, increasing the value, and returning to the original starting point. Expressed in formula:

$$G \text{——} w \bigg\langle \begin{array}{c} Pm \\ A \end{array} \cdots P \cdots w' \text{——} G' \qquad\qquad (1.6)$$

(2) Reproduction and Circulation of Social Capital

Ⅰ Simple reproduction of social capital

The simple reproduction of social capital refers to the reproduction of the social production scale on the original basis. Under the conditions of simple reproduction, all surplus value created by workers is used by capitalists for personal consumption, and there is no capital accumulation.

According to the principle that the total social product is divided into c, v, and m, and the social production is divided into two major categories according to the physical composition of the total social product, it is assumed that the constant capital of the first class is 4000 and the variable capital is 1000. The surplus value rate is 100%, the surplus value is 1000, the constant capital of the second class is 2000, the variable capital is 500, the surplus value rate is 100%, and the surplus value is 500. The composition of total social products throughout the year can be represented by the following diagrams:

$$\text{I} : 4000c + 1000v + 1000m = 6000 \text{ (production materials)}$$
$$\text{II} : 2000c + 500v + 500m = 3000 \text{ (consumer information)} \quad (1.7)$$

In order for the second year to be able to reproduce at the original scale, all products of the two major categories must be exchanged to achieve value compensation and physical compensation. There are three major aspects of the exchange between the various parts of the two major social products.

First, intra-class exchanges. $4000c$ of Part I , the physical form of this part of the product is the means of production. At the beginning of production at the beginning of the year, the Class I prepaid means of production with a value of $4000c$ were all consumed by the end of the year and turned into real products for society. At the beginning of next year's social production, compensation must be made with products within this category (that is, $4000c$). The specific method is: a small part of the product in $4000c$ directly enters the company's reproduction process, and those consumed as compensation for production materials A constant capital element. The other part of the product is to be compensated through the exchange between the capitalists of the enterprises within the first category.

Second, intra-class exchange. In terms of value, $500v$ and $500m$ of Class II are consumer funds used to pay workers' wages and personal consumption as capitalists. They will all be used to purchase consumer materials. In physical form, they are consumer materials. Therefore, the products of category II can be realized by the internal workers and capitalists of category II purchasing various consumer goods of this category.

Third, the exchange between the two major categories. Through the above two major exchanges, there is still a surplus in Part I, which is used to compensate the $1000v$ of prepaid variable capital and $1000m$ representing the surplus value to enter the personal consumption of capitalists and workers, but the physical form of existence is indeed the means of production It needs to be exchanged with Class II , and the constant capital $2000c$ used to compensate for the consumption of Class II should be replaced by means of production, but their physical form is still consumption data, and they need to be exchanged with Class I . As a result of the exchange between the two major categories, the product value of the first category ($1000v + 1000m$) was realized, and workers and capitalists were provided with equal means of subsistence. In this way, the products of category I ($1000v + 1000m$) and $2000c$ of category II were realized.

The three major exchanges of the various components of the above two major categories can be represented by the following diagram. (①②③ represent the exchange relationship of the above three aspects).

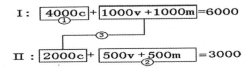

Figure1-1   The diagram of simple reproduction

It can be seen that in the case of simple reproduction, if the currency circulation as a medium is left aside, the realization of the total social product is carried out through the above three basic exchange relations.

The value compensation and in-kind compensation of the total social products are realized through the exchange between the two major categories and between the two major categories. In order to achieve the total compensation of the total social products, the various components of the total products must maintain a certain proportional relationship. . This proportional relationship is the condition for the simple reproduction of total social capital.

First, the sum of variable capital and surplus value in Part I should equal the constant capital in Part II, that is, I $(v + m) = $ IIc. This realization condition reflects the internal connection between the two major categories as prerequisites and mutual constraints. This is the basic condition for simple reproduction of total social capital.

Second, the value of all products in class I should be equal to the sum of the constant capital of the two major classes, that is, I $(c + v + m) = $ I$c + $ IIc. This condition indicates that the production of means of production must be balanced with the demand for the means of production of the two major categories. This is an important condition for examining the normal progress of simple reproduction of total social capital from the perspective of the supply and demand of the means of production of the whole society.

Third, the value of all products in category II must be equal to the sum of the variable capital and surplus value of the two major categories, that is, II $(c + v + m) = $ I $(v + m) + $ II $(v + m)$.

The first three implementation conditions above are basic, and the remaining two are derived from the first implementation condition. Each of them is from a different aspect, which reflects the two major types of production that must be followed in the simple reproduction process. Objective proportion.

II Realization of expanded reproduction of social capital

Capital accumulation is the basis for expanding reproduction. In order to convert the accumulated surplus value into additional constant capital and additional variable capital for extended expansion and reproduction, two basic conditions must be met, that is, there must be additional means of production in the total social product. And the consumption data necessary to maintain the additional labor force.

1. Prerequisites for expanded reproduction: First of all, in addition to maintaining the means of production necessary for the simple reproduction of Groups I and II, all products produced in Group I must have a balance. This balance is used to meet the needs of the two major sectors for the expansion of reproduction for additional constant capital. Therefore, the sum of variable capital and surplus value in Part I must be greater than the value of constant capital in Part II. This condition is expressed by the formula:

$$I\,(v + m) > IIc \tag{1.8}$$

Secondly, in addition to satisfying the consumption needs of the capitalists of the two major categories and the original workers, there must also be a balance for all the products of the second category. This balance is used to meet the needs of additional workers for consumption data when expanding reproduction in the two major sectors. This condition is expressed by the formula: $II\,(c + m - m/x) > I\,(v + m/x)$

According to the prerequisites for the expansion of reproduction mentioned above, the scheme for designing the expansion of reproduction is as follows:

$$\begin{aligned} I &: 4000c + 1000v + 1000m = 6000 \\ II &: 1500c + 750v + 750m = 3000 \\ &\ \ 5500c + 1750v + 1750m = 9000 \end{aligned} \tag{1.9}$$

In this scheme, $I\,(1000v + 1000m) > II\,1500c$, which meets the basic premise of expanding reproduction $[I\,(v + m) > II\,c]$, and has the possibility of expanding reproduction.

2. How the expansion and reproduction of social capital are carried out.

In order to expand reproduction, capitalists must accumulate after the first year of production. Accumulation first starts with the first category. It is assumed that the first category capitalists use half of the surplus value for accumulation and the other half for personal consumption by the capitalists. 400 of surplus value is converted into additional constant capital (indicated by $\triangle c$), and 100 is converted into additional variable capital (indicated by $\triangle v$). In this way, the parts of the value of the product in category I are regrouped according to their use as an expanded reproduction fund:

$$I : 4000c + 400 \triangle c + 1000v + 100 \triangle v + 500m / x = 6000 \quad (1.10)$$

Here $4000c$ is a compensation fund to compensate all the constant capital value consumed by Class I, $400 \triangle c$ is the part of the accumulation fund used to add constant capital, and $1000v$ is the consumption fund part of the original workers. $100 \triangle v$ is the consumption fund part of the accumulation fund for adding variable capital or additional workers, and $500m / x$ is the personal consumption fund of capitalists. Here I $(4000c + 400 \triangle c)$ can be realized and compensated through exchanges within this class. Part I $(1000v + 100 \triangle v + 500m / x)$ still needs to be exchanged with Class II. It represents a means of production with a total value of 1600, which is 100 more than the $1500c$ of means of production originally consumed by Class II. This 100 represents the production materials provided by the first category for the second category. The second category can be used for expanded reproduction. At the same time, the first category also requires the second category to provide more such consumption data for Increase the consumption of workers. In accordance with this, the second type of capital accumulation is as follows: first, 100 is taken from $750m$ as additional constant capital, and then the organic composition of capital is 2 : 1 (assuming that the second type of accumulation part is the organic composition of capital remains the same), and then take 50 out of $750m$ as additional variable capital. In this way, the parts of the product value of category II are regrouped according to their use as an expanded reproduction fund:

$$II : 1500c + 100 \triangle c + 750v + 50 \triangle v + 600m / x = 3000 \quad (1.11)$$

Here $1500c$ is to compensate the value of all the constant capital consumed by Part II, $100 \triangle c$ is the part of the accumulation fund to add constant capital, and $50 \triangle v$ is the consumption of the accumulation fund to add variable capital or additional workers. In the fund section, $600m / x$ is the personal consumption fund of capitalists. Among them, part II ($750v + 50 \triangle v + 600m / x$) can be compensated through internal exchange of this department; the product represented by part II ($1500c + 100 \triangle c$) is consumer data, and it passes Exchange of production materials worth 1600.

The exchange relationship between the two major categories can be represented by the following diagram:

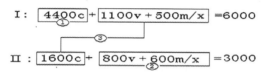

Figure1-2   The diagram of expanded reproduction

① and ② are the exchanges between the two major sectors of capitalist enterprises, and ③ are the exchanges between the two major sectors. After the exchange, all the social total products are compensated, and the expanded reproduction in the next year can be carried out. If the surplus value rate is still 100%, the result of the second year of production is:

$$I : 4400c + 1100v + 1100m = 6600$$
$$II : 1600c + 800v + 800m = 3200 \qquad (1.12)$$
$$6000c + 1900v + 1900m = 9800$$

The realization of products in the second year, as well as the expansion of reproduction and the realization of total social products in the years after the second year, can be deduced by analogy according to the above method based on the accumulation rate of Part I .

From the analysis of capitalist expansion of reproduction, it can be seen that I ($v + m$)> II c, II ($c + mm / x$)> I ($v + m / x$), only shows that it is possible to expand reproduction, only When the proportion of the total product of the society is maintained in balance, the total product will be fully compensated for value and replaced in kind. Only by expanding reproduction can it become reality.

3. In order for the total social capital to expand and reproduce normally, these conditions should be met:

First, the sum of the original variable capital of Class I plus additional variable capital, plus the surplus value of capital used by the capitalists for personal consumption, must be equal to the constant capital of Class II plus the additional constant capital. which is

$$\mathrm{I} \, (v + \triangle v + m / x) = \mathrm{II} \, (c + \triangle c) \qquad (1.13)$$

Second, the value of all products in category I must equal the original constant capital of the two major categories plus additional constant capital. which is

$$\mathrm{I} \, (c + v + m) = \mathrm{I} \, (c + \triangle c) + \mathrm{II} \, (c + \triangle c) \qquad (1.14)$$

Third, the value of all products in category II must be equal to the original variable capital of the two major categories plus additional variable capital, plus the sum of the residual value of capitalist personal consumption. which is

$$\mathrm{II} \, (c + v + m) = \mathrm{I} \, (v + \triangle v + m / x) + \mathrm{II} \, (v + \triangle v + m / x) \qquad (1.15)$$

Like simple reproduction, the first condition is basic and the other two conditions are derived. They all determine the smooth realization of the expansion and reproduction of social capital from different aspects.

1.1.7 Specific Forms of Capital and Surplus Value

(1) Profit

Ⅰ Turning surplus value into profit

Surplus value was originally generated by variable capital and was an increase above variable capital. However, the capitalist sees it as an increase above the cost price, i.e., an increase in the value of the total cost of capital. Therefore, the surplus value produced in the production process appears as a product of the capital expended. In this way, the original formula for expressing the value of a commodity: $W = c + (v + m)$ becomes $W = (c + v) + m$ or $k + m$. The conversion of surplus value into profit masks the true source of surplus value. It seems that surplus value is not generated by variable capital, but by all prepaid capital. This conceals the connection between surplus value and the surplus labor of workers. The result of spontaneous proliferation. At the same time, the formula for the value of goods is further transformed into $W = k + p$ (cost price plus profit). So the capitalist regards the cost price (k) as the intrinsic value of the commodity, and the surplus value (or profit) is expressed as the balance of the selling price of the commodity exceeding its intrinsic value. In this way, surplus value becomes a product in the process of commodity circulation. It seems that surplus value (profit) is generated in circulation, and its true source is further covered up.

II The rate of surplus value is converted into the rate of profit

Since the capitalist regards the surplus value as the product of the prepaid total capital, he does not compare the surplus value with the variable capital when calculating the size of the company's profit. The ratio of the total capital is called the profit rate. If P' is the profit rate, then $P' = =$ (the capital G represents the total capital paid in advance).

III Factors affecting profit margin

The level of surplus value: With the same amount of prepaid capital and the organic composition of capital, the higher the rate of surplus value, the higher the rate of profit; the rate of profit and the rate of surplus value change in proportion.

The level of organic composition of capital: The level of the organic composition of capital changes in the opposite direction compared to the change in the profit rate. An increase in the organic composition of capital will cause a decline in the profit rate.

Savings of constant capital: In the case where the amount of surplus value and the rate of surplus value have been determined, the constant capital is saved, the prepaid capital will be reduced, and the profit rate will be increased compared with the same amount of surplus value and a smaller amount of prepaid capital.

Capital turnover speed: When other conditions remain the same, the faster the capital turnover rate in a year, the more turnover of variable capital, the greater the amount of surplus value brought by the same amount of capital, and the higher the annual rate of surplus capital, The higher the annual profit rate (that is, the ratio of the surplus value of production to the total capital paid in one year).

(2) Industrial Capital and Average Profit

I Competition among sectors forms average profit margin

Inter-sector competition refers to competition among capitalists in various sectors in order to compete for more favorable investment venues. Under the capitalist system, because each production sector has a different rate of surplus value, a different organic composition of capital, and a different rate of capital turnover, it will inevitably result in different levels of profitability for each production sector. Now, we assume that the other conditions are the same in each sector, and that only the organic composition of capital is different to explain the difference in profitability.

Table 1-2 Average profit rate of each department

Production Department	Constant capital	Variable capital	Residual value	Commodity value	Average profit rate (100%)	Average profit	Difference between average profit and residual value
Food industry	70	30	30	130	20	20	−10
Textile industry	80	20	20	120	20	20	0
Machinery Industry	90	10	10	110	20	20	+10
Total	240	60	60	360		60	0

It can be seen from the Table 1-2 that the profit gained by the machinery industry sector is exactly the profit lost by the food industry sector. From all departments, the amount of profit has neither increased nor decreased, and the total profit is equal to the total surplus value. This shows that the process of forming average profit is a process in which capitalists in various sectors redistribution of surplus value through competition.

Therefore, the average profit rate is the profit rate calculated on the average of total social capital, that is, the ratio of total social surplus value to total social capital. The formula is:

$$\text{Average profit margin} = \frac{\text{total social surplus value}}{\text{total social capital}}$$

II The significance of average profit

Marx's theory of average profit and production price is of great importance. First, this theory scientifically reveals that obtaining the same amount of profit with the same amount of capital is nothing but the redistribution of surplus value among capitalists in different sectors, thereby providing an important theoretical premise for analyzing the profit, interest, and rent of capitalist enterprises. Second, this theory also has very important practical significance. It reveals the opposition between the entire proletariat and the entire bourgeoisie.

(3) Commercial Capital and Commercial Profits

I Formation and function of commercial capital

Commercial capital, also known as merchant capital, is a functional capital that plays a role in the field of circulation. The function performed by commodity capital is to sell commodities, convert commodity capital into monetary capital, realize the value and surplus value contained in commodities, and finally complete the cycle of commercial capital. This relative independence of the commodity capital function contains the possibility of making it independent from the industrial capital movement.

II The source and nature of commercial profits

Commercial profit rate, in the real economic life of a capitalist society, is essentially the average profit rate of functional capital. After commercial capital participates in the process of averaging the profit rate, new explanations must be made on the areas of average profit rate, average profit, and production price.

At this time, the average profit rate of industrial capital is transformed into the average profit rate of functional capital. which is:

$$\frac{\text{Average profit margin of functional capital}} = \frac{\text{total social surplus value}}{\text{total industral capital} + \text{total commercial capital}}$$

The average profit of industrial capital is converted into the average profit rate of functional capital, and is divided into two parts: industrial profit and commercial profit. Industrial profit = total industrial capital × functional capital profit rate; commercial profit = total commercial capital × functional capital average profit rate, the original production price = cost price + average profit, that is, $k + P$, now the average profit is decomposed into industrial profit and Commercial profit, $= p + h$, so the production price becomes: $k + p + h$, that is, cost price + industrial profit + commercial profit.

(4) Borrowed Capital and Interest

I Formation of loan capital

Borrowing capital comes from a large amount of idle currency capital generated by functional capital during the cycle and turnover process. Moreover, some capitalists also need to purchase goods and pay wages, or need to update equipment in advance, and often need to replenish monetary capital. So the capitalist who holds the idle money capital will lend it out for the capitalists who need the money capital urgently, and this part of the idle money capital becomes the loan capital.

II Interest and corporate profits

Borrowing capitalists are conditional on lending money capital to capitalists. Functional capitalists use borrowing capital to operate commodity production or commodity circulation. After obtaining an average profit margin, they must pay a portion of it to the borrowing capitalist as compensation for using the loan. That is interest. Interest is a part of the surplus value that the functional capitalist gives to the borrowing capitalist because of the use of the borrowing capital. It is a special conversion form of surplus value.

III Interest rate

The interest rate is the ratio of the amount of interest to borrowed capital over a period of time. Expressed by the formula: interest rate = $\frac{\text{the amount of interest}}{\text{borrowed capital}} \times 100\%$. There is a limit to the level of interest rates. Its highest limit is less than the average profit margin. The lowest limit of the interest rate is greater than zero. Otherwise, the borrowing capitalist is unprofitable and would rather store the money without risking the loan, and the borrowing capital would not exist. Therefore, the interest rate always swings between the average profit rate and zero. The change in the interest rate depends on two factors: first, the level of average profitability; second, the supply and demand of borrowed capital.

(5) Capitalist Rent

I The nature of capitalist rent

Capitalist rent is the excess of the average profit that land-leasing agricultural capitalists give to landowners to obtain land use rights. It reflects the relationship between landowners and agricultural capitalists exploiting agricultural workers. We are used to saying that rent is rent, which is somewhat different from real rent. Rent refers to the total amount of money paid by agricultural capitalists to landowners within a certain period. The real rent is the amount paid for simply using the land. In addition to rent in the true sense, rent also includes the following three aspects. First, rent includes depreciation and interest on fixed assets.Second, the rent sometimes includes part of the average profit of agricultural capitalists. Third, the rent sometimes includes the wages of some agricultural workers.

II Differential rent

Formation of differential rent: Differential rent is obtained by renting superior land, and the part of the excess profit owned by the land owner. The monopoly of land management caused by the limited land has severely hindered the competition of agricultural investors for better production conditions, so that those agricultural investors who operate better land can maintain their production Advantage, so as to be able to obtain long-term stable excess profits. The surplus labor of agricultural workers is the source of differential rent.

The first form of differential rent: The first form of differential rent (differential rent I) refers to the rent converted from excess profits due to the fertility and geographical location of the land. It is the result of investing the same amount of capital in the same area and under different production conditions due to different labor productivity. Taking three parcels of land of the same area but different fertility as an example, the list illustrates the formation of differential rent I.

Table 1-3 Differential Government Rent I

Land Type	Input capital (yuan)	Average profit (yuan)	Output	Individual production price (yuan)		Social production price (yuan)		Differential rent I
				All products	Per load	Per load	All products	
A(Excellent)	100	20	6	120	20	30	180	60
B (medium)	100	20	5	120	24	30	150	30
C(bad)	100	20	4	120	30	30	120	0
Sum	300	60		360			450	90

The second form of differential rent (differential rent Ⅱ) is a continuous additional investment in the same land. Due to the different labor productivity of each investment, the excess profit generated is converted into rent. The formation of differential rent Ⅱ is shown in table 1-4.

Table 1-4 Differential Government Rent Ⅱ

Land Type	Input capital (yuan)	Average profit (yuan)	Output	Individual production price (yuan)		Social production price (yuan)		Differential rent Ⅰ	Differential rent Ⅱ
				All products	Per load	Per load	All products		
A(Excellent)	100	20	6	120	20	30	180	60	
	add100	20	7	120	$17\frac{1}{7}$	30	210		90
B (medium)	100	20	5	120	24	30	150	30	
C(bad)	100	20	4	120	30	30	120		
sum				480			660		

The two forms of differential land rent are both closely related and show significant differences. The relationship between the two is shown in the following points: First, historically, differential rent Ⅰ is the basis and starting point of differential rent Ⅱ. Second, judging from the change in the amount of differential rent over a certain period of time, differential rent Ⅱ is also based on differential rent Ⅰ. The difference between the two types of land rent is: (1) Different investment methods. Differential rent Ⅰ is generated by investing in different land and expanding the area of cultivated land, which reflects the characteristics of extensive management. Differential rent Ⅱ is realized by continuous investment in the same land, which reflects the characteristics of intensive agricultural management. (2) There are different ways to convert excess profits into land rent. Differential rent Ⅰ was clearly stipulated to be owned by the landowner when the land owner and the agricultural capitalist signed the lease contract. Differential rent Ⅱ was owned by the agricultural capitalist during the term of the lease (this is the driving force for continuous additional investment by agricultural capitalists Where). When the lease expires and the lease is renewed, the differential rent II is transferred to the land owner in part or in whole by means of competition between the land owner and the capitalist.

III Absolute rent

1. Formation of absolute rent. Due to the monopoly of private land rights, the absolute rent that must be paid to rent any land is called absolute rent.

Table1-5 Absolute land rent   (Unit: Yuan)

Production sector	Organic composition of capital (C : V)	Surplus value	Average profit (P = 20%)	Product value	Production price	Absolute rent
Industrial	80:20	20	20	120	120	0
Agriculture	60:40	40	20	140	120	20

As can be seen from the table 1-5, because the organic composition of agricultural capital is lower than that of industry, 100 yuan is invested in agriculture, of which 40 yuan is the variable capital. When the residual value rate is 100%, the residual value is 40 yuan, and the value of the product It is 140 yuan; for the industrial sector, the same investment can get a residual value of 20 yuan and the product value is 120 yuan. According to the principle of equal profits for equal amounts of capital, both agricultural capitalists and industrial capitalists must obtain an average profit at an average profit of 20%. That is to obtain an average profit of 20 yuan each. In this way, the production price of industrial products and agricultural products is 120 yuan. However, the production price of agricultural products at 120 yuan is lower than the value of 140 yuan, and agricultural products are not sold at the production price, but at the value of the product. In this way, agricultural capitalists can obtain a balance of 20 yuan in addition to the average profit. This balance forms absolute rent. Therefore, absolute rent is the difference between the value of agricultural products and the price of production.

IV Land price is capitalized rent

The price of land is not a monetary expression of the value of the land, but a capitalized rent. That is the price of land is equivalent to such a sum of monetary capital, and the interest earned by depositing this monetary capital in a bank is equal to the land rent obtained after leasing this land. Therefore, the price of land is determined by two factors. One is the amount of land rent, i.e. the more the land rent, the higher the land price. Therefore, the price of superior land and closer to the market is higher than inferior land. Land far from the market. The second is the level of bank interest rates. The higher the interest rate, the lower the land price; conversely, the lower the interest rate, the higher the land price. It can be seen that the price of land and rent are directly proportional to change and inversely proportional to the interest rate of the bank. The formula for calculating land prices can be expressed as:

$$\text{Land price} = \frac{\text{land rent}}{\text{interest ratio}}$$

1.2 Chinese Practice of Marxist Political Economy

1.2.1 The Essence of Socialism is to Liberate and Develop Productive Forces

In Marx's view, productivity determines the production relationship, the economic foundation determines the superstructure, and the production relationship and the superstructure have an adverse effect. Among them, productivity is the most revolutionary and active factor, and those who master advanced technology and management methods play a core role in productivity. After the founding of People's Republic of China, especially after reform and opening up. The Communist Party of China unites and leads the people of all ethnic groups throughout the country, continuously deepens the reform of various systems and mechanisms, vigorously adjusts the factors restricting the development of productive forces in production relations, and promotes the tremendous progress of China's productive forces; its overall national strength and its ability to make technological innovation have been significantly improved.

After the Third Plenary Session of the Eleventh Central Committee, China moved towards reform and opening up. On the basis of summing up historical experience, according to the actual level and needs of the development of China's social productive forces, economic policies were adjusted based on actual conditions to achieve rapid economic development. In the 1980s, people had not completely stepped out of the ideological constraints of the planned economy era, and there were certain ideological differences regarding the socialist road. The second-generation leadership collective centered on Deng Xiaoping was able to carry out a new exploration of the socialist road with Marxism as the guideline and people as the center. In 1992, Deng Xiaoping's talks in the Southen tour put forward a new understanding and new judgment of the essence of socialism. "The essence of socialism is to liberate productive forces, develop productive forces, eliminate exploitation, eliminate polarization, and ultimately achieve common prosperity." Highlighting socialism is liberation. The development of productive forces not only deepened the understanding of socialism, but also demonstrated Marxist thought of developing productive forces, which is an inheritance and development of it.

After the reform and opening up, China has always placed the development of science and technology in an extremely important position. Vigorously develop higher education, deepen the reform of the scientific research system, and promote scientific and technological innovation in enterprises. Through the implementation of these policies and measures, China's scientific and technological innovation capabilities are among the highest in the world. The report of the 18th National Congress of the Communist Party of China emphasizes scientific and technological innovation, and for the first time puts forward the "Four Simultaneous" strategy for the simultaneous development of new industrialization, informatization, urbanization, and agricultural modernization. It also proposes for the first time that innovation-driven development, especially scientific and technological innovation is to improve social productivity. The key factor is also an important indicator for judging the comprehensive national strength. We must attach importance to the role of scientific and technological innovation. The Third Plenary Session of the Eighteenth Central Committee of the Communist Party of China implemented the system systematically, and proposed to establish a sound and innovative institutional mechanism, a sound market-oriented mechanism, and a collaborative innovation mechanism for industry, university, and research. Through deepening reforms in the field of science and technology, it stimulates the vitality of innovation and forms an atmosphere of innovation. Build a national innovation system. The assertions that "science and technology are the primary productive forces", "rejuvenating the country through science and education", "reinforcing the country by talents", and "innovation-driven development" are continuations and developments of the theory of developing productive forces and Marx's ideas on science and technology, with distinctive characteristics of the times. The report of the 19th National Congress of the Communist Party of China further proposed that the construction of an innovative country should be accelerated. Innovation is the primary driving force for development and a strategic support for building a modern economic system. We must aim at the forefront of world science and technology, strengthen basic research, and achieve major breakthroughs in forward-looking basic research and leading original results.

Table1-6 China Research and Experimental Development (R&D) funding (2013-2017)

Year	Input (100 million yuan)	Growth rate (%)	Input intensity (%)
2013	11846.6	15	1.99
2014	13015.63	9.9	2.02
2015	14169.88	8.9	2.06
2016	15676.75	10.6	2.11
2017	17606.1	12.3	2.13

Sources: Ministry of Science and Technology of the People's Republic of China, Bulletin on National Science and Technology Funding (2017).

1.2.2 Socialist Public Ownership

The ownership of the means of production refers to the sum of the economic and social relations formed by people in the possession, domination and use of the means of production in a certain society and economy. Marx believes that in a communist society, private ownership will be eliminated and common prosperity will be achieved. After the founding of the People's Republic of China, China has carried out arduous explorations on the road towards socialist construction, established basic economic systems in the primary stage of socialism on the basis of summing up both positive and negative experiences; inherited and developed Marx's ownership theory. The basic system with public ownership as the main body and other forms of ownership as the supplement.

First, Deng Xiaoping proposed a new criterion for ownership. He pointed out that to judge whether the ownership structure is reasonable in the primary stage of socialism, it can neither be determined by the nature of the ownership itself, nor by the scope and degree of public ownership. The criterion of judgment is to see if it can promote the development of productivity. If the ownership structure does not meet the requirements of the development of productive forces, it will hinder the development of productive forces.

Second is adhere to the fundamental principle of public ownership as the main body. The nature of the socialist country determines that China must always adhere to the dominant position of public ownership in economic reform. After the Third Plenary Session of the Eleventh Central Committee,

Deng Xiaoping repeatedly stated the importance of insisting on public ownership as the main body. A series of system reforms carried out in China, including policies such as opening to the outside world, combining planned economy and market economy, are in line with socialist principles, and require us to maintain the dominant position of public ownership in the reform.

Third, the non-public ownership economy is complementary. To implement a socialist market economy in China, we must mobilize the enthusiasm of all subjects in the market. Therefore, the non-public ownership economy is an important part of the national economy. Since the reform and opening up, China has continuously introduced foreign-funded enterprises and developed the private economy, which has greatly promoted the vigorous development of the economy. Deng Xiaoping proposed that the foreign capital economy is a necessary supplement to the public ownership, and further expanded the connotation of the non-public ownership economy. The Thirteenth National Congress of the People's Republic of China made a comprehensive discussion of the private economy, arguing that "a certain degree of development of the private economy is conducive to promoting production, activating the market, expanding employment, and better meeting the people's various needs in life. It is necessary and beneficial for the public economy supplement ".

Table 1-7 China's public and non-public economic assets structure (2004-2012)

Year	2004	2005	2006	2007	2008	2009	2010	2011	2012
Total assets (trillion yuan)	99.88	112.64	134.22	166.94	193.54	236.53	291.56	369.92	448.82
Public-owned economic assets (trillion yuan)	62.25	67.15	77.57	93.59	107.37	128.48	153.34	189.73	226.13
Non-public economic assets (trillion yuan)	37.23	45.49	56.65	73.35	86.16	108.05	138.22	180.19	222.15
Proportion of public assets (%)	62.73	59.62	57.79	56.06	55.48	54.32	52.59	51.29	50.44
Proportion of non-public assets (%)	37.27	40.38	42.41	43.94	44.52	45.68	47.41	48.71	49.56

Sources: Pei Changhong, Yang Chunxue, Yang Xinming, *China's Basic Economic System: From the Perspective of Quantitative Analysis*, China Social Sciences Press, 2015, p. 161.

Adhering to the socialist system with Chinese characteristics is the prerequisite for comprehensively deepening reforms. Xi Jinping believes that adhering to the basic economic system of Chinese socialism is conducive to the consolidation and development of the socialist system with Chinese characteristics. A series of innovative ideas have been put forward in practice.

First, the basic economic system is proposed as the foundation of the socialist market economic system. Since the reform and opening up, in the reform of the economic system, China's public-owned economy and non-public-owned economy have not only coexisted, but also have continuously formed strengthened ties, enhanced cooperation, promoted competition, and built the foundation of a socialist market economic system.

Second, a new strategy for consolidating and developing the public ownership economy. Xi Jinping stressed at the Third Plenary Session of the 18th Central Committee that the dominant position of the public ownership economy must be unwavering. On this basis, the vitality of the state-owned economy should be further released, the control and influence of the state-owned economy should be enhanced, and the leading role of the state-owned economy should be brought into play. It is necessary to continuously deepen the reform of state-owned enterprises, further improve the supervision system, improve the mechanism of state-owned capital flow, and improve the corporate governance structure. It is necessary to allow state-owned capital to play a greater role in achieving national strategic goals.

Third, new measures to encourage, support and guide the development of the non-public ownership economy. Xi Jinping pointed out that the development of the non-public ownership economy can effectively mobilize various economic entities to participate in the construction of economic development, and is a catalyst for the economy to maintain vitality and creativity. China is at the initial stage of socialism, the level of productive forces has not yet been fully developed, and the development between regions and between urban and rural areas is still unbalanced, leaving vast space for the development of non-public ownership economies.

Fourth, adhere to and improve the basic economic system and actively develop a mixed ownership economy. The development of a mixed-ownership economy is to allow non-state-owned capital to participate in state-owned capital investment projects, allow workers in mixed-ownership economies to hold shares, and allow the development of cross-shareholdings in state-owned, collective, and non-public capital. This can amplify the function of state capital in economic development, help maintain and increase the value of state capital, increase the competitiveness of state capital, and ensure the dominant position of state capital.

1.2.3 Socialist Income Distribution System

Marx's theory of labor value holds that value is the general indiscriminate human labor condensed in commodities, and labor is the source of value and the source of all wealth. Distribution is the distribution and redistribution of the full value created by a social labor. While criticizing the capitalist society's distribution according to capital, Marx proposed a distribution method that eliminates this form of exploitation in the future society: distribution according to work and distribution according to demand. Distribution according to work is the distribution method of the primary stage of future society discussed by Marx, while distribution according to demand is the distribution method of communism. Since the reform and opening up, the Communist Party of China has adhered to the Marxian distribution theory as a guide, continuously promoted the reform of the income distribution system, established and improved the income distribution system, and enriched and developed the Marxist distribution theory.

Socialism must adhere to the distribution system according to work. The egalitarian distribution method in the planned economy era not only violates the principle of distribution according to work, but also discourages laborers' enthusiasm for labor and seriously hinders the development of productive forces. Reforms in the area of income distribution were first carried out in rural areas. The Third Plenary Session of the Eleventh Central Committee proposed: "We must first mobilize the socialist enthusiasm of hundreds of millions of farmers in our country, and we must fully care about their material interests in the economy." In reality, good results have been achieved, and farmers' enthusiasm for production and production efficiency have been greatly improved. The reform of the city's income distribution system has been promoted simultaneously with the reform of the economic system. The central government pointed out that "serious egalitarianism in distribution" was the main obstacle hindering the development of enterprises. For enterprises to rejuvenate, they must "establish various forms of economic responsibility and seriously implement the principle of distribution according to work" to eliminate the adverse effects of egalitarianism.

With the deepening of reform and opening up, China has basically determined the basic distribution principle of distribution according to work as the main body and other forms of distribution as supplements. In response to the contents of the 14th National Congress of the CPC and the Third Plenary Session of the 14th CPC Central Committee, Jiang Zemin further emphasized the need to "regulate and improve other forms of distribution, production factors such as land, capital, and intellectual property rights, and participate in the distribution of income fairly according to relevant regulations". The 5th National Congress of the People's Republic of China proposed "combining distribution according to work and distribution according to production factors". The 16th National Congress of the CPC emphasized the contribution of production factors in social production, and further put forward the basic principles of participation of production factors in socialist distribution according to their contributions. The 17th National Congress of the CPC pointed out that the goal of deepening the reform of the income distribution system is to gradually reduce the trend of widening the income gap through a series of measures to achieve the protection of legal income, the suppression of illegal income, and the adjustment of excessive income. In order to achieve this goal, " it is important to increase the income of low-income earners, and gradually raise the standards for poverty alleviation and the minimum wage". The report of the 18th National Congress of the CPC states that to achieve the people's shared development results, the most fundamental and most important thing is to continue to promote The reform of the income distribution system is also a matter of most interest and reality for the people. The report of the 19th National Congress of the CPC pointed out that adhere to the principle of distribution according to work, improve the system and mechanism of distribution according to factors, and promote more reasonable and orderly income distribution.

Chapter 2
Theory of Socialist Market Economy

2.1 Basic Principles of the Market Economy

2.1.1 The Essence of the Market Economy

(1) Scarcity and Allocation of Resources

The scarcity of resources is also called the law of scarcity, which means that relative to the diverse and unlimited desires of human society, economic resources or the production of goods and services that meet the needs are always insufficient. The finiteness of resources and the infiniteness of needs forcing human beings to make choices. The so-called choice is how to use established resources to produce economic goods of high quality and quantity so as to better meet the infinite needs of human beings. Specifically, choice must answer three basic problems: what to produce, how to produce, and produce for whom. The three basic economic problems caused by the scarcity and selectivity of resources are called resource allocation problems, which are the core problems of economics. Economics is actually designed to solve these problems. Resource allocation runs through the whole process of social reproduction, and the four links of production, distribution, exchange and consumption involve the scarcity, selectivity and allocation of resources, so the essence of social production and reproduction is the allocation of resource.

(2) The Allocation Method of Resources

There are two main ways of resource allocation: planned allocation and market allocation.

Planed allocation is the dominant resource allocation method in the planned economic system. It is the allocation of resources through the role of the planning mechanism. In this resource allocation method, the decision maker of the resource allocation is the central planning agency, and the means of allocation is the plan indicators issued layer by layer in the form of prescriptive plans and administrative orders.The signal which displays the scarcity of the product is the difference or gap in the plan's balanced decision.

Market allocation is a way of allocating resources by the market and the market mechanism. It resolves the three basic economic issues of what to produce, how to produce, and produce for whom through the market and the market mechanism. The characteristics of the market allocation method are: decentralized decision-making; marketization of resource flows and production structure and scale; competition for resource and product allocation. Market allocation is based on a highly developed commodity economy, which obviously has many advantages over planned allocations, but the market is not a panacea and market allocation also has its limitations.

(3) The Essence of the Market Economy

In real economic life, the economic systems of many countries are a combination of planned allocation and market allocation to varying degrees. This combination is called "hybrid economic system" by economists. The market plays a decisive role in the allocation of resources, which is the essential requirements of a market economy. It includes the following layers of meanings. First, market allocation plays a dominant role in resource allocation and plays a decisive role. What is produced, how it is produced, and for whom it is produced are mainly determined by the market. Second, the economic connections and economic activities between people are mainly carried out in the market. Third, market mechanisms and price signals are the main basis for economic decision-making. Four, income distribution is mainly determined by market supply and demand. Five, while the market plays a decisive role in resource allocation, the government still plays an important role in monitoring the operation of the market economy, including formulating rules, maintaining order, promoting competition, providing public goods, protecting the environment, and maintaining fairness and stability.

The market mechanism is a set of systems for the allocation of resources through the coordination of the relationship between production and demand

and the flow and distribution of production factors through changes in market prices and supply-demand relationships and competition between economic entities. Its core is the market price mechanism and competition mechanisms.

2.1.2 The Formation and Development of Market Economy

(1) The Market Economy is the Product of the Development of the Commodity Economy to a Certain Height

The market economy is appeared with the emergence of socialized mass production and capitalist production methods. The commodity economy includes commodity production and commodity exchange. Marx pointed out that the emergence of the commodity economy has two conditions, social division of labor and private ownership. The social division of labor requires exchanges. The existence of private ownership makes equivalent exchanges required during the exchange process. The historical development of social division of labor and private ownership determines the historical changes of the commodity economy.

The emergence and development of the commodity economy is first based on the division of labor in society. The three major social labor divisions in history, which is known as the separation between animal husbandry and agriculture, handicrafts and agriculture, and commerce and agriculture, gave birth to the currency and commerce. As the result, the development of commodity exchanges was promoted and a special economic form appeared. However, in the long history of the disintegration of the slave society and the feudal society from the primitive society, the self-sufficient natural economy was the dominant economic form. The scale and development of commodity exchange are very limited. With the development of production, especially the industrial revolution, the large machine industry replaced simple collaboration and workshop handicrafts. The traditional self-sufficient production method and the feudal system completely disintegrated, followed with the emergence and development of capitalist mode of production. The capitalist mode of production made the commodity-money relationship and the rule of value dominate, so the market mechanism became the most basic means of regulating the allocation of social resources. It can be seen that capitalist mode of production and market economy are the products of the commodity economy and social productivity that achieve certain development.

(2) Two Major Stages of Market Economy Development: Classical Market
Economy and Modern Market Economy

The market economy evolved with the development of productive forces
and changes of socio-economic conditions. The earliest market economy
was called the "classical free market economy" and it originated from the
period when the capitalist workshop handicraft industry and the handicraft
industry transformed to the large machine industry. This completely laissez-
faire market economy was once an ideal pursued by bourgeois classical
economists. In this laissez-faire market economy, economic operations are
completely regulated by market mechanisms, and the role of the government
is limited to maintaining the external law enforcement. At most, it only
undertakes certain public works and minimal social security, and does not
interfere with the economy. With the development of socialized production,
the contradiction between the socialization of production and capitalist
private ownership has become increasingly acute. The Great Depression of
western economy in 1929 to 1933 fundamentally shaken the market economy
system of laissez-faire capitalism. It come with the national interventionist
policies and theories marked by Roosevelt's New Deal and Keynes' *The
General Theory of Employment, Interest and Money*. As a result, a laissez-
faire market economy began to be replaced by the market economy
intervened by the government. Under this condition, the role of government
is not limited to implementing laws and orders. Instead, it is involved in
the production, distribution, and circulation of the national economy to
a large extent, and it is called an important force to promote economic
development.

The market economy under the intervention of modern government is
a development of the classical laissez-faire market economy. In this
market economy, on the one hand, the market mechanism is mature and
continuously improved. On the other hand, the government's macro-
economic control remedies the deficiencies in allocating resources by market
mechanisms and creates conditions for the effective operation of the market
mechanism.

2.1.3 Basic Characteristics of the Market Economy

From the perspective of reflecting the essence and generalizing the overall
structure of the market economy, the basic characteristics of the market
economy are summarized as follows.

(1) Free Enterprise System

In a market economy, as the main body of market exchange, enterprises must be commodity producers and operators who operate independently and bear their own profits and losses. They can flexibly respond to the market supply and demand and price changes. Besides, independent property rights and rigid budget constraints are the core of free enterprises system. Independent property rights means that in a market economy, enterprises have full autonomy in decision-making in terms of what they produce, how much they produce, and how they produce. Rigid budget constraints mean that the budget principles of the company's revenue and expenditure restraints the economic behavior of the enterprise and determines the production and development of the enterprise. Therefore, if the enterprise has to bear risks and responsibilities, it will inevitably make a flexible and effective response to changes in market supply and demand, competition, and prices. The market thus becomes an effective regulator of resource allocation.

(2) Perfect Market System

In a mature and developed market economy, the market system is perfect, in the following seuse: market competition is adequate and the market structure is complete, not only including the commodity market, but also the production factor markets such as capital, labor, land, and technical information. The united and open market replacing region-separated market and a flexible price system are the basic condition for the efficient operation of the market economy.

(3) Developed Market Contract Relationship

The market economy is a kind of contract economy, and the contractual relationship (clear property rights) of free competition and equal exchange between market transaction subjects is a basic feature of the market economy, and this equal and free contractual relationship must be protected by the government through laws. This is the basic guarantee allowed by the market economy policy. In this sense, the market economy is a legal economy.

(4) Openness of the Economy

The market economy is a highly developed commodity economy based on large-scale socialized production. The characteristics of a modern market economy must be the internationalization of labor, production, market circulation, and the flow of production factors. A market economy with free competition are in essence with no national borders, and companies can participate in international competition on an equal basis.

2.1.4 Limitations of the Classical Market Economy (and the Need for Government Intervention)

The capitalist economic crisis in the 1930s exposed the serious flaws of the classical market economy, that the market was not a panacea.

(1) The Market Mechanism cannot Solve the Problems of Unemployment and Economic Cycles

Classical economics believes in the "Say's Law", that is, "supply creates demand". The spontaneous adjustment of the "invisible hand" of the market mechanism can completely resolve various contradictions in the economy, and will not cause a series of macroeconomic problems led by imbalances between supply and demand. However, the economic crisis of the 1930s completely broke the omnipotence and perfection of the "invisible hand" praised by classical economics, and the "laissez-faire" was replaced by Keynes' "government intervention" later. The reason is that market regulation is a kind of after-the-fact regulation, with a certain degree of spontaneity and blindness. In this way, it must be solved by the government through macroeconomic means such as fiscal and monetary policies from the overall situation of economic operation.

(2) Reduced Efficiency of Resource Allocation in Imperfect Competitive Market

Economics believes that under the conditions of a perfect competitive market, the market mechanism has the highest level of efficiency in resource allocation, but a perfect competitive market is just an ideal model. Although it is perfect, it does not exist in reality. The result of competition will inevitably lead to a monopoly. In order to obtain monopoly profits, monopolistic manufacturers must decrease the production and force up the price, which reduce the efficiency of resource allocation. To this end, the government is required to shoulder the responsibilities of anti-monopoly and maintain fair market competition to create a good competitive environment for enterprises.

(3) The Market Mechanism cannot Solve the Problem of Public Goods Provision and Externalities

In many fields of public goods, such as the provision of public goods like national defense, education, infrastructure (energy, transportation, communications, etc.), the market mechanism is powerless and can only provide the goods rely on the government or under the government's guidance because of the phenomenon of "free-riding". In the market economy, the behavior of an individual or business having an impact on others or society without paying or being compensated for it is called the externalities of economic activity, and is divided into positive externalities and negative externalities. The economic activities with positive externalities such as new inventions, vaccination, education investment, national defense, road construction, etc.. bring benefits to inventors and producers, but more brings benefits to others in the society. Examples of negative externalities are factory exhaust emissions, individuals smoking in public places, loud noises, etc.. The solution to externalities must rely on government systems, laws and regulations, reward and punishment systems, etc..

(4) The Market Mechanism cannot Solve the Problem of Inequality in Income Distribution

The market economy follows the rule of "survival of the fittest", with the principle of "allocating according to production factors". This will inevitably lead to uneven distribution and social instability. It is possible that such conflicts between economic goals with social goals will further inhibit the role of the market economy. To this end, the government needs to redistribute income appropriately and adjust it through taxation, social welfare, relief and other methods to achieve the unity of efficiency and fairness.

2.2 Establishment of a Socialist Market Economy

2.2.1 The Necessity of Socialism Implementing Market Economy

(1) The Planned Economic System, which was Originally Regarded as the Basic Special System of Socialism, Severely Hampered the Development of Social Productive Forces, thus Socialism Inevitably Chose a New Resource Allocation Method

China's traditional planned economy system was established in the 1950s, basically based on the former Soviet Union's centrally planned economic model in the 1950s. Of course, it also mixed some of our own experiences of the supply system implemented in revolutionary wartime and the transformation of capital in the transition period. The basic characteristics of the traditional planned economic system show as follow.

The decision-making structure: The allocation of resources is made centrally by the central planning agency representing the interests of all members in the society, and it is managed hierarchically in a pyramid-like structure. The information structure: The information flow is vertical, the content of information is mainly physical indicators. Planning and statistics are the main transmission tools, thereby forming a centralized and bureaucratic vertical management system. Motive structure: Economic operations rely on government's directive plans and administrative orders to promote, which lack the necessary economic incentives. In order to implement the plan, the government always adopts the method of administrative supervision. Coordination structure: The coordination of economic decision-making is completed by the central planning agency in advance.

It should be noticed that this economic system plays a certain positive role in the early years of the new China, because at that time we were faced with the implementation the missions of national fiscal unification, socialist transformation of agriculture, handicrafts, national capitalist industry and commerce, developing a large-scale economic construction with opportunities. This management method guarantees the establishment of the material basis of China's socialist public ownership economy and promotes the development of productive forces. However, with the basic completion of socialist transformation and the further development of socialist economic construction, the disadvantages of the traditional planned economic system gradually exposed, the main drawbacks of this system show as follow.

First, it excludes the function of the market, and the industrial structure and product structure formed by using administrative planning to allocate resources are severely disconnected to the demand structure, result in the low resource allocation efficiency. Besides, the plan that is anxious for success is removed from the national conditions and surpassing national strength, and ultimately led to the marked ups and downs of the national economy. Second,without distinction between government and enterprises, state-owned enterprises have become affiliated to administrative organs. Losing the autonomy, the enterprise cannot operate autonomously and sole-responsibility for its own profit and loss, which led to the lacking of vitality of the whole economy. Third, severe equalitarianism existed in allocation, people eat from the same pot, getting an equal share regardless of the work done. People's life cannot improve continuously with the development of production. This situation restraints the enthusiasm, initiative, and creativity of enterprises and employees, bring into a lack of vitality of the socialist economic system. An important reason why the superiority of our socialist system has not been fully exerted is that a rigid model that is incompatible with the development of social productive forces has been formed in the economic system.

In response to the above-mentioned shortcomings from 1959 to 1978, we carried out a large reform of the traditional planned economic system and also achieved some goals and experience. However, fundamental problems such as that decision-making power was concentrated in the state administrative organizations, the enterprises lacked autonomy and the economy is managed by administrative measures, had not been resolved. The main reasons include: first, independent commodity producer status for company has not been established; second, denying the function of economic leverage (costs, prices, profits, wages, bonuses) in economic management and economic accounting; third, being obsessively secretive about the concept of market and the market economy that they have not been able to raise fundamental questions such as "resource allocation efficiency", but only tinkered within the framework of the planned economic system, whose purpose is only to improve it.

(2) The Market Economy will Bring Huge Economic Vitality to Socialism, and Give Full Play to the Superiority of Socialism

The theory and practice have sufficiently proved that the market economy is superior to the planned economy. From a theoretical perspective, the market economy is significantly better than the planned economy in terms of power structure, information structure, scientific decision-making, and innovation capabilities.

The market economy has intrinsic motivation for incentives and innovation, while serious compatibility issues of incentives exist in the planned economy. Economic motivation is an inherent issue of the interests of the economic subject. The interests of the economic subject determine its behavioral goals. In an economy, the clearer the subject's goals and the more direct the benefits, the better it is for optimizing resource allocation and conducive to technological progress and capital accumulation. The market economy has a strong driving force for development, which is from the company's pursuit of maximum profit and the individual's pursuit of the maximum benefit. The rooted cause of the lack of motivation or serious compatibility problems of incentive in the planned economy is that the objective functions of the planning authority, manager, and employee are different. The difference in individual interests makes the manager and the employee to harm the overall interests in order to maximize their own interests. The asymmetry of information creating great difficulties for the authority to change the objective function of managers and employees by necessary rewards and punitive measures. In the economic system, output often become the main assessment indicators in a series of performance indicators, while indicators of benefits and cost are often ignored. Therefore, under the planned economic system, all economic entities, including planning authorities, lack motivation to provide economic efficiency.

The market economy has the most efficient information transmission channels and processing mechanisms, while the planned economy has serious problems of information asymmetry. Information is important for decision makers, and its role is to provide factual basis of information for making decision. By reducing uncertainty, the information improves decision-making efficiency and reduces decision-making costs. From the perspective of the entire economy and society, the effectiveness of the flow and use of information in social networks fundamentally determines the efficiency of the entire economic system. Thus, whether the information can be obtained at low cost, decides the quality of economic decision, and therefore becomes one of the key factors that determine the efficiency of economic system. In a market economy, due to decentralized decision-making, each decision-maker does not have to understand all the events that occur and what the impact of these events will be, the only thing that needs to be understood is what kind of changes have occurred to the relative price, and the price mechanism minimizes the importance of information in a specific time and environment. In addition, the market economy is an economy that can use information at the lowest cost, while the information in the planned economy is very expensive. As the result, the use of information in planned economy is more inadequate, and lacks the information that required for decision-making.

(3) The Market Economy has Great Potential of Progress and Innovation, While the Planned Economy is Bound to Stagnation and Decline

Practices at home and abroad have proven that the market economy is better than the planned economy. China's economic construction experience in the 1950s has proved that the disadvantages of the planned economy have become increasingly serious, which has greatly hindered the rapid development of the national economy. After the reform of the economic system in 1978, the decisive role of market mechanism was continuously stimulated in resource allocation and the improvement of productivity has been promoted effectively. Consequently, China's economic development has achieved world-renowned achievements. International experience has also strongly proved that the market economy is superior to the planned economy in the role of promoting economic development. The economic growth of the Four Asian Tigers 20 years ago has largely depended on the market economy. On the contrary, the former Soviet Union and the socialist countries of Eastern Europe, which have long adhered to the planned economy, failed to duly change the mechanism of resources allocation, and generally realize the transformation from a centralized planned economic system to a socialist market economic system under the background of commodity economy increasingly developing, especially the increasingly internationalized commodity economy. As a result, the lacks of vigor and vitality that blocking the rapidly and healthily development of domestic economy, and the slow development of people's living standards, eventually lead to the breakup of the country.

(4) Socialism has a Deep Foundation for Implementing Planned Economy, and the Implementation of a Market Economy is an Inevitable Result of the Development of a Socialist Economy

The market economy is a highly developed commodity economy. First of all, it has two basic prerequisites: social division of labor and the independence of producers on property rights and business activities based on this. In addition, there are two other important conditions: socialized mass production and the marketization of production resource allocation based on it. These prerequisites and conditions are all contained in the socialist economy.

(5) The Deepening of Understanding the Market Economy and the Development of Theory will Inevitably Lead to the Establishment of Market Economy in China

The transformation of China's planned economic system to a market economy is the inevitable result of the continuous development of understanding the market economy by the national leadership, theorists, and the cadres and the masses in Guangdong. Since the reform and opening up, the process of understanding the economy has gone through the following stages. In 1979, the idea of setting planned economy as the mainstay and market regulation as the supplement was established and the Twelfth National Congress was used as the symbol. In 1984, an organized theory of commodity economy was established on the Third Plenary Session of the 12th Central Committee. In 1987, the concept of "the state regulates the market and the market guides enterprises" was proposed on the 13th National Congress of the CPC; After 1989, in a special period of governance and rectification, the combination of a planned economy and a market economy was proposed; After Deng Xiaoping's southern inspection and speech in 1992, the 14th National Congress of the CPC clearly put forward setting the establishment of a socialist market economic system as the target model of China's economic reforms. The Third Plenary Session of the 14th Central Committee proposed 50 specific ways to establish a socialist market economic system in China, marking the leadership and the theoretical understanding of the socialist market economy is gradually deepening and mature. It is under the guidance of correct theories that China's economic system is reformed healthily and rapidly. It was gradually changed from the old planned economic system to the socialist market economic system. At the end of the 20th century, China initially established a socialist market economic system.

In short, choosing a socialist market economic system as the target model of our reform has its historicity and inevitability.

2.2.2 The Essence of the Socialist Market Economy

The socialist market economy is an economic system that organically combines the basic socialist system and the market economy and it is a new type of economic system that gives full play to the inherent advantages of the two. The socialist market economy has profound connotations. First, the market economy is used as an allocation method of resource in economic operations, and thereby get rid of the traditional concept that it is the unique characteristic of capitalism. The second is to use planning and market as the two methods of adjusting economy, and clarify that they have their own advantages and disadvantages in regulating economic activities. Under the conditions of socialized mass production and the existence of complex economic relations, the market economy has stronger adaptability, more significant advantages and higher efficiency for promoting economic development. Third, as a way of allocating resources, the market economy does not have a social system attributes, but the economic system formed by its combination with the pursuit of material benefitreflects the characteristics of the basic socialist system. Fourth, the organic combination of the development of a market economy and the adherence to the basic socialist system not only gives fully function the superiority of the socialist system but also gives full play to the important role of the market economy in effective resources allocating.

2.2.3 Basic Characteristics of Socialist Market Economy

(1) Contain the General Characteristics of a Modern Market Economy

Above all, the socialist market economy is a modern market economy. It shares similarities with market economies in other social forms, especially with the capitalist modern market economy, in its operating mechanism and mode of operation. It has the general characteristics of a modern market economy, mainly including: the market mechanism plays a decisive role in the allocation of resources; the main body of the market economy is an independent economic legal entity that operates independently and is responsible for its own profits and losses, self-development, and self-regulation; has a sound market system; the price of commodities is controlled by the market economy laws and market mechanisms to form and regulate; the government implements macro indirect regulation of the economy; has a strict and perfect market regulation system to ensure the normal operation of the market economy; has an extensive information system.

(2) The Inherent Characteristics of the Socialist Market Economy

The socialist market economy is a new type of modern market economy that combines the basic socialist system with the market economic system. The establishment of this market economy will be affected by the basic socialist system, the primary stage of socialist development, and the characteristics of large developing countries themselves and other factors. Therefore, the socialist market economy has some characteristics that are different from market economies in other social forms.

The socialist market economy is established based on a basic economic system that set public ownership as the main body and develop with multi-ownership economies together. Until now, the developed western market economies have been based on the private ownership of the means of production, while China's socialist market economy is based on the basic economic system in which the public ownership is the main body and the multi-ownership economy develops together. It is believed that the nature of public ownership and the market economy are both socialization, and the two can be organically integrated and compatible with each other. That is, the essential requirements of market economy can be achieved under the conditions of public ownership of the means of production while the essential requirements of a public ownership economy can also be met through the development of a market economy. First, in the initial stage of socialism, as a means of life for individuals, labor still has a considerable qualitative difference. Individual labor is far from being a component of the total social labor. This situation determines that under the premise that the fundamental interests are the same, the material interests of workers are different. Therefore, it requires that each economic unit also have independent economic benefits. The combination of public ownership and market economy can make the public ownership economy to gain more vitality and vitality. Second, public ownership requires the internal unity of fairness and efficiency to gradually achieve common prosperity. Market economy requires the realization of high efficiency in resource allocation based on fair competition, emphasizes efficiency first, and considers fairness. Combined, the public ownership economy can better achieve high efficiency, and at the same time, be more conducive to social fairness. Third, modern market economy is based on socialized large-scale production, and the public ownership economy also connects various economic units into an organic one through market contract forms, so as to get rid of the closed model of a strip-segmented traditional public ownership economy.

The socialist market economy is a market economy with distribution according to working performance as the main body, multiple forms of distribution coexisting, and the goal of common prosperity. Distribution relations is an important aspect of production relations, and the distribution of production conditions determines the distribution of personal income. The ownership structure that public ownership is the main body and develops with multiple ownership determines that the personal income is distributed mainly according to work, coexisting with multiple distribution methods and the goal of common prosperity. Under the socialist market economy system, because of the dominant position of public ownership economy, distribution according to work occupies the dominant position in the distribution mode. In a socialist market economy, if the market plays a decisive role in the allocation of resources, the market for production factors such as the capital market, labor market, land market, and technology market must be developed accordingly, so that it is also necessary to distribute according to production factors. The principle of giving priority to efficiency while giving consideration to fairness reflects the requirements of public ownership and market economy for personal income distribution. During the period of institutional transition, the trend of income gaps due to various reasons has widened. Thus, the state must adopt proper methods, such as income distribution policies and tax policies, etc., to adjust high income, guarantee the basic life of low income residents, prevent the disparity between the rich and the poor getting polarization and maintain social stability.

The socialist market economy is a market economy with a more complete and reasonable macro-economic control system. State intervention and regulation are important signs of the transformation of a free market economy into a modern market economy. The socialist market economy has the general characteristics of a modern market economy, and the country's macro regulation and planning guidance are the inherent requirements of a socialist market economy as well as a necessary condition for its healthy development. In addition, the socialist market economy is based on the structure of public ownership, the state owned economy led by it occupies the dominant position in the whole public economy, and the public owned economy dominates the economy. The fundamental goal of the entire market economy is to achieve common prosperity. Socialist countries implement macro-economic control to carry out market economy operations in accordance with the requirements for the sound and rapid development of the entire national economy on the side of fundamental interests of all people. The macro-economic control is fundamentally consistent with the interests of the dominant market economy subject under the socialist market economy, and the socialist countries can combine the current interests with long-term interests, local interests with overall interests, better utilize the advantages of the two market methods. This determines that the macroeconomic regulation and control in the socialist market economy is more effective and reasonable than in the capitalist market economy, which can better maintain the basic balance of the total national economy and promote the optimization of the economy structure, guides the sustained, coordinated and healthy development of the national economy and promote the overall progress of the society.

The socialist market economy is a market economy with a more complete legal system. The market economy is essentially a legal economy, especially the modern market economy, as the relationship in the process of economic operation is more complicated, market rules and development have also become more systematic. The socialist market economy is mainly based on the public ownership, and its fundamental goal of its operation is to realize common prosperity, which determines that the socialist market economy should be and may be a more perfect legal economy. In the socialism system, workers are the masters of the country, and all laws and regulations formulated by the state are based on the interests of workers. Thus, establishing market rules and regulations to ensure and promote the healthy development of the socialist market economy is also accord with the interests of the working people. Only when the socialist market economy operates in a healthy and coordinated manner can the entire socialist national economy develop rapidly, and thereby completely eradicate exploitation, eliminate polarization, and ultimately achieve a common prosperity to lay a strong material foundation. It can be seen that, the establishment and completion of laws and regulations system of the socialist market economy, is not only needed for the normal operation of the market economy, but also the requirement of the working people and the interests. The uniformity of the two makes the socialist market laws and regulations system an inherently unified and perfect legal system. Compared with the capitalist market economy law and regulation system, socialism market economy laws and regulations system is more complete.

2.2.4 The Basic Framework of the Socialist Market Economy System

The socialist market economic system we are going to build is integrated with the basic socialistic system. It has both similarities and fundamental differences with the capitalist market economy. The common point is determined by the market economy, and the difference is determined by the social system. Therefore, the basic framework of the socialist market economic system must reflect both the essence of the socialist economic system and the basic structure of the modern market economic system. After decades of reform and practice, China has explored the formed the basic framework of the socialist market economy system. It can be summarized in the following aspects.

(1) The Basic Economic System with Public Ownership as the Main Body and the Common Development of Multiple Ownership Economies

It mainly includes: unswervingly consolidating and developing the public ownership economy, optimizing the layout and structure of the state-owned economy, enhancing the vitality, control, and influence of the state-owned economy. Stabilizing and continuously improving the rural double-layered operating system which combines collective unified management and family decentralize management and based on family contracting and management in long term. Unswervingly encouraging, supporting, and guiding the development of the non-public ownership economy. Adhere to the equal protection of property rights, form a new pattern of equal competition among all forms of economic ownership and mutual promotion. Establishing a modern property rights system with clear property rights, separated rights and duties, strict protection, and smooth circulation. Developing a mixed ownership economy based on the modern property rights system.

(2) An Unified, Open and Orderly Competitive Modern Market System

The market system is a prerequisite for playing the basic role of the market mechanism in resource allocation. It mainly includes: forming a relatively complete factor market system including the labor market, capital market, real estate product market, and technology information market, to promote commodities and various factors flow freely and compete adequately across the country. Uniting urban and rural markets and connecting domestic and international markets together. Improving price formation mechanisms of production factors and resource, which reflects market supply and demand, resource scarcity, and environmental damage costs. Standardizing the development of industry associations and market intermediary organizations, establishing a sound social credit system.

(3) A Sound Macro-economic Control System

The socialist market economy must have a sound macro-economic control system to maintain the basic balance of the national economy at the macro level, promote the optimization of the economic structure, guide the sustained, rapid, healthy, and coordinated development of the national economy, and promote the overall progress of society. The means of macro-economic control mainly include economic, legal, and necessary administrative tool. The main contents of macro-economic control include: Establishing a comprehensive government-managed national economy system which contains overall planning, economic regulation, market supervision, social management, public services, and state-owned asset management. Playing a guiding role of national development planning, planning, and industrial policies in macro regulation and control, and improving the level of macro regulation and control through the comprehensive use of fiscal and monetary policies. Finalizing the market supervision system that combines administrative law enforcement, industry self-regulation, and public opinion supervision together, maintaining and improving the market order; Strengthening policy order for market entry, market competition, and market transaction, guaranteeing fair transactions and equal competition, and protecting the legitimate rights and interests of operators and consumers.

(4) Reasonable Income Distribution System

A fair and reasonable income distribution system is a powerful driving force for the smooth development of the socialist market economy, and is also an important sign of the superiority of the socialist system. It mainly includes: adhere to and improve the distribution system with distribution according to labor as the main body and multiple distribution methods coexist. Improve the distribution system that distribute according to the contribution of the production factors such as labor, capital, technology, management, etc.; deal with the relationship of efficiency and fairness in both primary distribution and redistribution, and put more emphasis on fairness in redistribution; standardizing the distribution order, strengthening the adjustment of income distribution and put emphasis on addressing the problem of income gap being excessively widening among partial social members. With the goal of common prosperity, the proportion of the middle-incomes and the income level of low-incomes should be increased, excessive income should be adjusted, and illegal income should be eliminated.

(5) Wide Coverage of Social Security Systems

The market economy cannot separate from a perfect social security system at any time. At present, our social security system is roughly composed of three major blocks: one is a social insurance program mandated by national laws, including pensions, unemployment, medical treatment, industrial injury, childbirth insurance and housing security, which is the main part of the social security system; the other one is a security project with national financial support, including public relief, social welfare, provide special assistance to entitled groups, and community services; and the last one is the commercial insurance projects that follow the voluntary principle and for the purpose of profiting, including personal insurance, corporate insurance and fraternal insurance, which is the main supplement of social insurance.

(6) Completed Legal System

The market economy is a legal economy, which means, from the allocation of production factors to the orderly, safe, fair, and efficient production, exchange, and distribution of commodities, laws are required to regulate it. In addition to the general characteristics of a market economy, a socialist market economy also has other characteristics required by the socialist system, that is to regulate the market economy through legal means to achieve social goals that the market mechanism itself cannot achieve. A complete legal system mainly includes: in accordance with the basic strategy of governing the country by the law, focusing on establishing a system, standardizing power and responsibility, protecting the rights and interests and strengthening economic legislation. Improve the legal system of market entities and intermediary organizations, standardize and rationalize product relations, and protect various types of property rights and interests. Improve the legal system of market transactions, guarantee freedom of contracts and transaction security, and maintain fair competition. Improve laws and regulations on budgets, tax, finance, and investment, regulate economic regulation and market supervision. Improve laws and regulations on labor, employment, and social security, and protect the legitimate rights and interests of workers and citizens properly. Improve laws and regulation in the field of society and sustainable development to promote overall development of society and economy.

(7) Good Social Credit System

The layout of the socialist market economy is combined with the basic socialist economic system and political system, together with the socialist spiritual civilization. Strengthening ideological and moral construction is an important prerequisite for the healthy development of the socialist market economy. The market economy is a credit economy. The general behavior of keeping promise is the prerequisite for the smooth progress of the transaction and the healthy development of the economy. Without credit, or lack of credit, contractual relationships cannot be maintained, and the networks and chains of socioeconomic relations will be disordered, imbalanced and even broken. A social credit system supported by morality, based on property rights and guaranteed by laws is a necessary condition for the construction of a modern market system and a fundamental strategy to standardize the order of the market economy. On the basis of strengthening the protection of property rights, it should be focused on monetary credit to build the modern market economy credit system which includes commercial credit, consumer credit, bank credit, and personal credit. At the same time, a punishment mechanism is established to punish breach of trust and breach of contract in accordance with law severely.

(8) Open Economy

The market economy is an open economy. Opening to the outside world is China's basic national policy, which mainly includes: combining active participation in globalization and adherence to independence, combining the "bringing in" strategy and the "going globally" strategy, making full use of the resources in domestic and international markets, forming a comprehensive, wide-ranging, and multi-level opening-up pattern. Improving the open economic system of internal and external interactions, mutual benefit, win-win cooperation, and safety and efficiency, forming new advantages for participating in international economic cooperation and competition under the conditions of economic globalization. Improving the opening-up system guarantees and accelerating the integration of domestic and foreign trade in accordance with the requirements of the market economy and WTO rules. Forms a stable and transparent foreign-related economic management system, creates a fair and predictable legal environment, and ensures the autonomy and equal status of various enterprises that engaged in foreign economic and trade. Manage foreign-related economic activities in accordance with the law, strengthen service and supervision functions, and further increase the convenience of trade and investment. Establish and improve a foreign trade operation monitoring system and a warning mechanism for international balance of payment to maintain national security.

(9) New Social Management System

The development of the market economy requires a new type of social management system that is compatible with it. It mainly includes: reforms of the social labor employment system, implement of active employment policies, and efforts to improve the entrepreneurial and employment environment. Establishment and improvement of the talent market system, and promotion of talent flow. Reforms of scientific and technological management system, acceleration of the construction of the national innovation system, promotion of the efficient allocation of science and technology resources throughout the society, and realization of the close integration of science and technology with economic and social development. Strengthening the government's public health management function, establishing a health care system that is compatible with the socialist market economic system. Deepening the culture institutional reforms, improving the cultural market system, and establishing a energetic production and management system of cultural product. Accelerating the formation of a standardized, coordinated, fair, transparent, clean, and efficient administrative management system. Further improving socialist democracy and the legal system. Strengthening and reforming the construction of the Communist party's conduct and integrity, and the formation of institutional guarantees that are conducive to the progress of economic, political, cultural, legal systems, and the whole society.

The content of the above aspects is an organic wholewith components interconnected and mutually restrained, and constitutes the basic framework of the socialist market economic system. The establishment and improvement of this framework involves all areas and aspects of the economy, politics, culture, and society. It is a long-term, complex, and arduous system project.

2.3 Carriers of Operation in a Socialist Market Economy

2.3.1 Micro-subjects in the Socialist Market Economy

The operation of the market economy not only involves a complete market system and market mechanism, but also requires a complete market body; because the essence of a market economy is that various market bodies are connected and interacted with each other in the market. Thus, the complete market body is particularly important for whether the market system can operate normally. The so-called "market subjects" (transaction subjects) are organizations and individuals who are directly engaged in trading activities and provide conditions and services for the smooth conduct of trading activities. In economics, the market transactions can be generalized abstractly as three categories: enterprises (manufacturers), residents (households), and governments (including non-profit organizations).

Enterprises are the most important economic entities of a market economy. Enterprises have dual identities, both as demanders of production factors and as suppliers of products and services. Enterprises purchase production factors to engage in production in order to obtain more profits, so their decision-making of production and operation (what to produce, how to produce, and produce for whom) must be market-oriented, and its costs, benefits, and profits must be constrained by the market. To achieve value, recover costs, and realize profit, enterprises will use market to transact the commodities and services it produce.

Residents also have dual identities, both as suppliers of production factors and as demanders of products or services. As suppliers of production factors, their purpose is to obtain remuneration for the production factors, some of which are paid to the government in the form of taxes, and the rest of disposable income is used for consumption and savings. The ultimate goal of consuming products and services is to achieve maximize utility. The purpose of savings is to obtain more interest or dividends. Therefore, the behavior of residents must be affected by commodity prices and market interest rates. The residents must be intrinsically linked to the market and become the subject of market economic activities.

The government and other non-profit institutions are the third pole that constitutes a tripartite situation between residents and businesses. Residents pay taxes to the government, and the government provides public goods and services for them, which is actually a transaction. In addition, as a third party of the transaction, the government will lead or participate in the construction of the market system and maintains the order of the transaction, playing the role of the market order maintainer. On the other hand, as a regulator of macroeconomics, it regulates or interfere with the economic operation by various financial means, in order to achieve the goals of stable growth of the national economy, realizing full employment, and ensuring the basic balance of international payments.

2.3.2 Market Mechanism in Socialist Market Economy

The market mechanism is the mechanism based on law of value. The price mechanism, the supply and demand mechanism, and the competition mechanism are the most important market mechanisms. To develop a socialist market economy, it is necessary to make full use of the function of the market mechanism, so that it can play a decisive role in the allocation of resources. In a market economy, the functioning of the market mechanism has the following characteristics.

(1) The Function of the Market Mechanism in Resource Allocation is Combined with Government Orientation

In the socialist market economy, the function of allocating resources for market value still plays a decisive role, but it is combined with the government's macro management of the national economy. That is to say, on the one hand, the government uses planning methods to allocate certain resources related to important issue such as national economy, people's livelihood and national security. On the other hand, the government uses macro-regulation to guide and adjust the role of the market mechanism in resource allocation.

(2) The Function of Market Mechanisms in the Regulation of Economic Interests is Combined with Social Coordination

In the socialist market economy, although the interests of the three parties, the countries, the enterprises and the individuals are fundamentally the same, due to the existence of external diseconomy, the pursuit of self-interest by enterprises and individuals may lead to excessive use of resources. Thus, the use and adjustment of market mechanisms may not always meet the requirements for the overall and long-term interests of society, which objectively requires the state to re-harmonize economic interests on the basis of regulating economic interests by market mechanisms on behalf or the whole society. This relationship is very obvious in the socialist market economy.

According to the requirements of the market economy, the government must give full play to the role of the market mechanism and further reform of the socio-economic system in order to create an economic and institutional environment that is more suitable for the functioning of the market mechanism. It mainly includes: building a unified, open, competitive, and orderly modern market economic system; promoting the reform and opening up of the capital market and steady development; developing markets for property rights, land, labor, and technology; creating an environment in which various market entities use production factors equally; reforming the social circulation system and developing modern circulation methods; standardizing disputes settlement procedure and regulating market economy orders, improving the social credit system of the modern market economy, breaking industry monopolies and regional blockades, and promoting the free flow of goods and production factors in the national market.

2.3.3 Market System in Socialist Market Economy

To give full play to the functions of the market mechanism, a sound modern market system base on the complete market system and adapt to the development requirements of China's socialist market economy is needed.

(1) Develop and Improve Commodity Markets and Production Factor Markets

The commodity market is the foundation of the socialist market system, and it is the basic platform and main form of transaction for goods and services in the national economy. According to the function of the commodity market, the commodity market can be divided into a consumption goods market and a production factors market. While developing the consumption goods market, the production factors market should be developed energetically as well, which mainly include: financial markets, technology and information markets, labor markets, real estate markets, and property rights markets.

(2) Develop and Improve Financial Markets

The financial market is at the core of the socialist market economy. Under the conditions of a modern market economy, a developed market economy will not exist without a developed financial market. To develop a socialist market economy, financial markets must be established and improved. The financial markets can be divided into a money market that provides short-term financing and a capital market that provides long-term working capital.

(3) Develop and Improve Technology and Information Markets

In the information economy era, as the important factors of production, science and technology and information have played an increasingly prominent role in the market. Practice has proven that the technology and information market is a link that promotes the integration of scientific research and production. The development of technology and information markets can make the scientific and technological achievements of scientific research institutions transform into commodity in time. This transformation not only serves the economic construction, but also strengthens these units, and greatly promotes the development of the socialist market economy. To develop and improve the technology and information market, it is necessary to introduce competition mechanisms, protect intellectual products, implement the rule of transferring technological achievements with compensation, realize the commoditization and industrialization of technology products and information; adopt incentive and supporting policies to attract enterprises to enter the technology market, improve technology and information trading regulations, and strengthen the management of technology and information markets.

(4) Develop and Improve the Labor Market

The labor market can promote the rational flow and distribution of labor. The market economy's function of the resources allocation and the distribution mechanism are implemented in the labor flow process. The main price signal of the labor market is work, which regulates the supply and demand of the labor market. China has abundant labor resources, but its employment pressure is high. Therefore, it is necessary to promote a rational flow of labor through developing the labor market and expanding the scope of employment for working population, so as to develop a socialist market economy.

(5) Develop and Improve the Real Estate Market

The real estate market is an important part of China's market system. Developing and improving the real estate market can contribute to the acceleration of China's urbanization process, driving the development of related industries, and promoting the adjustment of residents' consumption structure.

(6) Develop and Improve the Property Rights Market

The property rights market is a market that can provide various services such as corporate property rights transactions. Its development can activate corporate property rights transactions, enrich the way in which the company allocates elements, and reduce the cost of property rights restructuring. Besides, its development can help establishing a mechanism based on the principle of survival for the fittest, promoting the reform of enterprises, optimizing and adjusting the industrial structure, and integrating the industries.

2.3.4 Market Order in Socialist Market Economy

The socialist market economy is an efficiency economy and a legal economy. To ensure the efficiency of resource allocation in a market economy, market rules and market order must be established and improved.

Market rules are norms and rules of market behavior stipulated or expressed in the form of laws, regulations and credits, mainly including market entry and exit rules, market competition rules, market transaction rules, market arbitration rules, etc.. Market order is an orderly state of economic operation that is regulated, formed and maintained by institutional arrangements, legal systems, and social concepts. It mainly includes market subject order and market transaction order. Market rules and market order are closely related to market effectiveness. Therefore, they need to be established, refined and implemented effectively.

At the initial stage of China's market economy's development, the planned and natural economy still occupied a large proportion. Therefore, in the process of development, the phenomenon of shake-able market rules and the chaotic market order is hard to avoid. The key is to make it develop in a healthy direction through accelerating the economic system reform and legal system construction, improving market supervision and management. First of all, a good planning for market construction is need. Second, the construction of market laws and regulations should be strengthened, so that all market activities have a legal basis, which support using laws and regulations to regulate the behavior of market entities. Third, it is necessary to establish a policy of market entry, market competition, and market transaction order, to ensure fair transactions and equal competition, so as to protect the legitimate rights and interests of operators and consumers. Fourth, the higher level of market transactions openness, the establishment of authoritative market law enforcement and supervision institutions, strengthened management of the market, and the application of public opinion in supervising the market are needed.

2.4 Government Macro Control in Socialist Market Economy

Macro-economic control refers to the state's overall adjustment and control of the operation of the market economy, which is realized through various macro-economic policies, economic regulations from the perspective of the overall situation of economic operation. The subject of macro-economic control is the state. The objects of regulation are the process and result of the operation of the market economy. macro-economic control is the product of the development of the market economy, and is an economy category that closely linked to the modern market economy based on a highly developed social division of labor and socialized mass production.

2.4.1 Necessity of Government Macro-economic Control in Socialist Market Economy

The government's role in macroeconomic regulation and control is rooted from the requirements of large-scale socialized production, the normal operation of a market economy, and socio-economic development.

(1) Objective Requirements for Socialized Mass Production

The socialist market economy is built on the basis of socialized large-scale production, and there are complex social divisions of labor and close economic ties between various regions, departments and enterprises. The intention of coordinating the economic relations among the various regions, departments, enterprises and all levels of society to make social reproduction normal and make the national economy develop proportionally and coordinately, objectively requires macro-economic controlconducted by the government. This is unchangeable no matter in a capitalist market economy or in a socialist market economy, because they are both based on the socialization of production.

(2) The Inherent Requirements for the Normal Operation of the Market Economy

The market mechanism can play an effective role in the allocation of social resources, but it is not omnipotent. It has its own characteristics and deficiencies, that is, "market failure". Hence, government intervention in the economy and macro-economic control are necessary. The main manifestations of market failure include: imperfect competition, externalities, provision of public goods, incomplete information, and inequality in income distribution. These shortcomings in the market mechanism are an important cause of cyclical economic recession and other social contradictions in market economy countries, and the reason for the implementation and improvement of government intervention that are gradually appeared in various countries. The government's macro-economic control and policies and regulations are used to overcome the spontaneity, blindness and lag of the market economy itself. However, the government's macro-economic control under the conditions of a socialist market economy has fundamental differences from the government's management of the economy under the planned economy. Which means, the government no longer directly and comprehensively controls the socio-economy, but corrects market failures and achieves socio-economic development goals instead.

(3) Objective Requirements of the Socialist Economic System

Requirements for the public ownership economy. The public ownership economy, especially the state-owned economy, is belonging to the majority of working people. Its economic activities must conform to the purpose of socialist production. This requires the state to effectively use human, material, and financial resources in the entire society through macro-economic control, who helps to guide the development of production and public-owned economic activities accord with the interests of the working people generally.

Requirements of establishing a socialist market economy and accelerating economic development. As a developing country, if China only rely on the market itself to establish and improve its market economy, it will take a long time. On the contrary, if the government takes the initiative to adopt macroeconomic policies, formulate equal economic rules, protect and promote fair competition, then a sound market system and a competitive market order will be set up quickly.

Requirement to achieve common prosperity. The fundamental goal of carrying out the socialist market economy is to maximize the satisfaction of the growing material and cultural needs of the working people, and ultimately achieve common prosperity. Merely depending on the spontaneity of the micro-economy is impossible to achieve the goal, unless the national macro-economic control joining in.

2.4.2 Targets of Government Macro-economic Control in Socialist Market Economy

Under the socialist market economy system, the overall goal of macro-economic control is to strengthen the research and institution of property rights planning in national economic and social development, propose major strategies, basic tasks, and policies for development, focus on transforming the economic development mode, promoting structural adjustment, realizing a steady structure and total of social supply and demand, maintain stable and rapid economic development, improve the quality and efficiency of economic development, continuously improve people's lives, promote the construction of a harmonious society, and strive to achieve the unification of speed, structure, and efficiency, realize the development of national economy with quality and quantity. The overall goal of macro-economic control is achieved through working on specific objectives. The specific objectives comprehensively reflect the development level and operating quality of the national economy, and reflect the direction and trend of the national economy. The specific objectives of macro-economic control include four objectives, which are promoting economic growth, increasing employment, stabilizing prices, and maintaining the balance of international payments. Besides, it also include other objectives like optimizing the economic structure and achieving reasonable income distribution.

(1) Promoting Economic Growth

Economic growth is an important sign of increased social wealth and comprehensive national strength, the material basis for social development and the improvement of people's living standards, and the primary goal of macroeconomic control. Economic growth must be coordinated with the supply of resources and market demand, and maintained mmoderately rapid growth according to needs and possibility. Economic growth cannot be too slow, nor too fast. If it grows too slow, and the potential of economic growth cannot be fully reached, and many contradictions in economic and social activities are difficult to resolve. If it grows too fast, it will inevitably cause economic tension and the imbalance between agriculture, manufacturing industry and other industries, and cause economic changing radically. All in all,promoting economic growth properly is of great significance for consolidating the socialist system.

(2) Increasing Employment

Increasing employment means eliminating involuntary unemployment as much as possible, so that every capable and willing worker can have equal employment opportunities. For a long period of time in the future, the contradiction of oversupply of labor will be a long-term problem in China. Moreover, the economic system transformation and structural adjustment will highlight this contradiction. Therefore, it is an important task for China to increase more employment through macro-economic control.

(3) Stabilizing Prices

Under the conditions of a market economy, the overall level of prices is basically stable, that is, the price changes are kept within the range allowed by the smooth operation of the economy and the residents' tolerance, avoiding severe inflation and deflation. It is the necessary conditions for the sustained and healthy development of the national economy. Therefore, macro-economic control take price stabilization as an important goal.

(4) Keeping the Equilibrium of Balance of Payments

The equilibrium balance of payments mainly means that the balance of payments, including current accounts, capital accounts, and financial transactions, remain basically balanced. Under an open economy, balance of payments has an important impact on the balance of total social supply and total social demand. If the payments are seriously imbalanced, it will affect normal foreign economic activities and domestic economic activities. Therefore, maintaining the overall balance of domestic total supply and demand and the equilibrium of balance of payments is an important goal of macro-economic control.

(5) Optimize Economic Structure

Optimizing the economic structure is an important guarantee for the sustained and rapid development of the national economy. An irrational economic structure is not conducive to improving economic efficiency and promoting economic development. It goes against improving the employment structure and increasing residents' income, shrinking the gap of economic development between region, urban and rural districts. It also hinders efficient and optimized use of resources. Merely relying on market readjustment is difficult to optimize the economic structure, and may even lead to further distortions in the economic structure.

Optimizing the economic structure is to maintain a reasonable development ratio among industries, sectors, and products, coordinated development between regions, drive the national economy by conducting the industries, and continuously promote the optimization and upgrade of the industrial structure and product structure. It also refers to carefully formulating and implementing various industrial policies and regional development policies, djusting the existing industrial structure and regional structure, and giving preferential policies to key industries and regions, which will help promoting the upgrading of the entire industrial structure, help coordinating development of the regional economy, improve the efficiency of social resource allocation, and promote coordinated development of national economic.

(6) Achieve a Reasonable Income Distribution

Reasonable income distribution is an important manifestation of social fairness and justice, which is related to the healthy operation of the national economy and the full play of the superiority of the socialist system. Achieving a reasonable income distribution is conducive to ensuring social stability and creating a good social environment for reform and development. Besides, it also aids in stimulating the enthusiasm, initiative and creativity of the vast masses, promoting the provision of labor force and economic development. Under the conditions of a socialist market economy, it is necessary to take full advantage of the market readjustment in income distribution, as well as give full play to the role of the government in regulating income distribution. The distribution system of income in the primary stage of socialism should be implemented thoroughly to guarantee its positive rolein promoting economic development and social equity.

2.4.3 Means of Government Macro-economic Control in Socialist Market Economy

Under the conditions of a socialist market economy, the operation and development of the national economy are concentrated as the contradictory movement of the total supply and demand and structure of society. They have profound impact on economic growth rate, economic structure change, employment scale, income distribution, price level, and national income. To achieve the goals of macro-economic control, it is necessary to comprehensively use various means of macro-economic control to adjust and regulate the contradictory movement of the total and structure of social supply and demand. The report of the 17th National Congress of the CPC points out that "playing the guiding role of national development programming, planning, and industrial policies in macro-economic control, and comprehensively using fiscal and monetary policies to increase the level of macro-economic control".

(1) Economic Policy

Economic policies are guidelines and rules formulated by the government, which are to adjust the relations of interests between various economic entities, as well as guideand affect the economic activities. They are important means of macroeconomic regulation. The main economic policies are: fiscal policy, monetary policy, exchange rate policy, income distribution policies, etc.. Under the conditions of the socialist market economy, these policies should be used scientifically and flexibly in combination with different situations in the operation of the national economy in different periods. First, fiscal policies are formulated by the state based on social and economic development goals and economic conditions in a certain period of time. It is used to guide fiscal work and deal with fiscal relations, including fiscal revenue policies, fiscal expenditure policies. and total financial revenue and expenditure relationship policies. Second, monetary policy refers to the central bank's increase or decrease of the money supply to affect interest rates, and then investment and consumption. It mainly includes open market operations, statutory reserve ratios, and rate of rediscount. Third, income distribution policies are policies that regulate the initial distribution and redistribution of national income. Itis implemented through tools such as wages, fiscal budgets, taxes, etc.. Fourth, with the deepening of reform and opening up and the development of the socialist market economy, the contracts of the national economy with oversea parties have gradually strengthened, and the importance of the exchange rate has gradually increased. The role of the exchange rate is mainly reflected in the adjustment of international trade and balance of payments. It is necessary to continuously complete the RMB exchange rate formation mechanism, and maintain the basic stability of the RMB exchange rate at a reasonable and balanced level.

(2) Economic Plan

The development of the socialist market economy is inseparable from the guidance of the economic plan. Thus, the economic plan has become a necessary macro-economic control means. Under the traditional planned economic system, the mandatory plan occupies an absolute dominant position. In contrast, under the socialist market economic system, planning mainly refers to an instructive plan based on respect for the laws of the market economy. It embodies macro management objectives, tasks, various macro balances, and various relationships of basic proportion, and is composed of corresponding indicators system and policy measures. It is based on the role of market readjustment, and mainly guided by instructive plans and mid-to-long-term plans.

(3) Legal and Administrative Means

The market economy is a legal economy, and the law is the guarantee of implementation of macroeconomic regulation and maintaining the market economic order, but from the point of view that some legal provisions can also regulate the economy, the law can also be regarded as a macro-regulation tool. Administrative means for macroeconomic regulation and control mainly rely on mandatory orders adopted by administrative agencies, administrative tasks, or certain specific restrictions to regulate the operation of the economy. In a certain period, this means has its necessity.

Chapter 3

Government and Market

3.1 Economic Function of Government: The Theoretical Perspective

3.1.1 General Equilibrium and Welfare Economics

We start our introduction from a framework of general equilibrium, using the concepts from the Welfare Economics.

First of all, we should make clear the key concept of the Welfare Economics, that is, what does the word *welfare* mean? In fact, we use it widely in our daily life, from the speeches of political leaders to the analysis of news agencies, all of which is related to something about a group of persons.

(1) The Concept of Social Welfare

Now imagine you and some other children are dropped on a deserted island just as the scenario by the English novelist William Golding in his famous novel *Lord of the Flies*①. You and a few other children have to stay on the island for some period of time, waiting for the rescue from the adulthood world. Then when you realize and accept the situation, what is your first plan? What is the key point of your plan?

You have first to strive for living. You may try your best to seek for food, wild fruits, fishes and so on. During the process, as an excellent leader, you

---

① If you have never read the novel, I recommend you read it, for it is more like a political fable than merely a simple story of children.

may explore your wisdom to use what Adam Smith has referred in his *The Wealth of the Nation*, labor division, to make the best use of your human capital, making the one who is most suitable to do what he should do, in order to make the process of seeking food the most efficient.

However, is that enough for your smooth living? May not. You may soon find that, though there is enough food for all of you as a whole, once it comes to the distribution of food, there will still be difference in the viewpoint, even conflicts. The conflicts originate from obvious difference and non-satiety in people's preference. Each one prefers different foods from others, and he hopes he can own more in what he prefers. This ends up in a problem of equity in distribution.

Now we have reached the core of the concept *welfare*. We find that, if we want to live in harmony, we have to reach a balance of two aspects, efficiency and equity (you are now playing the role of a social planner or central planner). That is just the wisdom of the economists who focus on the Welfare Economics. The question then lies in how we can fulfill the requirements to derive both of them, at the same time, the balance between them.

(2) Social Welfare Maximization

Economists often use **Pareto Optimum** to evaluate economic efficiency[1], which means we cannot make anyone else better off without making anyone else worse. When the economy reaches the state of Pareto Optimum, there will be no possibility of Pareto Improvement. Economists prove that, if we want to reach the Pareto Optimum, we should fulfill the following three requirements simultaneously.

First, the optimum condition of production. Assume that we allocate all the production factors, labor (L) and capital (K), between producer X and Y, using a tool of Edgeworth Box, both of whom have their own production. According to what you have learned in your Micro Economics, you will get the condition of optimum, the equivalence of marginal ration of technical substitution (MRTS) of X and Y, which is the slope of the iso-quantity curve, for only in such a situation, there is no possibility of improvement (So we reach the state of Pareto Optimum). We call the curve connected by all the

---

[1] Of course, there are other standards to evaluate efficiency.

equilibrium points the Contract Curve of Production, which tells us all the way of factor distribution between X and Y. When we put the distribution of labor and capital into the production function of X and Y, we derive the production relation between product X and Y, which we directly call X and Y for convenience. We name the new curve the Production Possibilities Curve. It shows the social choice of production between X and Y, where there is an obvious tradeoff (See Figure 3–1).

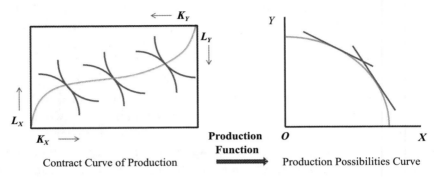

Figure 3-1   Contract Curve of Exchange

Second, the optimum condition of exchange. Now after X and Y are produced, they are owned respectively by A and B, and the quantity they occupy will be decided through a process of exchange with each other. Following the similar logic as the optimum of production and using the Edgeworth Box, we can derive the optimum condition of exchange, that is, the equivalence of marginal ration of substitution (MRS) of X and Y, which is the slope of the indifference curve, for only in such a situation, there is no possibility of improvement (So we reach the state of Pareto Optimum). We call the curve connected by all the equilibrium points the Contract Curve of Exchange, which tells us all the way of product distribution between A and B. When we put the distribution of X and Y into the utility function of A and B, we derive the utility relation between A and B consuming X and Y. We name the new curve the Utility Possibilities Curve. It shows the social arrangement of utility between A and B, where there is also an obvious tradeoff (See Figure 3–2).

Third, the optimum condition of combination. Now we have produced the product X and Y using labor and capital, and they are owned by A and B, who exchange what they own to determine the eventual allocation of their utility from consuming A and B. However, there is still something missing.

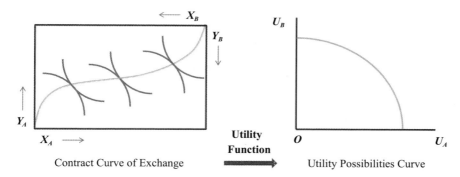

Figure 3-2   Utility Possibilities Curve

We have ignored the relation between the procedure of production and exchange. After all, if there is surplus of production or shortage from the demand of consuming more than what have been produced, the process of production and exchange is not in harmony. In Figure 3–3, we combine the production and exchange. Simple induction can give the optimum condition of combination. That is, people's preference for X relative to Y should be in accordance with the social production cost of X relative to Y, otherwise, we can always adjust the relative production quantity of A to B, to make sure there is neither surplus nor shortage, or in other words, there is no possibility of Pareto Improvement. We often use the MRS of X to Y to express people's preference for X relative to Y, and the marginal ratio of transformation (MRT) of X and Y to depict the social production cost of X relative to Y, so the optimum condition of combination is the equivalence of the MRS of X to Y and the MRT of X and Y.

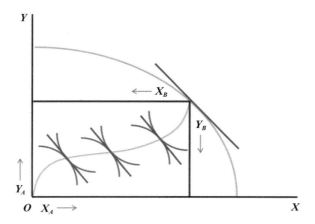

Figure3-3   General Equilibrium of Production and Exchange

After the discussion of economic efficiency, we now turn to the equity of income distribution. Economists use **Social Welfare Function** to depict the equity of income distribution, which is a function transforming heterogeneous individual utility into social utility as a whole and can be graphed as a social indifference curve just as the indifference curve of a single individual. The specific style of social welfare function is the key problem, which directly determines the best way of income distribution. However, there is significant difference in people's viewpoints towards the specific style of social welfare. For instance, as two opposite and extreme examples, under the Utilitarian Criterion, there is no inter-personal comparison and one person's utility is the complete substitute of another person, while under the Utilitarian Criterion, one person's utility is the complete complements of another one. As a result, any style of social welfare function is possible, leaving the equity in income distribution a subjective problem.

As a summary, we now combine the aspect of economic efficiency with the aspect of income distribution equity, to derive the solution of the social welfare maximization question. As depicted in Figure 3-4, the utility possibility frontier is combined, which stands for the economic efficiency and the social indifference curve, which stands for equity of income distribution, and the solution of the welfare maximization question is derived. Of course, you can use any shape of social indifference curve to express your own view of equity.

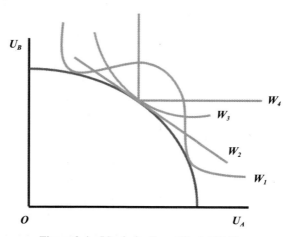

Figure 3-4   Maximization of Social Welfare

(3) The Fundamental Theorem of Welfare Economics

Now we introduce two important theorems by economists.

The First Fundamental Theorem of Welfare Economics: assume that: first, a market exists for each and every commodity; second, all producers and consumers are perfect competitors, then a Pareto efficient allocation of resources emerges. That is, when it comes to providing goods and services, free-enterprise systems are amazingly productive.

You can simply check the theorem by proving that all the conditions for Pareto Optimality will be satisfied naturally in the perfectly competitive market. The First Fundamental Theorem of Welfare Economics means that, when it comes to the problem of resource allocation, the free market is amazingly productive, and any interference by government or central plan is of no necessity.

However, the First Fundamental Theorem of Welfare Economics is silent about income distribution, for you can easily find that, in fact any point on the Contract Curve of Exchange is an equilibrium point satisfying the condition of Pareto Optimality. Therefore, the First Fundamental Theorem of Welfare Economics leaves the question of choosing the best allocation point of social resource. That will be resolved by the Second Fundamental Theorem of Welfare Economics.

The Second Fundamental Theorem of Welfare Economics: society can attain any Pareto efficient allocation of resources by making a suitable assignment of initial endowments and letting people freely trade with each other.

That is, by making a proper income redistribution and letting market play its role, we can reach any point in the Production Possibilities Curve, taking into account both efficiency and fairness. Thus at least in theory, the issues of efficiency and distributional fairness can be separated. Theoretically, it can be achieved through a lump-sum transfers among people, which can redistribute income and makes no distortion to the economy. As a result, when it comes to the problem of income redistribution, government can do some benefit.

3.1.2 Market Failure and the Function of Government

(1) Market Failure

The analysis above on the problem of social welfare maximization, especially the Fundamental Theorem of Welfare Economics, tells the possibility and the direction of government interference.

First, as shown by the Second Fundamental Theorem of Welfare Economics, when it comes to the problem of income distribution fairness, the function of market can do nothing, for the smooth function of market will give us numerous equilibrium without telling anything about the most equitable point.

Second, although the First Fundamental Theorem of Welfare Economics is silent about government interference, the assumption of the theorem still spares some space for the necessity of government intervention.

Although the First Fundamental Theorem of Welfare Economics proves that the free market has amazing ability to allocate resource efficiently, there are strict presumptions for it.

A market exists for each and every commodity. It means we can only use market to allocate those objects that can be exchanged through the mechanism of price. The presumption for this is that we can evaluate those objects by monetized value. Yet there are many objects in our economy that cannot be monetized, such as confidence, friendship, love, etc..

When the market mechanism is missing, some interesting phenomenon appears.

a. **Asymmetric Information:** Information is the core for trading efficiently, for the role of price mechanism can only play smoothly by checking the essential information by the traders. However, the distribution of information between the traders is not symmetric, with one side of the trade sometimes owning more information than the other. The asymmetric information leads to inefficiency in resource allocation. According to the timing of the asymmetric information, we call the specific sort of inefficiency moral hazards or adverse selection.

Moral hazard happens when there is asymmetric information after the trade.

For example, the board of the company hire a new CEO to manage the affair of the company. There is obvious asymmetric information between the board directors and the CEO, for only the latter masters the specific situation of the company affair. Under such condition, there is possibility that the CEO may do something to benefit himself while harming the benefit of the shareholders, which will end up in economic inefficiency.

Adverse selection happens when there is asymmetric information before the trade. The most famous example is the lemon market of used car by Economist George Akerlof. Because there is asymmetric information between buyer and seller of the second-hand car, with the latter owning more information about the condition of the car, misconduct of cheating may appear, which harms the benefit of the buyer. With time going on, there will be less and less trade in the market. Therefore, economic efficiency also produces.

Then how to restore efficiency? The economists contribute a lot of their wisdom to the question, one of which is the Theory of Information Economics, including various methods to design mechanisms to ease the degree of asymmetric information. However, because the market itself of course has friction, it is difficult to eliminate the asymmetric information completely by the mechanism of market, making the problem of asymmetric information an example of market nonexistence.

b. **Externality:** Externality is the benefit/damage you get from others without paying them or the cost you burden from others without asking them to pay for you. Externality is also an example of market nonexistence, for the externality often appears when it is difficult to define the border of the property rights. For instance, the difficulty in defining the property rights of air leads to the air pollution, and the difficulty in defining the property rights of river leads to the water pollution. Under the lack of property rights defining, using market mechanism to solve the problem of externality is impossible.

c. **Public Goods:** Public Goods are those goods that have the non-competitiveness in consumption and non-exclusiveness in benefit. The former means one person's consumption will not affect anther one's; while the latter means you cannot exclude anyone from consuming the goods. From national safeguard to law enforcement, we are surrounded by all kinds of public goods in our daily life. Yet unlike other commodities, there are special difficulties in supplying public goods by market.

First of all, the non-competitiveness in consumption means that the marginal cost of any one's consumption is zero. Under the competitive market, it means the efficient pricing of the goods should also be zero, except that you can use a monopoly to supply the goods, and at the same time, use the first level price prejudice to set the price. Second, the non-exclusiveness in benefit means you cannot exclude anyone from consuming the goods①. This makes collecting fees of consuming impossible. Both of the above features lead to the conclusion that, it is difficult to ask a single enterprise to supply the public goods in a competitive market. Then how about the people who consume the goods supplying public goods collectively? Considering the free-rider phenomenon, the collective supplying of public goods will also easily end up with collapse②.

The above shows the result of lack of market in allocating resources. As referred by the second presumption of the Second Fundamental Theorem of Welfare Economics, even there is market playing its role, sometimes, it cannot function well to allocate resources efficiently, the most important reason for which is the appearance of **Market Power**. Once there is market power, no matter it is **monopoly**, **oligopoly** or **monopolistic competition**, the pricing of commodities will surpass its social efficient level and the production quantity will be less than the social premium level, leaving inefficiency in resource allocation.

Besides the micro phenomenon above, on the macro level, the **short-run disequilibrium of aggregate demand and supply** of the economy is another important problem for the market to run smoothly to allocate resource, which is the main topic of Macro Economics.

All of the above phenomenon, asymmetric information, externality, public goods, market power and the short-run disequilibrium of aggregate demand and supply, as well as the absence of market in income redistribution, are examples of failures of market mechanism in allocating resource in the economy. We call such a phenomenon **Market Failure**, which aims to emphasize the malfunction or absence of market in allocating social resource to promote the economy function efficiently and fairly.

---

① Just as you have imagined, the progress of technology, such as the GPS, may make the exclusiveness easy to realize.

② Culture may contribute to the collective supplying of public goods, as you may see in some suburban areas.

(2) The Basic Function of Government

Government can use some remedies in face of market failure.

First, according to the Second Fundamental Theorem of Welfare Economics, we can fulfill the aim of income distribution equity through rearranging the initial endowment among people. However, it cannot be finished by the mechanism of market. Therefore, when it comes to the problem of income redistribution, we can invite government to do some benefit by transferring something from one person to another to fulfill the aim of income distribution fairness. Of course, the specific way of wealth transferring is another complicated problem.

Second, according to the First Fundamental Theorem of Welfare Economics, when all the presumptions are fulfilled, free market can play its role of allocating resources efficiently. However, when there is market failure, as we have mentioned above, asymmetric information, externality and public goods arising from the lack of market, or market power, such as monopoly, or on the macro level, the short-run disequilibrium of aggregate demand and supply, the assumptions of the First Fundamental Theorem of Welfare Economics are not satisfied, then the conclusion of the theorem cannot be guaranteed. As a result, free market is not enough for economic efficiency and the government interference is necessary.

Then we get to another question—based on the market failure, what can government do after all?

First, on consideration of the income redistribution function left for government in the Second Fundamental Theorem of Welfare Economics, government can do something to reach the aim of fairness in income distribution. For instance, government can collect taxes from the rich and transfer them to the poor, or directly subsidize those people in poor condition using the fiscal finance. Besides, government can install social security system to guarantee the basic protection of medical care, old-age care and unemployment care to those who are in need of them. All of the above shows the **income redistribution function of government** is to make sure that the income polarization is kept to a tolerable degree of the society.

Second, as to the contradiction of the assumption of the First Fundamental Theorem of Welfare Economics, government can also play its role to heal it. For the market power problem, government can make anti-monopoly laws to keep the influence of the monopoly in a certain degree to prevent its harm for the economic efficiency. For the problem of adverse selection under asymmetric information, government can take on the job of screening to protect the benefit of the traders, and when there is moral hazard, government can make laws to prevent serious cheating in the process of cooperation. For the problem of externality, government can use taxes and subsidies to fill in the gap between the social benefit and private benefit, or the gap between the social cost and private cost, to make the private production meet the best social level, to get rid of the harm for resource allocation of the externality problem. In the situation of insufficient supplying of public goods, government takes over the task. All of the above shows the **resource allocation function of government**, the aim of which is to heal the failure of market in making it efficiently.

Eventually, in the field of macro economy, government exerts its function of resource allocation to balance the aggregate demand and supply. In the short term, when there is disequilibrium of the demand side and supply side, there will be surplus or shortage, and the aggregate economy will show apparent volatility. Although there lies the possibility of reaching a new balance in the long term, if we cannot pay the high cost of unemployment or inflation in the short term, government can still function to balance the demand and supply side in the short term and stabilize the economy. The most used policy tools by government include fiscal policy and monetary policy, just as what you have learned in your course of Macro Economics. This is the so-called **economic stabilization function of government** for the macro economy.

The above is the generally accepted three functions of government.

3.2 Transformation of Government Function: The Historical Perspective

We have discussed the main government function: income redistribution, resource allocation and macro-economic stabilization. While these three aspects of function change over time in the history, they remain the basic functions of a modern government. Historically speaking, there is a long and complicated transformation of government function in the past thousands of years.

3.2.1 The Global Experience

The original form of people organizing their activities collectively is the prehistorical **Tribe**. The tribe leader was responsible for the safety of the tribe, and sometimes played the role as a justice of the court today to deal with the conflicts of different groups of people.

Then after hundreds of years of evolution, the tribe eventually turned into the preliminary form of **State**. The specific form of the complicated evolution process is the core of scholar's discussion and argument in social science. Scholars as Tilly believe that, war is an important contribution of the birth and building of a state, for the intensive demand for military materials in the war time results in the centralization of the social resource and development of the supporting institutional system, such as the bureau institution. Other explanations include the conflicts and bitter fighting among different social classes, and collective cooperation during the process agricultural production and so on, all of which explains the origin of the state from different perspectives. At that time, the main function of the state of lay in national safeguard. At the same time, emperor collected social surplus through the form of taxes and used it to support the basic need of the state, such as the expense of the bureau institution and army. Of course, a large part of the fiscal revenue was used to support the expense of the emperor himself and his family. Meanwhile, in the western world, for a long time, the Church also played important role in the distribution of fiscal resources.

Since the fifteenth century, through the movement of religious reform, Europe has gradually got out of the control of Church, and the **National State** emerged. The national state sought for the richness of the state to defeat their opponents in the competition of states. Under such strong ambition, the state not only tried their best to develop commercial activities to derive more fiscal revenues, but also used the fiscal resource they collected to support the exploration activities globally. An epoch of national competition started, the extreme form of which is the war. And just as what has been pointed by Tilly, warship gives birth to stronger national states. At that time, the function of the government was not constrained in the safeguard, many was governments played the role of economic management, especially under the thoughts of mercantilism.

With the development of the commercial activities, a new social class emerged, the Bourgeoisie. The increase of their wealth resulted in their demand for more political rights, and their fighting for that led to the birth of **Modern State**. In the modern state, the power of the governor was restrained. At the same time, the relationship between the governor and the citizen changed with taxation not only being a responsibility for the governor, but also a right to show their status as a certified citizen. Yet at that time, the state merely played limited role compared with modern governments, for example, safeguard, law making and enforcement. Under the thoughts of laissez-faire, for a long period of time, government also played limited role in managing economic activities.

Since the mid of the nineteenth century, the **Modern Welfare State** found its preliminary form. German built the world's first compulsory education system and the first social security system, although in most of the countries all over the world, governments did little to supply basic security for their citizens facing the uncertainty in their daily life. In fact, one can the get a glimpse of terrible daily life of an ordinary worker through the works of some famous novelists at that time, like Dickens. Besides the exposure to uncertainty, the working condition of ordinary workers was terrible. Meanwhile, some couldn't have a decent job, such as the household women, the infrastructure of the city was also in bad condition, which is an important contribution of the wide spread of illness.

The modern welfare state has paved its way since the beginning of the twentieth century, especially after the World War II. At the start of the twentieth century, under the limited role of government supplying social security and the wide criticism of the public towards those rich monopoly enterprisers, the private supporting philanthropy prospers, constituted an important supplement to the government supporting social security system. After World War II, under the background of the Cold War, the western world made great progress in improving their social security system, in trial to constitute an entire protection net covering one's life from birth to death, which is also called *from cradle to grave*. During the same period, in the socialist camp, countries built a nationalist social security system under the planned economy, in which the enterprise people worked for their whole life also supplied various living insurance for them, from state owned hospitals to state owned schools.

During the transformation of government function in the twentieth century, the 1929-1933 financial crisis is a key turning point. Before that, government held a laissez-faire attitude towards the economy activities. However, holding such viewpoint, the President Hoover faced terrible situation of high rate of unemployment and declining economic growth, making him eventually lose the political power. Following him, President Roosevelt's New Deal opened a new era. Through high expenditure on social welfare and public infrastructure, the new deal promoted the effective demand and regained a new balance of the economy. At the same time, the new deal broke the traditional doctrine of balanced fiscal budget, making deficit fiscal budget acceptable. From then on, the reasonability of government interference in stabilizing economy has entered the world history and opened a new field of government function.

3.2.2 The Chinese Experience

China is in the lead of building a centralized and effective bureau system, as early as time of Qin and Han Dynasty. At that time, the state has reached the primary level of the county to launch effective management. The leader of the primary level unit was responsible for collecting taxes and dealing with local conflicts. As the center of the empire, the central government was responsible for national safety and law making, as well as choosing the proper personnel to administrate the whole country.

China had kept such a mode of national management by the function division of central and local governments in almost two thousand years, from the Qin Dynasty to the Qing Dynasty, extending to the beginning of the twentieth century. Under such system, the peasants and the governors were put into their relative positions steadily, with one doing farming and perceiving paying taxes as purely a responsibility, and the other enjoying the power of collecting taxes and distributing them.

After decades of chaos and outer disruptions, China entered the planned economy system since 1949. From the beginning of 1950s to the end of 1970s, China underwent a highly regulated economic mode. Under such mode, the government centralized most of the social resources from the lowest level of the economy to the central level, and then allocated the resources to lower levels in accordance with the aim and the plan of the state. As the follower of the nationalism social security system of the Soviet Union, China also put its citizens under a national security system, mainly by the functioning of the state-owned enterprises, who shoulders many social burdens.

Since 1978, China has transformed its economic management mode from a planned economy to a market-oriented economy, which is the reform and opening-up. At the same time, the function of government also transformed.

First, the Chinese government removed many social burdens from itself to the society, reforming the state-owned enterprises and rebuilding the social security system. Second, government transformed its way of regulating economy from specific interference to macro regulation, and left the micro economic activities to the enterprises. Third, as to the fiscal supporting institutions, the main leading thoughts of distributing social resources changed from national finance to public finance, with the former viewing the nation as the main subject of allocating social resources to fulfill the requirement of national strategy, and the latter perceiving the market as the main subject of allocating social resources to fulfill the welfare of ordinary citizens.

China continuously reformed its government functions in the new century. After China joined the WTO in 2001, it played a more influential role in the global economy. In accordance with it, Chinese government devoted more resources to adapt to the international rules and tried to seize the opportunities granted by international competition. And as the supporting power, the domestic reform of state-owned enterprises and government administration was also underway.

3.2.3 The Pushing Power of the Transformation of Government Function

We have shown the history of government administration and function above, through the experience worldwide and in China. We have found significant time series change and cross section divergence in the function of government. The three main functions we have referred in the first part, namely efficiency in resource allocation, equity in income distribution, and stabilization of macro economy, are not shouldered by all governments in the history. In most of the time in history, national safety, lawmaking and enforcement are their main tasks. Only since stepping into a modern world, governments have devoted to building social infrastructure and managing economy. Now we will try to sum up the pushing power of government function transformation.

(1) Economic Development as a Pushing Power

Economic development is the utmost reason for the transformation of government function. In a long time in the history, the production ability of human being is limited, leading to little accumulation of social resources surplus. This results in the constraints for government function in two aspects.

First, low level of economic activities leaves no possibility for government to manage economic activities in large scale. Governments spend little time easing those conflicts in economic affairs and devote more time to military needs, which is more fatal to the state. Second, low level of economic activities produces low level of social material surplus, leaving less possibility of using the surplus to establish a social security system take like the modern state.

With the development of the economy, these two aspects become essential to the society.

First, with the increase in the scope of economic activities, the labor division is becoming more and more specified, leading to more complicated trading relationship, and the probability of conflicts in the process of trading is also going up. It then leaves a big problem of dealing with the conflicts. The task of law making and enforcement is granted to governments. Therefore, with the complication of economic trade, government gradually takes on its trade role as a mediator in the process. This is also the main logic by Wagner in his famous explanation for the fiscal expenditure increase of industrialized countries in the twentieth century, which is also called Wagner's Law.

Second, with the development of the economy, national wealth is accumulated, leading to citizen's demand for safe and decent life when they have overcome the threat of famine. This paves the path for government to build the social and physical infrastructure, for example, the compulsory education, medical care unemployment subsidy, as well as the improvement of public basic facilities. Through the structured change of the fiscal expenditure, we can witness the transformation of government devotion, with more expenditure devoted to social welfare instead of investment.

(2) External Impact as a Pushing Power

The external shock consists of two kinds, the military impact and the economic shock. We will discuss the effect of the two kinds respectively.

First, the military inpact often disrupts the normal functioning of the government and makes the government divert its attention and expense from regular activities to military needs. Meanwhile, preparation for war often makes government centralize the social resources and constrain the economy into a strong mode of regulation.

Second, the economic impact often brings new transform to the government function.

Take America as an example. The hit of the 1929-1933 Depression brought historical changes in the way the government managed economy. Before the Great Depression, government held the viewpoint of Liquidation, believing in the self-healing ability of the economy and launched a laissez-faire attitude towards the economy. The government function was constrained in basic service as national safeguard and law enforcement, and a balanced fiscal finance should be guaranteed, with public debt viewed as a burden to the later generations. The Great Depression divided the history of public policy and brought new possibilities to the action of government. The New Deal by President Roosevelt shows that if deficits of public finance can promote effective demand and brings more activities in the economy, it is wealth to the later generation instead of burden. From then on, people believe that the proper government intervention is necessary to the reviving of the economy. The time of Macro Economics and public policy emerged. The government has shouldered the responsibility of keeping macro economy stabilization since then.

Use China as another example. As a country in transition, China spent some time adaptly to the world popular way of managing economy since the reform and opening-up, trying to get rid of the mode under the planned economy. The Asian Financial Crisis in 1997 showed the preliminary maturity in Chinese policy of Macro Regulation. Before that, Chinese government used its public policy tools to mainly struggle with the domestic volatility, and since then China has gradually been used to dealing with the influence of external impact on the domestic economy.

We can also use the long-time stabilization of government function in the Middle Ages as an example. During thousands of years, the government function changed little. The main reason for it maybe that, though there were local conflicts from time to time, there were no radical changes like those later on brought by the Industial Revolution, which is more facilitative for the transformation of government function.

Finally, as a sort of economic impact, the technological progress sometimes also brought changes in government function. For instance, since the end of the twentieth century, the technology of the Internet has changed the economy from many aspects, making the regulation of the online world another task for government.

(3) Economic Management Mode as a Pushing Power

Economic management mode is another pushing power for the transformation of government function. We will mainly talk about the mode of free market and planned economy.

Under the traditional free market economy, although the government is responsible for the smooth function of the economy, the scope of its function is constrained. Besides the basic public service like contract enforcement and the macro regulation, anti-monopoly is an important task too.

On the opposite, the planned economy puts more emphasis on the centralized control of government. The government can be perceived as the core of the society and the economy. Using the channels of the bureaucratic system, the government collects social resources and then reallocates them to the individuals and enterprises to seek for its national aim and strategy. On top of that, the government supplies a social security net through the system of state-owned enterprises.

The significant divergence in the economic management mode under free market and plan economy makes the transitional countries experience radical changes in their style of regulating the economy in the end of the twentieth century. Most governments in the transitional economy adapt themselves to the rule of the market economy by releasing some of their former functions to market, and focusing on public service and macro regulation, which is a hard period in many former socialist countries.

(4) International Competition as a Pushing Power

International competition is a potential pushing power for the transformation of government function.

First, the developing countries are lagged behind by those developed ones. Yet they have to compete with them in the global economy. Therefore, for a developing country, the most emergent task is to catch up with their developed counterparts. Under such pressure of development, the developing countries show obvious feature in their government functions, among which the most evident is their centralization of social resources for the development strategy of the nation as a whole. Of course, the mode of the government action is supported by the Big Push Theory of many Development Economists. Under such theory, the pushing by the government in the primary period of the country's development is essential for the taking off of the economy; for under that situation, the private investment is inadequate to support the normal function of the market because of the poor condition of infrastructure. As a result, the government then plays the role as an engine promoting the economy by public investment.

Second, the Cold War showed another example of impact from international competition on the change of government function. The intense competition between the western world and the Socialist camp led to their mutual transformation in government function, absorbing each other's strength to adjust their own original modes. On the one hand, as a reaction to the challenge by the Socialist camp of their high level of national welfare, especially the protection for the benefit of the working class, after the World War Ⅱ, the western world devoted more social resources to social security and reacted more to the demand of the working class. On the other hand, under the strong pressure from the progress of technological progress and the likely use of that for military facility, the Soviet Union allocated more and more social resources to military use, and eventually it led to the ignorance of productive activities and the collapse of the whole economic system.

Third, in the times of globalization, international competition makes industry policy making and enforcement an important national strategy and crucial function of government. Nowadays, from the emerging economies to the developed countries, many governments perceive keeping their countries relative position in the international competition an important task, and promoting their ability of manufacturing production is the core task. As a consequenes, they make various forms of national strategies and programms to push the technological progress and the ability of manufacturing production.

3.3 Historical Changes of Chinese Government Functions

3.3.1 The Stage of Economic Development

The transformation of government functions can be divided into two parts: one is the content of the transformation of government functions, including the transformation of economic functions and the adjustment of functional structure; the other is the realization of the transformation of government functions, including the allocation of power, the change of management mode and the reform of institutions.

(1) Determination and Adjustment of Government Economic Functions (1978-1993)

After the reform and opening-up, China has entered a new era of economic development and institutional reform since 1978, and the functions of the government have changed profoundly. The Third Plenary Session of the Eleventh Central Committee of the CPC made a clear strategic decision to shift the focus of the work of the whole party to socialist modernization since 1979. It pointed out that: at present, one of the serious shortcomings of China's economic management system is that the power is too centralized, and local and industrial and agricultural enterprises should be given more autonomy in operation and management under the guidance of the national unified plan. We should start to simplify administrative organs at all levels, and transfer most of their functions and power to professional or joint companies of an enterprise nature. Following rules of the centralized leadership, we should solve the problem that the party, government and enterprise are not separated, and the party is the substitute for the government and the government is the substitute for the enterprise.

Under the guidance of this strategic decision-making, the situation that the government's economic functions are all inclusive under the traditional economic system has begun to change. Governments at all levels adhere to the economic construction as the center and realize the fundamental transformation of the focus of government functions, that is, from the original emphasis on class governance function to the emphasis on economic management function. Since the reform and opening-up, all previous governments have put the development of economy at the center, and government work has always been centered on economic construction. For example, the 1979 report on the work of the government pointed out that "at present and for a quite long historical period to come, our main task is to carry out socialist modernization in a systematic and planned way". In the years since then, every government work report has emphasized the core responsibility of the government's economic construction. It means that the basic functions of our government will be switched from political domination to economic and social management.

In October 1984, the Third Plenary Session of the 12th Central Committee of the CPC adopted the decision of the CPC Central Committee on economic system reform, which for the first time comprehensively and systematically discussed that in principle, government departments at all levels no longer directly managed enterprises and realized the separation of responsibilities between government and enterprises, the issue of changing the economic functions of the government, and made specific provisions on the main functions of the government in managing the economy. After the reform in 1984, most of the state-owned enterprises carried out independent accounting and self-financing in various degrees, and expanded their autonomy. As for enterprises, although the government still owned relatively heavy power, this kind of centralization was different from the past kind of highly centralized power. The government's economic and social management function mode, which was dominated by direct control, disintegrated and began to change to macro-control. This change has been proved to have a positive effect on practice. In 1986, the report on the Seventh Five-Year Plan adopted at the fourth session of the Sixth National People's Congress further summarized the government's economic management functions as: "overall planning, policy mastery, organization and coordination, service provision, economic means and inspection and supervision."

In 1990, in the proposal of the Central Committee of the CPC on the formulation of the ten-year plan for national economic and social development and the eighth Five-Year Plan, it was further clearly pointed out that the basic direction of deepening the reform of the economic system in the next ten years was to establish an economic operation mechanism combining planned economy and market regulation in accordance with the requirements of developing the socialist planned commodity economy. The main task of national economic management was to reasonably determine the plan, planning and macro-control objectives of national economic development, formulate correct industrial policies, regional policies and other economic policies, make a comprehensive balance, coordinate major proportion relations, and comprehensively use economic, legal and administrative means to guide and regulate the operation of the economy.

At the beginning of 1992, Deng Xiaoping delivered a speech on the southern tour, reiterating that planned economy is not equal to socialism, and capitalism also has plans; market economy is not equal to capitalism, and socialism also has markets. In 1992, the Fourteenth National Congress of the CPC clearly proposed that the functions of the government are to plan as a whole, master policies, guide information, organize and coordinate, provide services, inspect and supervise. Under the guidance of Deng Xiaoping's speech, the 14th National Congress of the CPC officially announced that the goal of China's economic system reform is to establish a socialist market economy system. The proposal of socialist market economy is undoubtedly a major breakthrough in the understanding of the relationship between the government, the market and enterprises, and also a new challenge to the transformation of government functions.

In November 1993, the CPC Central Committee made the decision on Several Issues concerning the establishment of a socialist market economic system. However, under the situation of inflation and corruption, the Central Committee had to take macro-control measures again, reduce fixed asset investment, withdraw bank funds within a time limit, and punish corruption. Although these measures were necessary, the negative impact was also very obvious, that is, the triangular debt of enterprises continued to expand, and the loss side of state-owned enterprises continues to increase. Some local governments again issued various kinds of tickets (food tickets, oil tickets, etc.) to strengthen economic regulation by traditional and habitual means of planning and administrative intervention.

(2) The Stage of Establishing Market Economy to Play a Fundamental Role (1994-2013)

From the Third Plenary Session of the 14th CPC Central Committee to the 18th CPC National Congress, with the deepening and development of reform, the functions of the government under the condition of socialist market economy, China has entered the period of establishing socialist market economy. Since 1994, the reform of finance and taxation has been carried out in an all-round way, the modern enterprise system has been established, and the functions of the government have changed. To establish a socialist market economy system is to make the market play a fundamental role in resource allocation under the state's macro-control. During this period, the government mainly formulated and implemented macro-control policies, did a good job in infrastructure construction, created a comfortable environment for economic development, and established a sound macro-control system mainly by indirect means. Its economic functions were resource allocation, fair distribution and economic stability. In the practice of 1994, the reform of finance and taxation went smoothly, and the new system operated normally. The financial and tax system changed from production, construction and operation finance under the planned economy to the public finance under the modern market economy, and a new financial and tax system with the tax sharing system as the core was initially formed. The financial system has broken away from the pattern of "financial cashier" in the planned economy period, and constructed a modern financial institution system, financial market system and financial regulation and supervision system in accordance with the needs of developing socialist market economy. Through the comprehensive use of fiscal and tax policies, monetary and credit policies and other economic and legal means to regulate economic operation, the government has effectively managed the serious inflation and deflation trend to a certain extent, and gradually accumulated useful experience in maintaining macroeconomic stability in the process of economic transition, but the construction of social security system lagged behind.

The 15th National Congress of the CPC put forward the idea of "making the market play a fundamental role in resource allocation under the macro-control of the state". The government is based on adapting to the market economic system, and the establishment of modern enterprises is the key. To realize the separation of government and enterprise, the power of enterprise production, operation and management should be effectively handed over to enterprises. The government plays a leading role in improving the macro-control mechanism of the market and improving the efficiency of government work. It is the development direction of government function in the new situation.

The 16th National Congress of the CPC set the goal "to give full play to the basic role of the market in resource allocation to a greater extent", turning the function of economic management to serving the market main body and creating a good development environment, and realizing the transformation of modern "people-oriented" government through economic regulation, market supervision, social management and public service. At the 17th National Congress of the CPC, it was put forward that "the basic role of the market in resource allocation should be better brought into play in terms of system". At the second plenary session of the 17th Central Committee of the CPC in 2008, the opinions on deepening the reform of administrative management system were adopted, which further emphasized that deepening the reform of administrative management system should take the transformation of government functions as the core, realize the transformation of government functions to create a good development environment and provide high-quality public services. At the 18th National Congress of the CPC, it was proposed that the market play a more fundamental role in resource allocation. In the 18th National Congress of the CPC, it was also proposed that the government's service and management functions be equally important. It was expressed as "to create a good development environment, provide high-quality public services, and maintain social equity and justice". To give better play to the role of the government, we should not only focus on service, but also on the management function of the government. "Only focusing on service but not on management is not enough. Management and service should not be partial. What should be managed by the government should not only be managed, but also be managed effectively."

With the deepening of scientific exploration carried out by the party, the appearance of the people, the appearance of the socialist country and the appearance of the party have undergone a new change, and China's position in the international community has been constantly improved. However, our country is on the way to establish the socialist market economy system, which is short of fashion, interwoven with old and new problems, and still faces many contradictions and even challenges. For example, the market order is not standardized, and the phenomenon of seeking economic benefits by improper means is widespread; the development of production factor market lags behind, and a large number of effective demands cannot be realized while the factors are idle; the market rules are not unified, and there are a large quantity of departmental protectionism and local protectionism; the market competition is not sufficient, which hinders the survival of the fittest and structural adjustment.

(3) Establishing the Decisive Stage of Market Economy (2014 to now)

From the end of 2013, Xi Jinping put forward the core issue of the government and the market, which is to make the market play a decisive role in the allocation of resources and a better role in the government. In many fields, it is emphasized that the relationship between the two parties is complementary and interdependent, and the government should respect the market rules, stimulate market vitality, reduce direct intervention and strengthen the implementation of key functions, with emphasis on the supply side in 2017. The major principle of structural reform is also to "make the market play a decisive role in the allocation of resources and better play the role of the government". The market role and the role of the government complement each other, and promote each other.

In November 2014, the Third Plenary Session of the 18th Central Committee of the CPC made an overall plan to comprehensively deepen the reform, firmly grasp the task of further promoting the reform of the socialist market economy system, and emphasize that "the reform of the economic system is still the key point of comprehensively deepening the reform, and the core issue of the reform of the economic system is still to deal with the relationship between the government and the market, and to allocate the originally advocated market in resources". We should deepen the "basic role" into "decisive role", and put forward a new orientation of "adhering to the direction of socialist market economy reform.

The core problem is to deal with the relationship between the government and the market, so that the market can play a decisive role in the allocation of resources and better play the role of the government". "[3] transforming the government's function is the core of deepening the reform of the administrative system, which should be solved in essence." It's about what the government should and shouldn't do, focusing on the relationship among the government, the market and the society, that is, what should be shared by the market, the society and the government, and what could be shared by the three. The key is to deepen the reform of the economic system, build a unified and open market system with orderly competition, so that the market can play a decisive role in the allocation of resources and better play the role of the government.

However, "(7) [1] he also repeatedly stressed the limits of the role of the market: "our country implements the socialist market economy system, and we still need to adhere to the superiority of our socialist system and the active role of the party and the government. The market plays a decisive role in the allocation of resources, not all of them. To reverse the lag of social system reform, we need to emphasize 'society' as an independent subject." For example, the unbalanced, uncoordinated and unsustainable development is still prominent; the ability of scientific and technological innovation is not strong; the industrial structure is unreasonable; the development mode is still extensive; the development gap between urban and rural areas and the income distribution gap between residents are still large; the social contradictions have significantly increased, in terms of education, employment, social security, medical care, housing, ecological environment, food and drug safety, production safety. There are many issues related to the vital interests of the masses, such as social security, law enforcement and justice. Some people are living in difficulties. Formalism, bureaucracy, hedonism and extravagance are not rare. Some areas are prone to negative corruption, and the situation of anti-corruption struggle is still severe.

"[8] the 19th National Congress of the CPC still places the market economy in the decisive position for the transformation of government functions. On the other hand, it emphasizes the need to "deepen the simplification of administration and decentralization, innovate supervision methods, enhance the public trust and executive power of the government, and build a service-oriented government satisfactory to the people", especially the need to "comprehensively implement the negative list system of market access, and clean up and abolish various regulations and practices that hinder the unified market and fair competition". To meet these requirements, we need to grasp the "deregulation service" reform to continue to promote the transformation of government functions. The basic feature of the development in the new era is the transition from the stage of high-speed growth to the stage of high-quality development. We must take the supply side structural reform as the main task to promote the development quality, efficiency and power reform. In this regard, deepening the streamlining of administration and decentralization can play an important role. There is an urgent need to explore a more effective regulatory model through innovative regulation, effectively maintain the market environment of fair competition and survival of the fittest, promote the transformation of old and new kinetic energy, and then eliminate invalid supply, increase effective supply and achieve high-quality development. Carrying out the management of the list of rights and responsibilities is not only the reform plan made by the Party Central Committee and the State Council, but also the system guarantees of deepening the reform of "releasing management service".

3.3.2 Reform of Government Institutions

The government function is the basis of the establishment of the institution, and the institution is the carrier of the function. On the one hand, the increase or decrease of government institutions is based on the adjustment of government functions. On the other hand, the reform of government institutions is the organizational guarantee for the transformation of government functions. The differences between the two are as follows: the transformation of government functions takes the adjustment of responsibilities as the main content, and the reform of government institutions takes the adjustment of institutions as the main content; the main purpose of the reform of government institutions is to ensure the internal coordination of the government, which is conducive to improving administrative efficiency; the main purpose of the transformation of government functions is to ensure that the responsibilities performed by the government meet the requirements of social development and change, which is conducive to better performance of political effect. Therefore, the transformation of Chinese government functions has been demonstrated since the reform and opening-up through the reform of government institutions. So far, China has carried out eight institutional reforms.

In order to cooperate with the reform of the economic system in 1982, the government carried out **the first reform.** In accordance with the principle of eliminating overlapping institutions and merging institutions with similar businesses, this reform has largely removed and merged economic management departments, changed some units with mature conditions into economic entities, and strengthened the comprehensive economic coordination departments. At that time, the reform of social management department was not put on the agenda.

In order to meet the requirements of deepening the economic system reform in 1988, the government carried out **the second reform.** This reform was centered on the transformation of government functions. The focus of the reform was still the economic management department, which had strengthened the macro-economic control department, simplified and weakened the professional economic department. However, the social management department did not make major changes. For example, the institutional reform of the State Council in 1988 and the pilot reform of local institutions after 1989 were carried out centering on the transformation of the economic functions of the government. In 1988, the State Council's institutional reform and the pilot reform of local institutions focused on the transformation of government functions.

In order to meet the requirements of the transformation from the traditional economic system to the market economic system in 1993, the government carried out **the third reform**. This reform was based on the principles of changing functions, straightening out relations, streamlining the administration and improving efficiency. The key points of the reform were to strengthen the macro-control and supervision departments, strengthen the social management function departments, transform some professional economic departments into industry management organizations or economic entities, and vigorously simplify the internal institutions of some basic industry departments related to the national economy and the people's livelihood, no longer directly managing enterprises.

The fourth institutional reform was carried out in accordance with the requirements of developing socialist market economy in 1998, changing government functions and realizing the separation of government from enterprise. In 1998, the State Council's institutional reform plan clearly proposed that the functions of the government should be effectively transformed into macro-control, social management and public services. This reform took a series of measures, which made a substantial breakthrough in the transformation of the government's economic management function. For example, the government no longer directly managed the enterprises, turning the enterprises into the main body of the market; the government's macro-economic control function was strengthened; the micro economic intervention was weakened; the government's administrative examination and approval items were reduced, and the working mode was changed. In terms of social affairs management reform, first, the Ministry of labor and social security was newly established; second, the drug administration was newly established; third, the State Environmental Protection Administration was upgraded to the General Administration; fourth, new progress was made in the decentralization of functions of education, sports and other departments. Through the adjustment of government institutions, the shift of government function structure and center of gravity could be realized. This time, for example, in the organizational reform, the management authority of each department was redivided, involving more than 100 adjustments of authority among each other, solving a number of long-term problems in the relationship between departments.

The fifth institutional reform of the State Council was carried out in in 2003, aiming at the realization of standardized behavior, coordinated operation, fairness and transparency, honesty and efficiency, and put forward the requirements of coordination of decision-making, implementation and supervision. The focus of the reform was to deepen the reform of the state-owned assets management system, improve the macro-control system, improve the financial supervision system, continue to promote the reform of the circulation system, strengthen the construction of the supervision system of food safety and production safety, and further transform the functions of the government. In this reform, the overall pattern of government institutions had remained relatively stable. Only by concentrating on solving the prominent contradictions and problems affecting reform and development in the administrative system, it focused on promoting the institutional reform of the State Council and further transformed the functions of the government, so as to provide organizational guarantee for promoting reform, opening-up and modernization. After the reform, in addition to the general office of the State Council, there were 28 constituent departments of the State Council.

In 2008, the main task of **the sixth institutional reform** was to explore a large-scale system with an organic unity of functions around the transformation of government functions and the rationalization of departmental responsibilities. It centered on reasonably allocating the functions of macro-control departments, focusing on improving people's livelihood, strengthening and integrating social management and public service departments, strengthening energy and environment management institutions, establishing the Ministry of industry and information technology, the Ministry of transportation, the Ministry of human resources and social security, the Ministry of environmental protection, the State Environmental Protection Administration, the Ministry of housing and urban rural development Ministry of construction. There were 15 institutions involved in the restructuring of the State Council, and four were reduced at the ministerial level.

The seventh institutional reform of the State Council, with the transformation of functions as the core in 2013, steadily pushed forward the reform of the large-scale department system, implemented the separation of the railway government and the enterprise, integrated and strengthened the health and family planning, food and drug, press and publication, radio, film and television, ocean and energy management agencies, and established the national health and Family Planning Commission, the State Food and Drug Administration, and the State Press, publication and radio. The State Administration of film and television, the State Oceanic Administration and the state energy administration, were reorganized, and the Ministry of railway, the Ministry of health, the state population and Family Planning Commission, the State Food and Drug Administration, the State Administration of radio, film and television, the State Press and publication administration, and the State Electricity Regulatory Commission were abolished. In this reform, the number of ministerial organs under the State Council had been reduced by four, and the number of constituent departments under the State Council was 25.

The eighth institutional reform was a reform that considered all kinds of institutional settings as a whole in 2018, scientifically allocating the power and responsibilities of the party and government departments and internal institutions. According to the report of the 19th National Congress of the CPC, in the final analysis, the reform of government institutions and administrative system is to "transform the functions of the government, deepen the simplification of administration and decentralization of power, innovate supervision methods, enhance the credibility and execution of the government, and build a service-oriented government that the people are satisfied with". If the institutional reform fails to drive the transformation of functions, or it is difficult to promote the innovation of government management, it is impossible to deepen the reform of administrative system.

After optimizing the setup of government institutions and the allocation of functions, the basic logic and remarkable features of the large-scale management system of "one kind of matters is in principle coordinated by one department, and one thing is in principle charged by one department" are realized. The specific organization was adjusted to establish the Ministry of natural resources. The Ministry of land and resources, the State Oceanic Administration and the State Bureau of surveying, mapping and geographic information was no longer retained. The Ministry of ecological environment was established. The Ministry of environmental protection was no longer retained. The Ministry of agriculture and rural areas was established. The Ministry of agriculture was no longer retained. The Ministry of culture and tourism was established. The Ministry of culture and the National Tourism Administration was no longer left. The National Health Committee was set up. The National Health and Family Planning Commission was no longer retained. The leading group office of the State Council for deepening the reform of the medical and health system was no longer established. The Department of Veterans Affairs was set up. Emergency management department was established. The State Administration of work safety was no longer retained. The Ministry of Science and Technology was reorgainized. The Ministry of Justice was reorganized. The responsibilities of the Ministry of Water Resources was optimized. The Three Gorges Project Construction Committee and its office under the State Council, the south to North Water Diversion Project Construction Committee and its office under the State Council were no longer retained. The responsibilities of the audit office were optimized. The board of supervisors of key large state-owned enterprises was no longer kept. The Ministry of supervision would be incorporated into the newly established national supervisory committee. The Ministry of supervision and the State Corruption Prevention Bureau was no longer retained. The State Council had 26 departments.

3.4 On the Future Functions of Chinese Government

From the historical process, it is revealed that, like other countries in the world, the functions of Chinese government are changing with the changes of external environment and social forces. In the market economy environment, the government function of a country is directly reflected in three aspects: resource allocation, income redistribution and economic stability. But the government function also includes indirect functions such as promoting economic growth and increasing employment. Compared with the government functions of income redistribution and economic stability, the most fundamental function of the government is to provide public goods. Looking back on the historical process, in the thousands of years of social development, the two government functions of income distribution and economic stability have not always existed, but if the government cannot provide public goods such as national defense, justice and personal protection, the society may not survive. Therefore, with the development of society in the future, the government functions of resource allocation, income redistribution and economic stability will gradually change.

3.4.1 International Issues may Change Government Functions

With the deepening of globalization, the government can use more government tools to fulfill its functions. In the past few decades, China's economy has developed rapidly. The government pays too much attention to expenditure and tax as fiscal policy when it realizes its government functions. In fact, there are other policy tools besides government expenditure and tax, especially the regulatory tools and government contingent liability related tools. Although the function of government is aimed at the role of governments at all levels of countries, with the accelerating process of globalization, the relationship between governments is getting closer and closer, and the "spillover effect" between countries is becoming more and more obvious, especially in transnational financial activities, such as the 2008 U.S. financial crisis. At present, the influence of a country's activities directly controlled by non-government is gradually increasing. The functions of resource allocation, income redistribution and economic stability are not limited to national level issues, but more and more international issues.

Under the influence of globalization, new technology, financial market development, economic and population growth and other factors, the international characteristics of resource allocation, income redistribution and stable economy become more and more important, which also shows that the space distance between one country and the other country before is shrinking, and the externality and relevance are increasing.

In today's world, global problems related to environment, finance, climate change and global warming, global infectious diseases, air and marine pollution, over exploitation of marine organisms, global terrorism, transnational crime, global disputes and so on all have the nature of global public goods (public dangerous goods), which can generate huge externalities between countries, depending on the fundamental of one country's government. There is no "invisible hand" for unified coordination at the international level. Therefore, a government can no longer only allocate resources according to the change of domestic aggregate demand, it needs to respond to externalities, provide public goods and reduce public hazards. Governments should jointly provide global public goods (or reduce public hazards) and increase the urgency of resource allocation.

Stable economy and income redistribution also have international characteristics. Traditionally, economic stability has been linked to specific national policies. In the past, Keynesianism believes that to stabilize the economy, the government should adopt counter-cyclical policy to play a role in it, that is, if the economy slows down, the government should implement expansionary fiscal policy and loose monetary policy to deal with the shortage of effective demand. The deepening of economic openness and financial market globalization reduces the effect of a government's counter-cyclical policy, and weakens a country's ability to take independent action, so each country is increasingly affected by other countries.

In order to improve the effectiveness of stable economic policies, international cooperation and coordination are becoming more and more important. Since there is no global government or a unified mechanism to ensure the joint action of all countries, heads of government and economic officials regularly convene international organizations, such as the International Monetary Fund, the organization for economic cooperation and development, the United Nations and other international institutions also play an increasingly important role, and this role will be further enhanced in the future. Therefore, a government must carry out its own government functions and contribute to the development of global government. China's "contract and construction of all the countries along the belt and road" is working towards global coordination.

In the 20th century, income redistribution plays an important role in China and other countries. It is also one of the main reasons to promote the growth of government expenditure. However, with the increasingly closer economic ties among countries, the negative externalities between countries have had a direct or indirect impact on the global income distribution. For example, the change of global industrial layout brings not only economic development to all countries, but also environmental pollution, global warming and other external problems. If rich countries can increase economic assistance to poor countries, help poor countries to develop their economies and create jobs, negative externalities will be greatly reduced. At the same time, the global distribution of wealth is very uneven, the Gini coefficient is very high, and the proportion of income of rich countries in the world's total income is far higher than that of the population of rich countries in the world. At present, no global government or international organization has the ability to promote the income transfer between countries. Even the international organizations such as the United Nations and the World Bank have limited role in this regard, as income redistribution is indeed a government function of an international problem. To a certain extent, the "community of shared future of mankind" proposed by our country also reflects the functional orientation of income redistribution on a global scale.

In view of the increasing importance of international factors, governments of all countries, including China, must take more international influence into account when taking actions. They can manage income and expenditure through international institutions and coordinate actions through some international agreements. In the future, such activities will become more common, which will change the existing government functions to a certain extent.

3.4.2 The Function of the Government in Dealing with Major Disasters should be Improved

With the increase of population, the degree of intervention of human activities on nature and society has deepened. The major natural or man-made disasters that human beings are facing have not decreased, and their impact on human beings is also growing. At this time, people want the government to intervene and play a leading role in the process of dealing with the disaster, so as to reduce the suffering caused by the disaster. But the government is often unprepared and spends more time, energy and resources than it did in the past. The Chinese government should make early warning preparations and measures in advance, so as to make the best efforts to intervene in time in the event of a major disaster. The Chinese government should formulate strict policies in advance to reduce the existence of incentives that may cause disasters. To formulate and implement early warning measures and policies is one of the important economic functions of the government. The government should not only strengthen the prevention of potential destructive events in advance, but also pay attention to the afterwards. The main policy tool for the government to perform the function of prevention is supervision. The means of prevention should not only be used in areas where disasters may occur, but also in occasions other than disasters. The government can accumulate the donation funds for major disasters, set up a special fund for special purpose, and maintain strong liquidity to ensure that it can be used to deal with major disasters at any time. At the same time, the government should give the military the responsibility of preventing and responding to domestic disasters, which will be more productive in the beginning of the military.

3.4.3 The Function of the Government to Prevent Risks is Expanding

When all countries choose to play the decisive role of the market in the economy firmly and effectively and the government plays the basic role, this means that when the market fails, the government will intervene appropriately and replace the market with the public sector. In case of that, it will concentrate a lot of efforts on adjusting in order to achieve fair results and equal income distribution, so it does not try to avoid market failure. In many cases, the reason why the market fails is that the government allows these markets to form an environment leading to market failure. For example, various new technologies (such as the Internet, animal cloning, gene therapy, genetically modified crops, nanotechnology, atomic energy, etc.) and new products (financial innovation products, etc.) have brought new and potential risks as well as continuous improvement of people's living standards and quality. Some of these new products and technologies are far riskier than their effectiveness. For example, some of them may lead to catastrophic consequences; some of the innovations of financial institutions will not focus on the well-being of the people, so national regulators should bear the responsibility and concentrate their efforts to avoid market failure, prevent potential risks and protect the people from risks, instead of repairing or correcting the market afterwards. Playing its economic role should be a fundamental principle for the government. Buchanan believes that the government should establish clear rules to guide people's behavior. This rule includes an indispensable tool, which is the political and legal framework. It not only clearly defines the market economy, but also clearly indicates which market failure should be corrected. It also includes policy tools and regulators. In order to protect citizens from potential risks, negative externalities and improper production and consumption behaviors, the government will have to undertake more and more regulatory functions in the future because of the stronger technological innovation ability and more and more use of new products. The government should pay more attention to the prevention of risks than the economic benefits.

Chapter 4

Industrialization in China

4.1 Introduction

Over the past four years, the Chinese economy has developed at an unprecedented pace. In ten years it may be the largest in the world. Our overview briefly introduces a few relevant topics: economic sectors, current challenges and opportunities, and top locations. Since the founding of the People's Republic of China in 1949, especially since 1978, China has transformed from a traditional agricultural society to a modern industrial society, and the pace of industrial restructuring has accelerated. China's industrial structure has developed in line with the industrialization goals aimed at reducing the proportion of agriculture, increasing the proportion of industry, and increasing the proportion of the service industry. Currently, industrial products produced in China range from capital goods to consumer goods, but some consumer goods are still in short supply [1].

China's factory production ranges from textiles to railway locomotives, jets and computers. China is the world's largest producer of cheap cotton textiles and exports large quantities of textiles and clothing. Food processing is very important and many agricultural products are exported. China is one of the world's largest cement producers. Steel production has been down recently, with production dropping slightly to around 44 million tons per year. Other industrial products include televisions, bicycles, cars, trucks and washing machines. Product quality and production technology lag behind Japan, the United States and European countries. The processing and production of

---

[1] Brandt, Loren, Ma, Debin, Rawski, Thomas, 2016, "Industrialization in China", IZA Discussion Papers, No. 10096, Institute for the Study of Labor (IZA).

chemicals, including fertilizers, petroleum products, and pharmaceuticals, is another large and expanding area of Chinese industry.

China has become an industrialized country to some extent. Column industries such as the automobile industry and the housing industry developed rapidly during the industrialization period. Iron and steel production are also important industries in China. The most important export products are machinery and electrical equipment. The most important import products are raw materials. In recent years, due to economic extroversion, China's industry has entered international competition, and as a result, the country's industrial development is increasingly influenced by international economic environments. On the one hand, exports are getting harder and export prices continue to fall. On the other hand, the market share of foreign products and products of foreign-owned enterprises continues to grow. The above two factors increase the difficulties of the country's domestic industry in terms of production and sale. State-owned enterprises are particularly affected. As a matter of fact, the growth of textile and other light industries has slowed down since 1985. Since 1989, the production capacity of durable consumer goods has become idle. After the mid-1990s, bottleneck sectors such as steel, oil and raw materials began to fall into market saturation. Large-scale IC chips only account for 40 percent of all IC chips made in China. 80 percent of the Chinese telecom equipment and instrument market is acquired by foreign companies.

In general, the technical level of China's industry system is relatively low. The hi-tech industry is still in its infancy. The main industrial sectors are technologically backward and lack autonomous equipment capabilities. The average life cycle of more than 2,000 leading products in China is 10.5 years, which is 3.5 times that of similar products in the United States. For example, fewer Chinese work in the field of information than American citizens. About 45% of the American workforce is engaged in information technology, but only 10% of the Chinese workforce is involved. China's industrial technology level needs to be improved, especially high-tech industries, so that Chinese industries will develop in the direction of knowledge economy in the 21st century.

4.1.1 The Industries Driving China's Economy

China is the world's largest emerging market economy, both in terms of population and economic aggregate. China is arguably the world's most important manufacturer and industrial producer. These two sectors alone account for more than 40% of China's gross domestic product (GDP). China is also the world's largest exporter and second largest importer, with the fastest growing consumer market. The main industries include manufacturing, agriculture and telecommunications services. As of 2015, this Asian giant is one of the most important economic powers in the world. But that's not always the case, just 50 years ago China was a country of extreme hunger, poverty and oppression.

China's communist government began implementing capitalist market reforms in 1978, and in the following years, the Chinese took a sharp turn from state-owned enterprises (SOEs). As of 2013, SOEs accounted for only 45% of all Chinese industrial output. This figure was about 80% in 1978; the remaining 22% were collectively owned businesses. The result is an economic expansion that catapults China into the world's second largest economy after only the United States.

Between 1978 and 2008, the size of the Chinese economy increased nearly 50 times, with an average annual GDP growth of around 10%. Initial reforms focused on agriculture, but soon spread to the services and light manufacturing sectors. All of these foreshadowed the prohibition reforms that led to perhaps the most important transformations in the Chinese economy in the 20th century.

4.1.2 Manufacturing

China produces and sells more manufactured products as compared to any other country. The scope of Chinese goods includes iron, steel, aluminum, textiles, cement, chemicals, toys, electronic products, wagons, ships, airplanes and many other products. As in 2015, manufacturing was the country's largest and most different industry.

China is a world leader in many kinds of designs and products made in China. For instance, nearly 80% of air conditioning units are manufactured by Chinese companies. The number of personal computers per capita in China is more than 45 times that of the rest of the world jointly. It is largest producer of solar cells, footwear, mobile phones, and boats as well.

China has a booming automobile manufacturing industry, although it has not received the same types of loans as Sweden, Germany, Japan or the United

States. Although the Chinese government claims to be the world leader, most investors are surprised that China is the world's third-largest automaker.

China's automobile industry originated from the nation's attention to automobiles in the 1990s, when the total automobile production of Chinese manufacturers almost tripled. Although automobile consumption finally became popular after 2005, most of these early cars were used in the export market because the vast majority of Chinese citizens were too poor to buy products on their own.

This is the common theme of China's manufacturing industry. Products are usually produced for government use or immediately shipped to foreign consumers. Compared with other countries, Chinese workers have historically rarely purchased their own high-quality manufactured goods; this problem becomes worse when the government depreciates the Chinese currency and has the effect of lowering China's real wages.

4.1.3 Services

As of 2013, only the United States and Japan had higher service output than China, which represented a major shift in China. A healthy service industry is an indicator of healthy domestic consumption and an increase in per capita welfare; in other words, the Chinese are reaching the ability to meet their own output.

Before the economic reform in 1978, there were no shopping centers and private retail markets in China. However, as of 2015, there is a young and developing service market. This supported the tourism industry and led to a proliferation of Internet and telephone products.

Large foreign companies such as Microsoft and IBM have even entered the Chinese service market. These measures will help accelerate the development of the telecommunications industry, cloud computing and e-commerce.

4.1.4 Agriculture

Another area where China sets global standards is agriculture. There are about 300 million farmers in China, more than the total population of all countries except China, India and the United States. Rice is China's main agricultural product, but the country is also very competitive in wheat, tobacco, potatoes, peanuts, millet, pork, fish, soybeans, corn, tea and oilseeds. Farmers also export large amounts of vegetables, fruits and new meats to nearby countries and regions, especially Hong Kong and China.

Regardless of China's overall agricultural production efficiency, comparative statistics show that, on a per capita basis, Chinese farms are among the least productive in the world. Some analysts attribute this part to unfavorable weather. However, a 2012 study by Deutsche Bank concluded that despite similar terrain and environmental conditions, South Korean farmers are 40 times more productive than Chinese farmers.

Others pointed out that the problem lies in the state's large-scale control of Chinese farms. Farmers cannot own and mortgage farmland, and cannot borrow to buy better capital equipment. These are two functions that encourage innovation and development.

4.1.5 Up and Coming Industries

The Chinese government's 2011-2015 fiscal year's "Twelfth Five-Year Plan lists seven strategic industries as high priority industries: biotechnology, information technology, new energy, environmental protection, new materials, high-end manufacturing and alternative fuels. The government has invested heavily in these areas.

An unidentified but noteworthy industry is China's health care industry. The rise of middle-class families and urbanization are driving a huge demand for health care, which is a promising sign of a booming economy. Reforms passed in 2011 allow competition in the health care market, including wholly foreign-owned organizations. This has attracted investment from major international companies such as Pfizer, Merck and Glaxo Smith Kline. China has one of the fastest growing health care industries in the world.

4.1.6 Industrialization in China

Although China's recent economic boom is widely regarded as a contemporary phenomenon, it is the result of a long process with deep historical roots. Here, we apply this perspective to analyze the trajectory of

China's transformation from an indecisive experiment in the 19th century to the world's largest producer.

Table 4-1 summarizes our core quantitative results. The astonishing speed of China's industrial growth after 1978 is well known. What is less known is that rapid industrial growth can be traced back to at least 1912. In the past century, China's manufacturing industry has grown at an annual rate of over 9%. Table 4-2 provides further comparative perspectives.

Table 4-1 Growth of industrial output, 1912-2008

Year	Growth rate (%)
1912-1936	8.0
1912-1949	4.1
1912-1952	6.2
1952-1965	12.3
1965-1978	10.2
1978-1995	11.6
1995-2008	13.8
1952-2008	11.9
1912-2008	9.5

Source: https://www.iza.org/publications/dp/10096/industrialization-in-china.

Table 4-2 Comparative industrialization of China, 1912—2008

	1912	1933	1952	1965	1978	1995	2008
Cotton Yarn Production (Mill.Lbs.)	221	990	1445	2860	5240	11928	38214
Electricity Production (Bill kWh)	0.1	2.8	7.3	67.6	256.6	1007.0	3496.0
Ingot Steel Production (Mill. Tonnes)	0.0	0.4	1.4	12.2	31.81	95.4	503.0
Cement Production (Mill. Tonnes)	0.1	0.8	2.9	16.3	65.2	475.6	1423.6
Industrial Employment (Millions)	0.7	1.1	5.3	16.6	53.3	147.4	126.3

However, China's experience shows that industrialization is more than just a surge in goods moving in and out of bakeries, mills, and machine shops. How growth occurs, the relative effects of intensive and broad profit rates, and the more general basic macroeconomic processes are the keys to maintaining the long-term momentum of industrialization and having an impact on the entire economy. The similar growth rate of the manufacturing industry may conceal the huge differences in the process of industrialization. We believe that the process of industrialization is essentially a macroeconomic process that enables companies and individuals to accumulate and deepen technical, operational, management and business skills so that they can competition in more fields. The market releases multiple streams of interest, which then resonate in the economy. China's planned economy period, spanning approximately 1952-1978, recorded an impressive growth rate of production, but it was achieved in a policy and institutional environment, ultimately limiting the pace of change to a small part of its potential. And it brings high cost and economy to the rest. Both institutional and political restrictions hindered early industrialization efforts in the late 19th century. Two factors have been the main driving force behind the global rise of China's industry: the opening to the international economy and the liberalization of the domestic market.

Openness is important because it allows the accumulation of new technology and knowledge through foreign direct investment (FDI), the import of intermediate products and capital equipment, and the movement of people and ideas. For a large mainland economy like China, the domestic market usually absorbs more than 85% of industrial output (Table 4-3). The definition of openness based on access to overseas markets alone cannot claim its significance. The opening of the internal market is an important resource for new opportunities. It is an important resource for existing companies and new entrants to upgrade through product improvements and cost reductions, thereby guiding resources to high-yield companies and industries.

For latecomers like China, modern industry includes labor-intensive production that initially requires only moderate skills. Over time, upgrades will encourage the transition to more skilled labor and capital-intensive products and processes. Our review of China's industrialization process for a century and a half shows that when the policy environment provides ample opportunities for complementary interactions between openness and market liberalization, escalation occurs most quickly, helping to remove institutional barriers that often hinder the deepening of industrialization.

Table 4-3 Chinese exports of manufactures:
Scale and share of production and overall exports, 1933-2008

	Unit	1933	1952	1965	1978	1995	2008
Total exports	RMB Bill.	0.989	2.71	6.31	16.76	1245.18	10039.49
Share of Manufactures in exports	Percent	27.5	15	45	55	85.5	94.6
GVIO, current prices	RMB Bill.	-	34.9	140.2	423.7	9189.4	60737.92243
Manufacturing Share in GVIO	Percent	83.4	88	88	88	88	88
GVIO Manufacturing	RMB Bill.	2.645	30.7	123.4	372.9	8086.7	53449.4
Share of Manufacturing output exported	Percent	9.3	1.3	2.3	2.5	13.2	17.8
Trade Ration [X+M]/GDP	Percent	8.8	9.6	6.9	11.8	38.7	57.3

Note: * 1933 data in billions of current pre-war yuan.

Although there have been huge differences in international openness and local liberalization in the past 150 years, we can identify several major aspects of industrial development that have continued to operate throughout the study period, albeit at different intensities. First, manufacturing activities and industrial capabilities are gradually spreading across China's vast territory. Factory production was initially concentrated in the southeastern coast of China, especially the Lower Yangtze area around Shanghai, and later concentrated in northeastern China. The wartime (1937-1949) brought an astonishing large-scale industrial expansion to inland China. The planned economy era (1949-1978) moderately expanded the regional distribution, especially through the third-line policy, because it restricted the country's investment in dominant regions that were previously considered military fragile and ideologically questionable, and developed inland industrial capabilities.

The second is the expansion of industrial product structure. Even without tariff protection, import substitution has emerged since the end of the 19th century, especially in the cotton textile sector. On a more moderate scale, import substitution has appeared elsewhere, especially in the machinery manufacturing industry. In the 1930s, Chinese companies produced a small amount of textile machinery, machine tools, transportation equipment, and light weapons.

The socialist plan will graft the entire industry, including trucks, oil refining, telecommunications equipment, and nuclear fuel, onto the inherited industrial foundation. Although reforms allow market forces to exert increasing influence on the structure of China's industrial products, government agencies continue to promote the import of computers, chemicals, machine tools, and other industries considered by the authorities to be basic components of economic development or of military significance.

Third, domestic upgrading have narrowed the gap between China's leading manufacturers and global standards. Even without strong official support, progress in this direction became apparent in the 1920s and 1930s, especially in cotton textiles. Chinese yarn manufacturers have surpassed the coarsest grades of cotton yarn, increased labor and machine productivity, and absorbed the management practices of British and Japanese competitors; the New Academy provides textile technology training courses, and NGOs hire foreign technicians to promote production and sales of Japanese-style hand-knitting equipment.

Starting in the 1950s, the government of the People's Republic of China used its new financial strength and technical support from the Soviet Union and the Eastern European Union to initiate the largest technology transfer in human history at that time. Although the characteristics of the Soviet Union focused on quality improvement and innovation, Since the knowledge, accumulation o, resources, and experience under the planned economy created potential for improvement. When the post-1978 reforms encouraged the revival of incentives and allowed greater flexibility in the resource distribution.

4.2 Quantitative Overview

Table 4-1 provides a comparative perspective on China's long-term industrial growth ending with 2008, the most recent census year for which firm-level data are publicly available. With the sole exception of Japan during its heyday of accelerated growth, the pace of Chinese industrial expansion exceeded that of India, Japan and USSR/Russia during every sub-period for which meaningful comparison is feasible. Table 4-2 uses information on physical commodity output and industrial employment to provide crude comparisons of the scale of industrial activity in China, India, Japan and USSR/Russia during the century beginning in 1912. These data portray early 20th-century China as an industrial pygmy, trailing India's production of cotton textiles and lagging far behind Japanese and Russian/Soviet production of electricity, steel and cement.

Data for 1933 and 1952 suggest rough parity between Chinese and Indian industrial activity. An international comparison of industrial energy use during 1936-1937 provides a clear ranking: industries in China (including the northeast China) and British India each absorb the equivalent of 19 billion kWh of electricity per year, one-third the figure for Japan and one-sixth the total for the USSR [1].

Manufacturing contributed 2.1 and 3.2 per cent of China1933 and 1952 GDP respectively (in 1933 prices); adding mining and utilities (but not handicrafts) raises the 1933 figure to 3.3 per cent[2]. PRC compilations showed a rapid increase in the GDP share of industry (including mining and utilities), which rises to 44.1, 41.0 and 48,6 per cent in 1978, 1995 and 2008 [3].

4.3 China's Pre-1949 Industrial Development

4.3.1 Overview

We observe three stages of industrialization before 1949: the slow development in the late 19th century, including formal incentives and private commercial efforts, and then the more dynamic, market-driven expansion triggered by the Shimonoseki Treaty (1895), barriers to private enterprises.

---

① U.S. Department of State, 1949, *Energy Resources of the World*, Washington: U.S. Government Printing Office, pp,96-97.

② Liu, T.C. and Yeh, K.C., 1965, *The Economy of the Chinese Mainland: National Income and Economic Development, 1933-1959*, Princeton, N.J.: Princeton University Press, p. 66.

③ Compendium, 2009, *Xin Zhongguo liushiwuman tongji ziliao huibian* [China Compendium of Statistics 1949-2008], Beijing.

Subsequently, Japan's military pressure led to the Sino-Japanese War (1937-45) and Civil War (1945-1949), leading to increased state intervention. During this period, the government became the main driving force of industrial development, leading to an increase in the share of military-related activities and an increase in the share of production in the hinterland.

The Nanldng Treaty that ended the Opium War (1839-1842) forced China to open five ports for unrestricted trade, limit tariffs to 5%, and exempt foreigners from complying with Chinese laws. Subsequent agreements doubled the number of "treaty ports" and granted similar privileges to citizens of many European countries, as well as the United States and Japan. The resulting mandatory free trade system lasted until China regained tariff autonomy in 1929.

Declining international transportation and communication costs, coupled with rising trade volume, gradually adjusted China's price structure, showing significant local integration before the Opium War[1], with global values[2], The resulting changes include price drops (cotton yam, ferrous metals) and price increases (cotton, silk, tea) , As well as substitutes for domestic traded goods and new products (machinery, kerosene, matches) that affect the prices of complementary products.

4.3.2 Slow Development during the First Half-century of Openness

The opening aroused strong opposition in parts of the Chinese economy, such as tea farmers in Fujian[3]. However, production has developed slowly, whether it is a semi-official enterprise led by a prominent regional leader or a private enterprise specializing in silk and other agricultural products processing, some of which include foreign entrepreneurs. Although the Jiangnan Arsenal left a deep impression on Japanese tourists, and China's Hanyeping Complex introduced modern ferrous metallurgy before the Yawata Factory in Japan, the formal related measures mainly focused on

① Wang, Y.C., 1992, "Secular Trends of Rice Prices in the Yangzi Delta, 1638-1935", *Chinese History in Economic Perspective* (Eds. Rawski, T.G. and Li, L.M.), Berkeley: University of California Press, pp. 35-68.

② Brandt, L,, 1985, "Chinese Agriculture and the International Economy, 1870-1930: A Reassessment", *Explorations in Economic History*, 22, 168.

③ Gardella, R., 1994, *Harvesting Mountains: Fujian and the China Tea Trade, 1757-1937*, Berkeley: University of California Press, p.74.

defense-related production, which produced limited results. The sector hardly has any spillover effects.Early literature mistakenly attributed this slow growth to the inability of modern factory products to compete with Chinese traditional industrial products[1]. In fact, modern technology has allowed factory products to surpass many traditional products in terms of price and quality. Given that Japan's industrial progress has been faster under similar trade and treaty arrangements, it is equally unconvincing to attribute limited manufacturing growth to Western imperialism[2].

System and ideological restrictions consume the potential profits of emerging industrial enterprises and constitute a major obstacle to modern industry. With the decentralization of power that may accompany the Taiping Rebellion[3], the established local interest groups have been strengthened to hinder potential competition from newcomers by blocking access to supplies (soybeans, cocoons), storage facilities, and transportation.

4.3.3 Accelerated Growth from 1896 to 1937

As more and more trade ports opened up to foreign manufacturing activities, the disastrous military defeat in the hands of a small underestimated neighbor, Japan, led to a comprehensive reconsideration of traditional attitudes and structures. The rapid withdrawal of the government, and perhaps more importantly, the unofficial restrictions and prejudices, became a topic at the time, and even conservative leaders agreed to comprehensive reforms. The new company law introduced limited liability; the traditional examination system gave way to the new direction of modern education; Confucian-educated elites turned to constitutionalism, parliamentary democracy, and chambers of commerce as possible ways to reverse China's decline.

---

① Murphey, R., 1977, *The Outsiders: The Western Experience in India and China*, Ann Arbor: University of Michigan Press; Huang, P.C.C., 1985, *The Peasant Economy and Social Change in North China*, Stanford, Calif :Stanfbrd University Press.

② Esherick, J., 1972, "Harvard on China: The Apologetics of Imperialism", *Bulletin of Concerned Asian Scholars*, 4, 9-16; Moulder, F.V, 1977, *Japan, China and the Modern World Economy: Towards a Reinterpretation of East Asian Development ca. 1600~ca. 1918*, Cambridge: Cambridge University Press.

③ Brandt, L, Ma, D. and Rawski, T., 2014, "From Divergence to Convergence: Reexamining the History behind China's Economic Boom", *Journal of Economic Literature*, 52,45-123.

This year promoted the formation of industrial enterprises to speed up. From the 1880s to the 1890s, the number of newly established private factories in modern China more than doubled, from 42 to 99, and to 437 in the first decade of the 20th century. This wave of entry, coupled with the increase in foreign direct investment [1], initiated decades of rapid industrial growth, which continued into periods of division, war, and depression. It was not until 1937 that industrial growth before the war stagnated due to the outbreak of an all-out war with Japan, surpassing the growth of Japan, India and Russia/Soviet Union. Research by Chinese scientists found that Shanghai is also developing rapidly. From 1895 to 1912[2], Shanghai was the center of pre-war production.

The rapid growth from a small grassroots does not turn China into an industrial country. At the peak of the pre-war period in 1936, factory production accounted for only 3.1% of GDP-far lower than Japan's comparable figure of 25.1%. Even though Willow's estimate of 1933 production was significantly lowered[3] Compared with the situation in Japan from 1900 to 1910, handicrafts accounted for nearly half of the industry's total output value (and added value) in 1933[4].

4.3.4 Key Features of Early 20th-century Industrialization

The production of labor-intensive consumer goods dominated China's early industrial pattern. Textiles, clothing, and food processing accounted for two-thirds of industrial production in 1933, regardless of whether there were

---

[1] Remer, C.F., 1933, *Foreign Investments in China*, New York: Macmillan; Hou, C.M., 1965, *Foreign Investment and Economic Development in China, 1840-1937*, Cambridge: Harvard University Press.

[2] Ma, D,, 2008, "Economic Growth in the Lower Yangzi Region of China in 1911-1937: A Quantitative and Historical Analysis", *Journal of Economic History*, 68, 355-392.

[3] Liu and Yeh assign all non-factory production for food processing and textiles to the handicraft segment of China's 1933 industrial sector. Their estimate of "industrial" output thus includes non-commercial household production for self-consumption. Our attempt to remove non-commercial handicrafts from the industrial total focuses on the largest segments, textiles and food processing. We assume that commercial handicraft textile production in 1933 amounted to 90 per cent of factory textile output and that commercial handicraft food processing activity amounted to 100 per cent of factory output in that sector, with output measured by gross value in both sectors.

[4] Ohkawa, K. and Shinohara, M., 1979, *Patterns of Japanese Economic Development: A Quantitative Appraisal*, New Haven: Yale University Press.

handicrafts or not.

Industrial activities are concentrated in the region. Approximately two-thirds of the industrial output value in 1933 was concentrated in the southeast coastal provinces, while Shanghai and the neighboring Jiangsu provinces were reduced by half. Another 10% are located in Northeast China and rely heavily on Japanese investment. Data from newly established private factories before 1911 show a similar regional clustering pattern.

Extreme geographic concentration resulted in large variations in industry's GDP share. For Shanghai and the adjacent Lower Yangzi region, an area with a population of 60 million, the GDP share of modern industry during the early 1930s may have reached 15 per cent, three times the national total and comparable to the role of industry in Japan by the late 1920s[1]. Vast regions, especially in the west, experienced very limited development of modern industry prior to 1937.

Domestic entrepreneurs were soon able to overcome their initial disadvantages, namely, lack of expertise, weak financing, and treaty provisions to exempt foreign companies from many taxes in China. Although 90% of factory output in 1933 was sold domestically, global market forces had a strong influence on Chinese manufacturing in the pre-war period. New domestic producers often face the task of grabbing market share from foreign manufacturers, which are attracted by offering alternatives to traditional products (yarn instead of handicrafts, cigarettes instead of pipes, and kerosene instead of vegetable oil for lighting) and "new" products. Therefore, China's pre-war factory production is closely related to its economic comparative advantage.

Cotton textiles was the leading industry in China before the war, which illustrates the close connection between the global market and the development of pre-war factories. The import of artificial yarns and fabrics formed a market niche, which was later taken over by local manufacturers. Yarn imports fell sharply after peaking in 1903 and 1914, and China became a net exporter of cotton yarn since 1927. Fabric imports peaked in 1913; in 1932-1936, their share of domestic consumption fell to 8%, and in 1910-

---

[1] Ohkawa, K. and Shinohara, M., 1979, *Patterns of Japanese Economic Development: A Quantitative Appraisal*, New Haven: Yale University Press, p.37.

1910 it exceeded 25%[1].

International influence penetrates into the development process. Chinese textile entrepreneurs hire foreign-trained technicians, purchase imported equipment on the advice of foreign experts in Shanghai, send their son to study abroad, and borrow money from foreign banks.

The competition between imported goods and domestic goods from foreign and Chinese-owned factories has led to market segmentation. Chinese companies initially competed for products that serve lower-price and quality market segments[2]. Chinese textile entrepreneurs initially produced yarns instead of fabrics and focused on low-count varieties, leaving better quality to foreign competitors[3].

Market evolution and competitive pressure urge enterprises to upgrade. In the 1920s, changes in Japanese machinery and local demand encouraged spinning companies to shift their focus from "coarse and low-count yam" to "high-quality, high-quality, high-content fine yam" varieties[4]. Forcing independent store owners and installing technically-trained managers has enabled some companies to ensure substantial increases in productivity[5]. Between 1924 and 1936, Chinese yam producers kept up with the increasing productivity of Chinese and Japanese companies and surpassed their British competitors; in terms of factory weaving, missing data showed that Chinese companies would Production increased from 59% of the level recorded by

① Hsiao, L. L., 1974, *China's Foreign Trade Statistics, 1864-1949*, Cambridge, MA: East Asian Research Center Harvard University, distributed by Harvard University Press, pp.38-39; Kraus, R. A., 1980, *Cotton and Cotton Goods in China, 1918-1936,* New York & London: Garland, pp.116, J-3; Feuerwerker, A., 1970, "Handicraft and Manufactured Cotton Textiles in China, 1871- 1910", *Journal of Economic History*, 30, 338-378; Brandt, L., 1989, *Commercialization and Agricultural Development: Central and Eastern China, 1870-1937*, Cambridge; New York: Cambridge University Press.

② Sutton, J., 2012, *Competing in Capabilities: The Globalization Process*, Oxford: Oxford University Press.

③ Hou, C.M., 1965, *Foreign Investment and Economic Development in China, 1840-1937*, Cambridge: Harvard University Press, p.153.

④ Koll, Elisabeth, 2003, *From Cotton Mill to Business Empire: The Emergence of Regional Enterprises in Modern China*, Cambridge MA: Harvard University Asia Center, p.265.

⑤ Cochran, S.G., 2000, *Encountering Chinese Networks*, Berkeley: University of California Press; Compendium, 2009, *Xin Zhongguo liitshiwimian tongji ziliao huibian* [China Compendium of Statistics 1949-2008], Beijing: Zhongguo tongji chubanshe, pp.l91ff; Zeitz, P., 2013, "Do Local Institutions Affect all Foreign Investors in the Same Way?", *Journal of Economic History*, 73, 117-141.

Japanese industry leaders to 84% [1].

Match presents a similar situation, with imports being replaced by domestic production, first by foreign companies and then by Chinese companies. Liu Hongsheng, the Chinese "King of Matches", started his business in a small city and was ignored by foreign competitors. Customers value price and quality. Later, he challenged Japan and Sweden in the Shanghai market, China's largest market[2]. Start-ups of China Telecom Equipment (Huawei) and Construction Machinery (Sany Heavy Industry, Liugong) have recently successfully entered the global high-end market initially dominated by leading multinational companies, leveraging their skills accumulated by selling inferior products to less demanding markets Caterpillar and Ericsson [3].

4.3.5 Impact on Handicrafts

The scale and growth of the process are difficult to predict, but several propositions are clear. Forced free trade and factory expansion disrupted some handicraft sectors and brought new life to other sectors. The overall effect may be beneficial: between 1875 and 1928, the export of some handicrafts increased by an average of 2.6% per year, and between 1912 and 1931[4], the total export of 67 kinds of handicrafts increased by an average of 1.1% per year. Cotton textiles explain the result of this mixing. Handcraft was hit by the double blow of the fall in raw yarn prices and the rise in cotton prices, resulting in a sharp drop[5]. However, the same low price of factory yarn has strengthened the booming hand-knitting, the combination of factory and home knitting[6]. Grove discussed the Japanese proposal and the

---

① Zeitz, P., 2013, "Do Local Institutions Affect all Foreign Investors in the Same Way?", *Journal of Economic History*, 73, 117-141; Chao, K., 1977, *The Development of Cotton Textile Production in China*, Harvard University Press, p.313.

② Cochran, S.G., 1992, "Three Roads into Shanghai's Market: Japanese, Western, and Chinese Companies in the Match Trade, 1895-1937", In *Shanghai Sojourners* (Eds., Wakeman, F. and Yeh, W.H.). Berkeley; Institute of East Asian Studies, 35-75.

③ Brandt, L. and Thun, E,, 2010, "The Fight for the Middle: Competition and Upgrading in Chinese Industry", *World Development*, 38, 1555-1574.

④ Hou, C.M., 1965, *Foreign Investment and Economic Development in China, 1840-1937*, Cambridge: Harvard University Press, p.171.

⑤ Feuerwerker, A., 1970, "Handicraft and Manufactured Cotton Textiles in China, 1871-1910", *Journal of Economic History*, 30, 338-378.

⑥ Reynolds, B.L., 1974, "Weft: The Technological Sanctuary of Chinese Handspun Yam", *Ch 'ing~ shihwen-t'i*, 3, 1-19

key role of Japanese intermediate technology (iron-tooth wood handloom) in the expansion of small-scale fabric production in northern China[1]. Despite rapid industrial growth, handicrafts were still the main component of industrial output value until 1955, when they accounted for about 20% of total industrial output value[2].

Hyperinflation undermined private manufacturing and limited the implementation of industrialization plans, especially for Chiang Kai-shek Nationalist government. Consumer manufacturing centered on Shanghai suffered catastrophic reductions in capacity utilization: operating rates in flour milling fell by nearly 90 per cent between 1936 and 1945; in textiles, the decline was even steeper. Official industrialization efforts, however, moved forward despite the travails of war. Indeed, rapid manufacturing growth immediately following the cessation of civil war in 1949 reflects substantial wartime increases in manufacturing capacityexpansion that pushed 1952 output to double the 1933 level and 65 per cent above the 1936 figure. Wartime investments also altered China's industrial structure, raising the share of producer goods from 25 to 42 per cent of manufacturing output, increasing the share of central, southwest and northwestern regions from 8.8 to 21 per cent, and sharply reducing the Herfindahl index for provincial 1933 and 1952.

4.3.6 Pre-1949 Outcomes

A century after the British arms free trade system was implemented, China was still mainly an agricultural economy in 1949. Although industry grew rapidly at the beginning of the 20th century, the share of production in total output was still small. Nevertheless, China has made significant progress in industrialization. After decades of slow expansion, the impact of military failures and the 1895 treaty provisions that allowed foreign investment to set up factories in China's trade ports have set off a wave of reforms. The ensuing entry and growth momentum provided China with a modest set of manufacturing industries, some of which (especially the cotton textile industry) had global visibility, employing more than 1 million workers in

---

① Grove, L,, 2006, *A Chinese Economic Revolution: Rural Entrepreneurship in the Twentieth Century*, Lanham: Rowman and Littlefield.

② Chen, N.R., 1967, *Chinese Economic Statistics: A Handbook for Mainland China*, Chicago, Aldine, p. 210.

1933[1].

China's leading industrial areas, the Shanghai area and the Northeast, reflect different sources of growth. In the Lower Yangtze area of Shanghai, the private sector was the main driver of pre-war industrial growth. Beginning in the 1900s, the rapid expansion of the consumer goods manufacturing industry promoted the entire economic transformation consistent with Japan's previous path. Expand the production of consumer goods such as cotton products, food, matches, etc., encourage backward connections with engineering and chemicals, encourage the development of commodity and financial exchanges, and encourage banks to expand finance to manufacturing and even agriculture[2]. Before 1931, government intervention was mostly indirect; especially important was the support of modern banks, "this sector has benefited the most from agreements with the state[3]. This became a threat after 1931, and then the reality of the war with Japan forced the Chinese government to strengthen its control. Industries and markets that were mainly affected by private activities in the past have directly injected themselves into the distribution and development of industrial resources.

In contrast, in Northeast China, the government's direction is clear, with a large amount of actual investment coming from Japanese-controlled companies whose actions respond to Tokyo's economic priorities. Reflecting this situation, chemicals, machinery, and metals in 1936-core components of a detailed formal plan dating back to the 1950s-became the largest contributors to the added value of the factory[4].

These developments occurred in an open economy, with free trade (from 1842), substantial price integration with global markets (from the 1880s), minimal restriction of FDI (from 1895), rapid expansion of new forms of education and overseas study, and considerable return migration by overseas Chinese. Extensive openness magnified both the disruption (e.g. to handicraft

---

[1] Liu, T.C. and Yeh, K.C., 1965, *The Economy of the Chinese Mainland: National Income and Economic Development, 1933-1959*, Princeton, N.J.: Princeton University Press, p.428.

[2] Rawski, T.G., 1980, *China's Transition to Industrialism: Producer Goods and Economic Development in the Twentieth Century*, Ann Arbor: University of Michigan Press; Ma, D., 2008, "Economic Growth in the Lower Yangzi Region of China in 1911-1937: A Quantitative and Historical Analysis", *Journal of Economic History*, 68, 355-392.

[3] Kirby, W. C., 1984, *Germany and Republican China*, Stanford: Stanford University Press, p. 80.

[4] Chao, K., 1982, *The Economic Development of Manchuria: The Rise of a Frontier Economy*, Ann Arbor: Center for Chinese Studies, University of Michigan, p.83.

spinning) and the opportunities resulting from the growth of international links.

State action, initially focused on sponsorship of semi-official enterprises during the late 19th century, and subsequently emphasized indirect actions that smoothed the path of private ventures: passing a corporation law, identifying and disseminating commercially promising technologies, and pursuing tariff autonomy.

As a result, China's pre-war economy displayed many features of a market system. Prices were flexible and generally market-determined. There were few man-made obstacles to domestic or international mobility of goods, people, information and ideas. Formal and informal entry barriers declined over time. Low revenue and, after 1911, weak central control restricted the state's ability to regulate and intervene.

This began to change soon after the Guomindang established the Nanjing government in 1927. Although restricted by weak finances and limited territorial control, the new administration set out to follow Japan and other rising powers by systematically deploying the levers of state power to build a modem industrial economy. Japan's assault on China's territorial integrity, which signaled a growing likelihood of all-out war, hastened the Guomindang's shift from supporting a largely private economy toward an emerging vision of a planned economy in which official direction of investment and state-owned enterprises (SOEs) would occupy leading roles.

The outbreak of the war in 1937 led to a large-scale expansion of the Guomindang's economic bureaucracy in China. This led to the nationalization of many existing industrial operations and plans to produce and distribute necessary war materials[1]. By 1944, public sector enterprises accounted for more than half of the total industrial output, its share in heavy industry is even higher[2]. As Japan's failure reignited China's long-suffering internal conflict, the Guomindang and the Communists had a common vision of a military force led by government technocrats and dominated by state-owned enterprises.

---

[1] Kirby, W. C., 1990, "Continuity and Change in Modem China: Economic Planning on the Mainland and on Taiwan, 1943-1958", *Australian Journal of Chinese Affairs*, 24, 121-141.

[2] Bian, M.L., 2002, "The Sino-Japanese War and the Formation of the State Enterprise System in China: A case study of the Dadukou Iron and Steel Works, 1938-1945", *Enterprise and Society*, 3, 80-123.

4.4 Chinese Industry under Socialist Planning, 1949-1978

With the end of hostilities and the establishment of China in 1949, the Chinese economy recovered rapidly. In the mid-1950s, China succeeded in further institutionalizing and expanding the system left over from the previous World War I era. Two characteristics that are particularly prominent in industry are: state-owned and planned systems replace the market. Industry under socialism is not only a continuity story, but also a change story. State ownership emerged in the 1940s. The remaining nationalization of private enterprises in the early 1950s and the concentration of new investment in the state sector only strengthened this dominance. From 1957 to 1978, the state-owned sector provided more than 80% of GVIO, and the rest came from a large number of small urban collective enterprises, and even more rural collective enterprises began in the late 1950s.

Through the expanded and integrated version of the independent planning bureaucracy inherited from the former Kuomintang and Manchu government, China began to replace the market with pure administrative resource allocation. Decisions about output, inputs, and investments are now in the hands of planners. Although China's planning system is similar to that of the Soviet Union, there are also important differences. The planners distributed fewer commodities nationwide than the Soviet Union. China's system is more decentralized, with large amounts of resources controlled by provincial and county governments[①]. This localization reflects a series of initiatives that began in the mid-1950s and continued for the next two decades. This characteristic of the economy before 1978 had an important impact on the trajectory of the system's reform era[②].

The main purpose of the new system is to mobilize resources that planners can use to achieve strategic goals. Controlling prices is crucial: by setting the price of the final product higher relative to the input price (including wages), planners can concentrate profits in the hands of state-owned enterprises. Low profit retention rates—companies must remit more than 95% of their

---

① Wong, C., 1985, "Material Allocation and Decentralization: Impact of the Local Sector on Industrial Reform", In *The Political Economy of Reform in Post-Mao China* (Eds, Peny, E.J. and Wong, C.), Cambridge, MA: Council on East Asian Studies/Harvard University, pp. 253-278.

② Maskin, E., Qian, Y.Y., and Xu, C.G., 2000, "Incentives, Information, and Organizational Form", *J Review of Economic Studies*, 67, 359-378.

profits—provide a source of revenue for the government, which accounts for a large portion of fiscal revenue.

Security issues and the desire to narrow the gap with the West have made the investment and expansion of China's manufacturing industries such as steel, machine tools and chemical industries highly valued. Like the Soviet Union, in stark contrast to the first three decades of the 20th century, China's planning closely followed industrial development without reference to comparative advantages. In addition, in addition to the vast equipment, technology, and expertise of the Soviet bloc in the 1950s, Chinese leaders also restricted the country's connections to the global market. Reflecting the combination of ideological beliefs and the impact of the US-led trade embargo, it has promoted international isolation. China's trade rate is far below the level of the 1930s.

4.4.1 Achievements

These institutional arrangements provided three years of rapid industrial expansion that exceeded the previous growth rate. After doubling the economic boom from 1949 to 1952, industrial production grew at an annual rate of more than 11% between 1952 and 1978, while employment increased nearly tenfold, from 530 in 1952. to 53.3 million in 1978.

According to the planner's purpose, the quantitative expansion has led to a significant shift in the industrial structure, shifting from the previously dominant consumer manufacturing industry to intermediate and production products. Brand new industries have emerged, such as the manufacture of trucks, tractors, radios, telecommunications, and power generation equipment. Machinery increased from only 6.2% of industrial production in 1952 to 25.7% in 1978, highlighting the direction and magnitude of structural changes. By the 1970s, the sectoral composition of industry was similar to that of countries with significantly higher GDP per capita; Japan in the late 1950s.

The downward trend in spatial concentration that had occurred between 1933 and 1952 continued in the socialist planning environment. China's first five-year plan (1953-1957) concentrated investment in the interior, bypassing the pre-war manufacturing-dominated coastal areas. Planners also moved personnel and factories from the military fragile coastal cities to inland areas. It continued in the 1960s under the "Third Front" program, which placed industrial facilities in remote internal spaces to prevent potential US or Soviet attacks[1]. With these changes, the Industrial Production Index of Herfindaal Region continued the downward trend that began in the 1930s, from 0.09 in 1952 to 0.06 in 197. Outside the cities, and largely outside official plans, development represents an unusual feature of China's industrialization. Most rural enterprises are operated by agricultural collectives, aiming to serve agriculture and use local resources to meet local demand for cement, fertilizer, machinery, electricity, and coal. The promotion of rural industry began in the mid-1950s, experienced explosive but extremely wasteful growth during the Great Leap Forward (1958-1960), and reappeared after major post-splash damage in the late 1960s. In 1978, rural industries (including mining, construction, and manufacturing) employed 19.7 million workers[2]. Rural industries have been particularly successful in the slums of large coastal cities, which developed the largest non-agricultural sectors before 1949. These areas were ignored in China's early investment plans and later third-tier policies.

By the 1970s, China's manufacturing industry was no longer limited to the production of low-quality, labor-intensive consumer goods, but almost covered the entire industrial activity, including oil refining, nuclear weapons, and complex operations involving earth satellites. Despite the short duration, aid and trade flows from the Soviet Union and its Eastern European Union countries ensured unprecedented international technology transfer and accelerated China's efforts to expand its domestic manufacturing footprint. In addition to the increase in output and the expansion of the product structure, the socialist plan also brought about a huge expansion of industrial capacity. The accumulation of manufacturing experience and popularization of popular education have increased the stock of factory-level technical skills and human capital. In addition, the planning system provides a significant expansion of institutions, resources, and personnel for advanced technical education and research. Various ministries and large state-owned enterprises have established a network of universities, technical schools, and R&D institutions. By the end of the 1970s, there were more than 700 research and development institutions with more than 500,000 scientists and engineers,

---

[1] Naughton, B., 1988, "The Third Front: Defense Industrialization in Chinese Interior", *The China Quarterly*, 115, 351-386.

[2] Gu, S.L., 1999, *China's Industrial Technology: Market Reform and Organizational Change*, London: Routledge, pp. 56-58; Nolting, L.E. and Feshbach, M., 1981, *Statistics on Research and Development Employment in the U.S.S.R.*, Washington DC: U.S. Dept, of Commerce, Bureau of the Census, p.44.

almost as many as the United States[1].

4.4.2 Shortcomings

Despite significant progress, the achievements of Chinese industry during the planning period are far from reaching its potential. The most obvious indicator is slow productivity growth, despite many favorable conditions: unprecedented official stimulation of industrial development, massive influx of Soviet technology and capital goods, massive increase in public R&D expenditure, and rapid expansion of primary education and primary health care.

Due to the substantial increase in investment expenditures, the growth of capital per worker coincides with the surprisingly slow growth of industrial output per worker[2] in most industries/workers-all industries including metallurgy experienced a decline in labor productivity between 1965 and 1978[3]. The factor of human capital improvement points to TFP negative growth[4]. This "disappointing" result means that "the rapid expansion of output is almost entirely due to the huge increase in labor, especially capital input." The obvious implication is that the beneficial effects of multiple sources of productivity growth have been stifled by institutional bottlenecks and policy failures. The investment used to offset the decline in TFP has increased as a proportion of GDP, and consumption has weakened. Chinese observers quickly emphasized the institutional source of bad results. An editorial in 1982 explained that "the root causes of low (industrial) labor productivity" include "low morale, bureaucracy and lax discipline" in many factories.

① World Bank, 1985, *China: Long-term Development Issues and Options*, Baltimore: Johns Hopkins University Press, p.1-10; Chen, K. et al., 1988, "Productivity Change in Chinese Industry: 1963-1985", *Journal of Comparative Economics*, 12, 570-591.

② Chen, K. et al., 1988, "Productivity Change in Chinese Industry: 1963-1985", *Journal of Comparative Economics*, 12, 570-591.

③ Field, R.M., 1982, "Slow Growth of Labour Productivity in Chinese Industry, 1952-8", *China Quarterly*, 96, 641-664.

④ Zhu, X.D., 2012, "Understanding China's Growth: Past, Present, and Future", *Journal of Economic Perspectives*, 26, 103-124.

4.5 Chinese Industry during the Reform Era, 1978-2008

4.5.1 Early Reforms, 1978-1995

Beginning in the late 1970s, successive reform attempts gradually gave way to a mixture that combined key elements of planning, state ownership, and formal management with the open, private, and market-based institutions of the 1920s and 1930s. This new arrangement continues the rapid growth under the old planned system, but combines quantitative expansion with market opening, deep integration with the global market, and rapid upgrades, bringing more and more Chinese manufacturers closer to the global technological maturity and product limits . quality. We divided the reform period into two periods, and the breakthrough point was 1995.

China's early reforms included selective opening to the global economy, especially through the establishment of special economic zones (SEZs), welcoming foreign investment and allowing duty-free imports of materials used to produce export goods, and the gradual reform of state-owned enterprises. However, the key element of the early reforms was market liberalization, which proceeded along multiple axes.

Price and quantity determination, formerly the near-exclusive preserve of official plan bodies, moved toward market outcomes. Separate initiatives empowering firms to arrange the disposition of above-quota output and establishing "dual pricing", i.e. market pricing of non-plan exchanges, injected scarcity-based marginal values into a formerly rigid pricing system By 1991, "market forces surpassed" state order in determining prices of "production materials"; in 1995, the share of market forces reached 77.9 percent. Introduction of partial profit retention (for firms) and bonuses (for workers) reversed the plan system's destruction of incentives and weakened the corrosive impact of soft budget constraints among state-owned firms. Reforms began to dismantle plan-era restrictions that had limited the mobility of people, goods, technology, funds and infomiation across China's internal and international boundaries. These initiatives sparked what was developed into vast flows of migrant labor to coastal industrial centers; they also undermined protectionist policies aimed at retaining local materials and blocking inflows of manufactures. Finally, early reforms reduced impediments to entry and exit in a growing array of industries, although SOE monopoly persisted in some sectors , others opened up for entry by non-state actors urban collectives, rural township and village enterprises (TVEs), private domestic ventures and foreign-invested firms.

Price and quantification were once the almost exclusive domains of official planning agencies, but now they have turned to market results. A separate measure authorizes companies to supervise output exceeding quotas and establish "dual pricing", that is, market pricing on unplanned exchanges, and inject marginal value based on scarcity into the rigid pricing system in advance[1]. In 1991 ("market forces" surpassed the "national order" in setting prices for "materials of production"; in 1995, the share of market forces reached 77.9%[2]. The role of the planned system was reversed. The destruction of the incentive mechanism has weakened the corrosive effect of soft budget constraints on state-owned enterprises. These measures have triggered an influx of migrant workers into coastal industrial centers. It also undermines protectionist policies designed to protect local materials and prevent manufacturers from entering. Finally, the early reforms lowered entry and exit barriers in more and more ways. Although the monopoly of state-owned enterprises continues to exist in some areas[3], other areas are open to non-state actors such as urban collectives, rural areas and village and township enterprises (TVE), domestic private enterprises, and foreign-funded enterprises.

4.5.2 Outcomes to 1995

Although planned allocations and prices continue to exist, incentives, domestic trade, and the recovery of market pricing have enabled manufacturers to change product mixes, choose alternative suppliers, or expand sales efforts into new markets without the need for cumbersome bureaucratic approvals. New entrants operating outside the planning system may occupy a niche of the market overlooked by the planning agency. The

---

① Naughton,B., 1995, *Growing Out of the Plan: Chinese Economic Reform 1978-1993*, Cambridge: Cambridge University Press.

② Rawski, T.G., 2000, "China's Move to Market: How Far? What Next?", In *China's Future: Constructive Partner or Emerging Threat?* (Eds, Carpenter, T.G. and Dorn, J.A.), Washington DC: Cato Institute, 317-339.

③ Haggard, S. and Huang, Y.S., 2008, "The Political Economy of Private Sector Development in China", In *China's Great Economic Transformation* (Eds, Brandt, L. and Rawski, T.), Cambridge and New York: Cambridge University Press, 337-374.

increase in the supply of unplanned materials and services encouraged specialization and reversed excessive vertical integration in the planned environment. At the same time, the increase in openness has steadily expanded its global influence on China's previously isolated and largely self-sufficient industrial sector; this faces the prospect of acquiring overseas innovation accumulation dating back to the 1930s. Between 1978 and 1995, manufacturing exports exceeded USD100. Imports of capital equipment, raw materials and industrial components account for a large proportion, most of which are delivered to the factory sector, reflecting China's increasing participation in the global supply chain.

Foreign direct investment has increased sharply, especially in companies led by entrepreneurs with ties to Hong Kong and Taiwan and with experience in the production and export of consumer products, which constitute the majority of IUU enterprises. These companies specialize in the assembly and export of textiles, clothing, footwear and electronic products, and have become the main source of China's exports. However, during this period, the share of foreign-related enterprises in industrial production—the share of exports in the sales of manufactured goods and the share of foreign direct investment in total investment remained below 15%.

But tariff and non-tariff barriers, remnants of the industrial planning system, temporary (especially private) business interruptions, and inadequate infrastructure (frequent power outages, overcrowded railways, poor roads, primitive telecommunications) limit the economic response to these opportunities. Ten years ago, 1937. The ability of private actors to respond was limited due to similar local restrictions.

At the beginning of the reform, industrial growth was slightly higher than that in 1965-1978, and textile and food processing increased significantly. From 1978 to 1995, the shares of machinery, chemical industry and metallurgy did not change much. The percentage of industries and products that China had comparative advantages from 1978 to 1995.

The growth mainly occurred outside the government sector, with state-owned enterprises reducing their share of output from 80% to 49% between 1978 and 1995. Township and village enterprises have become the main source of new power. Once again concentrated in the vibrant coastal areas, mainly owned and managed by town and village governments (some of which are actually private), these companies absorbed the labor released by the increase in productivity accompanying the land reform and sold it. An

expanding network of local products and trade to obtain equipment, supplies and expertise. Strong incentives, limited technical expertise and strict budget constraints have made township and village enterprises focus on labor-intensive consumer goods[1]. The township and village enterprises are flexible, ambitious and in line with China's comparative advantages. They quickly entered the international market, accounting for 16.3% of total exports in 1990 and 28.9% in 1995.

With wave after wave of new entrants slashing returns in the consumer sector, Chinese leaders have begun to rethink the position of the state sector. Industries such as garments and beverages are designated as "competitive industries", which means that market competition can determine the fate of state-owned Chinese companies in these product groups. Planning increasingly focuses on a limited number of "strategic" departments that seem to deserve special attention and support. Despite the reforms, between 1981 and 1995, state-owned enterprises in the secondary industry (industry and construction) absorbed more than half (usually more) of total investment expenditure each year. State-owned enterprises benefit from preferential access to bank loans. The licensing of advanced technologies and joint ventures with overseas multinational companies such as Beijing Jeep and Shanghai Volkswagen provide additional support for expanding the technological capabilities and competitiveness of state-owned enterprises. Despite these advantages, state-owned enterprises lag behind other companies in terms of financial returns[2] and productivity growth[3]. This inspired efforts to expand reform efforts that began in the mid-1990s.

4.5.3 Reforms since 1995

On the domestic front, the government (mainly insiders) has been privatized or shut down many small, unnecessary or underperforming state-owned enterprises: more than 75,000 state-owned enterprises disappeared, and with them 15 to 20 million workers work. Between 1995 and 2008, the

---

[1] Whiting, S.H., 2001, *Power and Wealth in Rural China: the Political Economy of Institutional Change*, Cambridge; New York: Cambridge University.

[2] Holz, C.A., 2003, *China's Industrial State-owned Enterprises: Between Profitability and Bankruptcy*, New Jersey: World Scientific.

[3] Jefferson, G.H. et al., 2000, "Ownership, Productivity Change, and Financial Performance in Chinese Industry", *Journal of Comparative Economics*, 28, 786-813.

share of the state sector in industrial production increased from 48.6% to 24%. Many policy initiatives have tried to make state-owned enterprises more commercial and innovative: control and management of state-owned assets.

The SASAC was established to lead the reorganization of large state-owned enterprises to consolidate the management of state-owned property interests and improve their competitiveness[1]. The government has invested resources to promote "domestic innovation," which will make China (rather than past buyers) a producer of cutting-edge technology. The state has also increased overseas direct investment orders to promote Chinese enterprises that give priority to state-owned enterprises to "go global" in order to deepen market experience and accelerate the absorption and development of advanced technologies.

Legal reforms that clearly affirmed the legitimacy of private enterprises stimulated the rapid expansion of private manufacturing, including the formation of new enterprises and the privatization of township and village enterprises and urban collectives. Restrictions on the movement of people and goods have been further weakened. Externally, a number of measures (reducing tariffs and non-tariff barriers, new measures to encourage foreign direct investment, allowing large numbers of companies to enter international trade, and providing exporters with more generous currency holdings) brought China back to the world in 2001[2]. Reform leaders have seen the close connection between reforms at home and abroad. They see China's WTO agreement as "a credible commitment to maintaining market results, and local participants, especially large state-owned enterprises, will have to adapt". The benefits of joining the WTO.

4.5.4 Outcomes since 1995

Industrial growth accelerated during this period. Although the share of textiles and food processing continued to decline, the share of machinery was

---

① Naughton, B., 2015, "The Transformation of the State Sector: SASAC, the Market Economy, and the New National Champions", In *State Capitalism, Institutional Adaptation, and the Chinese Miracle* (Eds, Naughton, B. and Tsai, K), 46-71.

② Lardy, N.R., 1983, *Agriculture in ChinaModern Economic Development*, Cambridge and New York: Cambridge University Press; Branstetter, L. and Lardy, MR., 2008, "China's Embrace of Globalization", In *China's Great Economic Transformation* (Eds, Brandt, L. and Rawski, T.). Cambridge and New York: Cambridge University Press, 633-682.

almost halved. The southeast coast continued to advance, and the production trap increased by 20% to 45.8%.

With the rapid growth of manufactured goods exports, China's rapid expansion, fierce competition, and increasingly demanding domestic market absorbed more than 80% of the increased production output during the two sub-periods of the reform period. For most manufacturers, This is an opportunity to sell. The domestic market is the world's largest market for automobiles, mobile phones and nuclear power equipment, providing the greatest driving force for growth. Domestic companies have achieved strong competitiveness in certain fields (beer, home appliances, heavy construction equipment), and the regained market share was initially transferred to foreign operators. As of 2008, domestic companies accounted for four percent of the total industrial output value. above over three- fourths.

Reforms have increased the incentives for companies to invest in capacity building and their ability to upgrade. The increase in innovation and upgrading has allowed companies to close the productivity gap between local and international leaders, similar to recent developments elsewhere in Asia and China's long-term catch-up since the late 19th century. Foreign direct investment accelerated after Deng Xiaoping went south in 1992 and has maintained a high level since then, making a significant contribution. A large part of foreign direct investment comes from relatively local Anren in Hong Kong and Taiwan. Large multinational companies such as Boeing, General Electric, Hitachi, and Volkswagen have also established important businesses in China.

Foreign companies initially focused on using Chinese land and labor to reduce the production costs of parts and final products sold overseas. "Processing" export is a regulation that allows duty-free import of materials and components, accelerating China's engagement with the global production chain. As foreign companies become familiar with the growing capabilities of Chinese manufacturers, they turn to domestic suppliers to purchase more and more products. This increases the distribution of international standards and advanced business practices (inventory management, production planning, quality control, etc.) among domestic manufacturers, because the supply chain of a single vehicle or electrical equipment assembly plant can span thousands. Finally, due to the expected rapid increase in income and the growing middle class, foreign direct investment is increasingly turning to serve the growing domestic market, a shift that has intensified competition in many domestic product categories.

The experience of Chinese companies in telecommunications and construction equipment proves the contribution of openness and liberalization to industrial progress. Huawei, initially regarded by Chinese planners and partners of multinational corporations as technologically weak, follows the path of China's pre-war "king of the game and develops expertise in neglected markets (first small cities in mainland China, then Africa) . Products that later entered the high-end market at home and abroad[1]. Reflecting the spillover effect of China's increased R&D expenditure[2], research engineers designed cheap concrete pumps, enabling Sany, an unknown Hunan company, to develop into an internationally competitive construction equipment manufacturert[3].

The ever-increasing market penetration and rising unit value confirm the increasing complexity and rapid upward migration of China's finished product exports on the international price/quality ladder[4]. The domestic (Chinese) content of exports has increased significantly, reflecting the deepening of local supply chains and capabilities[5].

The ever-increasing market penetration and rising unit value confirm the increasing complexity and rapid upward migration of China's finished product exports on the international price/quality ladder. Manufacturing productivity growth is mainly driven by the entry of new companies and is now parallel to the success of other successful economies during the period of rapid industrial expansion[6]. The most dynamic results appear in areas where competition is fierce, foreign investors are easy to enter and hinder

---

[1] Brandt, L. and Thun, E., 2013, "Going Mobile in China: Shifting Value Chains and Upgrading in the Mobile Telecom Sector", *International Journal of Technological Learning, Innovation and Development*, 148-180.

[2] Hu, A.G.Z. and Jefferson, G.H., 2008, "Science and Technology in China", In *China's Great Economic Transformation* (Eds, Brandt, L. and Rawski, T.), Cambridge and New York: Cambridge University Press, 286-336.

[3] Brandt, L. and Thun, E., 2015, "Constructing a Ladder for Growth: Policy, Markets and Industrial Upgrading in China", *World Development*, 80, 78-95.

[4] Schott, P., 2008, "The Relative Sophistication of Chinese Exports", *Economic Policy*, 53, 5-49; Mandel, B., 2013, "Chinese Exports and U.S. Import Prices Staff Reports", Federal Reserve Bank of New York, No 591.

[5] Kee, H.L. and Tang, H.W., 2015, "Domestic Value Added in Exports: Theory and Firm Evidence from China", *American Economic Review*, Forthcoming.

[6] Brandt, L., Van Biesebroeck, J. and Zhang, Y.F., 2012, "Creative Accounting or Creative Destruction? Firm-Level Productivity Growth in Chinese Manufacturing", *Journal of Development Economics*, 97, 339-351.

domestic companies from entering or exiting[1].

At the same time, there are large-scale inefficiencies in individual industries: Hsieh and Klenow concluded that reducing the productivity gap between companies in the industry to the level of the US manufacturing industry can make the productivity of Chinese factories in the period 1998-2005 Increase by 30-50%[2]. Priority access to capital, energy, and other key inputs may be the culprits of these costs, usually in the form of overcapacity in enterprises and industries. It shows that there are large differences in productivity dynamics among sectors where the output share of state-owned enterprises is higher or lower than 50%. For the sectors where state-owned enterprises contributed most of the output in 1998, the result was consistently weak: sustained enterprises had a negative contribution to productivity growth, and new entrants, including new private enterprises—that is, new enterprises were Enter at the productivity level of existing enterprises. For industries where the share of state-owned enterprises was less than 50% in 1998, the situation reversed with the increase in productivity, mainly because the entering enterprises achieved above-average performance, which improved the performance of the entire industry.

Our investigation ended with a profound contradiction. As China achieved results that exceeded everyone's craziest dream in the fourth decade of transformation, the strategy of placing state-owned enterprises at the center of the national development plan reappeared. Although the current government clearly adheres to the traditional policy of using state-owned enterprises to dominate the economy, we must ask whether the economic momentum is sufficient to cover the costs associated with state-owned enterprises.

① Brandt, L., Rawski, T. and Sutton, J., 2008, "China's Industrial Development", In *China's Great Economic Transformation* (Eds, Brandt, L. and Rawski, T.), Cambridge and New York: Cambridge University Press, 569-632; Brandt, L. and Thun, E., 2015, "Constructing a Ladder for Growth: Policy, Markets and Industrial Upgrading in China", *World Development*, 80,78-95.
② Hsieh, C.T. and Klenow, P., 2009, "Misallocation and Manufacturing TFP in China and India", *Quarterly Journal of Economics*, 124, 1403-1448.

Chapter 5

Reform and Development of Chinese Enterprises

5.1 The Breakthrough for Chinese Enterprises: The Transformation of the Planned Economy into a Market Economy

The establishment of China's socialist market economy belongs to a huge project laid on the history of a backward, traditional agricultural power. At present, China is the only country in the world's reality and history to adopt such a development model. This is one of the characteristics of Chinese socialism.

5.1.1 The Planned Economy Allows the People's Republic of China to Recover from the Ruins in a Powerful Way

In the end of the 19th century and the beginning of the 20th century, many economic crises broke out in capitalist countries. On the surface, it was an excess of production materials and an economic waste caused by insufficient consumption power of residents. So some people have come up with the method of a planned economy and planned production of materials according to demand to avoid the economic crisis. The Soviet Union relied on the means of the planned economy to greatly revitalize its economy in a short period of time, especially to gain first-line status in the world, second only to the United States. The founding of the People's Republic of China (PRC) experienced various hardships and suffered severe economic losses. As a member of the socialist camp, China chose to draw on the successful Soviet experience. Seven years after the founding of PRC, China has gradually embarked on the track of a planned economic system. Its basic formation process can be roughly divided into three stages.

The first stage (October 1949 to June 1950) was the nascent stage of the planned economy system. At the end of 1949, China confiscated 2,858 bureaucratic capitalist industrial enterprises, established state-owned industries (accounting for 78.3% of national industrial funds), grasped the lifeblood of the national economy, and began to establish socialist public ownership. Soon, adjustments were made to non-public ownership of private industry and commerce, so that private enterprises were initially included in the planned production track. In terms of organization, the Central Finance and Economic Committee was established in October 1949. Later, other specialized central agencies responsible for plan management were successively established. For example, the National Establishment Committee, the National Warehouse Materials Clearing and Allocation Committee, and the People's Bank of China designated as the head office of the national cash dispatching agency. Through these institutions, the state began to implement direct management of administrative instructions for economic activities. In the winter of 1949, the central government decided to implement the unified national fiscal and economic management policy, and through the National Financial Conference held in February 1950, proposed the "six unifications" in a prescriptive manner, namely, unification of fiscal revenue and expenditure, unification of public grain, unification of taxation, unification of establishment, unification of trade, unification of banking. During this period, certain plans and measures for developing the national economy have begun. Such as grain, lint, coal and other planned indicators for production in 1950. During this period, trial work on some annual plans was also carried out. For example, the "Draft Estimates of National Fiscal Revenue of 1950" was compiled at the end of 1949. In May 1950, the "Overview of the 1950 National Economic Plan", including more than 20 contents including agriculture, industry, culture, education, health, etc., was trial-edited, and experience was explored for the later compilation of medium and long term national economic plans. The Third Plenary Session of the Seventh Central Committee of the Communist Party held in June 1950 held that during this period of reorganization of the old socio-economic structure to varying degrees, the old liberated areas "especially in the northeast have begun planned economic construction". But in the new liberated area "the conditions for planned economic construction have not yet been obtained".[1]

---

[1] Zedong Mao, "Fight For Improvement of National Financial Economic Situation", *People's Daily* June 13.

The second stage (June 1950 to August 1952) was the initial stage of the planned economic system. After the Third Plenary Session of the Seventh Central Committee of the Communist Party, it began to create conditions for planned economic construction nationwide. In August 1950, the central government held the first national planning work conference to discuss the preparation of the 1951 plan and the three-year goal. Each department is required to first set a three-year goal and a one-year plan, and then the central government will draw up a comprehensive national plan.After the conference, although the three-year goal of struggle did not form a plan, it has initially formed the embryonic form of the hierarchical structure of China's planned economy system. That is, the decision-making power belongs to the state, and the distribution of decision-making power adopts administrative methods to form a hierarchical structure of division.

First, the central government strengthened the planning and management of state-owned industrial production and capital construction. "In the factory, the implementation of the production plan is the center, and the unified leadership of the party, government, and industry groups is implemented."[1] In terms of capital construction, the construction unit is divided into two types of specific investment amounts: "above the limit" and "below the limit", and the focus is on the construction of transportation.

Second, with regard to the planning and leadership of agriculture and handicraft industry, at the first mutual assistance and cooperation conference held in September 1951, it was proposed to overcome the difficulties in the decentralized management of farmers by launching a mutual assistance and cooperation campaign in areas where land reform was completed, and to ensure the realization of the national agricultural production plan. And actively promote the experience of the "combined contract" system of the production mutual aid group and the supply and marketing cooperatives, so that the mutual aid group can produce and consume in a planned manner, and the supply and marketing cooperatives can achieve planned operation. For the production of handicraft industries, the central government requires all localities to incorporate and develop plans for handicraft production cooperatives into local industrial plans, and to take orders from the state and superior cooperatives as the key to the development of handicraft production.

---

[1] China Institute of CPC Literature Research, The Political Bureau of the CPC Central Committee expanded the main points of its resolution, Important documents since the founding of the People's Republic, 2,1992:200-251.

Third, based on the adjustment of private industry and commerce in 1950, it was required that private industry and commerce comply with the production and marketing plan formulated by the government. One of the purposes of the "Five Antis" struggles at that time was to "thoroughly investigate the situation of private industry and commerce, in order to unite and control the bourgeoisie, and carry out the country's planned economy. The situation is unknown, and it cannot be planned".[1]

Four, in terms of market management, state directives require state trading companies to properly implement price policies. In short, after the Third Plenary Session of the Seventh Central Committee of the Communist Party of China, the decision-making structure of China's planned economic system was initially formed. Under the centralized and unified leadership of the country, comprehensive planning management has been implemented for all aspects of the national economy in the form of a prescriptive economic development plan, and the planned economic system has been initially formed. By August 1952, the tasks proposed by the Third Plenary Session of the Seventh Central Committee had been completed in advance. Mao Zedong announced at the Standing Committee of the First National Committee of the CPPCC: "After two and a half years of struggle, the national economy has now been restored and planned construction has begun."[2]

The third stage (September 1952 to December 1956) was the basic formation stage of the planned economy system. In September 1952, Mao Zedong set the goal of "basically completing socialism in 10 to 15 years". In order to achieve this goal, the planned economic system was further improved and legally confirmed. On the basis of various specialized plan management institutions that had been established, the National Planning Commission was established in November 1952, and in April 1954, the central government set up a working group to compile the draft five-year plan. Based on several trial compilations since 1951, the group guided the transitional general line as the guide to form the first draft of the five-year plan. After the statutory approval process, the "First Five-Year Plan" was promulgated by the State Council in the form of an order, requiring all localities and departments to comply with it. In 1954, China enacted and promulgated the first constitution, in which Article 15 states: "The state uses economic plans to guide the development and transformation of the national economy, to continuously increase productivity, to improve the people's material and cultural life, and

---

① *Selected Works of Mao Zedong*, People's Publishing House, 5, 1977, 120-121.
② *Selected Works of Mao Zedong*, People's Publishing House, 5, 1977, 230-231.

to consolidate the state Independence and security." This shows that the planned economic system has become China's legal economic system.

In short, in the early days of the founding of the country, after the socialist transformation of property rights, the pursuit of the goal of socialist public ownership was basically achieve. In the form of management of economic activities, the First Five-Year Plan for the development of the national economy was formulated and issued by administrative orders,and at the end of 1956, most of the targets scheduled in the First Five-Year Plan were completed ahead of schedule. This planned economic system, which operates in real economic life, has been explicitly recognized by the Constitution of PRC as the national legal economic system. Therefore, by the end of 1956, China's planned economy system had basically formed and had some characteristics of its own.

5.1.2 Merits and Demerits of the Five-Year Plan

(1) The First Five-Year Plan (1953-1957)

China has basically completed the tasks of socialist transformation of individual agriculture, handicraft industry and private industry and commerce, established the preliminary foundation of socialist industrialization, and basically established socialist production relations. In the total national income, the proportion of state-owned economy, cooperative economy and public-private partnership economy increased from 21.3% in 1952 to 92.9%. A large number of important projects have been completed. Total industrial output value increased by 128.6% over 1952.

(2) The Second Five-Year Plan (1958-1962)

The Second Five-Year Plan goals show as follows. Industrial output value will double, agricultural total output value will increase by 35%, steel output will reach 10.6 million to 12 million tons in 1962, and total investment in capital construction will double about the First Five-Year Plan period, the average income of employees and farmers increased by 25%—30%. However, the Second Five-Year Plan has shown a serious aggressive tendency in the formulation and implementation. In August 1958, the Beidaihe CPC Central Committee Political Bureau Enlarged Meeting raised the goal of the struggle and proposed that Chinese Socialist Construction can be completed during the Second Five-Year Plan, which can create conditions for transition to communism. By 1962, a strong independent and complete industrialization system will be built, and will surpass Britain and catch up with the United States in terms of several important products and output.

Due to the "Great Leap Forward" and "Anti-Righting" movements, fiscal deficits have occurred year after year, and people's lives have encountered great difficulties. China's economic construction can no longer continue to develop in accordance with the deployment of the Second Five-Year Plan. In September 1960, the Central Committee of the Communist Party of China proposed the "eight-character policy" for the adjustment, enrichment, consolidation, and improvement of the national economy in the "Report on the Control of National Economic Plan 1961". And the Eighth Ninth Plenary Session of the Party was officially approved in January 1961.

The planned economy is an economic operation system operated by government coercive means. When the situation inside and outside the country is stable, good planning will allow the economy to develop at a very high efficiency. When the situation inside or outside the country is unstable, or when the government makes a plan that does not meet the economic situation, it will greatly damage economic development and lead to financial collapse.

5.1.3 Transformation to a Market Economy is an Objective Requirement for the Development of Productive Forces

After the founding of PRC, the planned economy has made great contributions to our economy in a certain period of time. However, as China's productivity level has been greatly improved and the development of the commodity economy has been promoted, the planned economy at this time no longer meets the development requirements of productivity. In this period, choosing a market economy is of great importance to China's social and economic development. The Third Plenary Session of the Eleventh Central Committee of the People's Republic of China will slowly begin the prelude to a new economic system reform. China's chief leaders have begun to deeply look back on the traditional system. Therefore, if we want to handle some of the deeper contradictions in the basic contradictions of society, we must reform the economic system. The most crucial point of this reform is how to understand and handle the relationship between the planned economy and the market economy. At the beginning of China's economic system, market factors began to gradually influence the periphery of the planned economy.

The market economy is a demand-oriented economic system that is based on demand and produces everything based on demand, the purpose of production is to meet demand and resources are allocated according to the actual conditions of the market, and efficiency but relatively fair are not enough.

There are several differences between the planned economy and the market economy in nature. (1) The mechanism of economic operation is different. The planned economy is where the state arranges everything. And the market economy is the market mechanism. It uses the relationship between prices, supply and demand, competition, and interest rates to operate the market. (2) Different means of regulating the economy. The former are mainly administrative means, while the latter are mainly economic and legal means. For example, the most impressive thing about the planned economy of PRC is the various kinds of tickets, such as food tickets, meat tickets, and cloth tickets. The economic means of the market economy are like macroeconomic regulation and legal means, such as purchase order[①]. (3) There are different ways to regulate the economy. The former is direct state regulation of enterprises; the latter is state regulation of the market and the market guides enterprises. (4) Ownership structure is different. The former has a single ownership structure and the public ownership stands alone; the latter has a diversified ownership structure. At present, China adopts a form of ownership with public ownership as the main body and multiple types of ownership developing together. (5) The distribution of benefits varies. The former has serious egalitarianism, and the latter is based on the contribution of various factors of production in production. The pursuit of the largest income opportunity stimulates producers to continuously improve technology, strengthen management and increase the productivity of various factors of production to promote the continuous development of the company.

5.1.4 The Process of Converting Single Public Ownership to Mixed Ownership

Before 1978, Chinese enterprises operated under the planned economy

---

① Ticket supply is not the earliest use in China. After the October Revolution in the Soviet Union, the country was unstable, civil wars continued, and commodities were lacking. It adopted a planned distribution of commodities and issued various commodity tickets. The earliest Soviet ticket was a 1916 shoe ticket.

system. At that time, the allocation of various resources in society depended on administrative means through national centralized and unified plans. An industrial enterprise as a basic-level production unit is merely a subsidiary of administrative organs at all levels, just like the workshops or teams under the entire large-scale production factory of the society. It is not a true independent enterprise. What they produce, how much they produce, how they produce them, and who they produce them are all arranged by the state plan. The people, commodities and materials needed for production are all allocated according to the state plan, the products are also divided by the state, the sales income is turned over to the state, and the wages of employees are uniformly regulated by the state. As a result, the vitality of the company was constrained, and a fundamental problem that could not be avoided was the need to reform the enterprises under the traditional system into market competition subjects that met the needs of the socialist market economy. Therefore, China's enterprise reform has gone through a difficult process. Since 1978, under the guidance of Deng Xiaoping's thought of building socialism with Chinese characteristics, China has begun to explore new paths for economic development and enterprises have begun to implement reforms, after five stages of gradual reform, China's economic system has truly completed its transition from a socialist planned economy to a market economy with socialist characteristics that has subsequently achieved world-wide shocking results.

(1) The First Stage (1978-1980) was a Pilot Stage to Expand Corporate Autonomy

In the fall of 1978, Sichuan Province took the lead in conducting pilot projects to expand the autonomy of enterprises, which opened the prelude to the reform of industrial enterprises across the country. In April 1979, the state decided to expand the autonomy of enterprises. In May of the same year, the state decided to select eight companies, including the Capital Iron and Steel Company, in Beijing, Tianjin and Shanghai to conduct trials to expand the autonomy of enterprises. In July of the same year, the State Council issued documents such as "Several Provisions on Expanding the Autonomy of State-owned Industrial Enterprises in Operation and Management" and other documents, affirming the reform direction of expanding autonomy of enterprises in various regions, and required regions and departments to conduct trials in a small number of enterprises. Since then, the pilot work on corporate reform centered on expanding corporate autonomy has gradually expanded to all parts of the country. By the end of June 1980, there had been more than 6,600 enterprises in the country expanding power, accounting for 16% of industrial enterprises in the national budget at that time, and output value and profits accounted for 60% and 70%, respectively. Under the premise of the national plan, according to the supplementary plan of production construction and market demand system, production is arranged independently; within a certain range, some products can be sold by themselves at the price set by the state, which is an attempt to reform the management system of the enterprise under the traditional planning management system in China, which is divided, allocated and collected. At the same time, the enterprise has certain independent distribution of financial resources and economic benefits, and gradually linked the good and bad of the company's operations with the material benefits of employees, mobilizing the enthusiasm of production and operation of the enterprise and employees, and promoting the improvement of enterprise labor efficiency and economic benefits

(2) The Second Stage (1981-1982) was the Stage of Piloting the Economic Responsibility System

In April 1981, the State Council affirmed the profit-and-loss contract method of retaining various profits as the content of the corporate economic responsibility system. And it is clearly pointed out that the industrial economic responsibility system must not only be linked to profit, but also to product output, quality, variety, cost, etc.. Require enterprises to establish a clear and specific economic responsibility system in production, technology, and management. Establishing an enterprise economic responsibility system includes two steps. First, it is necessary to correctly handle the relationship between the state and the benefit distribution of enterprises, solve the problem of enterprises eating the country's "big pot rice", and hang the economic benefits of the enterprise to the business results; the second is to correctly handle the distribution of benefits between enterprises and employees, solve the problem of employees eating "big pot rice" of enterprises, and link the economic benefits of employees with their labor contributions. The pilot at this stage, although not long, and various economic relations outside the enterprise have not yet been smoothed out, have clearly learned many characteristics of the enterprise contracted management responsibility system, and provided practical experience for the large-scale promotion of the contracted system in the future.

(3) The Third Stage (1983-1986) is the Stage of Implementing Profit-taxation Reform and Deepening Internal Reform of Enterprises

The first step from profit to taxation was implemented in April 1983, its main content is that all profitable state-owned large and medium-sized enterprises pay 55% of income tax based on realized profits, part of the profit after tax is paid to the country, and the other part is left to the enterprise at the level of retained profits approved by the state. The implementation of the original eight-level excessive progressive tax on small enterprises aims to rationalize the distribution relationship between the state and enterprises, correctly handle the interests of the country, enterprises and employees, mobilize the production enthusiasm of enterprises and employees, and ensure the stable growth of national fiscal revenue.

The second step from profit to taxation began in September 1984, its main content is that divide the industrial and commercial tax into product tax, value added tax, salt tax and business tax, the state-owned enterprises' profits paid to the state finance have been changed to pay taxes to the state according to 11 tax types, and the distribution relationship between the state and enterprises has been fixed by tax law. The second step is to change the profits from taxes to the form of taxation. The aim is to standardize the distribution relationship between the state and enterprises by rationally determining tax items and rates, and on this basis, the relationship between the responsibility and rights of the state and the enterprise is rationalized, and the vitality of the enterprise is gradually increased. This reform is designed in accordance with the principle of "the state gets the largest share of profits, the enterprise gets the middle share of profits, and the individual gets the small share of profits". To a certain extent, it overcomes the disadvantages of bargaining between the state and enterprises in the distribution of benefits in the process of implementing the economic responsibility system. However, from the results of implementation, due to the incomplete macro-reforms and the defects and deficiencies of the two-step profit-taxation reform. As a result, enterprises generally lack the ability of self-reform and self-development, forming a situation of "rising water and rising ship" and "whipping fast cows", affecting the enthusiasm of enterprises and employees, and ultimately affecting the country's fiscal revenue.

At this stage, the internal reform of the enterprise continues to develop in depth. In May 1984, the State Council promulgated the "Regulations on Wisdom of Further Enhancing the Autonomy of State-owned Industrial Enterprises", which for the first time clarified the autonomy of enterprise management through administrative regulations. From January 1985 to July 1986, the State Council piloted total wages in line with economic benefits, implemented horizontal unions, reformed material supply and product sales measures, reduced regulatory taxes, separated administrative functions from corporate functions, simplified administration and decentralization. A series of documents have been issued to some large enterprises for their direct external operation rights and the implementation of labor contract systems. All these reforms have undoubtedly played a positive role in improving the internal operating mechanism of the enterprise and improving the external operating environment of the enterprise. In September 1986, the Central Committee of the Communist Party of China and the State Council promulgated three regulations, which made it clear that the factory director is the legal representative of the enterprise, formed a new enterprise leadership system of "the factory director is fully responsible, the Party committee supervises and guarantees, and the staff democratic management", which made is a big step forward of the enterprise reform.

(4) The Fourth Stage (1987-1991) is the Stage of Improving the Operating Mechanism of the Enterprise and Fully Implementing the Contracted Management Responsibility System

After the two-step profit-taxation reform, enterprises generally lack motivation and stamina, and economic benefits have declined for 22 consecutive months, which has greatly affected fiscal revenue. At the same time, according to the characteristics of different industries and enterprises throughout the country, various explorations have been conducted to transform the operating mechanism of the enterprise, such as the contract system, lease system, shareholding system, and asset management responsibility system. In particular, especially the enterprises represented by the Capital Iron and Steel Company that implement the contract system, which has obviously enhanced the vigor and vitality. In March 1987, the government clearly stated that the focus of economic system reform should be on improving the operating mechanism of enterprises, and that various forms of contracted operating responsibility systems should be conscientiously implemented in accordance with the principle of separating operating rights from ownership. In April of the same year, the full implementation of the enterprise contracted operation responsibility system was started. Since then, the reform of enterprises focusing on the contract system has developed into a new stage. In February 1988, the State Council promulgated the "Regulations on the Implementation of the Contractual Management Responsibility System for Industrial Enterprises Owned by the Whole People", which put the implementation of the contracting system on a standardized and regulated track. Since 1987, more than 95% of large and medium-sized enterprises have gradually implemented contract system. The large-scale implementation and in-depth development of the contract system has reversed the situation of continuous decline in fiscal revenue, which not only promoted the development of production and the improvement of economic benefits, but also caused profound changes in the operating mechanism of the enterprise, and promoted reforms in the internal leadership system, distribution system, labor system, cadre system, organizational structure, etc.. Meanwhile, it has accumulated experience and created conditions for the entire economic system reform. In April 1988, the State promulgated *The National-owned Industrial Enterprise Law*, which is a fundamental law that establishes the basic system of Chinese enterprises, stipulates the legal status of enterprises, and protects the legitimate rights and interests of enterprises. It summarizes the practical experience of corporate reforms since the reform and opening up, and clearly specifies the principles and directions of corporate reforms in China, and played an important guiding role. The practice of enterprise reform has proved that most of the enterprises that do well are those that can make full use of the production and operation autonomy given by *The National-owned Industrial Enterprise* Law and actively face the market. However, because the supporting reform measures are not fully in place, on the whole, it is difficult to implement the autonomy of production and operation of most state-owned enterprises. Therefore, in September 1991, the state also proposed 20 policies and measures to deepen various supporting reforms, which made new progress in enterprise reform.

(5) The Fifth Stage (1992-Present) is the Stage of Implementing Deng Xiaoping's Important Talks during the Southern Tour, Comprehensively Transforming the Operating Mechanism of the Enterprise and Gradually Establishing a Modern Enterprise System

At the beginning of 1992, Comrade Deng Xiaoping, the chief designer of China's reform and opening up, made an important speech during the southern tour. This has brought reform and opening up into a new stage. So this opportunity was seized throughout the country to accelerate the pace of corporate reform. In November 1993, the Third Plenary Session of the Fourteenth Central Committee of the Communist Party of China passed the "Decision of the Central Committee of the Communist Party of China on Several Issues concerning the Establishment of a Socialist Market Economy System", which is a summary of the experience of the reform and opening up centered on economic construction over the past ten years. It systematizes and specifies the reform objectives and the basic principles for the establishment of the socialist market economy system proposed by the Fourteenth National Congress of the Communist Party of China, and clarifies the reform direction of the state-owned enterprises in China. So far, China's enterprise reform has entered a new stage of establishing a modern enterprise system. This means that the deepening of corporate reforms will change from policy adjustments to corporate system innovations, and reforms will undergo new changes from goals to content and from methods to intensity. This also signifies that China's state-owned enterprises will eventually get rid of the shackles of the traditional planned economic system and truly become the subject of market competition. It is not only a fundamental change in the microeconomic foundation, but also a comprehensive and profound reform involving the macroeconomic system.

Due to the implementation of reform measures, China's industrial economy has achieved rapid development. The industrial production value was 141.74 billion yuan in 1978 and 14.14 billion yuan in 1993, an increase of 8.9 times; the average monetary salary of employees was 644 yuan in 1978 and it was 3,236 yuan by 1993, a four-fold increase, and people's living standards have improved significantly. Beginning in July 1994, *The Company Law* has been implemented nationwide. It regulates and reflects the basic contents and requirements of the modern enterprise system in the form of law. It condenses the achievements of the enterprise reform since the reform of China's economic system, which focuses on enhancing the vitality of enterprises and transforming the operation mechanism of enterprises. It marks that the establishment of the modern enterprise system in China has stepped into the track of standardization and legalization. It plays an important role in establishing a standardized enterprise system, safeguarding the rights and interests of the enterprise, maintaining the social and economic order, and safeguarding and promoting the healthy development of the socialist market economy. It is necessary to continue to establish a modern enterprise system with public ownership as the main body, fully implement the requirements of the State Council on "clear property rights, clear powers and responsibilities, separate government and enterprise management, and scientific management". The focus of the work is on the separation of responsibilities between government and enterprises, strengthening of internal management of enterprises, and the establishment of a social security system. It is necessary to carry out various reforms and carry out comprehensive management, and at the same time continue to carry out "transition mechanisms, grasp management, practice internal strength, and increase efficiency" in enterprises to promote turning losses into profits. China's enterprise reform is a gradual process of exploration and improvement, and there will be various new situations and problems in the future. Therefore, all our reform measures should be based on China's national conditions, to support and reform, truly separate the responsibilities of government and enterprises, so as to gradually straighten out the relationship of property rights, standardize the internal leadership system and organizational system of enterprises, seek an effective way to combine public ownership and market economy, promote the transformation of business mechanism, improve economic efficiency, and accelerate the health development of socialist market economy.

5.1.5 Socialist Market Economy and American Capitalism

In 1978, China's industrial production had only two economic components, one was collective ownership, the other is an economy owned by the whole people, with no other economic component at all. But in 1990, in addition to the two leading economies, other economic components also had a 9.8% share. After China's reform practice has achieved greater development, market regulation has played a greater role. This requires the allocation of resources through the market. China's earliest SEZs and coastal cities with market regulation have achieved remarkable results. The economic structure of our country at this time includes not only the public ownership economy, but also other economic components. Many large and medium-sized state-owned enterprises are no longer bound by the traditional system and are moving towards marketization. In order for our country to enter the international economic circle and catch the train of the world economy, we must engage ourselves in the international large market. After entering the market economy, we starts to cultivate and establish a socialist market system.

China's mixed ownership is actually close to the current capitalist society in the United States. State-owned enterprises can be compared to Fannie Mae in the United States. In 1938, the government funded the establishment of Fannie Mae to engage in financial business to expand the flow of funds in the secondary housing consumer market. In 1968, Raymond H. Lapin became the president of Fannie Mae. During his 30 years in office, he modified the company's system to make it a private joint-stock company and was listed on the New York Stock Exchange in 1970. However, in the sub-prime mortgage crisis, Fannie Mae was severely hit due to the loss of 70 billion U.S. dollars, asking the US federal government for help. The US government funded and held approximately 80% of Fannie Mae's shares. Similarly, Freddie Mac sold its 80% shares to avoid bankruptcy.

Although the U.S. government defines such enterprises as Government

Sponsored Enterprises, in terms of the number of shares held by the U.S. government, Government Sponsored Enterprise is a complete state-owned enterprise. In addition, the United States federal government also controls large enterprises such as the United States Postal Service (USPS) and the Federal Deposit Insurance Corporation (FDIC), it also includes small professional companies such as the Federal Financing Bank under the Ministry of Finance and the Federal Prison Industries under the Ministry of Justice. These publicly owned economies account for about 5% of GDP in the United States.

It can be seen that, despite being a country claiming market-oriented freedom, in a certain period of time and certain political needs, there also needs to be a public ownership economic component in order to maintain national domination and social stability. China's socialist market economy is also adapting to the economic system tailored to local conditions and flexibly borrowing successful experience.

5.1.6 The Private Economy that Drove the Economy to Take off, Gradually Gaining Government Recognition

The 16th National Congress of the Communist Party of China for the first time in 2002 proposed "unswervingly encourage, support and guide the development of the non-public economy", which further consolidated the status of private enterprises. Representatives of the Private Entrepreneur Party made their first appearance at the 16th National Congress of the Communist Party of China, and their political status was recognized by all sectors of society. In 2004, the National People's Congress passed an amendment to the Constitution. Article 11 of the Constitution was amended to read: "The state protects the legitimate rights and interests of non-public ownership economies such as individual and private economies; the state encourages, supports and guides the development of the non-public economy, and supervises and manages the non-public economy in accordance with the law." In March 2007, the National People's Congress passed *The Property Law of the People's Republic of China*, proposing equal protection of state, collective and private property rights, so that the development achievements of private enterprises have legal protection.

The 18th National Congress of the Communist Party of China in 2012 proposed to "unwaveringly encourage, support and guide the development of the non-public ownership economy". The Third Plenary Session of the

Eighteenth Central Committee pointed out that the basic system for the common development of public ownership and multi-ownership economy is an important pillar of the socialist system with Chinese characteristics and the foundation of the socialist market economic system. Public-owned economy and non-public-owned economy are both important components of the socialist market economy, and are important foundations for China's economic and social development. For the first time ever, the words "important pillar" "foundation" "important component" and "important foundation" were used to emphasize the role of the non-public economy. The Third Plenary Session of the 18th CPC Central Committee also emphasized that "public-owned economic property rights are inviolable, and non-public-owned economic property rights are equally inviolable", and further pointed out that guaranteeing the equal use of production factors according to law in various ownership economies, participating in market competition openly, fairly, and justly equally protected by law.

After more than 40 years of reform and opening up, private investment has continued to grow and develop, and its contribution to China's overall investment growth has gradually increased. From the perspective of growth rate, before 2014, the yearly growth rate of the fixed asset investment across the country was more than 20%, the average value was more than 25%, and in certain years it was more than 30%, state-owned and state-holding enterprises' fixed asset investment remained below 20% in most years, fluctuating around 15%. However, the growth rate of private fixed assets investment and private enterprises' fixed assets investment is between 25%-90% and 28%-60% respectively. From 2006 to 2013, the growth rate of private fixed assets investment and private enterprises' fixed assets investment is 1.5-3 times of that of state-owned and state holding enterprises, and 7 and 6 times of that in 2005. After the second half of 2006, the growth rate of fixed assets investment of private enterprises was much higher than that of private fixed assets. With China's economy entering the new normal, since the second half of 2014, under the background of national supply side structural reform and economic downturn, under the influence of multiple factors such as increased operational risk, decreased return on investment, industry access restrictions, poor financing channels, and complex international situation, the growth rate of private investment and private enterprise investment has declined rapidly from a high of more than 25%, especially to single digits in 2016. However, private enterprise investment is about 6 percentage points higher than private investment. At the same time, the investment growth rate of state-owned and state-holding enterprises has rapidly climbed from more than 10% to more than 20%, showing a phenomenon of "national advance and people retreat". However, with the support of the central government's encouraging policies for two consecutive years in 2016 and 2017, the growth rate of private investment and investment by private enterprises is picking up month by month and stabilizing to more than 6% and 10%.

In terms of proportion, the cumulative proportion of private fixed asset investment in the total social fixed asset investment has increased from 20% in 2004 to more than 60%, and stabilized at this level after 2012, with the proportion reaching 65% in 2015. The investment proportion of private enterprises has increased from 13% to more than 30%, and the investment proportion of state-owned and state holding enterprises has continued to decline from 50% to about 30%; The proportion of private investment in urban fixed assets investment has increased from about 30% in 2004 to more than 60% at present. The above data shows that private investment has become the leading force of Chinese investment and a ballast stone for the steady growth of China's economy. The growth rate of private investment and private enterprise investment has become one of the important weathervanes for judging the quality of the economy.

5.2 Liberation of Five Social Production Factors

Factors of production markets provide transactions for all types of factors of production. In the development process of the market economy, the factor market has a very important position. Without a developed market for factors of production, the fundamental role of market mechanisms in the allocation of resources cannot be achieved. This is because the process of social reproduction is actually the process of allocating production factors. If the market for production factors is not fully developed, the allocation of production factors may be distorted. At the same time, in a market economy, enterprises are constrained by the development of the market for factors of production. Only by forming a perfect market of factors of production, making the output of enterprises face the market, accepting the examination and choice of the market, making the input of enterprises face the market, obtaining all kinds of factors of production needed from the market, and being regulated by the market price and competition mechanism, can the economic behavior of enterprises be truly dominated by the market, and the survival of the fittest function of the market mechanism be brought into full play. In the context of a planned economy, the market for factors of production is in a secondary position and is not valued. All factors are in the hands of the government and are not transferred. In the process of gradually transforming the planned economy into a market economy with socialist characteristics, the five elements were gradually liberated, releasing their energy to the economy.

Marx says: "labor productivity is determined by a variety of factors, including the average proficiency of workers, the level of scientific development and its application in technology, the social combination of production process, the scale and efficiency of means of production, and natural conditions."[1] He also said that land "provides a foothold for workers and a place for their process activities".[2] Among these discussions, "workers" are the factors of labor; "the level of scientific development and its application in technology" are the factors of knowledge; "natural conditions" are the factors of natural environment; "the scale and efficiency of means of production" are the factors of capital; "social integration of production process" is based on the factors of information (there was no word "information" at that time, Marx put it "capital productivity").

5.2.1 Labor Market Elements

The labor factor is the most important economic resource and production factor. In a market economy, its allocation and price formation must be realized through the market. "Labor is the substance and intrinsic measure of value, but it has no value in itself."[3] Wages are not a monetary expression of the value of labor factors, but a performance of labor prices. Under capitalist conditions, labor becomes a commodity and has value. The value of labor depends on the value of the means of subsistence necessary to reproduce the labor, and the combination of labor and capital is achieved through the employment relationship in the labor commodity trading market. Wages are manifested in the form of remuneration for labor, which is essentially a monetary expression of the value of the means of living necessary for workers to reproduce labor. Under socialist conditions, labor enters the market as a factor of production, and through the contractual relationship between supply and demand in the market, the combination

---

① Karl Heinrich Marx, *Das Kapita*, The Commercial Press, 1, 1936, 98-99.

② Karl Heinrich Marx, *Das Kapita*, The Commercial Press, 1, 1936, 99-100.

③ Karl Heinrich Marx, *Das Kapita*, The Commercial Press, 1, 1936, 103-104.

of laborers and public means of production is achieved. In the socialist public ownership economy, the principle of distribution according to work is implemented, and the essence of wages is the monetary performance of laborers distributing the value of personal consumer commodities according to work.

Labor elements are laborers who have a clear purpose of labor and know the contents and methods of labor; labor objects include "natural objects and raw materials used for production" ,etc.; labor materials include "labor tools, power systems, transportation systems, information transmission systems and labor fields, etc.". This is the theory of "Three Factors of Productivity".[1]

(1) Employment Pressure Provides Opportunities for Labor Liberation

For a period of 20 years from 1958 to 1978, due to various reasons, the Chinese economy has been in a stagnation and lingering state for a long time. With the end of the ten-year catastrophe, in urban areas, more than 10 million knowledgeable young people across the country have returned to the city, and millions of graduates are not fully employed every year. Due to limited positions in government agencies and state-owned enterprises, employment placement has become the first social problem. In order to ease employment pressure in cities and towns, the state allows some idle laborers with formal urban hukou to engage in individual labor in handicrafts such as repairs and services. Forced to make a living, knowledgeable young people returning to the city can only rely on stalls to solve the problem of food and clothing. In rural areas, Xiaogang Village in Anhui Province, risking its life, began to explore how to solve the problem of food production and food consumption by contracting production to households. The government acquiesced in the existence of these phenomena.

(2) The State Recognizes the Private Economy and Breaks the Limit on the Number of Employees

In 1978, the state began to recognize the legitimacy of the private economy and opened the era of China's private economy. Private enterprises have begun to survive in the gaps, looking for opportunities in the gaps in the state-owned economy. In urban areas, in February 1979, the Central Committee of the Communist Party of China and the State Council approved

---

[1] Karl Heinrich Marx, *Das Kapita*, The Commercial Press, 3, 1936, 44-45.

the first report on the development of the individual economy, allowing "all localities may, according to the market demand and after obtaining the consent of the relevant competent business departments, approve some idle labors with official hukou to engage in repair, service and individual labor of handicraftsmen", and the individual industrial and commercial households in urban areas came into being. In rural areas, after 1978, the Household Contract Responsibility System was widely promoted throughout the country, which greatly stimulated farmers' enthusiasm for production, and self-employed households began to appear, and gave birth to the rise of a large number of township enterprises. Around 1980, the first batch of self-employed businesses obtained business licenses legally. In July 1981, the state recognized the legitimacy of the existence of self-employed businesses for the first time. After the 1980s, with the development of the individual economy, the number of large individual businesses, namely private enterprises, with more than seven employees is also increasing. The "capable people" in some state-owned enterprises began to accumulate assets through contracting state-owned enterprises and gradually became private enterprises.

(3) Entrepreneurial Development of Private Enterprises, More Labors Engaged in Private Economy

In 1982, officials began to loosen controls on private enterprises. Private enterprises began to shift from underground (informal) to above-ground (recognized by the government), and the number increased rapidly.

In June 1988, the State Council promulgated the "Interim Regulations on Private Enterprises", which stipulates the nature of private enterprises: "Private enterprises refer to profit-making economic organizations whose assets are privately owned and employ more than 8 people. In April 1988, the seventh session of the National People's Congress passed an amendment to the Constitution, Article 11 of the Constitution added: "The state allows the private economy to exist and develop within the scope prescribed by law. The private economy is a supplement to the socialist public ownership economy. Protecting the legitimate rights and interests of the private economy, and guiding, supervising and managing the private economy"[1], legally establishing the status of private enterprises.

---

[1] The First Session of The Seventh National People's Congress Passed the Amendment to The Constitution, China, April, 1988.

Under the great wave of reform and market economy, a wave of entrepreneurship has been set off rapidly. A large number of government officials, scientific researchers, employees of state-owned enterprises, returnees, etc. have jumped out of the system and resigned to start enterprises, forming a new wave of entrepreneurship after China's reform and opening up. The Ministry of Human Resources and Social Security has done statistics. In 1992, more than 120,000 people resigned to start a business, and more than 10 million people joined the business community. Many people in the system started business, and many college students also consider entrepreneurship as their dream after graduation. Entrepreneurship became a distinctive brand in the 1990s, which also greatly promoted the vigorous development of private enterprises. For example, Guangdong Feipeng Group began to contract aluminum products factories at this time, using the sensitive sense of entrepreneurs to the market, and the low labor cost at that time, to produce high-quality and low-cost aluminum products, sell domestic and even Russian markets, and obtain the first barrel of gold for enterprise development.

5.2.2 Liberation of Land Market Factors

Land as a category of production factors is a collective term for various natural resources that have not been transformed by human labor, including not only general arable land and construction land, but also forests, minerals, water, and the sky. Land is an economic resource that any economic activity must rely on and utilize. Compared with other economic resources, its natural characteristics are mainly its location immovability and durability, and the difference between abundance and location. Compared with other economic resources and production factors, land is the most difficult to increase, and its scarcity is more significant than other production factors. Especially with the increase of the population, the expansion of economic activity scale and the in-depth development, the scarcity of land has an objective trend of significantly strengthening.

In the early days of the founding of the People's Republic of China, China moved in the direction of a public-owned economy. During the period of 1950-1952, land reform and farmers' land ownership were implemented. Land was received from the landlords, which was beneficial to the restoration of agricultural production and development. Then in the "Three Great Reconstructions" periods of 1953-1956, the private ownership of farmers' land was further transformed into the public ownership of land, and the land ownership system was centralized to maximize the realization of the principle of focusing on major issues. In just a few years, new China quickly recovered its vitality and solved the problem of people's food and clothing. However, after the Great Leap Forward, the Cultural Revolution and other radical measures to promote the public ownership economy, the leaders found that this transitional state-owned land policy was not conducive to the enthusiasm of the working people. Therefore, under the leadership of Deng Xiaoping and referring to foreign experience, he innovatively created a system of paid land use.

(1) The Invention and Birth of System of Compensated Land-use

The System of Compensated Land-Use refers to a system in which land users should pay certain fees in accordance with the law. Each country has established this system. After the founding of the People's Republic of China, China had a long history of unreasonable land use without compensation. Article 2 of the amendment to the Constitution, adopted at the First Session of the Seventh National People's Congress on April 12, 1988, stipulates that "no organization or individual shall occupy, trade, lease or illegally transfer land in any other form" as mentioned in paragraph 4 of Article 10 of the constitution. It is revised to read: "no organization or individual may occupy, trade or illegally transfer land in other forms. The right to the use of the land may be transferred in accordance with the provisions of the law." This is the basic legal basis of the System of Compensated Land-Use. Before that, the Special Economic Zone had tried out the System of Compensated Land-Use. The State shall levy land taxes on state-owned land users and collective land owners in accordance with the law; levy land use fees on construction land in accordance with the law; pay land compensation fees and resettlement subsidies for state-owned construction land acquisition; and pay compensation and rehabilitation fees for temporary land users. The compensated use of land is an important measure to use economic leverage to implement land conservation, rational use of local resources, and effective protection of land resources and the environment. The "Interim Regulations on the Transfer and Transfer of Urban State-owned Land Use Rights" and the "Interim Measures for the Administration of Foreign-invested Development and Management of Land" issued by the State Council on May 19, 1989 stipulate the specific content of the compensated land use system, such as land use right assignment, transfer, lease, mortgage, termination, appropriate, etc..

(2) The Marketization of Land Ownership has Catalyzed Real Estate

After the "Provisional Regulations on the Transfer and Transfer of Urban State-owned Land Use Rights in the People's Republic of China" stipulated for the System of Compensated Land-Use, the sale of commercial housing became possible, and China's real estate industry emerged at the historic moment. In the early 1990s, a mainstream consensus was basically formed throughout the country, and it was necessary to vigorously develop the private economy, collective economy, joint-stock economy, and cooperative economy. Except for a few important industries that support national economy and people's livelihood, other industries are basically allowed to enter, and real estate is one of them.

At the most basic industry entry threshold, although the primary land market is controlled by the government, this industry does not have access restrictions and does not require various approvals from the Development and Reform Commission. During this period, private housing companies were the earliest groups to directly negotiate land with farmers, village committees, and local governments. They were also the earliest learners from Hong Kong to use the "throw a sprat to catch a herring" development method with a small amount of their own funds to leverage hundreds of millions of real estate projects using bank financing channels. For example, Guangdong Feipeng Group entered the real estate industry at this time and took over the bad land reclamation projects in the hands of banks. Through the advantages of private enterprises, operate flexibly, revitalize the project, carry out five connections and one level, and fund roads in the construction zone and surrounding areas, greening projects, water supply and drainage projects, high and low voltage power projects, fill soil projects, flood drainage rivers, sluices, typhoon shelters, fishing People's wharf, etc., use public supporting facilities to reclaim land. By creating value for fishermen and the government, Feipeng has obtained a large amount of land development rights and has grown since then.

With the relatively loose space provided by the system and the sensitivity to prices and innovation, private real estate companies are here to open up the Blue Ocean Market. Because there is no entry threshold and the profits are high, numerous enterprises rush into the real estate industry, which can even be described as "white hot". Especially in the years before and after the housing marketization in 1998, the real estate industry was highly market-oriented, with state-owned enterprises accounting for only 8% of the total market share. According to public data such as the results of the national economic census, by the end of 2004, there were 59,000 legal entities in real estate development enterprises across the country. By the end of 2008, this number had grown to 88,000. Judging from the amount of investment in commercial housing, the investment in commercial housing in 2010 was only 5,270 billion yuan, and in 2020 it was 17,360 billion yuan. From 2010 to 2020, the amount of money flowing into the entire industry actually exceeded 6 times.

(3) Economic Benefits of Real Estate

Ⅰ Role of investment

Investment is the behavior that investors integrate the existing capital into the project construction and hope to obtain more economic benefits from the project. The real estate construction project involves many contents, sometimes it needs to integrate multiple investors' capital for construction. In terms of real estate investment, investment behavior can be divided into development investment and real estate investment. Development investment refers to the behavior of using scientific algorithm to calculate the estimated economic income of the project in the initial stage of real estate, comparing the investment and income, and investing according to the comparison results. Real estate economic profit space is large, many investors will choose to develop investment, and to obtain more economic benefits. Real estate investment is the investment behavior of real estate transaction, lease, exchange and other activities. Both ways of investment can stimulate the vitality of the national economy and make it grow steadily. According to the latest data, at present, the amount of real estate investment in China is still in a state of continuous growth, indicating that in the future, China's national economy will maintain a high dynamic and sustained growth.

Ⅱ Role of production

The real estate industry involves many fields, each of which has its own unique economic characteristics and represents the current development of each field. The growth of the real estate economy can promote the growth of economy, and then realize the rapid improvement of the national economic level. For example, in the construction stage of a real estate project, the active cooperation of building materials production industry and logistics transportation industry is needed. The production of building materials needs a large number of raw materials, and logistics transportation needs to be equipped with professional drivers. At the same time, construction needs a lot of labor force, which makes the economy of the whole region in a highly active state. And the construction period generally lasts for a long time. Before the completion of the project, the active cooperation of multiple departments is needed, which can make the regional economy maintain sufficient vitality in a long time, and then promote the rapid development of the local economy. In addition, after the completion of the real estate project, a large amount of human resource is also needed to cooperate in the sales and property management stages. At the same time, when users purchase houses, refit houses and buy new furniture, they will drive the economic development of the real estate subsidiary industry, and make the national economic growth enter a virtuous cycle.

III Role of consumption

The growth source of real estate economy is the consumption of national economy. Developers encourage people to buy houses by creating a comfortable community environment, setting a reasonable sales price, and formulating preferential policies. In order to improve the comfort of accommodation, people will decorate the house according to their needs. Decoration needs to involve all kinds of raw material procurement, which will stimulate the economic growth of the building materials industry. For the relatively remote residential area, all the purchased raw materials need to be delivered by a logistics company, which will also stimulate the economic growth of the logistics industry. At the same time, in order to further improve the comfort of the living environment, the residents will purchase the furniture they like and drive the economic development of the furniture industry. Even in daily life, the normal use of water and electricity and the purchase of consumables will generate corresponding costs. These are important means to stimulate people's consumption. After the completion of the real estate project, a complete consumption chain will be formed. People will meet their own needs for quality of life and spiritual aesthetics through consumption, which will play a role in promoting the economic growth of the consumption industry involved, and further promote the overall national economic growth.

IV Role of employment

Real estate projects can be divided into design, construction, sales and property management stages. In the design stage, the feasibility of the project is evaluated scientifically. The project design needs to be reviewed by a professional organization. If the project is large in scale, more manpower is required to audit to ensure the feasibility of the project implementation. The construction stage of the project is the stage with the most labor input, including Xitong construction personnel, technical construction personnel, site management personnel, site supervision personnel, etc. different types of labor correspond to different job requirements, especially the large demand for basic construction personnel, which provides employment opportunities for more people. After the completion of the real estate, the real estate enters the sales stage. Before the complete sale of the housing, the corresponding staff is required to carry out the real estate sales, providing employment opportunities for some people. After the completion of the community, developers need to be equipped with a corresponding number of property management personnel to be responsible for daily community facilities maintenance and household problem solving. The real estate project is designed and put into use. In this process, a large number of labor is required to participate. Well and the project life cycle (from the beginning of the project to the putting into use is called a life cycle) is long, which can provide employment opportunities for more people, stabilize the social employment structure, and promote the stable development of regional economy.

V Improve the level of social consumption

The real estate industry can not only provide people with comfortable living space, but also promote the rapid development of urban economy as an important industry to promote social and economic development. Before the formal construction of the real estate, the relevant departments need to make compensation policies for the people involved in the construction area and compensate the residents for the demolition costs. The improvement of people's economic ability will also change people's material pursuit, and the liquidity of related industries and urban capital will also increase, which will speed up the improvement of urban economic structure and further improve the economic income of relevant departments. In addition, the tax paid by users when buying houses is also an important part of our fiscal revenue, which can stimulate consumption in many fields and effectively improve the level of social consumption.

VI Promote the development of related industries

Real estate project is not a single sector can complete the project, from the beginning of the project to put into use, need to participate in a number of industry areas, effectively promote the economic development of related industries. In practice, a lot of investment and capital planning are used to create a good development environment for the development of the rain industry and related financial industries. In the process of building construction, it can effectively promote the rapid growth of economic level in the architectural design and construction sectors. And in the process of construction, all raw materials and production equipment need to be purchased from outside. The purchase of steel bars, sandstone and cement in raw materials can effectively promote rapid economic development of steel industry, sandstone processing industry and cement industry. In the user decoration stage, the purchase of decoration materials and furniture can effectively promote the development of interior decoration industry, building materials industry and furniture production industry.

To sum up, the improvement of real estate economy can promote the rapid development of other industries, and it is of great significance to improve the growth rate of China's national economy.

5.2.3 Financial Factors

(1) Connotation of Financial Market

The financial market refers to the places where financial commodities are traded, such as places for borrowing money and funds, places for the issuance and trading of stocks and bonds, places for trading gold, etc. It is the basis for the central bank to use the monetary policy tools to indirectly regulate the economy. It is a system premise that is based on the market, rationally allocates limited capital and capital resources within the entire society, and improves the efficiency of capital and capital use. At the same time, it is also a channel and place to play the role of a reservoir of capital stock and convert savings into investment in a rapid and flexible financing method. The state and the central bank carry out macroeconomic control of the national economy based on the information sent by the financial market. At the same time, financial institutions and enterprises can also make corresponding decisions based on financial market information.

(2) Composition of Financial Markets

Financial markets are mainly composed of three basic elements: participants, financial instruments and organizational methods.

(3) Financial Market Participants

There are five main types of participants in the financial market: government, central banks, commercial banks and non-bank financial institutions, enterprises and individual residents.

First, the government mainly acts as the demander and manager of the financial market. Second, the central bank is the Bank of a bank, the lender of last resort of a commercial bank and the provider of funds in the financial market. It directly regulates the money supply by handling securities in the financial market, affects and guides the operation of the financial market, and is the maker and executor of monetary policy. Third, commercial banks and non bank financial institutions, as financial intermediaries, are the most important participants in the financial market. Both the supply and demand of funds are financed through these intermediaries. Therefore, they are actually the centers of financial commodity transactions. Fourth,enterprises are both suppliers and demanders of capital in the financial market. Idle funds formed in the operation of enterprises are important sources of funds in the financial market, and the demand of enterprises for funds constitutes the main part of the demand for funds. Fifth, residents are mainly fund suppliers in the financial market, and also provide part of the capital demand.

(4) Financial Instruments

Financial instrument, also known as credit instrument, is a tool to carry out financial transactions in the financial market. It is a written proof of the relationship between the creditor's rights and debts of both parties to the capital transaction. It is a kind of financial contract with legal effect. There are many kinds of financial instruments, generally divided into two categories. First, credit and debt certificates, such as bills, bonds, etc.; second, ownership certificates, such as stocks, etc.

(5) Organization of Financial Markets

The organization of financial markets refers to the methods adopted by financial exchanges. There are three main types. The first method is to conduct transactions in a fixed place, in an organized, systematic, and centralized manner, such as an exchange transaction method; the second is to conduct face-to-face, decentralized transactions, such as over-the-counter transactions, on the counters of financial institutions; the third is the way of over-the-counter trading, which is not a fixed place or direct contact, but mainly completed by means of telecommunication.

(6) Classification of Financial Market

First, according to the different types of financing methods, financial markets can be divided into two categories; namely direct financing markets and indirect financing markets. In the financial market, direct financing is mainly to raise long-term capital, while indirect financing is mainly to raise short-term working capital. Second, according to the length of the financing period, financial markets can be divided into two categories: money markets and capital markets.

(7) Financial Market Prices

In the process of capital financing, there is a price for capital transfer, which is reflected in the price of capital elements in the market operation. There are two kinds of capital element prices. One is the price of borrowing capital, expressed as interest. Interest is not the expression of capital value, but the unreasonable price form of capitalization income. Interest is a form of expression in which the owner of loan capital lends out the right to use the capital to share the surplus or profit of production, which is essentially a kind of capitalized income. Its source is a part of surplus value created by labor. Another one is the virtual capital price, such as the price of stocks, bonds and other securities. The stock itself has no value, "just represents the right to obtain income", is essentially the monetary performance of dividend capitalization income, and is a more illusory and unreasonable price form than the loan capital price.

(8) History of the Development of China's Financial Market

In the 40 years after the reform and opening up, with the transition from the planned economy to the market economy, our financial undertakings have changed greatly and achieved more outstanding achievements. A systematic and complete financial organization system has been established. For a long time, there was only one financial institution in China, namely the people's Bank of China, which not only undertook the task of the central bank but also handled most of the banking business. China has initially established a new financial institution organization system with complementary functions and coordinated development. It is under the macro-control of the people's Bank of China, supervised by the CBRC, the CIRC and the CSRC, with state-owned commercial banks and other new commercial banks as the main body, and policy banks, non bank financial institutions and foreign financial institutions coexist. It can be said that most of the financial institutions owned by the advanced countries in the world have been established. Financial institutions not only have a wide range of types, but also a large number, which greatly meet the growing financial needs of people. It is particularly important that, in addition to policy financial institutions, other commercial financial institutions basically implement the share-holding system, establish a modern enterprise management system, conduct strict management in full accordance with the rules of the market economy, significantly improve the operation efficiency of institutions, and better adapt to and serve the economic and social development.

From 1977 to 1981, the state began to strengthen the rectification of banking institutions, strengthen the leadership to rectify rules and regulations, and strengthen financial work. In 1977, the banking order was basically restored, the quality of banking work was guaranteed to be improved, and the necessary conditions were created to ensure the role of banks in the national economy. In March 1979, the Agricultural Bank of China resumed its establishment. In March 1979, the Bank of China decided to separate from the people's Bank of China, as a specialized foreign exchange bank designated by the state, to operate and centrally manage the foreign exchange business of the country. In March 1979, the State Administration of foreign exchange was established. In October 1979, China International Trust and Investment Corporation was established, which opened the prelude to the development of trust industry. On January 1, 1984, the Industrial and Commercial Bank of China was established. The people's Bank of China will no longer handle credit business for enterprises and individuals, but will become a government institution specialized in financial management, formulation and implementation of monetary policies. The industrial and commercial credit and savings businesses undertaken by the people's Bank of China in the past are professionally operated by the Industrial and Commercial Bank of China.

On November 14, 1984, after the reform and opening up, the first stock issue was approved by Shanghai Branch of the people's Bank of China, and Shanghai Feile audio Co., Ltd. issued the non-repaid shares to the public. This is the first real stock after China's reform and opening up, marking that China has opened the mysterious veil of capital market after the reform and opening up. On January 1, 1985, the new credit fund management system was implemented, which was a credit fund management system of "unified plan, division of funds, actual loan and actual deposit, mutual accommodation". In July 1986, the Bank of Communications was established. The first joint-stock commercial bank, Bank of Communications, was established.

In November 1990, Shanghai Stock Exchange, the first stock exchange, was established. Since then, the development of China's stock market has begun a new chapter. From March to April 1994, the three policy-oriented banks of China Development Bank, Export Import Bank of China and Agricultural Development Bank of China were established, marking the establishment of the basic framework of the policy banking system. Beginning in September 1996, rural credit cooperatives and county federations were delinked from the Agricultural Bank of China, and more than 50,000 rural credit cooperatives and more than 2,400 county federations across the country gradually delinked from the Agricultural Bank of China. In November 1998, the China Insurance Regulatory Commission was established. This is a major reform of the insurance supervision system, which indicates that China's insurance supervision mechanism and the division management system have been further improved. In May 1999, the Shanghai Futures Exchange was officially established. In July 1999, *The Securities Law of the People's Republic of China* was officially implemented, which played a huge role in the development of the capital market.

China officially joined the World Trade Organization in December 2001. The pace of financial industry reform has accelerated and it has officially opened to the outside world step-by-step. In December 2001, the "Interim Measures for the Administration of Domestic Securities Investment by Qualified Foreign Institutional Investors" jointly issued by the China Securities Regulatory Commission and the People's Bank of China was formally implemented, and the QFII system kicked off in China. This is the first step of incorporating Chinese capital market into the global capital market system, although it also brings huge capital market risks. On March 10, 2003, the decision on the institutional reform plan of the State Council approved the establishment of China Banking Regulatory Commission (CBRC) by the State Council. So far, the pattern of "one Bank, three Commissions" has been formed in China's financial supervision. In December 2003, the Central Huijin Company was established to clarify the property rights of state-owned banks, improve the corporate governance structure, urge banks to implement various reform measures, and establish a new state-owned bank operating mechanism. In 2004, *The Securities Investment Fund Law* was officially promulgated and implemented. Since July 21, 2005, a managed floating exchange rate system has been implemented. China has started to implement a managed floating exchange rate system based on market supply and demand, with reference to a basket of currencies for adjustment. The

RMB exchange rate is no longer pegged to a single USD, forming a more flexible RMB exchange rate mechanism. On November 28, 2009, the inter-bank market clearing house Co., Ltd. was established.

On June 19, 2010, the reform of RMB exchange rate formation mechanism was restarted. A spokesman for the people's Bank of China said that according to the economic and financial situation at home and abroad and China's balance of payments, the People's Bank of China decided to further promote the reform of the RMB exchange rate formation mechanism and enhance the flexibility of the RMB exchange rate. This time, on the basis of the exchange rate reform in 2005, we will further promote the reform of the RMB exchange rate formation mechanism, focusing on the adjustment based on market supply and demand and referring to a basket of currencies.

In recent years, China's financial market continues to develop rapidly. Since 2010, China's financial market has continued to operate healthily and steadily. The transaction in the money market is active, and the market interest rate is restrained first and then raised; the bond market index is rising steadily, and the bond issuance scale is growing steadily; the stock market volatility is picking up, and the stock financing is increasing substantially. In the first three quarters of 2010, the total financing volume of domestic non-financial institutions (including households, non-financial enterprises and government departments) was 8.6 trillion yuan, down 23.3% year on year. In terms of financing tools, the dominant position of loan financing has declined, the proportion of stock financing has increased significantly, corporate bond financing has continued to increase, the strength of national debt financing has not decreased, the role of direct financing in the allocation of funds has been further improved, and the financing structure has been significantly optimized.

In 2011, the scale and activity of China's financial market maintained steady growth, the function of the financial market was further deepened, the operation differences of each sub market increased, the market structure changed significantly, the innovation of financial market products and trading methods continued to advance steadily, and the market system was further improved. From 2011 to 2021, the financial market developed rapidly.

(9) Problems in China's Financial Market

Although China's financial market has achieved rapid development, compared with foreign mature financial markets, there are still many places that need to be improved, which are mainly manifested in the following aspects.

First, financial structure imbalance. Although China's financial institutions are constantly optimizing, the existing structural state still cannot meet the inherent requirements of market economy development and the needs of economic globalization, which has even seriously restricted the improvement of financial efficiency and international competitiveness.

Second, weak financial innovation. Compared with developed countries, China's financial innovation is still very backward, and financial innovation is too reliant on the government. With limited financial innovation, progress in various fields is unbalanced. All these have reduced the efficiency of financial resources and weakened the innovation competitiveness of China's financial institutions.

Third, there are outstanding problems in financial supervision. From the internal point of view, financial institutions are facing the same dilemma as state-owned enterprises, that is, how to truly solve the problem of incentive and restraint mechanism; from the external supervision, the first performance is that the construction of financial laws and regulations is lagging behind. After years of revision, the current laws on financial supervision in China have been relatively systematic and perfect. However, due to the lack of solid legal basis, lack of experience in financial supervision, the coverage of the law is not extensive, and the limitations of the law are serious, especially some temporary management conditions and implementation methods, lack of consistency, continuity and authority, which is extremely unfavorable to the development of the financial market.

Fourth, because the money market and the capital market are not connected, they are artificially separated, which forces the funds to be connected in disguise, hinders the linkage effect between the money market and the capital market, blocks the transmission of the monetary policy, weakens the effectiveness of the monetary policy, and makes the development of the money market unable to effectively promote the development of the capital market. And the separate operation and supervision of banking institutions and non-banking financial institutions cause some supervision vacuum in the financial market.

(10) Development Trend of China's Financial Market

Ⅰ Deepening the reform of state-owned commercial banks

Under the background of profound changes in the financial system and financial market, the state-owned commercial banks should establish a real modern enterprise management system in strict accordance with the requirements of the company law, fundamentally change the existing management mode, and finally make it a modern financial enterprise with perfect corporate governance structure, sound internal control mechanism and market-oriented mechanism. At the same time, it is also necessary to innovate the system of joint-stock banks, establish a strict internal control, standardized and efficient operation mechanism and management system in accordance with the standards of modern commercial banks, and comprehensively improve their operation and management level and profitability.

Ⅱ Establishing a perfect insurance market operation mechanism

It is necessary to change the business model, completely change the status quo of relying on low compensation rates to maintain high growth rates, improve the market operation mechanism, and effectively change the focus of insurance companies' work to improve internal control, strengthen management, innovate products, and improve service quality. It should be that insurance companies voluntarily and actively adapt to the needs of market mechanisms.

Ⅲ Establishing an effective financial supervision system

The development of financial markets has been accompanied and promoted the reform of the financial regulatory system. The basic principle for judging the effectiveness of a financial supervision system should be whether it can gradually deregulate, reduce administrative approval, and provide a good environment for financial institution business innovation. Therefore, it is necessary to earnestly transfer the supervisory function to mainly serve market players and create a good development environment. By means of industry planning, policy guidance, market supervision, information release, and regulation of market access to regulate and control financial markets, prevent and resolve risks, and thereby promote the sustainable, healthy, and rapid development of financial markets.

Ⅴ Regulating the behavior of securities market entities: the first is the investment entity

China's securities market is experiencing a transition period from the coexistence of retail and institutional investors to institutional investors as the main investment subject. Developing and improving securities investment funds and gradually allowing insurance funds and other investment securities markets are the main ways for investment entities to deepen. The second is the financing subject. Create positive conditions for the circulation of state-owned shares and corporate shares, and gradually realize the flow of asset stocks; on the basis of standardization, promote the strategic reorganization of large and medium-sized state-owned enterprises; expand the scale of bond issuance of state-owned enterprises, improve the capital structure of state-owned enterprises, and change excessive reliance on bank credit; increasing external pressure on the operation of state-owned enterprises, prompting them to switch operating mechanisms and improve management quality. Finally, it is the securities company. Establish a long-term mechanism for risk control, strictly prevent securities companies from misappropriating customers' funds in the system design, and establish an effective margin trading mechanism; improve the safe custody and repayment system of customers' margin to ensure the safety of customers' assets; achieve strong integration through acquisition and merger, and enhance the ability to resist risks.

5.2.4 Information Market Factors

Information is a kind of understanding and of knowledge of people about external things in order to eliminate uncertain knowledge. It is a result of human understanding[①]. Economic information is human's understanding of the characteristics and regularity of social production, exchange, distribution, and consumption. Some of these contents have special use value and should be used as commodities for market transactions.

(1) Use Value and Value of Information

In a market economy, the information put into market transactions is economic information with commercial value or economic function. This kind of economic information has practical economic application value. It can bring actual economic benefits to the economic activity subject who masters this information, and improve the level of economic activity. This is the use value of information products. From the perspective of the production

---

① The concept of "information" has not yet been universally defined. In the book "The Mathematical Theory of Communication", the founder of information theory, Shannon argued that "information is used to eliminate uncertainty"; Wiener in his book "Cybernetics" think of information as "the name of the content that is exchanged with the outside world"

of information products, information products, especially information products with economic functions, are generally produced specifically after consuming human labor and are parts of the fruits of human labor.

As an indispensable productive labor, the labor engaged in information collection, processing, and creation also needs to achieve compensation in some way. This requires the commercialization of information products, and labor compensation and corresponding benefits through market transactions. When information products become commodities, a market with information commodities as the trading object is bound to form an information market.

(2) The Composition of the Information Market

The information market is mainly an information consulting market. The industry that carries out activities such as the production, distribution, and service of information products is the information consulting industry, which is an important part of the information industry. In a modern economy where science and technology are increasingly playing a role in production, the information industry has gradually become the leading industry of the entire society and economy, and is known as the "fourth industry".

(3) The Price of Information Commodity

Information commercialization can not only compensate the consumption of information production, but also promote the production and circulation of information, optimize the allocation of information resources, and improve the economic benefits of the whole society. In information transaction, the price of information commodity is based on the production and processing cost of information commodity and the amount of social labor consumption, on the other hand, it has a great relationship with the economic benefits of information commodity. The price of information commodity deviates greatly from its direct cost. On the one hand, the labor consumed in information production is a very special high-level and complex labor, and the unit labor consumption will form a greater social value. On the other hand, it is mainly because of its potential economic benefits and greater market demand.

(4) China Actively Integrates into the Globalization Process, and the Competitiveness of Private Enterprises has Greatly Increased

On November 10, 2001, the Fourth Ministerial Conference of the World Trade Organization (WTO) considered and approved China's application to join the WTO, and China officially became a WTO member since December 11, 2001. China's entry into the WTO has enabled China to integrate more rapidly into the globalization process, providing opportunities for Chinese private enterprises to participate in the globalization process, participate in international competition, and develop and grow in international competition. After the 16th National Congress of the Communist Party of China in 2002, the process of "going-out" of Chinese enterprises has accelerated. At the same time, the economic strength of private enterprises has greatly increased, and the number of large private enterprises and enterprise groups has increased significantly. Focus on the use of international and domestic "two markets, two resources", from domestic to international development, the degree of internationalization has greatly increased, "going-out" investment, mergers and acquisitions behavior is increasing. In 2001, among the 500 enterprises with the largest volume of import and export there were only 5 private enterprises, which increased to 44 in 2010. According to the data of the all China Federation of industry and commerce, in 2010, a total of 137 enterprises among the top 500 private enterprises carried out overseas investment, with 592 investment enterprises and projects, and the amount of overseas investment reached USD 6.177 billion, an increase of 174% over 2009. In 2010, the number of mergers and acquisitions of overseas enterprises by the top 500 private enterprises increased significantly. It fully shows that Chinese private enterprises are not only increasing in scale, but also increasing in competitiveness.

5.2.5 Development of Technical Factors

Technology is the knowledge and skills that are created and invented by humans through experience, scientific research, and experiments, which can directly improve production or improve life. Technology generally exists in the form of knowledge. In production, technology is creative and unitary, it is sustainable in use and consumption, and can be improved in use and consumption. Technology has use value and is also the fruit of human labor. If it is exchanged in the market, it will naturally appear as a commodity.

(1) Conditions for Technology to Become a Commodity

In order for a technological achievement to become a commodity, it must have the conditions of advancedness, maturity, applicability, and economy; technological advancement means that new technology must be superior to the original technology; technological maturity means that new technology must be stable and reliable; the applicability of technology means that the new technology can meet the production and market needs of users, adapt to the production technology conditions and environment of users, and can be digested and mastered by users; the economy of technology means that the transfer price of technology should be reasonable, the application cost and investment should be borne by users. The difference between technical commodities and common commodities is that the trade of technical commodities has continuity and repeatability.

(2) Circulation of Technical Commodity

The circulation of technology commodities is represented by technology trade. There are many specific forms, the most typical of which is technology transfer. Technology transfer is the activity of transferring scientific and technological achievements, including patented and proprietary technologies, with a certain level of technology and practical value from one party to another. The most important form of technology transfer is license trade. License trade refers to a technology transaction conducted by both parties in the form of a license agreement. Specifically, there are three forms. The first is exclusive license trade. It requires the Licensee to have exclusive use of the purchased technology in the identified area, and the Licensor and any third party cannot use the transferred technology to manufacture and sell products in the area. The second is exclusive licensing trade. It is characterized by the exclusive use of the purchased technology by the Licensee to manufacture and sell the products in the determined region, and no third party is allowed to use the transferred technology to manufacture and sell the products in the region. However, the Licensor still reserves the right to use the transferred technology to manufacture and sell the products in the region. The third is the general license trade. Its characteristic is that the Licensor is allowed to use the purchased technology to manufacture and sell products in the specified area, and at the same time, the Licensor still reserves the right to resell the same technology to a third party in the area.

(3) Technical Commodity Prices

The price of technology commodities refers to the technology use fee obtained from the technology transferee after the technology is transferred. The particularity of the formation of technical commodity prices lies in the fact that, first of all, the labor that forms the value of technical commodities is high-level complex labor, which is cumulative simple labor. Second, the labor that forms the value of technological commodities must include not only the labor consumed by the Applied Technology Research Institute, but also the labor consumed by the basic research institutes directly related to it. Thirdly, the labor that forms the value of technological commodities is expressed by the amount of labor saved after the application of technology, that is, the added economic benefits of a technological product. In the specific process of price formation and change, the relationship between supply and demand, the cost of technical goods, potential economic benefits, life cycle, transfer times, development and promotion risks, practicability and implementation conditions, as well as the payment method of price and technology circulation mode, all have different degrees of actual impact.

(4) Labor-intensive Enterprises are Gradually Declining, and There is an Urgent need to Transform to Technology-based Enterprises

In the process of public ownership becoming mixed ownership, labor factors, land factors, and information factors are gradually being liberated. However, due to the low technological starting point of Chinese enterprises and low labor and land costs, Chinese private enterprises have largely undertaken Southeast Asian industrial production, which are mainly concentrated in traditional industries and at the middle and low end of the industrial chain. Influenced by the international financial crisis in 2008 and the downward pressure of domestic economy, private enterprises, especially private small and medium-sized enterprises, are generally faced with such problems as rising labor cost, rising raw material price, rising financing cost and falling profit level, and the pressure of survival and development is increasing. From 2010 to 2016, the profitability of private enterprises continued to decline, and the net interest rate on sales, net interest rate on assets, and return on net assets continued to decline. Data show that in 2012, the net profit growth rate of the top 500 private enterprises reached -3.39%. Transformation and upgrading have become the only way for the survival and development of private enterprises. Facing the severe and complicated economic situation at home and abroad, the 2015 Central Economic Work Conference proposed that supply-side structural reforms should be the main line in the future, and private enterprises should enhance total factor productivity by strengthening technological innovation, management innovation, product innovation, business model innovation, brand building and other ways. This accelerated the pace of transformation and upgrading, showing a trend of moving from the low end of the industrial chain to the high end, and from the traditional industry to the emerging industry.

(5) Imitating and Innovating, Making Chinese Internet Enterprises Rise Suddenly in the World

From 1994 to 2000, China launched the first tide of Internet entrepreneurship development. The Internet economy quickly entered all aspects of the economy and society, and becoming a popular form of entrepreneurship. Yahoo, NetEase, Sohu, Sina, Baidu, Alibaba and other private enterprises were born. After nearly 20 years of development, these companies have grown into the leaders of Internet economy in China and even in the world. They have bred a number of world-class Unicorn private enterprises represented by Alibaba, and more and more people have invested in Internet entrepreneurship. Their exploration and growth is precisely because they realize that the technical foundation of the country itself is poor, and they adopt the imitative and innovative way to realize the overtaking on the curve. The concept and method of imitation innovation is based on its own resources and technology, and it is improved by introducing advanced technology at the same time, rather than simply cutting and copying, let alone bringism. The purpose of imitation innovation is to make enterprises attach importance to innovation through imitation, knowing that innovation is a long-term model for enterprises to maintain vitality. In this process, enterprises will complete the necessary technology accumulation and capital accumulation. Imitation innovation is not the denial of independent innovation, imitation innovation is the practical way of independent innovation. Wu Xiaobo put forward a dynamic model of secondary innovation, which is "imitation innovation, creative imitation, improved innovation, and post secondary innovation"[1]. The imitation object of the imitation enterprise cannot be limited to one enterprise, but can imitate multiple enterprises, which can make breakthrough progress in innovation and leap development in competitiveness.

Foreign companies are also many cases of imitating innovation. Such as the famous multinational company Nike early imitation of ASICS Tiger running shoes, now Nike has become the world's largest sporting goods company. DELL Computer Company was originally in DIY (Do it yourself) mode. Inspironone, the latest LCD integrated machine in 2009, was also accused of imitating AppleMac. DELL became one of the world's largest computer manufacturers and a leader in e-commerce mode. Japan's Toyota A1 sedan imitates the Dodge sedan and Corolla imitates the Opel Kadett sedan. Toyota surpassed GM to become the world's largest car company, and

---

① Xu Qingrui, Wu Xiaobo, "The Process of Secondary Innovation", *Proceedings of DICMET91*, IEEE Inc. 1991, 622-627.

Corolla became one of the most successful models in the world. Panasonic is known as the "imitation company", Sanyo imitates the Hoover turbo jet washing machine, Panasonic and Sanyo have become world-renowned electrical companies, in 2008 Panasonic acquired Sanyo. Early Hyundai in South Korea imitated GM and Ford, KIA, SSANGYong and others imitated Mercedes-Benz. Although Korean cars already have global influence, many existing products still have imitations of famous European and American brands. It can be seen from the above cases that imitation innovation is a common way for many international large enterprises to enter the new field and an effective way from weak to strong, which has a positive reference for Chinese enterprises.

(6) A Large Number of Private Enterprises Enter into Emerging Industries, and the Pace of Diversified Layout is Accelerated

From 2012 to 2017, energy conservation and environmental protection industry, new materials, new energy industry, new generation information technology industry, high-end equipment manufacturing industry, biological industry and new energy automobile industry have become the key areas of private enterprise investment, and the number of private enterprises has increased significantly. Private enterprises have increased their distribution in modern logistics, financial services, financial leasing, e-commerce and other emerging productive services. According to the survey data of all China Federation of Industry and Commerce, in 2016, 46.8% of the top 500 private enterprises took the initiative to transform, upgrade and eliminate excess capacity; 71.8% of the top 500 private enterprises kept a reasonable inventory scale; 66.2% of the top 500 private enterprises took the initiative to take measures to reduce or maintain a reasonable leverage ratio. The market competitiveness of private enterprises in financial leasing, new energy, communication equipment manufacturing and other emerging economic fields has been continuously enhanced, which has become the most dynamic economic type.

(7) Awareness of Brand Protection of Private Enterprises Reaches New Heights

In 2018, the total number of domestic and foreign trademarks owned by the top 500 private enterprises reached 145,959, an increase of 42,049 over the previous year, an increase of 40.47%. Among them, the total number of domestic trademarks was 119,555, an increase of 47.76% over the previous year, and the total number of domestic trademarks was 3,407, an increase of 14.81% over the previous year. In 2018, the average number of trademarks owned by each enterprise reached 292, an increase of 84 from the previous year, an increase of 40.47%. Details show on table 5-1.

(number)

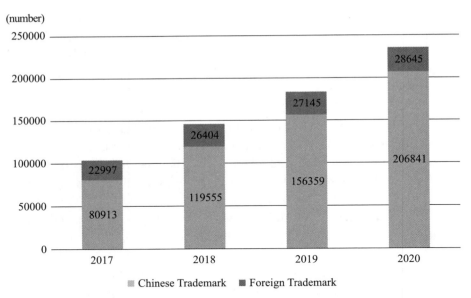

Table 5-1 **Number of registered trademarks of top 500 private enterprises in 2015-2018**
Source: All-China Federation of Industry and Commerce.

At the beginning of the founding of the United States, the United States attached great importance to intellectual property rights and continued to improve intellectual property legislation. In 1790, the first copyright law was passed. At that time, it was limited to maps and books. After the revisions of 1835, 1870, and 1909, it has completely covered all types of works. In 1998, in order to adapt to the development of digital information technology, Congress passed *The Millennium Digital Copyright Law*, which extended the scope to all the copyright objects closely related to modern film, video recording, computer software and other technologies according to the major revision of copyright fee in 1976.

(8) Private Enterprises Attach Importance to Innovation Capabilities and Increase Investment in Research and Development

Through the transformation and upgrading, the awareness of independent innovation of private enterprises has been greatly enhanced, the ability of independent innovation has been gradually improved, and private enterprises are undergoing a new round of transformation and upgrading. Take the top 500 private enterprises as an example. From 2015 to 2018, the R&D investment of private enterprises continued to strengthen. The number of enterprises with R&D personnel accounting for more than 3% increased from 299 to 328, accounting for 65.6% of the total enterprises, with an average annual growth of about 3.2 percentage points. By 2018, the proportion of enterprises with R&D intensity exceeding 1% was about 37%; the proportion of private enterprises whose key technology comes from independent development and research has increased from 78.80% in 2015 to 82.80% in 2018.

In 2016, the number of domestic patent applications increased by 55.65% compared with 2013, and the number of international patent applications increased by 80.56% compared with 2013. In 2016, the R&D expenses of private manufacturing enterprises accounted for 43.5% of the total R&D expenses of manufacturing industry among 34000 key tax source manufacturing enterprises with an annual tax payment of more than 10 million yuan, an increase of 5.8 percentage points over the same period last year, providing a strong impetus for the sustained and rapid development of private manufacturing industry. In the "2016 global enterprise R&D investment ranking" released by the European Commission, Huawei surpassed Apple, ranking eighth with 8.358 billion euros of R&D expenses, and Chinese enterprises such as Baidu, Lenovo, Tencent and Midea were all listed.

Table 5-2 Proportion of R&D personnel and R&D intensity of top 500 private enterprises in China from 2015 to 2018

Proportion structure	Proportion of R&D personnel (Number of enterprises)			
	2017	2018	2019	2020
≥10%	189	184	190	191
3%-10%	116	144	145	148
1%-3%	64	54	55	53
<1%	26	27	20	18
Total	395	409	410	410
Proportion structure	R&D intensity (Nomber of enterprices)			
	2017	2018	2019	2020
≥10%	6	6	8	9
3%-10%	65	63	69	68
1%-3%	111	116	115	114
<1%	223	229	220	222
Total	405	414	412	413

Sources: China's Top 500 Private Enterprises Report, China Minsheng Banking Research Institute.

5.3 Establishing Modern Enterprise System and Standard Market Order

5.3.1 Modern Enterprise System

The modern enterprise system is a standard that absorbs the advanced experience of the share-holding economy of developed countries in the West, and is based on China's status quo for the reform and construction of our enterprise system.

Its content has two aspects. First, reconstruction and reconstruction of existing enterprises. In accordance with the scientific and reasonable method formulated by the state, a specialized organization shall conduct clearing and verification of capital and asset evaluation of the enterprise, and clearly define the measurement and ownership of the existing assets of the enterprise. In particular, the state-owned assets should be clearly identified and implemented by specific departments to represent national interests. According to the national regulations and their own conditions, enterprises rationally choose a certain organizational form, such as a company limited by shares or a limited liability company, with independent accounting and independent management as a legal person, so that the enterprise truly becomes an active cell in the economic society.

Second, establish a standardized property rights market, such as a stock exchange, through fair transactions and fair competition in the property rights market, to reflect changes in the value of enterprises in a market economy, to achieve the necessary restructuring, mergers or auctions, and to optimize the allocation of social resources, and get the best socio-economic benefits.

(1) Basic Characteristics of Modern Enterprise System

Separation of ultimate ownership and corporate ownership, that is, separation of legal ownership and economic ownership. This duality of capital ownership, that is, separation of corporate property into physical ownership and value ownership, separates and separates their sovereignty and movement. The legal ownership of capital becomes equity and is owned by shareholders. Shareholders are the ultimate owners of corporate property and enjoy the rights to participate in management, income distribution, and rights to buy and sell equities transferred from the exercise of equity, but lose the actual possession and control of corporate assets. The economic ownership of capital, that is, the completely independent management right, is the ownership of the physical assets of the enterprise owned by the corporate legal person. As long as the firm is not bankrupt or unliquidated, no investor can withdraw capital or directly intervene. Therefore, under the modern enterprise system, the company can truly achieve independent operation, self-financing, and have the conditions to achieve self-development and self-restraint.

Shareholders bear limited economic responsibility for corporate assets and liabilities. This means that when a company goes bankrupt or dissolves, shareholders only bear the company's debts with the shares they own, and have nothing to do with other shareholders' assets. This feature is conducive to mobilizing the investment enthusiasm of shareholders and eliminates unlimited joint worry.

Equity equality and benefit sharing. In an enterprise, one share has one right and the same share has the same interest. If the shareholders want to have more control, they need more shares, but they don't have to own all of them, only need more than 50%. Equity can be transferred and sold, and investors enjoy full investment freedom. The operation of the securities market breaks the solidification and closed state of the real assets, makes the social resources flow fully, and it is very easy to realize the optimal allocation.

It is an important feature of modern enterprise system that legal person holds and shares with each other. The mutual ownership of legal persons is mainly the need of mutual control and cooperation between enterprises, which leads to the mutual ownership of enterprises. Corporate ownership reduces the amount of pure private capital in enterprises, makes capital more socialized, and forms the mechanism of mutual restriction among enterprises.

The stock form of modern enterprise system is conducive to absorbing foreign capital and capital to invest in foreign countries, forming multinational companies. It is also conducive to China's participation in the flood of world economic development and meeting the challenges.

Stock exchange leads to diversification and decentralization of stock rights. The shareholders of an enterprise include not only natural persons, but also enterprises and institutions, government departments, foreign natural persons and legal persons. The diversification and decentralization of stock rights will inevitably separate the ownership and management rights of enterprises. For example, General Motors has as many as 2 million shareholders, with a total number of 400 million shares, each holding an average of 200 shares. No one shareholder can hold 1% of the shares, and it is difficult for any individual to control the operation of the company based on the equity. With the decline of personal role, it can be considered that enterprises are becoming more and more social enterprises.

(2) The Western Joint-stock System Provides Us Experience

As early as in the ancient Greek and Roman era, the western stock system had the sprout of partnership management and distribution according to capital. At the beginning of the 17th century, the United Kingdom and other countries established joint-stock companies such as "Moscow Company" and "East India Company", which were recognized as independent legal persons. The shareholding system has more than 100 shareholders, with a share capital of tens of thousands or even millions of pounds. At the end of the 18th century and the beginning of the 19th century, the British joint-stock system developed in banking, insurance, transportation and some public sectors, and gradually became the main organizational form of enterprises, with rapid economic development. In the 20 years from 1850 to 1870, the coal production in Britain increased from 49.8 million tons to 112 million tons, pig iron from 2.24 million tons to 6.1 million tons, and cotton from 590 million pounds to 1.08 billion pounds. In 1870, Britain accounted for 32% of the world industry and 25% of the world trade, ranking first in the world. After the implementation of the joint-stock system in the United States, the effect is also amazing. Take the railway construction as an example. In 1842, 2808 kilometers of railway in the United States increased to 60,000 kilometers in 1865, 270,000 kilometers in 1890, and 400,000 kilometers in 1916, accounting for one third of the total world railway mileage at that time. It is inconceivable that the huge investment of these constructions will leave the way of stock financing. As Marx said, the concentration of capital through the joint-stock company completes this matter in a flash. In the second half of the 19th century, the United States generally adopted the organizational form of joint-stock companies in the industrial sectors of steel, coal, machine manufacturing, etc. through the joint-stock system, capital was rapidly concentrated, old enterprises were expanded, new large enterprises were built, and economic development quickly leaped to the forefront of the world. After the 1860s, the stock system of western developed countries has become more and more common and standardized, and the laws and regulations of the stock system have become more and more strict and perfect. In order to ensure the normal and orderly operation of social economy, western developed countries have formulated a relatively complete set of laws and regulations. These laws and regulations embody the requirements of commodity economy and socialized mass production, and form a complete set of socialized management and supervision system. For example, securities law, securities exchange law, investment company law, securities investor protection law, company law, bankruptcy law, etc.. The joint-stock system is gradually maturing. From the development of the joint-stock system in the developed capitalist countries in the west, we can see its great role in promoting economic development.

We must study and analyze carefully for our own use: First, it is conducive to raising huge amount of funds for the long-term development of the enterprise. Second, it is conducive to the independent operation of the enterprise, free from all kinds of interference, and able to develop itself according to economic laws. Third, it is conducive to the social production of economic development. Fourth, it is not the patent of developing capitalism, but the necessity of developing market economy. Fifth, we must complete the construction of laws and regulations as soon as possible to ensure healthy development. We should not only learn from western experience, but also combine it with China's national conditions.

(3) China's Modern Enterprise System is a Natural Result

Since the reform and opening up, many people of insight in China have raised the issue of shareholding system for a long time. In the 1980s, the government also carried out pilot projects, but due to the lack of fire, it failed to form our own set of things and promote great development. Over the years, China's own multi-faceted practical experience and exploration have finally formed a consensus from the top to the bottom, and determined that Chinese enterprises take the road of modern enterprise system reform. It should be said that at present, it is a natural result.

First, scholars in the field of economics constantly introduce the emergence, development and current situation of the western stock system, which plays an important role in promoting economic development. And combined with the reality of our country, it repeatedly explains the feasibility of the stock system under the socialist conditions of China, demonstrates that the stock system is not private ownership, will not destroy the public ownership, and will strengthen the control of the public ownership over the national economy. At the same time, over the years, China's joint-stock enterprises and securities market pilot has accumulated considerable experience.

Second, the state-owned economy has been troubled for a long time. Although some achievements have been made in the past reform, the basic approach is simply "delegating powers and benefits", which has not fundamentally touched the institutional reform of enterprises. As a result, the problems such as the separation of government and enterprise, the ambiguity of property rights, the lack of self-restraint mechanism, and the non implementation of independent rights have not been fundamentally solved, thus the economic benefits are difficult to improve. After thousands of turns, we finally realize that in order to truly realize the transformation of enterprise management mechanism, we must effectively reconstruct and reconstruct the existing enterprises according to the requirements of modern enterprise system.

Third, enlightenment from rural township enterprises and urban private enterprises. The fact that these enterprises have flourished since the early 1980s tells us that independent operation is the foundation of enterprise vitality. Township and village enterprises and private enterprises were initially small and weak, which were incomparable with state-owned enterprises. However, they have the autonomy to operate, so they can take the opportunity to act in the market, act in accordance with the laws of the economy, grasp the right market, sell the production, network talents, and independently develop new technologies and products. Their success is in stark contrast to the problems of state-owned enterprises.

At the same time, the development of township enterprises and private enterprises also exposed the problems of self-development and self-restraint, such as product quality, scale difficulties, financial discipline is not strict. This shows that the development of enterprises cannot be achieved only by liberalizing the management autonomy, but also by comprehensively standardizing the enterprise system. Not only the state-owned enterprises should carry out the reform of modern enterprise system, but also the township enterprises and private enterprises should be further developed according to the modern enterprise system.

(4) Modern Enterprise Management cannot be Ignored

When it comes to the reform of modern enterprise system, people tend to focus on the definition of property rights, which is right, but not all. The modern enterprise system also requires a series of modern management within the enterprise.

The general meeting of shareholders and the board of directors of an enterprise shall earnestly exercise their power in accordance with the procedures and methods stipulated in the articles of association of the enterprise, which shall not be a mere formality: they shall learn and be accustomed to acting in accordance with the law, completely eliminate the influence of the government and enterprise indiscriminate and shadow cabinet, so that the enterprise legal person can be truly established and become a grass-roots cell full of vitality.

Enterprises should be carefully selecting competent general managers, deputy general managers, chief engineers, chief accountants, chief economists and secretaries. This person should be some special talents and entrepreneurs. The general manager is the general director of the daily business of the enterprise appointed by the board of directors. The deputy general manager assists the general manager in his work and acts for him in his absence. The chief engineer, chief accountant and chief economist assist the general manager in charge of technology, finance and overall benefits. The secretary is not a general secretary, but an officer of the nature of the Secretary General. An enterprise shall also have competent functional department managers and production and sales branch managers, each of whom shall be competent and conscientious. The general manager must have a clear division of responsibilities and reward and punishment rules for his subordinates. The superior shall be rewarded and the inferior shall be punished. The general manager shall be responsible for and report to the board of directors, and the board of directors has the right to replace the general manager. In order to ensure the normal operation of the enterprise, the enterprise must also set up a board of supervisors, which is the enterprise supervision organization under the leadership of the general meeting of shareholders. The board of supervisors, in parallel with the board of directors, supervises the board of directors and the general manager's administrative management system. The members of the board of supervisors are composed of a number of professional members from the shareholders, staff representatives and external financial, accounting, legal and other aspects. Party organizations, mass organizations and social organizations in an enterprise can participate in the work of the board of supervisors in the name of the organization or in the name of the employees of the enterprise, and play their due role. The work of the board of supervisors must be implemented, which cannot be regarded as an empty one. The quality of the work of the board of supervisors is very important, which directly affects the board of directors and the general manager's administrative management system.

The internal management of modern enterprises, that is, the internal power of enterprises, is our weak link. After solving the external environmental factors of enterprises, enterprises must work hard to improve the internal power, so as to ultimately achieve the purpose of improving economic benefits.

5.3.2 Significance of Establishing and Regulating Market Order

Market order refers to the general term for various rules of conduct and codes of conduct that must be followed in the operation of the market. Including two aspects of market rules and market management. Market order is the basic condition for ensuring that the law of value functions and the orderly operation of the market.

First, establishing and regulating market order can promote the normal functioning of the market mechanism. If the market order is chaotic, the market operates without rules, and speculative fraud, bullying, and counterfeit and shoddy goods flood the market, the market mechanism will be difficult to function, and the market development will be adversely affected. Second, the establishment and standardization of market order are conducive to ensuring the country's macro-control of the operation of the national economy. Under the conditions of a market economy, the country's macro-control is mainly achieved by guiding enterprises through economic levers such as taxes, interest rates, and prices. Only by establishing a standardized market order can companies respond correctly to changes in economic leverage and enable the state's regulatory goals to be successfully realized. Third, the establishment and standardization of market order will help strengthen the vitality of enterprises. Under the perfect market order, the economic behavior of enterprises can be based on law and live without chaos. If the market order is chaotic and the performance rate of economic contracts is low, it will not be possible for enterprises to flexibly adjust production and operation based on market supply and demand. Fourth, establishing and regulating market order is a necessary condition for economic opening. If the market order is chaotic, it will damage the image and international reputation of a country, damage the investment environment, and affect foreign investment. At the same time, if counterfeit and shoddy goods are exported, the reputation of the country's goods will be seriously damaged and exports will be hindered. Without a standardized market order, it will not be possible to proceed smoothly to opening up.

5.3.3 Market Rules

To maintain market order, we must have sound market rules. Market rules refer to various rules and regulations formulated by the state to ensure the orderly operation of the market, including laws and regulations, contracts and conventions. Market rules include market entry and exit rules, market competition rules, market transaction rules, and market arbitration rules.

Market entry and exit rules are codes of conduct and norms for market subjects and market objects (that is, commodities) to enter or exit the market. The components include the follows. First, the qualifications of market entities to enter the market. That is, according to the regulations, the qualifications and conditions of market entities are reviewed, legal entities are allowed to enter the market, and illegal entities are rejected from entering the market. The second is the regulation of the nature of market entities, which mainly includes clarifying the nature of the market entities, registered capital, operating projects and business scope. The third is the norm for market entities to withdraw from the market. Market participants must abide by certain procedures and perform necessary procedures. The fourth is the regulation of market objects entering and leaving the market. Commodities that enter the market must not only be consignment commodities, but also must meet relevant regulations in terms of quality, measurement and packaging.

Market competition rules are the behavior rules and norms that market subjects must abide by in market competition. It is the system embodiment of the competition relationship of equal status and equal opportunity among market subjects, which is mainly composed of the following three parts. First, operators are forbidden to use deception, coercion, inducement, slander and other means against the fair competition rules to engage in market transactions and damage the interests of competitors. Second, operators are prohibited from abusing their market advantage and market power, or more than two operators are allowed to coordinate with each other in terms of transaction price, sales, trading conditions, etc. through agreements and other ways, thus hindering fair competition and damaging the interests of competitors. Third, operators are forbidden to exclude competitors, monopolize, control and dominate the market in a comprehensive and long-term way through monopolization, merger and exclusive transaction.

Market transaction rules are the rules and norms that market subjects must abide by when they carry out market transaction activities. The main contents include: first, the regulation of market transaction mode, such as trading in an open place, clearly marking prices, open competition, using money as the medium, prohibiting black market trading and underground economy. The second is the regulation of market transaction behavior. For example, it is forbidden to buy or sell by force, cheat or cheat, lack of weight, adulterate or make false, hoard or hoard, bid up prices and make huge profits.

Market arbitration rules are the rules and norms that market arbitration institutions must abide by when they arbitrate the economic disputes between market subjects. The purpose is to solve the economic disputes among market subjects fairly and openly. The most important thing of the arbitration rules is to follow the principle of fairness; both parties involved in the dispute must be treated equally without partiality to either party.

5.3.4 Market Management

In order to ensure that the market is orderly and operates in accordance with the rules, in addition to establishing and improving various market rules, standardized management of the market is also required. The market management includes the market management organization and the market supervision system. There are three main types of market management organizations. The first is the state-established organization that specializes in market management, including relevant government departments and relevant institutions of the political and legal system, such as finance, taxation, business, statistics, auditing, banking, price and other institutions. The second is related technical management agencies, such as measurement standards, testing, quality appraisal agencies, and so on. The third is about social and mass management institutions, such as consumer associations, quality supervision associations and other non-governmental organizations. The market supervision system mainly includes four aspects: administrative law enforcement, industry self-regulation, public opinion supervision, and mass participation.

In 2005 and 2010, the State Council successively issued "Several Opinions on Encouraging and Supporting the Development of Non-Public Ownership and Private Economy" and "Several Opinions on Encouraging and

Guiding the Healthy Development of Private Investment", regulations and policies hindering the development of private enterprises were cleared and revised, market access conditions were relaxed, and 18 industries such as infrastructure were opened to private enterprises, In 2005 and 2010, the State Council issued several opinions on encouraging, supporting and guiding the development of non-public economy such as individual and private enterprises and opinions on encouraging and guiding the healthy development of private investment. Laws, regulations and policies hindering the development of private enterprises were cleared and revised, market access conditions were relaxed, and 18 industries such as infrastructure were opened to private enterprises. The market environment of fair competition and equal access has been greatly improved, and private enterprises' investment and financing, tax, land use and other policies have been put forward in succession. In 2004, 2006, and 2009, the SME Board, the New Third Board, and the Growth Enterprise Market were respectively established, and the financing channels for private enterprises were further expanded. This series of major policies and events has promoted the large-scale development of private enterprises and made China a "world factory".

5.3.5 The Horn of All-round Reform Sounded, and the Development Environment for Private Enterprises Continued to Improve

The Third Plenary Session of the 18th Central Committee of the Communist Party of China has opened the prelude to comprehensively deepen the reform. China has entered an era of all-round reform focusing on economic system reform. The external environment for the development of private enterprises has never been taken seriously by the state before. The central and local governments have introduced policies to support small and medium-sized enterprises and small and micro enterprises in finance and taxation, investment and financing systems, market access, credit policies, property rights protection and other aspects. At the same time, efforts should be taken to optimize and improve the business environment and encourage the development of private enterprises.

In 2014, the State Council proposed "mass entrepreneurship, mass innovation", and launched the reform of administrative examination and approval system such as "streamlining administration, delegating power, strengthening regulation and improving services"; the reform of commercial system such as "separation of certificates and licenses", "integration of three certificates" and "integration of five certificates"; Since 2015, the State Council and the Central Committee of the CPC Central Committee have held eight meetings to discuss the issue of optimizing the business environment; In March 2016, General Secretary Xi Jinping proposed to build a new type of political and business relationship, that is, to pro-clear the relationship between government and business; In 2016, the CPC Central Committee and the State Council issued "the opinions on deepening the reform of investment and financing system", on the basis of "the revision of the catalogue of investment projects approved by the government" in 2013 and 2014, the State Council issued a new version of the catalogue of investment projects to ease the entry of private enterprises in related fields; the restrictions on the entry of private capital into the financial sector have been lifted, and 17 private banks have been approved to set up; policy guarantee companies were established in various places to provide guarantees for private enterprises, at the central and local government levels, special funds were established to support the development of private enterprises; carry out "business tax instead of value-added tax" in an all-round way, reduce enterprise tax and raise income tax threshold for small and micro enterprises; implement a unified market access system, eliminate hidden barriers, and formulate a negative list of market access; promote mixed ownership reforms and encourage private enterprises to invest in state-owned enterprises.

The State Council announced on October 8, 2019 that the "Regulations on Optimizing the Business Environment" will be implemented on January 1, 2020 to minimize the government's direct allocation of market resources and minimize government's direct intervention in market activities. It is of great significance to further improve the fairness and fairness of market order.

Chapter 6

New Urbanization Developments in China

Urbanization describes the process of rural-to-urban transformation. With the deepening of social divisions of labor and the expansion of industrialization, urbanization has become the dominant trend of the era and its study has become increasingly important. Most under-developed nations in Africa, Asia and Central and South America have experienced high levels of rural-to-urban migration, due to lack of employment possibilities in rural area. The migration has resulted in urban slums, such as non-existent urban services, deplorable health conditions, reliance upon the informal employment sector and poverty. The rural-urban income inequality and within urban income inequality is severe. The environment of urbanization development is undergoing profound changes in both China and globally.

China's urbanization has its own characteristics due to the unique household registration system (hukou system). This unique path to urbanization has avoided many of the traditional pitfalls, although the process has also involved high costs of various kinds. This chapter first briefly reviews the historical process of Chinese Urbanization and defines the new urbanization in this era. Then we examine some of the changes in urbanization that are currently underway in China.

The literature indicates that to draw a definition of new urbanization, most scholars tend to start from are refection on traditional urbanization and compare the background, concept and goals of new and traditional urbanization. We follow the same routine by reviewing the historical background of urbanization in China. Our discussions are divided into two aspects: supply side and demand side. Moving from abstract to concrete definitions, although differences exist among scholars, some consensus has been reached on two aspects. The first is sustainable development, which is an inevitable choice for new urbanization and the goal of all countries in the world. This is what we categories into a supply side problem. The second is people-centered urbanization, which is an essential property of new urbanization. The phenomenon of valuing materials more highly than people in urbanization needs to be changed so that people's employment patterns, lifestyle, living environment and so on can be urbanized. This is what we categories into a demand side problem.

Traditionally, scholars understood the concept of sustainable development as the harmonious coexistence of humans and nature, embodied in the effective utilization and protection of natural resources and the environment. In fact, sustainable development, in a broad sense, also essentially includes sustainable organizational forms and institutional arrangements. This kind of sustainability manifests in the synergy between and balancing of the population, economy, natural resources and the environment, as well as sustainable institutional and planning arrangements. It entails not only the proper concentration of population and sustained economic growth, but also the efficient use of natural resources and environmental protection while demanding social fairness and harmony in institutional arrangements and rational spatial structure in urban planning.

6.1 Historical Background of Urbanization

The traditional mode of urbanization is simply pursuing urban population growth and scale expansion. The extensive development resulted in high consumption and high pollution, which is unsustainable as they created many social and economic problems. This has led to a search for a pattern of sustainable urbanization—the idea of "new urbanization". New urbanization is characterized with effective resource utilization and environmental protection.

6.1.1 Inefficient Production and Envromental Issues

The main stimulus of China's traditional urbanization process is industrialization, which is reflected in its export and investment-oriented economic growth mode. This development mode has made tremendous contributions to China's rapid economic development and growth over the past few decades.

However, overreliance on investment and external economic environment for economic development is not sustainable. The RMB 4 trillion rescue plan initiated in response to the Global Financial Crisis (GFC) in 2008 is a case in point. Although government-led investment in infrastructure and real estate boom iron the depression cycle, but it not only failed to solve the substantive problems in economic development, but also worsened structural contradictions and caused overproduction and other problems. The current development condition in China poses a severe challenge to the momentum of growth.

The mode of extensive industrial production caused a series of economic and social problems, including serious resource waste and environmental pollution especially. The inefficiencies inherent in the traditional model of production and urbanization are summarized as follows.

High energy consumption. For example, in 2015, China's gross domestic product (GDP) accounted for 15% of the global total, however, its primary energy consumption accounted for about 22.9%. Most of China's energy consumption occurred in its cities. At present, China faces a double disadvantage of high energy consumption and low utilization efficiency. Urban energy consumption will grow year by year with increasing urbanization. The International Energy Agency (IEA) showed that, in 2015, China accounted for 79% of city energy consumption—nearly 23% higher than the urbanization rate of 56.1 % in that year—and will soar to 83% by 2030.

High water consumption. China has serious water shortage and pollution problems. Rapid urbanization has seen urban water use shift from industrial demand to household use. The efficiency of urban water usage directly determines the quality of urbanization. According to China's Ministry of Water Resources, nearly 400 of 661 cities are in a water deficit, and among those more than 100 cities are experiencing a serious water shortage.

High land consumption. Urban sprawl is a common occurrence in China. According to the National Bureau of Statistics (NBS), urban built-up areas in China amounted to 12,856 square km in 1990 and surged to 49,772 square km by 2014, with an average annual growth rate of 5.56%, while the urbanization rate in the same period increased from 26.4% to 54.8%, an average annual growth rate of only 2.96 %, which means the growth rate of built-up areas is nearly two times that of urbanization. This demonstrates that the speed of land urbanization is much faster than that of population in China.

High pollution. According to the Ministry of Environmental Protection's 2015 China Environmental State Bulletin, among the first 74 cities implementing its new Ambient Air Quality Standards, the average number of days in which that standard was met in 2015 was about 260, with a standard-reaching rate of only 71.2%. The average annual concentration of particulate matter (PM) 2.5 is 55 µg per cubic meter, which is 1.57 times that of China's secondary standard (35 µg per cu m). Among these 74 cities, only Zhoushan, Fuzhou, Xiamen, Shenzhen, Zhuhai, Jiangmen, Huizhou, Zhongshan, Haikou, Kunming and Lhasa fully met the air quality standards. In addition, according to China's surface water environment monitoring data, water with quality types I, II and III accounted for 64.5% of the total, while nearly 40 % did not meet the water quality standards in 2015.

Therefore, the traditional processes promoted by traditional manufacturing industries are facing difficulties. In response to these pollution and over-capacity problems, it is imperative to achieve industrial transformation and upgrading and take a new road of urbanization with sustainable economic growth. Premier Li Keqiang has said the new urbanization should follow an intensive and low-carbon development mode, emphasizing the efficient utilization of natural resources and energy. New urbanization should take the road of green urbanization and green governance.

In addition, the deepening trend of population ageing has led to a declining demographic dividend, a dilemma for the labor-intensive production, especially in export-oriented manufacturing industry, in which cheap labor is the main competitive advantage.

The results of the sixth census (2010) of China indicate that the number of people over the age of 60 is 178 million, 13.26% of the total population, and an increase of 2.93% compared with 2000. Moreover, under the influence of China's fertility planning policy, the proportion of the population born in the 1990s and 2000s is far below the current proportion of middle-aged and elderly people. The disappearance of the demographic advantage has already had an impact on China's export-oriented economy, which previously developed vigorously thanks to an unlimited supply of cheap labor. In addition, China's export-oriented economy, dominated by manufacturing industries, is at the lowest point of the 'smiling curve' and can obtain only extremely meager profits in the global value chain. Therefore, with the rise of labor costs and the shortage of external demand caused by the GFC, the outsourcing demand of manufacturing industries in Europe and the United States has shifted to others developing countries such as Vietnam and India, which have lower labor and land resource costs. The export-oriented development mode can no longer be regarded as an economic engine of China's future urbanization.

6.1.2 Social Welfare and Income Distribution Issues

The household registration (Hukou) system disadvantages migrant workers in urban areas, resulting in unequal distribution of public services between urban residents and rural and regional migrant workers. Therefore, China's traditional pattern of urbanization has reached a turning point in its development and faces a crucial transformation. Working out how to break through the dilemma of the traditional mode of urbanization and embark on a path of new urbanization with Chinese characteristics, a sustainable and people-oriented model of urbanization, have become important tasks for China in the new era.

First, in 2014, the proportion of the rural population in China's total population was as high as 45%, while total output from the agricultural sector was only 16% of the national total, with a downward trend. At the same time, the urban population (including migrant workers from rural areas) represented only 55% of the total population, but generated 84% of national output, with a growing trend. It means 45% of the population received only 16% of total national income, while 55% of the population received 84% of total income, which indicates the paradox of socioeconomic development in China—that is, the coexistence of rising national income and rural poverty.

In fact, urbanization in China is not as simple as transferring of status from rural residents to urban citizens. The obstruction caused by the Hukou system is one important reason for this paradox. Under the Hukou system, large numbers of migrant workers cannot fully realize their citizenship in urban areas, nor can they enjoy basic public services in the city, including education, housing and medical care, pension insurance and housing security, which cause social problems for the children and elderly people left behind in rural areas. For example, in the Pearl River Delta, 20 million migrant workers were unemployed and without social security because of the GFC in 2008.

Second, the geographic distribution and scale structure of urbanization are imbalanced. More people are moving to eastern areas, while the resources and spaces in middle and western regions are not utilized effectively and efficiently. Associated problems, such as "urban diseases" and land disputes, have caused major social concerns.

For example, the urbanization rate in the east of the country is much higher than in the central and western regions. According to data released by the NBS, in 2014, the urbanization rate in eastern China was 61%, while that in central China was 53 % and 49.7% in the west. The regional differentiation of urbanization levels is obvious, so it is imperative new urbanization addresses this issue. Mega-cities are agglomerated mainly in eastern China, which is also where urban diseases are mainly concentrated due to population expansion and relatively low level of city governance capacity. In central and western China, the development of mega-cities has been inadequate and the distribution of small and medium-sized cities and small towns is relatively loose. Due to low levels of infrastructure and public services, socioeconomic development capacity is also hampered in central and western China. Tis spatial imbalance has led to large-scale regional population migration to the east and social problems associated with it, including for the children of migrants and elderly people left behind.

Moreover, capital cities in all provinces have enjoyed rapid development due to favorable urban policies and resource levels, essentially creating a population–industrial agglomeration effect. However, the spillover effects of these cities on surrounding cities are weak. Therefore, further development of urbanization should prevent the urban diseases and improve the city governance capacity. Metropolitan cluster development shall be adopted as the main strategy of promoting new urbanization in order to construct polycentric metropolitan areas and to promote the trans-regional mobility of production factors. At the same time, development strategy should be implemented in light of local conditions and characteristics, embarking on a path of regional and urban–rural coordinated new urbanization with reasonable spatial structure.

In sum, deepening people's urbanization and pursuing social harmony and justice, reasonable spatial structure, effective resource utilization and environmental protection are essential. This entails reform of the Hukou and land systems from the institutional level.

6.2 Defining New Urbanization

New urbanization is inevitable in the era of globalization and post-industrialization. At present, all countries in the world experiencing the wave of globalization have begun the transformation from traditional to post-industrialization processes, including in urbanization. As a national development strategy, China's urbanization transformation has been concentrated in the development of new urbanization. This, together with industrialization, informationally and agricultural modernization, has created a path for synchronizing the 'four modernizations' of sustainable development with Chinese characteristics.

6.2.1 Requirement for New Urbanization

Among the four modernizations, urbanization has special status, and accelerating that process is now a major task for China. First, in the face of the highly carbonized and unsustainable traditional mode of urbanization, new urbanization, which incorporating effective resource utilization and environmental protection, is essential. Second, the traditional mode of urbanization has not only failed to achieve common prosperity, but also caused social injustice and a widening of the gap between the rich and the poor. Pursuit of social justice and harmony has become an inevitable requirement of the new urbanization, by putting people at the core.

In view of these shortcomings, China has carried out a major rethink of its existing policy for urbanization. Both academia and government departments have reached consensus on a new pattern of intensive, smart, low-carbon and green urbanization. To achieve the new urbanization, industrial transformation and upgrading from traditional manufacturing to modern service industries must be realized. Premier Li Keqiang pointed out that the new urbanization requires, in particular, the development of service industries. Currently, service industries in developed countries account for more than 70% of total output value, which can absorb the maximum number of urban employees, and also helps to achieve the upgrading of the industrial structure. The impetus behind new urbanization is not traditional investment and exports, but domestic 'green' consumption and the synergistic development of urbanization, industrialization, informationalism and agricultural modernization.

After the eighteenth National Congress of the CPC explicitly proposed a road to new urbanization with Chinese characteristics, the State Council promulgated its "National New Urbanization Plan 2014–2020", which has positive strategic significance for the sustainable development of urbanization. Since then, the thirteenth five-year plan has also put forward requirements for accelerating the pace of new urbanization. The new urbanization has therefore entered a new phase and its importance to China's future development is self-evident.

6.2.2 Concept of New Urbanization

All in all, the concept of new urbanization is rare in other countries. The most significant concept of urban renewal in the Western world is the theory of new urbanism, which emerged in the 1990s against the issue of urban sprawl, and which is considered the most influential global urban design trend of the past two decades. Although the theory of new urbanism has some value for the development of China's new urbanization, there are some essential differences with China in terms of the stage of medium-level development and rapid urbanization and the definition of the concept of new urbanization. The study of urbanization in China has moved through conceptual stages— from urbanization, to urbanization with Chinese characteristics, to new urbanization and to new urbanization with Chinese characteristics—each stage of which is closely linked with national policies. Academics have been discussing the differences and connections between the concepts for a long time.

This chapter focuses on new urbanization, for which an accurate definition is a prerequisite for carrying out research. If there is no comprehensive and systematic understanding of new urbanization, some aspects may be over-emphasized while others are neglected in urbanization practice, resulting in a situation in which some old problems are solved but many new ones arise. Despite the name, new urbanization is not a new concept, even though it does not yet have a unified definition. The basic idea is to explore a more quality-oriented approach to sustainable urbanization, developing what is useful from traditional urbanization and discarding what is not. The approach to sustainable urbanization has become a heated topic, and the existing literatures shows that different scholars hold diverging views.

6.3 The Executions of National Urbanization Plan (2014-2020)

To better guide its urbanization, China's National Development and Reform Commission putted forward the "National New Urbanization Plan (2014-2020)" (here in after referred to as "Plan 2014-2020") in March 2014. Upon the writing of this chapter, it is the last year of executing the Plan 2014-2020. China has unfolded a very comprehensive top-down campaign of new urbanization construction. Hence, we review the up-to-date policies and implementations since the release of the Plan and provide a preliminary assessment of Plan 2014-2020.

The strict urban-rural dual household registration system has started to be changed into a residence permit system. However, the implementation of the Plan is also facing many challenges. The most important thing is that the bottom-up factors should be more emphasized and combined with top-down factors in future plan implementations. This is to say, peasant-workers will need to be taken into proper consideration. People-oriented new urbanization should position peasant-workers at the center. Also, China's transformation of new urbanization is comprehensive, complex, dynamic, and long term. It should not be expected that this transformation will be completed during the short six-year planning period.

First, the institutional reform of Hukou system is one of the most concerned institutional factors in China's new urbanization. Since 2014, the central government has issued three documents directly covering the Hukou system: further speeding up the pace of Hukou reform, releasing the interim regulation on residence permits, and a notice on promoting 100 million people without urban Hukou who settled in cities. The first document claims that accelerating the pace of Hukou reform is necessary and imperative to adapting to new urbanization, and calls for relaxing restrictions on access to urban Hukou. On the one hand, the government has tried to help migrant workers who can find stable employment, live in cities, settle in urban areas, and get an urban Hukou. The conditions for getting an urban Hukou were simplified and classified into four types (Table 1). On the other hand, basic public services were expanded to allow access to all residents, whether they have an urban Hukou or not, including migrant workers. The second document focus on the latter, while the third highlights the former.

For example, cities of different scales have generally relaxed restrictions on the transfer of agricultural populations to towns. One kind of measure, the residential permit system, is generally implemented to help the urban resident population enjoy basic public services. In 2015, the number of peasant migrants reached 277.47 million, of whom the amount owning pension, health care, unemployment, and industrial injury insurance was 55.85, 51.66, 42.19, and 74.89 million, respectively.

Table 6-1 The conditions for getting an urban Hukou

Urban type (Urban scale)	Conditions to settle
Small (<50)	Have a legal and stable residence in an urban district, or resident town of a county government, or other designated town
Medium (50–100)	Have legal and stable employment as well as a residence in a city, together with participation in urban social insurance for a certain number of years, which is no more than three years according to the national regulation
Large (100–500)	Have legal and stable employment for a certain number of years as well as a legal and stable residence in a city, together with participation in urban social insurance for a certain number of years, which is no more than five years according to the national regulation
Mega city (>500)	Having legal and stable employment as well as a residence, participation in urban social insurance and years of continuous residence as main indexes, establishing and perfecting points system for household registration according to the overall carrying capacities of cities and needs of economic and social development and indicates that cultivating and developing the housing rental market is an important part of housing system reform; it is also a path to achieving the objective of everyone having housing (owned or rented)

Source: http://www.gov.cn/zhengce/2015-12/14/content_5023611.htm.

Second, new districts, which are given special economic and developmental support by the government, are not a new phenomenon. The first new national-level district was Shanghai Pudong New District, which was founded in 1992 and became a benchmark of regional economic growth. The pace approved by China's central government has accelerated dramatically since 2014. Between 1992 and 2013, there were only six new districts at the national level. However, China has approved 12 new national-level districts since 2014. Five were approved in 2014, including Xixian, Guian Guizhou, the West Coast of Qingdao, Jinpu of Dalian, and Tianfu of Sichuan. Five were approved in 2015, including Xiangjiang, Jiangbei of Nanjing, Fuzhou, Dianzhong, and Haerbin. Two had been approved at the end of November 2016, including Changchun and Ganjiang. According to the incomplete statistics, there are at least nine cities seeking the title of new national-level district, including Changjiang of Wuhan, Changjiu of Jiangxi, Zhengding of Shijiazhuang, Wuxiang of Nanning, Binhu of Hefei, Cuiheng of Zhongshan, Shen Fu of Shenyang, Yellow River of Jinan, and Dongjin of Xiangyang. In addition, there are thousands of new local-level districts emerging in almost every city. There are even media reports that "over 3500 new districts have been built in cities, with plans to house a total population of around

3.4 billion". Furthermore, two documents about housing construction were issued. A three-year action program for the reconstruction of urban shantytowns, dangerous houses in rural areas, and supporting infrastructure was formulated. The target is, between 2015 and 2017, rebuilding shantytown houses (18 million) and dangerous houses (10.6 million) in rural areas. The other document focuses on the rental housing market, and indicates that cultivating and developing the housing rental market is an important part of housing system reform; it is also a path to achieving the objective of everyone having housing (owned or rented).

Third, the major driving force for urbanization and rural-to-urban migration is employment in non-agricultural industries. Therefore, industry development and industry-city integration are regarded as important factors. The Chinese government issued four documents, focusing on three aspects. (1) Plot areas for industry-city integration were founded (about 60 nationwide). The government attempted to switch industrial parks from a single function to a comprehensive type: this involved the development of industries, complete urban services, and clear area boundaries. (2) Migrant workers are encouraged to go back home, supported in undertaking business in urban or rural areas. This work had been carried out in two batches. At present, China has agreed to carry out pilot projects for returning migrant workers and other personnel to start their own businesses in combination with the new urbanization in 116 counties (cities and districts). These pilot projects cover 27 provinces (municipalities and autonomous regions) in China. (3) One of the documents issued by the State Council stresses the integration of the first, second, and third industries in rural areas while promoting integrated new urbanization and urban-rural development.

Fourth, the institutional supports of new urbanization are also very comprehensive. It contains three main aspects: the establishment of the Joint Committee of 15 ministries, the preparation of sub-national planning, and experimental zones.

(1) Joint Committee of 15 Ministries

China's central government established an inter-ministerial Joint Committee to promote new urbanization on July 7, 2014. The Joint Committee has three main responsibilities: (1) promoting plan implementation and policy execution; coordinating major issues; proposing annual work arrangements; dividing up tasks; and ensuring the realization of the development goals of new urbanization under the leadership of the State Council. (2) Strengthening consultation and information sharing; research; promoting the key tasks in population management, land management, taxation, and financial reform; and so on. (3) Undertaking the functions of supervision, inspection, tracking assessment, summary, and reporting to the State Council. There are 15 ministries on the committee: the National Development and Reform Commission, State Commission Office for Public Sector Reform, the Ministry of Education, the Ministry of Public Security, the Ministry of Civil Affairs, the Ministry of Finance, the Ministry of Human Resources and Social Security, the Ministry of Land and Resources, the Ministry of Environmental Protection, the Ministry of Housing and Urban Construction, the Ministry of Transport, the Ministry of Agriculture, National Health and Family Planning Commission, the People's Bank of China, and the State Statistical Bureau. The National Development and Reform Commission is taking a lead role.

(2) Sub-national Planning

After the issuance issue of the Plan, a conference on promoting the construction of new urbanization and experimental zones was held on September 16, 2014. Premier Li Keqiang stressed that "New urbanization is of great importance in the overall situation of China's modernization. The word "new" is the highlight of the Plan, and "people-oriented urbanization" is the core of the Plan. Solving the "three-100-million" was a breakthrough point. This involved bringing migrant workers into the scope of urban housing and social security to facilitate 100 million peasant workers settling down in cities; improving the construction of public ancillary facilities to renovate shantytown housing for 100 million people; and favoring the central and western regions to guide the mode of proximate urbanization for 100 million people near their hometowns. A document entitled "Several opinions about deepening new urbanization construction" was issued by the central government on February 2, 2016. China's new urbanization is one of the biggest potential factors in domestic demand. It is an important engine of economic growth, as well as a huge project for people's lives.

Moreover, the provincial governments are responding actively and rapidly compiling new plans to promote the transformation development of new urbanization in the scope of provincial regions. Except for three coastal municipalities, all provincial governments have finished their plans. As a very big country, significant regional differences are present in China: different regions present their own distinct restrictive factors along the road of new urbanization. These plans combined with actual local situations, guide the development mode's transfer to new urbanization.

Additionally, urban agglomeration planning has also been carried out by the national and local governments. Since 2014, 6 urban agglomerations have drawn up blueprints for national-level plans: "Beijing-Tianjin-Hebei Urban Agglomeration" "Yangtze River Delta Urban Agglomeration" "Pearl River Delta Urban Agglomeration" "Middle Yangtze River Urban Agglomeration" "Harbin-Changchun Urban Agglomeration" and "Chengdu-Chongqing Urban Agglomeration".

(3) Experimental Zones

The National Development and Reform Commission has announced three batches of experimental zone based on the various modes of new urbanization in different regions, of different types, and at different scales. The total numbers of experimental zones, including provinces, cities, and towns, are 62, 59, and 111, respectively, in the two batches (232 in all). By setting experimental zones, China is attempting to break the previous uniform design of the urbanization path from top to bottom, and to fully use market mechanisms in resource allocation. Experimental zones were constructed jointly by the central government and local governments, in which the latter played the more important role. Local governments, awarded with the preferential right of the initiative and creativity, tried valiantly to explore the innovation model of new urbanization. Since 2014, the reform work has been in full swing, and in the midterm, 2017, the experimental zones are supposed to propose reasonable and applicable experience on the work of new urbanization, and gradually to 2020, those experiences will expand across the whole country. The reform involves multi-dimensional works such as cost sharing for population urbanization, diverse financial support, a public administration system, and so on. The experimental zones in total cover 103.83 km^2, occupy 10.82% of the land area, and contain 232.83 million people, which is 17.08% of the permanent national population.

6.4 Achievements and Challenges of New Urbanization

6.4.1 Achievements of New Urbanization

In recent years, in response to the strategic disposition and new urbanization plan announced by the Party Central Committee and the State Council, various regions and relevant departments have devoted much effort to actively carrying out measures and policies. Up to now, the new urbanization process has shown obvious progress and been promoted vigorously.

First, the experimental zones of new urbanization have been continuously promoted and have already achieved some regional modes and experiences. The new urbanization pilot areas paved the way for some initial results. The National Development and Reform Commission and 11 ministries and departments jointly implemented 3 batches of new urbanization pilot areas, covering 2 provinces and more than 200 cities and towns. All pilot areas carried out the construction of new urbanization in three aspects. Firstly, they compiled implementation plans and assigned tasks to subordinate departments. Secondly, they improved the leadership system, which is generally led by party and government leaders from pilot areas, with the comrades of primary departments of municipal government acting as members. Thirdly, they established specialized offices; the leading group offices for pilot areas are mainly located in government offices or development and reform departments, with others in the housing construction sector. The pilot areas have created a number of local modes and experiences for the development of new urbanization, such as relaxing the conditions for settlement, improving the value of residence permits, improving the investment and financing mechanism for urbanization, promoting the links of urban and rural construction land use, and redeveloping urban low efficiency land.

Second, Urbanization in Central and Western China is faster, with a balanced trend in the urbanization level in four regions In 2005, the urbanization rates of Central and Western China were 36.54% and 34.52%, respectively, which soared to 49.79% and 47.37%, respectively, in 2014.

In addition, the Belt and Road initiative provided the chance to develop Central and Western China. For the western part, the State Council has approved Dongxing, Ruili, and Manzhouli as vital developments and opened up pilot areas, pushing for reformation of the mechanism and system, cooperation on foreign economy and trade, the construction of infrastructure, and the development of industries with unique advantages. As for the central part, taking advantage of two vital urban agglomerations, the capital cities of the six provinces can be built into inland economic highlands.

In another aspect, there are 16 new national districts with preferential policies nationwide, of which are located in Central and Western China, reflecting the importance of these areas' development. Since the reform and opening-up of China, national construction has emphasized the Eastern coastal region; however, in recent years, the nation has focused on the equal development of the whole country and has given more privileges to any regions lagging behind, which definitely enhanced the development of Central and Western China.

6.4.2 Challenges of New Urbanization

First, Many unique Chinese phenomena indicate that people-oriented urbanization has not been completely implemented: the difficulty peasant workers have with entering cities; the annual Spring Festival transportation problem; exorbitant housing prices; and the neglect of old people, women, and children. Once the migrant workers are old or find it hard to find a suitable job in a city, they will return to rural areas and use the land as much as possible to feed themselves. The government needs to respect this right of farmers, allowing the retreat of migrant workers who cannot afford to stay in a city. Currently, the promotion of new urbanization is still in a government-centered, top-down form. As the main focus of people-oriented urbanization, migrant workers do not play a full role.

Second, given that land urbanization was the key to the previous orbit, land centered urbanization has posed many adverse impacts, such as the loss of arable land, the phenomenon of "ghost cities," and the urban heat island effect. The core of new-type urbanization is the change from a land-centered to people-oriented stance. However, land urbanization is still developing rapidly. Moreover, in the new period, land urbanization has introduced many new factors. These new factors increase the rash risks of land urbanization, especially the government-led financing and guarantee risks. These plans including new towns and districts, urban agglomeration planning, and characteristic town planning, which often open up new areas based on the original urban areas to implement new development activities and build infrastructure. This greatly reduces the accessibility and publicity of the cities and wastes capital and scarce resources. Some city governments vigorously carry out land urbanization on the grounds of new urbanization; this aggressive situation needs to be further curbed. More recently, bottom-up forces have increased dramatically, such as the appearance of the middle class and the increasing autonomy of local governments. The focus of government efforts should incrementally shift from land urbanization to the efficient utilization of developed land.

Last but not least, the Chinese economy has entered a new moderate-speed growth stage, and industrial transformation and upgrading have created greater pressure. In recent years, China's GDP growth has slowed significantly, showing a downward trend. Since the reform and opening up, China's GDP had always maintained a 2-digit growth rate, but recently it has dropped to 1 digit; GDP growth in 2015 was only 6.9%. The downward trend in China's macro-economic growth is obvious. China's economy has entered a period of adjusting to the new normal. In the future, the economy will gradually transform from high-speed growth into medium-speed growth. The development mode will transform from the single pursuit of economic growth to the coordinated pursuit of economic, social, and ecological development. The type areas of the new normal economy have obvious geographical clustering characteristics. Coastal areas will enter the stage of structural upgrading; low-speed economic growth will be a long-term characteristic. Northeast China, facing the risk of an integrity recession, will enter a deep adjustment period where its economic structure and system reform will change. Shanxi, Hebei, and other provinces with a large chemical industry need more time to output surplus productivity. Although the central and western regions have growth potential, the downwards economic trend will not change. With the continuous improvement of China's economy, the slowdown in economic growth is in accordance with the objective laws of international economic development. Compared with most countries in the world, China is a special country with a large population and powerful economy. It is remarkable that China can maintain an average growth rate above 5%. In addition, the spatial transference of global manufacturing is an objective law. With the increase in China's labor costs, land costs, and other costs, there have been quite a few manufacturing transfers to Southeast Asian countries. Economic growth and industrial development are important driving forces of urbanization. Therefore, how to use China's new-type urbanization to promote its healthy development is a longer-term proposition. Certainly, by seizing the strategic opportunity of new-type urbanization and exploiting the potentialities of innovation-driven development, market consumption, new industries, and infrastructure investment, China still has the power to maintain steady growth under the new normal economy.

Chapter 7

Rural Vitalization and Poverty Alleviation

7.1 Introduction

China is still largely an agricultural state, with the largest number of rural populations in the world. At the year of 2017, totally 770 million people were considered as labor force, in which around 350 million came from rural areas. The prosperity of rural areas is an important part of the prosperity of China as farmers are important components of Chinese population, an important source of the country's labor force. A great many of them moved to cities. The Central Economic Working Conference in 2017 stated that poverty alleviation is one of the three tough battles in the following years. The 19th National congress of the CPC has put forward "Rural Vitalization" as one of the fundamental policies in the next five-year plan. In 2018, according to the "CPC Central Committee and the State Council's comment on the implementation of rural vitalization strategies", the current objective is to accelerate the transformation from a large agricultural country to a strong agricultural country, whereas the specific task is to strengthen the basis of agricultural productivity and to construct the ecosystem to promote the integration of various sectors (agriculture, industry and services).

The world hails the great achievement of development of Chinese rural areas. The income per capita of a rural person has been increasing rapidly. The expected disposable income of a rural population has reached 13,432 yuan, equivalent to 1,918 dollars, out of which 10,995 yuan is consumed by an average rural population. The number reached around 3,500 dollars in Zhejiang province. The growth speed of disposable income has been greater than an urban population since many years ago. A standard rural family is now equipped with a refrigerator, a television, a personal computer and Internet. Almost everyone owns a mobile phone. Many families own cars or tractors. However, Average income is still low compared with the world average.

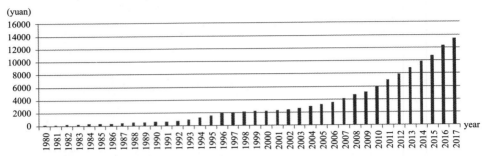

Figure7-1 Expected disposable income per capita in rural China

Source: National Bureav of Statistics of China (http://www.stats.gov.cn).

China used to be the country with the greatest number of poor populations in the world. Now China is ranked after Nigeria and India. Most poor people live in the remote, hilly regions or deserts, especially in west China. According to the newest poverty line, there are 485 state poverty countiesin China. The government encourages investment in state poverty counties. By the end of 2019, State-owned enterprises in Beijing totally invested 22.9 billion yuan in over 200 projects. The population living in poverty is 82.5 million in 2013, 55.7 million in 2015 and 30.4 million in 2017, which is roughly 2.5% of total population. By July 2007, China has built 62898 HOPE primary schools. The illiteracy rate in China is 5.28%, lower in the eastern provinces and higher in the west provinces. From 2001 to 2011, the percentage of university students coming from rural areas increased from 48% to 61%.

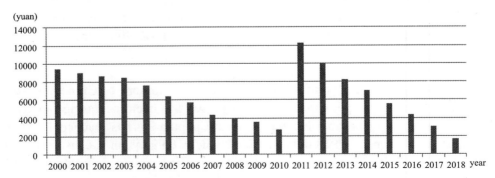

Figure7-2 Rural Population living in Poverty in China

Source: National Bureav of Statistics of China (http://www.stats.gov.cn).

During the same period, the poverty line is renewed each year, according to the price index and the households' income. In 2011, Chinese government raised sharply the poverty line, from 1,274 yuan per year to 2,300 yuan per year. As the result, population living in poverty increased from 26 million to 122 million. In 2018, poor population is around 16.6 million.

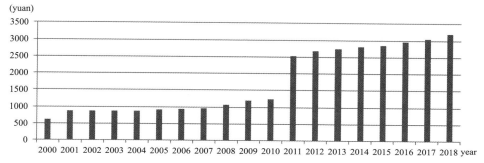

Figure7-3 Rural Population living in Poverty in China

Source: National Bureav of Statistics of China (http://www.stats.gov.cn).

The world pays attention to the ongoing urbanization in China. The World Bank forecasts that China's urbanization rate will reach 66% by the end of 2030. By the end of 2017, its rural population was 577 million, around 41.48% of the total population. The percentage of rural population fell from 46.27% in 2013 to 42.65% in 2016. A very important question facing farmers and the governments is the role of rural areas. This widening imbalance between urban areas and rural areas leads to a natural question of how are economies of rural areas able to sustain such growth with continuous loss of population.

7.2 History of Poverty Alleviation

7.2.1 Early Exploration on Poverty Alleviation from 1921 to 1949

In the old land tenure system, land is owned by lords and rented to tenants (farmers). Since the outbreak of opium war in 1840, China had been deeply involved in various wars and gradually became a semi-colonial and semi-feudal society. As the result of social unrests, heavy taxation and poor public services, many peasants lost their land and lived in miserable conditions. Meanwhile, considerable amount of resources fell in the hands of the bureaucrats and some oligarchs. The economic state of farmers was continuous worsening. Marx and Engels pointed out that the movement of the proletariat belongs to the majority and fight for the interest of the majority. With the vast majority of the population being farmers, many reformers agreed that China's problem was essentially the problem of peasants.

Elimination of poverty and collective prosperity has been an everlasting goal of the Chinese communist party. In 1922, the CCP proposed to confiscate the properties of warlords and some bureaucrats and redistributed them to poor farmers. By 1949, around 166 million farmers in liberated areas were involved in the reform.

7.2.2 Social Reforms from 1949 to 1978

Since the founding of the People's Republic of China, the party led land reform in which around 700 million mu（a mu is approximate to 0.66 hectare.）of farmland are assigned to 300 million farmers. The old feudal ownership of land is abolished. The new system returns land to farmers and waiver their tenants. The new system also aims to eradicate poverty caused by the social inequity and thus is able to release more productivity and pave ways for industrialization. Rural communes were founded. Farmers formed cooperatives, shared land, tools and the final outputs. By the end of 1952, land reform had been largely implemented. By the year 1956, 540 thousand rural communes have been founded and with 87.8% of farmers being members. From 1949 to 1952, crops were sold at the market price or "centralized prices" prescribed by the government. From 1953, market prices were replaced with centralized prices. However due to limitations in agricultural technology, by the end of 1978 around 250 million farmers (or 30%) still lived in poverty.

7.2.3 Policy Transitions from 1978 to 1985

As a cornerstone of the reform and opening up policy, the Household Contract Responsibility System (HCRS) was first tested in several communes, and then spread to the entire country. The Xiaogang village of Fengyang county is the first village to introduce the new mechanism. The HCRS has several features which sets it apart from the cooperative system and private ownership. Sticking to the collective ownership of land, households make their own decisions about what to grow and how to grow, and keep a large part of output. The HCRS greatly solves the incentive problem of farmers. In what follows, the central government drastically raised the wholesale price to purchase crops from farmers. The central government then encouraged circulation of production factors, including reforms of agriculture markets, encouraging rural labor forces to work in urban areas. Thanks to many great efforts, population living in poverty deceases from 250 million in 1978, to 125 million in 1985. The poverty rate fell from 33.7% to 14.8%.

7.2.4 Helping Poverty-stricken Counties from 1986 to 1993

A series of policy reforms facilitate economic growth in most areas. However, some regions with better economic basis grew faster than many other regions. Poverty is stratified within each province, with most poor population living in mountainous areas, desert areas, the loess plateau and areas with endemic diseases. In 1986, the agricultural output accidentally fell, calling for deeper reform. In the same year, 331 counties were assigned as "key poverty-stricken counties" by the Chinese government. This number reached 592 in 1987. Population living in poverty decreased from 125 million to 70 million, with the percentage falling from 14.8% to 7.7%.

7.2.5 Plan of Assistance to Impoverishment 1994 to 2000

The state council resolved to in 7 years pull the remaining 80 million population out of poverty, to narrow the income gap between western provinces and eastern provinces and eliminating illiteracy. By the year 2000, population living in poverty was reduced to 32 million, less than 3% of the total population. By then, 95.5% of overall administrative villages have installed electricity devices, 67.7% of them have installed telephones. The plan was proved to greatly improve living conditions of rural household.

7.2.6 Village Reconstruction 2001-2012

Early in 2001, the government published "the outline of elimination of poverty in China 2001-2010". The government has chosen 150 thousand poor villages from the 592 counties. The primary goal is to integrate useful resources to solve food and clothing problems, to set up long-term mechanisms for sustainable development of poor villages, and to strengthen the capability of endogenous economic growth of these villages. In 2011, China has raised the poverty line to 2,300 Yuan (using the 2010 prices). Under the new standard, the number of poor populations reached 165 million. By the end of 2012, 98.8% of villages in the "key poverty-stricken counties" have been able to use electricity. 93.2% of them have installed telephones. Youth literacy rate (between 7 and 15 years old) was 97%.

In 1996, China's arable land was 1.95 billion Mus. The 3rd version of "Outline of National General Planning for Land Use (2006-2020)" has stipulated that the arable land minimum is around 1.8 billion Mus. This law aims at balancing economic growth and the problem of food shortage. The "Measures for punishment of acts in violation of land management regulations" stipulates that if illegal occupation of arable land reaches 15% of overall occupation of arable land for construction usage, then the primary leaders of the local government who is responsible for this act, will receive warnings or punishment.

7.3 A New Stage since 2012

China has population of 1.3 billion, which makes it the largest food producer and consumer in the world. According to data from State Statistical Bureau, the rural population living in poverty is around 99 million using 2010 prices under new criteria. Most poor people live in remote areas, with the lack of natural resources, and areas inhabited by ethnic minorities. Their expected annual income is 4,732 Yuan, around 60% of the rural average. Behind these numbers are success stories with new phenomena and challenges intertwining each other.

7.3.1 The Status Quo

Rucheng county lies in the southeast of Hunan province, close to the border of three provinces (Hunan, Jiangxi and Guangdong province). The county has no railway and no highway. Most of its land is in remote mountainous areas covered by forest. Because of the continuous mountains, it is very expensive to build rural roads reaching each village. Also, providing clean water is a hard issue for the local government. As the result of the stagnant development, school children from mountainous villages used to spend 2-3 hours walking to the school. Dropping out of school is not a rare scene. As a result of the economic underdevelopment, young people move and work in larger cities, leaving land to their parents and friends.

Daliangzhou is a prefecture-level city in Sichuan province, famous for its "rugged mountainous beauty" and low temperatures throughout the year. Many Yi people, (Yi is an ethnic group) lives isolated lives in this region, to escape from wars. 11 out of 17 counties are key poverty-stricken counties. 1618 villages are poverty-stricken, 166 out of which are extremely poor. Many rural young people do not speak Chinese mandarin or even illiterate. Birth is out of control in some areas, especially in poor families. Drugs are rampant. In 2016, media reported "villages on the cliffs" in Zhaojue County, Daliangzhou city. One village lies on the cliff, 800 meters from the ground. For villages to leave the village, they resort to 218 interlinking ladders fabricated by vinesfalling from the cliffs to the grounds. Nobody understood why 72 households choose this habitat. In Daliangzhou, there are 85 such villages. Over 1600 villages lie in areas with stony desertification. In 2016, Fiber-optical devices are installed some cliff-villages. Villagers were by then able to watch high-definition TVs and use 4G networks.

Lintao is a county in Dingxi city, Gansu province. Because of being landlocked and high altitude, the climate in Lintao has been characterized by cold winter and little precipitation, making most of its land not arable. Farmers in Lintao used to grow wheat, corn and potatoes but were not able to feed themselves. Some farmers attempted to grow Lily, a plant used in home decoration and gardening, and succeeded. Soon similar practices were promoted to the entire county. Farmers cooperate with Pingan group, who has been assisting them in building a platform for farmers to sell Lily.

7.3.2 Separating Rural Land Ownership Right, Contract Right and Management Right

The Chinese reform started in rural areas, the reform in rural areas started with "Household Contract Responsibility System". Any new policy must follow the guideline "Practice is the sole criterion of truth". It must also be insisted that land circulation follows farmers' willingness, guarantee safety and increase farmers' income. The HCRS and "Centralized-Decentralized System" are two cornerstones of rural policies and were written in *The Law of the People's Republic of China on Land Contract in Rural Areas* in 2002. According to *The Land Administration Law*, land in urban areas is under state ownership. Except expressively written in laws, land in suburbs rural areas is under collective ownership. The contracting right grants the person the right of having contracts with land. The right of land management grants the contractor the right to occupy and use the land, and the right of making profit and receiving punishment generating from the land he has contracts with.

The new system clarifies the relationship among land ownership right, contracting right and land management right. The three rights are protected by laws. By the end of 2015, land circulation with transfers of management right has reached 443 million mu, 33.3% of total land under HCRS. Data from ministry of agriculture shows that by the end of June 2016, over 70 million farmers are involved in land circulation. Many lease their land to family farms, high-tech firms. Separating of three rights is an important institutional innovation after the HCRS.

7.3.3 Deepening Rural Land Reforms

The second round of land contracting started from 1993 and finished in around 1999. According to 30 years of lease term, most contracts will end between 2023 and 2029. The new contract involves agricultural land of 1.5 billion mu and around 200 million farmers. The State Council has made it clear in a document that the farmers' contracting right is protected by the law and the lease can be protracted for another 30 years. New contracts provide policy foundation for rural vitalization and agriculture modernization.

The new **land shareholding cooperative system** is based on collective ownership and members' management rights. The new system will allow the division of land management rights into shares owned by individuals or collectives. These shares can be traded for money or shares in third-party firms. The system allows a new form for land circulation. Prominent examples are Nanhai, Wenling, Suzhou and Shanghai. Some tests were made in Fengxian district of Shanghai in 2018. Past tests showed several key parts: proper configuration of shares according to land areas; Proper procedures for collective decision making; founding members' congress, board of directors and board of supervisors; a commensurate financial system for management and supervision

7.3.4 Amelioration of Agriculture Protection System

For many years, the Chinese government purchases agricultural products from farmers under "centralized" prices and sell them in many domestic markets. Starting from 1980s, the government gradually allowed flowing prices. In 2004, the State council lifted many restrictions on agricultural markets. Almost at the same time, the government sets up "minimum purchase price" policy (initially for rice and wheat), giving farmers an alternative choice. During financial crisis in 2008, international prices of maize and soybean plunged. As a result of the plunging prices, similar practices (temporary purchase and storage policies) were implemented for maize.

New issues continued to emerge. From 2008 to 2014, Chinese agricultural products are gradually losing price advantages compared with their foreign counterparts. With foreign products entering the Chinese market, the government-set minimum prices are constantly greater than international prices and are even increasing by year. From 2008 to 2014, the minimum prices for maize in Inner Mongolia and Liaoning have increased 48.68%, with the 2014 price 60% greater than international average. Soaring prices drastically add inventory cost to the government and production cost to some downstream industries, resulting in lasting high stockpiles and many firms quitting the market.

In 2014, temporary purchase and storage policies were no longer in use. In some target regions, the new "target price" system was first tested on cottons and soybeans. The same practice was implemented on maize in 2016. The new system is different from the old system in several aspects: the government no longer maintains the minimum prices and let all trades follow the market price. Besides, a target price is set in some target regions. When prices fall below the target price, certain subsidies will be given according to the price difference, land area, total output and sales.

The target prices will be renewed year by year right before dissemination takes place. With little intervention from the government's part, farmers take their own risks. Investigations show that the impacts of the new practice vary. Small-scale household outside target regions tended to give up and switch to new species. Large-scale household tend to enlarge the growing. The world also worries about food supply in China, who has population of 1.3 billion. The enormous size implies that the world is not able insure China's risk of food shortage. Some scholars have concern about how the new system can guarantee the food provision under turbulent prices. Stabilizing prices is still an import goal.

Table 7-1 Policy Transitions of China's Rural Industries

Year	Main Motivation	Content
1980-1984	De-collectivization and promoting agricultural commercialization	Approve Household Contract Responsibility System. Design circulation mechanism for agricultural products
1985-1992	Deepening commercialization and marketization reform on AGRO goods	Moving from centralized prices to market prices of agricultural products. Propose structure adjustment of agricultural sectors
1992-2007	Promote Agriculture Marketization	Support leading agricultural firms
2007-2017	Develop Modern Agriculture	Promote land circulation. Construct demonstrative zones of agricultural industries
2017-2018	Rural Industry Vitalization	Implement quality-first strategy to revitalize agriculture. Promote connection of small household and modern agriculture

7.3.5 Agricultural Subsidization

Some scholars believe that the main challenge China faces is no longer shortage of food, but structural changes. Improper target prices bias farmers' choices about what to grow. Besides insisting on marketization of agricultural products, further amelioration requires subsidies in more general senses. **Green box policies** usually refer to subsidies on the usage of agricultural technologies, hydraulics, building bridges or roads. Green box policies do not directly affect market prices. **Yellow box policies** usually refer to subsidies on seeds, chemical fertilizer, marketing loans and fallow, etc. In various regions, farmers can receive 30% off the payment of agricultural machinery, such a tractor.

Since 2004, Chinese farmers started to receive three types of subsidies. First, a subsidy to improved crop species refers to the subsidy if farmers select seeds of better strains to grow. Better seeds often come at higher prices. According to documents released by Linxia government, for each breeding sheep from a superior species in **Linxia city**, Gansu province, the herdsman is able to receive 800 yuan. Second, a direct subsidy on production refers subsidy on growing crops. As long as the land is not let uncultivated, the farmer can receive such subsidy. In Hunan province, a farmer is able to receive 105-175 yuan for each Mu of land depending on the type of crops and total land areas. Third, agricultural general subsidies refer to subsidies on seeds, chemical fertilizers, agricultural machinery and many other items. In Liaoning province, price-based insurances are offered to farmers to insure them from any price fall. The government covers around 50%-75% of total insurance fees, which is another type of subsidies. All these subsidies aim to promote agricultural products, increase agricultural productivity and income of farmers.

The marginal performance of the three subsidies drops year by year. Lately, many subsidies deteriorated into pure income transfer. In 2016, the Ministry of Agriculture and the Ministry of Finance Agricultural subsidization decreed that the three types of subsidies are merged into "agricultural support & protection subsidy". New measures promotes greener, more ecological use of land such as organic fertilizer, discourages chemical fertilizer and the burning of straws. New measures also encourage large-scale farming, and call for a more mature financial system to support modern farmers.

7.3.6 Supply and Marketing Cooperatives

Supply and marketing cooperatives (and cooperatives after) were founded in the 1950s serving as platforms providing people in rural areas with goods, services and information about agricultural products and policies. As the name "platform" suggests, farmers could sell agricultural products to the cooperatives. In 1954, its first congress was held in Beijing. In 1959, the state council advised that besides procurement services, cooperatives should be multifunctional: organize meetings and actively guide trades in the market, lead communication between urban and rural areas and promote the growth of rural economy. During the 1960s and 1970s, due to resource shortage and rationing, cooperatives served as a bridge linking rural areas and urban areas, many helping farmers to purchase rare items even from distant regions.

A movie shot in 1965 named "Red Backpack". The protagonist Yanxiang Wang is the person in charge of cooperatives. Farmers lived deep inside the mountains. In 1958, for farmers' convenience, Wang decided to let his colleagues travel and dispatch the goods in turn. At the end, Wang received word of mouth.

Following the economic development, farmers have greater demand for goods than before. In Document No. 1of 1983, the government proposed to recover the commercial nature of cooperatives. A report of the Ministry of Commerce in 1992 stated that the goal of cooperatives is to promote economic growth in rural areas, guided by the market and led by high-technology. Nowadays more and more young people move to work in cities. With more means of purchasing goods and transportation, farmers more often resort to large department stores in the city or online platforms. Many believe that cooperatives are falling.

In April 2014, the state council chose Hebei, Zhejiang, Shandong and Guangdong province as locations for experiments. From 2014 to 2016, many new cooperatives are founded. The main tasks of new cooperatives are: offering consumption goods to farmers; upgrading marketing network to farmers; offering consulting services helping leading agricultural firms to grow; assisting in the formation of industry chains. Later reforms in Xinjiang proved to be successful: around 4,000 cooperatives were operating in 2017. Following steady reforms, total revenue reached 65 billion Yuan, 15% larger than the number 2016; realized profit was 984 million, with a growth rate of 19.2%. By the end of 2017, total 300 thousand offices are operating, greatly facilitating lives in rural areas.

7.3.7 Residence Land and Operational Construction Land

Rural residence landrefers to land used by rural households to build residence, which is different residential land in urban areas. Since the founding of PRC, its regulations have undergone several transitions. *The Law of Land Reform* that passed in 1950 decreed that ownership of rural residence land belongs to farmers. Lately the other document stipulated that agricultural land, heavy agricultural tools and draft animals belongs to the collective. Later in1962, the system of people's commune was implemented in rural areas, and the ownership of rural residence land was then assigned to production teams, with the right of usage assigned to farmers. Construction of new residence on arable land is not permitted.

The new constitution in 1982 stipulated that the ownership belongs to the collective. Later in 1984, another law stipulated that trades on the right of usage must undergo official procedures. Laws limit the use of rural residence land by urban residents. If the person is from urban areas and has the right of usage, he has no right to reconstruct or refurbish existing houses without following some procedures. Later in 1988 *The Law of Land Management* stipulated that residents from urban areas must have permits from the county government to be authorized to construct residences in rural residence land.

The Law of Land Management was then revised in 1998, and in 2004. The newer law no longer allowed application of rural usage right (of rural resident land) by urban applicants. From 1999, urban residents are not allowed to purchase houses in rural residence land (namely, the right of usage). Laws decree "one household and one house", "free allocation", "legal fixed area" and "no circulation", leading to wasting of land. On one hand, lots of young people move to cities and leave the residence empty and land unused during these years. On the other hand, many rural residents are in need of larger houses which they are unable to afford.

In order to fix this missing market, the upcoming law in 2020 permits and even encourages voluntary exits of those moving to live in cities. Exits are compensated by cash, normally at the price of 30-50 thousand per mu. After exits, the collective can redistribute the land to whomever in need of the land. Baishan is a village in Changping districtof Beijing. Within several months in 2017, 882 households have signed contracts agreeing to return their residence land to the collectives. Various issues arose while handling exits, such as illegal land occupation, obscure ownership.

Rural construction operational land refers to land used by rural enterprises or other operational units and owned by the collectives. While plenty of rural land is in the hands of collectives, little land is left for local governments for economic growth. Expropriation cost is too high for the government, who pass it to firms and consumers. An attempt was made in 2015 to authorize 33 districts in China to trade or lease rural construction land. The new policy applies only to operational construction land, not land for residence. The purpose is to lessen wasted rural land, making land use more efficient. 33 districts include Daxing, Nanhai, Yucheng etc.. By the end of 2018, over 10 thousand sites have been traded, with market value around 25.7 billion yuan.

Reforms try to break down the rural-urban dual system, the major cause of unbalance in development. With more and more land supplied to the market, the primary economic impact is that prices of industrial land falls, lowering down firms' fixed cost. The second impact is that, with more land leased to firms, farmers become wealthier than ever. Reforms reduce income inequity, enhance economic efficiency and promote innovation.

7.4 Land Circulation

7.4.1 Household Contract Responsibility System

On November 24th, 1978, eighteen farmers gathered in the cottage of Lihua Yan, lying in Xiaogang village, Fengli commune of Fengyang County. A private meeting was held to discuss about the future of the village. The consequence was a signed decision letter, agreeing to redistribute collective arable land to each household. In 1978, starvation was an issue for around 200 million poor people. Nobody would agree with the boldness of these folks, which turned out to be the outset of a new era. Later in 1979, yearly yield of Xiaogang village was 66 tons, sum of total yield from 1966 to 1970. People who first did not agree or even criticize their behavior gradually accepted that this responsibility system is different from private ownership. From 1980 to 1984, the average annual growth of agricultural production increased 12.3% by year in Shaanxi province. In 1984, crops yields of Shannxi province hit a record high of 10.2 billion kilograms. Total domestic agricultural yield in China has increased by 42.23% from 1978 to 1984. The gallant tale of Xiaogang farmers stayed in everyone's memory. Household contract responsibility system is a great innovation by Chinese farmers.

During an important talk in 1980, Deng publicly agreed with the behavior of Xiaogang village. Rural reform was near. Document No.1 of 1982 clearly pointed out that "distribution to each household" is also a form of collective ownership. In the years that followed, China continuously stabilized and refined such system.

The new household contract responsibility system has the following content. The collective acts as the contracted person whereas the household acts as the contractor. According to the contract, the household needs to hand over a fixed amount of crops (ding gou liang) to the collectives, a form of agricultural tax. The advantage of the new system is obvious. Suppose that Wang is a master in chili growing, and is able to increase yields by 2 tons. However, with 10 members sharing the increment, at most Wang is able to obtain 200 kilograms. Therefore, Wang may not want to share his expertise. Under the new system, Wang can voluntarily contract himself with all land suitable to grow chili. The overall increment of chili production may exceed 2 tons.

Household contract responsibility system has two main versions. The first version of the system is "contracting output to household". This version is based on collective ownership of land and sharing of tools. According to the contract, land and tools are assigned to each individual household, as well as tasks. If total yields exceed what has been written in the contract, the surplus will be left to the household. If total yields have not met the contract's requirement, the household has to cover the shortage. The new system solved the incentive problem of households and proved to be very successful to stimulation of economic growth.

The second version is "contracting work to household", an enhanced version of the previous one. Again, the version is based on collective ownership of land and other production factors. Each year, the household hands in fixed amount of yields according to area of land assigned to it. Each household decides on its own what to grow and how to grow. After handing in the fixed amount, the household keeps all remaining yields at its disposal. Many sell them in the market. The main difference of the two versions is that households cannot decide what to grow in "contracting output to household", and can decide on this issue in "contracting work to household". Households are contracted on yields on the first version, and are contracted on rights of management in the second version. "Contracting work to household" endows households with more autonomy.

In coordination with the household contract responsibility system, the state council released a document "several issues in current rural economic policy" in Jan. 1983. This document approved free trade of agricultural products. Farmers could then sell crops in the market, in exchange of whatever in need. In 1985, centralized tradewas finally abolished. New policies helped facilitate rural marketization, and specialization of production. Households now grow whatever they have comparative advantage. From Jan. 1ˢᵗ of 2006, agricultural tax was abolished, aiming at reducing gap between urban areas and rural areas.

7.4.2 Rural Construction Operational Land

For long time, Chinese cities have been expanding. For a large city such as a provincial capital, it is not abnormal to see that its urban area increases by many folds. In many cities, rural areas resemble urban areas in many aspects. Sometimes, it is difficult to tell the difference just from appearance.

However, existing laws prohibit any entity from urban areas to obtain management rights or operating rights of rural land. For rural land to enter the market, its ownership must be transferred to the state. The urban and rural dual system has been seriously slowing down development of rural economy. Changes are being made. The government was testing a new policy in 33 counties allowing rural construction operational land to enter the "urban" market. During the 13th national people's congress in 2019, a committee member said the government may push the reform to the whole country after further revises of the law.

In the revised *The law of Land Management*, in order to authorize outsiders (entities or individuals from another cooperatives or from urban areas) to use such land, the land must be registered under legal procedures, and must secure the accordance of over 2/3 of members of the cooperatives. Once authorized, the "outsider" can transfer the land to another entity or use the land as mortgage. So far, such land has been used for many purposes: industrial production, education and residences.

The "new" land may be used as an alleviation of the rising housing prices. In October 2019, three sites in Daxin, Beijing catch many audiences' attention. All three sites are announced to be used to build sharing ownership housing. Earlier in September, the official website showed that one site (with around 48 thousand square meters) had been traded at 1.51 billion. Experts estimated that around 1000 apartments with sharing ownership will be built, and will enter the market in 2022, with the term of usage to be 70 years, the same as other urban land used for residence. Now it is too early to infer whether such entries help controlling housing prices and whether such experience is replicable.

Some remarkable cases took place long before the new law, but are more limited to large enterprises. Huawei, the technology giant based in Shenzhen, recently moved its terminal headquarters, R&D department and laboratory to a site named Songshanhu in Dongguan. The site has 600 thousand square meters, with 6 blocks and 50 units. Huawei has invested over 10 billion in Songshanhu for its smartphone services. Around 20 thousand researchers works here, providing technology support for over 1000 mobile network operators, generating data over 5000TB each day. Songshanhu is a natural reservoir, inside town of Dalang. Later, the government of Dongguan reintegrates land of the three towns (Dalingshan, Liaobu and Dalang) contiguous to the reservoir, and found a development zone.

For many enterprises, the new policy provides a more convenient channel to move their business to rural areas, a solution to the "urban malaise". Operating cost is much lower than before. Ideas are simple. Before, rural land usage by outside users must undergo two main procedures: transfer from collective ownership to state ownership; transfer of management right and operating rights from the state to other entities. The first step must involve accordance of all members, usually with large compensation. The second step often involves auctions. Entities bid price in order to obtain the land. Both procedures are too costly, for the government and for entities. Worse still, bidders' high bidding prices very often drives the housing price in nearby neighborhood to high levels. High cost is disadvantageous for many high-tech firms, because their business is already very risky. Finally, all cost will be passed to employers and consumers.

The new policy is also beneficial to education. Land is too expensive in cities. For this reason, many new schools are being built on the old sites. Before, the government must "purchase" land from the farmers. A recent example is from Shandong University, who planned to build a new campus in Zhangqiu, Jinan. Till mid-2017, six out of eight villages have agreed with the relocation plan. The new campus will cover an area of 8,000 mu, in which 6,000 mu are teaching zone, and 2000 mu are living zone, equipped with supermarkets, hospitals and cinemas. HKUST planned a new site in Guangzhou. The government of Guangzhou is responsible for provision of land and facilities. Experts estimate that under the new policy, more schools will enter rural areas, attracting more elites and narrowing the gap between urban and rural areas.

7.4.3 Rural Residence Land

Looking around the world history of agricultural development, no matter in ancient times or modern ages; in developed countries or developing countries, the main body of a fundamental unit of agricultural production is a household. At the moment, the government requires strict implementation of the one-household-one-house policy, meaning that each household is guaranteed a house but no more. Upon building a new house, the household must return the old one to the collectives. With one of the following qualifications, the household can apply for new residence land: first, the applicants are newly married couple with no residence land. Second, the applicant is a registered immigrant with no residence land. Third, the applicant is obliged to move to a new region as a result of natural disasters, village or town re-planning or construction of new infrastructures.

Villagers in the following situations cannot apply for new residence land: first the applicant is an adolescent less than 18 years old. Second, the applicant already owns residence land meeting all criteria. Third, the applicant has ever sold or rented a house to other people.

In short, the resident land cannot be inherited, but the residence (namely the house) can. When somebody passed away, the heir can inherit the right to use the residence. If the heirs are members of the collectives, thy still have chance to use the land. If not, they keep the right of using the house or they can sell the house to other members of the collectives. In the former situation, the heir has no right to reconstruct or refurbish the house. When the house falls down or breaks apart due to natural reasons, the residence is returned to the collectives. Even without land ownership, if the land is wanted by the government, the heir is able to receive compensation, even if the heir is from urban areas.

More restrictions are imposed on usage and trade. Residence cannot be built on permanent agricultural land. If some agricultural land must be used for residence, the household must follow conversion procedures according to the law. Urban residents are not allowed to build villas or private houses on rural resident land.

Large-Scale Rent Services in Urban Villages

By June 2019, the total number of immigrants in Guangzhou reached almost 10 million, with around 5 million living in urban villages. Urban villages are villages near urban areas. Land of urban villages belongs to collectives. Except this difference, many urban villages have tall buildings, department stores, schools, libraries and even cinemas. Sometimes, they are very crowded with immigrants. Urban villages in Guangzhou generate garbage of 9,000 tons in a single day. In total, there are 4.8 million apartments for rent, mostly in urban villages. Hygiene is a big issue.

One step is to identify sources of pollution. So far around 50 thousand polluting sites have been identified; many illegal constructions are dismantled; Chebei and Dayuan village are listed as key sites of pollution removal. The other step is dredging. 141 urban villages started the installation of pipelines. So far, 1,300 kilometers of pipelines have been installed. The difference is that new pipelines directly connect each source and the sewage plant. In July 2019, 16 cities were selected as testing sites of residence renting market.

The other issue is that the landlords are often clueless about the actual experience of living in the apartments. In order to improve life quality, and provide convenience to the tenant, Guangzhou encourages professional renting services to enter urban villages and help in improving the environment. These professionals rent apartments from villages, refurbish them and rent it to the tenants. Professionals help screening the tenants, and offer various services, such as cleaning, fire protection and public security.

7.5 Small Households, Big Market

7.5.1 What is Internet +

"Internet plus agriculture" is the combination of modern logistics, big data, e-commerce and agricultural production, which increases agriculture modernization, optimizes resource configuration, removes information asymmetry, and accelerates agricultural production (and modernization). The new concept hast three main components:

(1) Artificial Intelligence

Researchers install cameras and other sensors in the fields to supervise the growth of crops. Sensors generate data and transmit it into computers. Even mobile apps are offered to customers to watch the crops. With data analysis, households are able to learn actual condition of crops and make accurate predictions about yields. Sensors replace human labor force, help make the right diagnosis and lower down production cost.

In the summer of 2017, orchard farmer Lianquan Liu introduces an innovation for his peaches. The innovation is a sorting machine proposed by Zhongxiang Zhou and his three fellows from Beijing University of Technology. The machine sorts peaches according to their shape, size, color and luster. Inside the machine is machine learning algorithms. After learning 6,400 peach photos, the algorithm is able to infer the grade of each peach with degree of accuracy of 90%. The machine is even able to self-learning.

After learning more photos, it becomes cleverer. The set of equipment saves Lianquan Liu 30 thousand yuan each year on hiring workers.

(2) E-Commerce

Households can use on-line platforms (such as Taobao and eBay) to sell agricultural products. So far there are over 30 thousand such shops in platforms. These shops sell machines, fertilizers, agricultural chemicals and seeds. Platforms are aggregators who have many advantages: first, many niche products are only available in on-line platforms. The reason is that niche products are for the niche market with few consumers, and are hence too costly for brick-and-mortar stores to list. Second, concentration of products in on-line platforms leads to more intense competition, reducing prices and increasing welfare. Third, on-line platforms often allow comments of consumers, helping those avoiding defective products.

(3) Cordyceps Sinensis

It is a fungus that grows on larvae of insects. The insect is a species of ghost moths coming from Tibetan Plateau between elevations of 3,000 meter and 5,000 meter. The fungus lives in the larvae, kills it and then a stalk body emerges from the corpse and stand upright. Cordyceps sinensis is traditional Chinese medicine and traditional Tibetan medicine, which is said to increase energy, stimulate the immune system. The province of Qinghai accounts for around 60% of overall production in China. The price of this herb is 38-45 per piece.

In view of its special lifestyles, between April and June each year, farmers harvest the herb. people in Qinghai have long before noticed the amazing effect of Cordyceps sinensis on human bodies. The first issue is that the local market is too small with production level much higher than consumption level. The second issue is that demand is unpredictable, making sellers difficult to know how much to produce. Recently, these herbs start to appear in Taobao and JD. Starting from April, retailers in other provinces reserve herbs on the platform. Then from April, Qinghai farmers know how much to harvest. By May 2017, around 32 thousand pieces have been reserved. According to estimation, total production in 2017 will be around 30 tons, with only 1 ton in stock.

(4) Internet Finance

When banks set a high standard, it is harder for SME (Small Medium

Enterprise) to obtain loads. It is even harder for rural households to obtain loans. A natural question will be that, are banks really setting high standard for these people? As we know, banks make loans only when they are quite certain that the person will pay back the loans. The default risk is calculated from the person's income and cash flow. When rural households do not have any proven cash flow or even a bank card, the bank is unable to calculate the risk. For this reason, they are not able to obtain loans. Data shows that only 25% of rural population is registered in the central credit system, only 18% are evaluated.

One solution is to set up a platform, in which rural households trade on. A credit score can be calculated from the platform's data for each household. Then loans can be made according to scores. This is exactly what Alibaba was doing. Ant financial groupis cooperating with over 2,300 rural financial institutions. On one hand, it provides channels for rural users to purchase products. On the other hand, Ant financial group provide data analysis to financial institutions, who offer loans to households enabling them to consume more than their income. Jiebei is the credit service of Ant financial group, using a complicated algorithm to determine a person's Sesame credit score. If one's score is higher than 600, he can normally borrow money from many sources.

In 2015, JDis launching the JD-Agriculture channel which offers seeds, agricultural chemicals, fertilizers and agricultural tools. In 2016, JD worked with rural agricultural enterprises and found offline service centers, providing funds to local farmers. According to JD's plan, 1,000 such offline shops has been opened in 3 years from 2016 to 2019.

Different from traditional loan services, these "financial institutions" offers everything: loans, marketing and technical support. According to many experts, the reason for this composite service is that agricultural yields still depends a lot on temperatures and precipitation, which is largely uncertain. Agriculture risk is too high for interest to cover.

So far is the supply side. As for the demand side, modern agriculture requires high technology, economy of scale and a complete set of industry chain, all of which requires financing.

7.5.2 Relevant Policies

In the document No.1 of 2015, the government sends a signal to the public that China should strengthen information use in agriculture. In March 2015, in a report, the prime minister mentioned a plan of "Internet+". The "Eight measures of E-commerce" released in 2015 suggested integration of internet and agriculture, and introduction ideology of industry chain, value chain and supply chain. This document proposes "1-village-1-brand", that is, each village pushes a brand to the outside market. Trading agricultural products in on-line platforms is encouraged. The document also suggests that forestry bureau in each county support trading forest products in on-line markets; establish credit system for trading forest products, establish forestry exchange centers. A document named "Comments about accelerating development of rural E-commerce" insist on letting the market guide resource configuration, suggested that rural economy should adapt to the "new normal" economy and proposed actively integration of on-line and off-line markets. It also proposed that by the end of 2020, the government develop a few counties who excel in "E-commerce", for other counties to follow.

7.5.3 Prominent Cases: Three Squirrels

Liaoyuan Zhang is CEO of Three Squirrels limited. At a young age, Zhang was fascinated with the movie "Heroes". He did not enter university, and instead at the very early stage, tried many jobs. He sold optical-disc seller, cloth, worked as an electrician and a motor driver. At the age of 36, he opened up his own business of selling nut fruits. In 2012, his firm received investment of 1.2 million dollars from an angel investor. It takes three squirrels only 63 days to grow from daily revenue of zero to 100 thousand. Since the 65th day of its birth, it became the largest seller of nut fruits in TMall.

Three Squirrels cooperate with various suppliers, domestic and oversea. Foreign suppliers come from many countries such as USA, Australia, Kenya and Iran. Domestic suppliers are mainly from Guangdong and Zhejiang for nut fruits and Xinjiang for dried fruits. Ming Wang from Almas vineyard, Turpan, Xinjiang is one of its suppliers. Wang ships hundreds of tons of raisons to three squirrels each year. Almas vineyard possesses over 2000 mu of vineyard. Cooperating with Three Squirrels has two main advantages: first, after fixing the channels, farmers no longer worry about selling the grapes. Second, Three Squirrels follows strictly trade rules and is willing pay higher prices for better quality. The agreed trade price per kilo is two yuan greater than the outside market.

Lower circulation cost is another advantage of Three Squirrels. After packaging, products are usually in circulation segments. Each segment takes away a portion of overall profit, similar to adding a markup to the price. If the cost of producing a pack of nut fruits is 4 yuan, adding up the markups will push the price to 10 yuan. Worse still, the process leads to long sales cycles. Internet direct marketing saves circulation cost and shortens sales cycles. Another marketing strategy used by Three Squirrels is that its salesperson always calls its client "master".

The firm has configured a cloud platform for quality control. Web crawlersgrab data from the internet, most consumers' comments. Using data analysis, web crawlers track the comments and identify their sources. Web crawlers are also able to find out characteristics of each user group. Actually, many enterprises such as Tencent and JD are using similar systems.

As one source of the profit, Three Squirrels spent 30 million yuan to shoot an animation with 104 episodes. The animation is named three squirrels. In the future, the firm plans to build a squirrel town near the Yangtze River. The theme town will receive revenue from tourism, entertainment and shopping.

7.6 Modern Agro Industries

7.6.1 Regulations and Policies

In 2019, a document from the state council named "Suggestions on promotion of rural industry vitalization" lists the following guidelines for industry development in rural areas.

First, each rural area should stick to industries that it has comparative advantages. Today, traditional farms face competition from modern farms, which has higher productivity. At the same time, more and more urban people prefer spending holidays in suburbs. On Friday, many drive a car to a nearby farm, rent a lodge where rural restaurants are able to offer organic food. A new term "Agritainment", or "agriculture plus entertainment" is an abbreviation for such activities. Except food, pick-our-own, pets and many other services are also offered.

Second, local government should play a supportive role in development, which should be guided by the market. Normally, the government serves as a platform. On one side of the platform are firms; on the other side are production factors (land, labor forces, etc.). Besides, development under the guidance of market can ensure efficient allocation of economic resources.

Third, local government should accelerate integration of resources and formation of industry chain and value chain. For those industries that rely heavily on resources coming from rural areas, the government should encourage them to stay in rural area and hire rural population. This measure help reduces rural unemployment and income inequity.

Lastly, new requirement puts less emphasis on GDP than before, and insists on the idea that lucid waters and lush mountains are invaluable assets. Development should be innovation-driven rather than value-driven. Moreover, arable land minimum of 1.8 billion mu must be respected.

For each sector of the economy, the document proposed the following suggestions: first, planting and Breeding industry should develop in the direction of large-scale, less pollution, standardization and branding. Second, feature industry should be based on the region's unique features, such as food, artifacts and culture. Any intangible cultural heritage is a potential target. Third, insisting on building high-quality projects of rural tourism (leisure agriculture) including multiple functions: forest, lodges and food.

7.6.2 Case Study: Fanhua Food Limited

Chili is very common in Chinese cuisine. In Hunan, Jiangxi, Sichuan and some provinces in southwest China, Chili is extremely popular. Chili appears in many forms in our cuisine. It can be either water-based on oil-based. The water-based Chili has two usual forms, chopped chili pepper or pickled pepper. Chili can also appear in the form of Chili sauce. In 2015, total production of Chili sauce in China reached five million tons, around 5% larger than the number in 2014. Another form is chili oil, used by hot pots. Demand for chili products is huge and stable over time.

Fanhua Food Limited is a producer of Chili sauce in Rucheng county of Hunan. In total, it has three sites. The original site is founded in July 2007, integrating breeding, cultivating, purchasing, storage, R&D, processing and marketing. The company has a mission "Use Chili to Eliminate Poverty and Serve China". The second site is located in Dongguan, with a brand operating center and production and research center. The Dongguan factory is able to process 65 thousand tons of chili per year. Fanhua is successful in marketing. In Pearl River Delta, seven out of ten Hunan restaurants use its chili sauce. The third site is in Changsha, the province capital of Hunan. This site focuses on research and marketing.

When Fanhua was founded, the most serious issue is average cost. In economics theory, in order to minimize average cost, minimum efficient scale must be reached. The price for bottled chili sauce has been stable for many years. At first, the firm purchase chili directly from rural markets. When market price fluctuates for various reasons, total production of chili fluctuates and the firm takes all the risk. To offset risks, the firm began to sign contracts with farmers, or even rent arable land to grow chili. The contracts set protection price. When market price is higher than the protection price, protection price is used for procurement. This ensures that Fanhua almost always have enough production to meet the marker's demand. Fanhua also offers technical support to farmers.

Year after year, the Fanhua marketing group manages to find many clients for its products. They are sold in normal markets, in chained stores, chain restaurantsand on-line platforms (Taobao, TMall and JD). The gross revenue of Fanhua reached 700 million yuan.

In 2018, Fanhua introduced a special species of chili to Rucheng County, benefiting more than 6,011 household with population of 17,800. Their gross revenue reaches 112 million. This act received support from Rucheng government. Besides, growing chili in Hunan province is more difficult than in provinces in north China for climate and topography reasons. With support from Chenzhou government, large-scale production becomes possible. Recently, Fanhua build a new plant in Sanxing, Rucheng, capable of processing 500 thousand tons of chili per year.

7.6.3 Case Study: Thermal Spring in Rucheng

In Rucheng County, there is a town named Reshui (in English, hot water). As its name suggests, the town has a thermal spring. Rucheng thermal spring has the highest temperature in south China, with the average temperature varying from 91.5℃ to 98℃ depending on the season. Tractable records about the spring date back to Song dynastic. The water is characterized by high temperature, low mineralization and alkalescency, with numerous substances (silicon, sodium, potassium, calcium, strontium, etc.). The spring water is rich in radon, an element beneficial to metabolism.

Surrounding the thermal spring is a succession of mountains, covered by green forests. The region has lower temperatures in summer than many cities with the same latitude. When it is 36 Celsius degree in Changsha, it reaches only 25 Celsius degrees in Reshui. In summer, it is windy and Diurnal temperature fluctuations are large. Living cost is low. Reshui attracts many tourists who spend their summer there.

Local investment has turned Reshui into a huge touristic zone, containing the thermal-spring village and a sanatorium. By now, total investment has reached around 10 billion yuan. The Feilaizhai has a waterfall, and an ancient battlefield of Huangchao's army. The Yao ethnic group and She ethnic group (She zu) live in this region. In 2016, Reshui Town received 600 thousand tourists, and revenue of 450 million.

7.7 Education

Most children in rural China do not have sufficient education, compared with their urban counterparts. According to a recent survey by Tsinghua University, among 3,400 new students, only 656 of them come from rural area. This is not the end of the story. Out of these 656 students, 379 enter Tsinghua University through special plans, that is to say, less than 10% of the students enter the university through normal channels.

Think deeply about difference in education. Rural parents do not spend as much in their kids as urban parents. To understand this, the first aspect is from attitudes towards education. Back to the old days, many rural parents believe that Children are one source of labor force which can increase family income. And many others believe that school work is already sufficient for children's education. When urban parents take their children to tutorial classes or remedy classes on weekends, urban parents leave their children playing at home.

The second aspect is from family income. Rural parents have less income than urban parents. Many rural parents work in cities and return home only during the New Year. They don't have time to educate the kids. Those kids are left to their grandparents, who have no knowledge about the courses. It is reported that in 2017, the number of such children was 15.5 million, whereas the other 14.06 million follow their parents to cities. Private teachers in rural areas are almost as expensive as in urban area. The reason is that rural teachers face less competition than urban ones. As a result, those kids are left alone and fall behind the urban kids.

The third aspect is the lack of education resources in rural areas. Auxiliary books are hard to find in rural areas. In many rural schools, teachers must be versatile enough to cover several courses (literature, math, English, etc.). As more and more young people move to cities, rural teachers are on average getting older. Finding a young teacher from urban areas is a mission impossible for rural schools. According to "Report on development of China's rural education" published by Ministry of Education and Northeast Normal University, during 2016 and 2017, over 8,000 rural school shut down.

7.7.1 HOPE Schools

All the above has for many years raised the government's concern. By now, several measures have been taken: first, the government is pledged to spend more money on rural education, construct more roads connecting schools and villages, and ensure students' safety. Second, the government is pledged to introduce more schools and teachers in rural area. For those willing to teach in rural areas, higher wage will be paid. Third, an emerging phenomenon is that many aged urban population flow to rural areas. The government can set up funds, and selectively dispatch some retired teachers to rural schools, on a voluntary basis.

In May 1990, the first hope primary school was built in Jinzhai, Anhui. The school lies in Nanxi Town of Jinzhai County, and was funded by "China Youth Development Foundation" and the local government. During the first 19 years, the school has received donations valued at 5 million. By now, the school has 21 classes, 48 teachers and 1,366 students. The school's library has a volume of over 20 thousand books.

7.7.2 A Modern Quota System

To help rural students enter better universities, from 2012, the government launched special plans, basically a quota system. The government requires universities to set quota for students from rural area. The quota system has three types: one type is called "National Special Plan", the second type is called "Local Special Plan", whereas the third type is called "University Special Plan". Some universities use another name. In Tsinghua University, the plan is called "self-strengthening plan", allowing a deduction of at most 60 points.

National Special Plan is exclusively for key poverty-stricken counties and four prefecture-level cities in Xinjiang and targets college/university directly under ministries and commissions of the central government. Besides, it puts no restrictions on whether students are from urban areas or rural areas. Each applicant should bear domicile from one of these regions for in the last three years without interrupt, and one of his parents or custodian's domicile should also be in one of these regions. Admission often takes place before the admission of Class I universities.

Local quotas system, normally, is for provincial key universities. The local government has the authority to determine the area this plan is applied for. The Ministry of Education requires that the enrollment from the local special plan must be no less than 3% of total enrollment of Class I universities, and the enrollment from the university special plan must be no less than 2% of total universities enrollment.

University Special Plan is exclusively for rural population from remote, poor regions or ethnic groups and targets the college/university under ministry of education. The domicile requirement is nearly the same as the national special plan.

From 2015 to 2017, enrollment through special plans increased steadily by year, reaching 63 thousand in 2017.

7.8 Environment Protection

On one hand, the ongoing trend is that heavy industries are retreating from large cities to small cities and from small cities to rural areas. On the other hand, there is a need for rural areas to develop economy. Except these, rural areas have their own environmental problems. Here we list a few issues.

The first issue is that, farmers have insufficient knowledge about environmental problems. Industry waste usually consists of waste gas, waste water and waste residues. According to a survey in Changzhou cityin 2016, over 1/3 of rural residents have no ideas about what they are. And most of them don't know its damage. Most of them are conscious about greenhouse gas, and around 80% of them know that burning straws will aggravate the greenhouse effect. About pesticide bottles, 78.7% of them say that these bottles are just thrown away in random places or with domestic garbage.

The second issue is that, rubbish bin are hardly been seen in rural areas. Because of high fixed cost, garbage disposal service normally avoids rural market. Depending on the type of garbage, domestic garbage should follow separate treatment. What are commonly seen are toilets with two floors. The ground floor is used as toilets whereas the basement is to store waste from human livestock and poultry, used to generate methane. The methane is then used for heating and what remains is used as fertilizers. Despite its efficiency, this way of disposal raises a problem of hygiene.

The third issue is the use of fertilizers. Many farmers are not aware of the detrimental effects of fertilizers to humans and land. Organic fertilizers take longer time for effects to appear. Meanwhile, fertilizers imported from foreign countries are too expensive to use. In order to save time and production cost, many resorts to cheap fertilizers. The consequence is that some land and water is polluted. And the pollution is irreversible.

There are many other issues. Forests which are not taken care of are very often victims of uncontrolled lumbering. Many species of wild animals such as pangolinand alligator, are in danger because of unmanaged hunting.

Since the Central Economic Work Conferencein 2017, environment protection and management has become one of the three main tough battles for the central government and any policy change must stick to the principle of "lucid waters and lush mountains are invaluable assets". In many rural areas, it is forbidden to burn straws in autumn. Laws against hunting of wild animals are now implemented. In Weiyuan county of Gansu province, the local government organized rural households to plant trees in barren ridges. In the last few years, the county has achieved 66.2 thousand mu of plantation, with a forest coverage rate of 15.6%.

Chapter 8

Chinese Macroeconomic Policies and Performances

This chapter discusses the Chinese macroeconomic policies and performance in the business cycle frequency. Apart from the economic growth, the stable cyclical fluctuation is also an important goal of macroeconomic policies. Therefore, the macroeconomic policies that we discussed in this chapter are the business cycle management policies. The three important goals of Macroeconomic policies are: maintaining sustainable economic growth; remaining at a moderate inflation; low unemployment rate. The same as other countries and regions in the world, Chinese macroeconomic policies are also aiming to achieve these three macroeconomic policies goals. For the first goal in business cycle frequency, the tasks are to maintain a smooth cycle, namely, preventing economy from overheating in an economic boom and recovering economy growth in an economic recession (even depression). According to the theories of Phillips Curve and Okun's Law, the fluctuations of inflation rate and unemployment rate are associated with cyclical economic growth, which means that management of the second and the third goals go together with the first goal, which may complicates the macroeconomic managements in some cases. To achieve these, the counter-cyclical macroeconomic policies implementations are usually required. While in practice, it is, in many cases, hard to achieved, even in well developed economies with sophisticated macroeconomic management system.

Meanwhile, Chinese business cycle patterns exhibited some unique characteristics, which increase the difficulties of macroeconomic policies decision-makings and implementations. As an over two-digit high speeding growth economy, investment is one of the most important components in national income account. The rapid growth of investment with the support of expansionary policies, usually cause the dramatic fluctuation of various asset prices, which might boosting the inflation rate more than generally observed in developed economies. When contraction policies were implemented in this case, the economic growth first responses by slowing down. But due to the sticky price (inertia of inflation), inflation rate might remain at a high level or even keep increasing. To bring down the inflation, it would cause the slowdown of growth rate more than expected. The overcapacity caused by excess investment in the early stage, may also exaggerate this dilemma. To recovering from the recession, the investment is again boosted when expansionary macroeconomic policies are implemented. Then a new cycle began. This is a typical business cycle mode in China.

As Chinese government has learned in the past years' practices and is pacing into gradually improvement of its pro-cyclical patterns of macroeconomic policies implementations. But the over-volatile business cycle remains in current stage, like most of other emerging markets and developing economies. The balance of long run economic growth and the short run business cycle management in developing economies, like us, increase the difficulties of macroeconomic managements. Generally, due to the complicacy of economic environments of a large-scale economy, it is well believed by most of economists in the world that the macroeconomic policies management in China is of great success in the past thirty years, especially when we have achieved near 10 percent economic growth rate with approximately 3% annual inflation. The improvements of macroeconomic policies design and implementation are an important and difficult challenge in near and long future.

The structures of this chapter are organized as follows. In the first section, we briefly review of history of Chinese macroeconomic performances since 1990s. In the second and the third section, we discuss the design and implementation of monetary policy and fiscal policy, respectively. And the last section concludes.

8.1 The Briefing History of Chinese Macroeconomic Performance

In the past 30 years, China has experienced dramatic rapid economic growth, due to the high saving rate, flexible labor market, and the favorable technology shock. The rapid advancement in total factor productivity is the main driving force of Chinese economic growth. However, in business cycle frequency, China has also experienced the economic over-heating and the slow-down. The aggregate demand management has multiple aims, including maintaining the efficient use of economic capacity, eliminating the influence of business cycle fluctuation and relieving the impacts of external shocks. Although China has become a market-orientated economy, the transformation has not yet completed. State-own enterprises and local government still are the main market participants. State-own banks dominate the banking system. The situations impede the efficiency of credit allocation and production. The process of financial liberalization is still on going. Therefore, the design and the use of the macroeconomic policies tools have to consider the special characteristics of our market economy, especially the frictions in the policy transmission.

The chapter mainly discusses the policy performance starting from 1990s, which were the periods that can be considered as the market oriented economy. We divided it into five sub-periods: 1990-1997, 1998-2003, 2004-2008 and after-2009. The division of periods are not based on the separation of each business cycle, but based on the switch points of policy regimes.

8.1.1 The Period 1990-1997

In early 1990s, it is a period of high inflation. Although the inflation rate had already declined after 1980s, but GDP growth was impeded by the high inflation, with the lowest growth rate ever since 1978, of 4.1% appeared in 1990.

In 1992, Chairman Deng Xiaoping called for further openness and reform of Chinese economy, which set up for a new beginning of rapid growth. But with the support of the expansionary policy, it also brought a new round of high inflation. The growth rate of investment in 1992 and 1993 were amazingly high as 42.6% and 58.6%, respectively. Hence, the corresponding GDP growth rate in 1992 and 1993 were also rocketed to a high level of 14.2% and 13.5%, respectively. After the dramatically boosting of demand, the high inflation followed. The inflation rate in 1992 rose to 6.4%. Successively in 1993, it rose to 14.7% dramatically.

The investment mainly flowed to the real estate sector. The growth rate of real estate investment in 1992 and 1993 were astonishingly high as 93.5% and 124.9%. It rose the systemic risk of financial sector. The high inflation and real estate price bubble would cause severe risk of financial crisis. Therefore, the domestic credit was strictly controlled and cut-down since

Aug 1993, by the vice-prime minister and head of central bank, Zhu Rongji. The growth of aggregate money supply slowed down since 1993.

But due to inertia of price, the inflation rate in 1994 was still as high as 24.1%, which is the worst peak since 1979. The causes of 1994 hyper-inflation is multi-folded, not only due to over booming of the real estate, but also attribute to the reasons including the reform of administrative fees and charge, the shortage of grain supply in the year, the temporal increase of transaction cost of agricultural products transaction due to reform, the increase of foreign reserve due to the capital inflow, and so on. Basically, several disorders of price system happened together just during 1993 to 1994.

The People's Bank of China (PBC) continued to restrict the money supply in 1995. In 1996, there was over-supply in manufacturing industry, which drove down the price of manufacturing goods. The inflation rate started to drop quickly from the 1994 peak. In 1996, the PBC started to relieve the control of domestic credit by setting down the deposit and loan rate, first time since 1993.

In 1997, real GDP and inflation rate both declined. The economic conditions dramatically deteriorated. It was also partially due to the negative external environment, such as Asian Financial crisis. In Oct 1997, the PBC again adjusted down the deposit and loan rate. This was a strong signal shown that monetary policy was turning from contraction to expansion again. Despite the expansion of monetary policy, the money growth and domestic credit growth still declined suddenly in 1997, due to the contraction and unrest of financial system during the turbulence of Asian Financial Crisis. In the end of 1997, the GDP growth rate and the inflation rate are 8.8% and 2.8%.

8.1.2 The Period 1998-2003

In 1998, due to the impact of the Asian Financial Crisis, Chinese export growth declined dramatically, succeeded with the drop of the investment growth. Although government loose the money again, but GDP growth rate was dropped to below 7% in the first half of 1998.

Another worth-noting phenomenon was the growth rate of money supply and domestic credit kept dropping during 1997 to 2001, the lowest point was 13% and 11%, respectively, in the fourth quarter of 2011, even when central bank relax the reserve requirement rate from 13% to 8%. This implies a large drop of money multiplier. The whole banking system was reluctant to make loan.

As the response to this situation, the government turned to the expansionary fiscal policy in the second half of 1998. The active fiscal policy proved to be effective. The annual GDP growth achieved 7.8%. At the same time, the inflation rate was dropped to the -0.8% in 1998, which is the first time that the inflation rate turns to a negative value within one year. Although one of the macroeconomic policies' goals is to pursuit moderate inflation rate, but for moderate, it usually means around 2% inflation rate in international standard. Under the nominal rigidity, below 2% inflation rate, not to mention a negative inflation rate in 1998, hurts the lenders, which partially explains the shrink of money multiplier during the period.

Deflation also has some severe unstable effects on macroeconomics. Therefore, to deal with the deflation, central bank implemented some policies to encourage the collateral lending, which started to take effects in 2000. A strong and amazing rebound of real estate investment took place, with the growth rate rose from negative value in 1997 to 13.7% in 1998, and was further rising to 21.5% in 2000. This real estate investment growth was critical improvement to the perspective of economic growth in this period.

The economic growth started to speed up in the second half of 2002. This speed-up was still relying on the strong investment growth. This increase was due to the response to the lack of infrastructure investment and physical investment in some important industries. The GDP growth rate returned to 9.1% in 2003.

8.1.3 The Period 2004-2009

The investment boom started and continues to grow since 2002. The real estate investment became the key driving force of gross investment and GDP growth. In Oct 2003, central bank raised the policy interest rate for the first time after 1997. This shows the turning point of expansionary policy regime to the prudent contractionary policy regime. The fiscal policy was turning to a relative neutral stance.

Even the monetary policy has leaned against the wind. The investment booms continued. As a response to the potential over-heating, the Chinese government used not only the conventional macroeconomic policy, but also various command policies, to cool down the investment. After a series of adjustments taken placed in 2004, the growth rate of money supply and the domestic credit dropped rapidly to 13.5% and 10.9%, respectively.

In early 2005, due to the strong growth of investment from 2002 to 2004, the over-capacity problems were emerged in some industries. The profitability of enterprises was decreasing, correspondingly. It seems that the rebound of economic growth started from 2002 has come to an end. Some economist suggested that economic policies should turn from moderate contraction to moderate expansion. But the expected economic growth slowdown did not happen in 2005. The monetary growth and domestic credit growth also picked up from a low level in 2004. The innovation and productivity growth absorbed the over-capacities temporarily. In fact, the export growth astonishingly rocketed to 220% in 2005, which actually was due to the over-capacities in many major industries. Although the over-capacity was prevailing, the GDP growth rate remained strong, and together with investment growth. Meanwhile, the net export growth was as high as 41.4%.

Therefore, central bank announced the reform of exchange rate system and allowed the floating of RMB against US dollar. The RMB appreciated by 2.1% in Jul 2005.

The strong economic growth in 2006 may due to the facts that 2006 was the first year of the 11th Five-Year Plan, and it also was the last year before the new election of provincial governors. Local governments and state-own enterprises have the incentive to maintain splendid performance and the promising perspectives.

With the dramatic growth of net export, there were excess current account surplus and capital account surplus, which creates the massive liquidity in domestic banking system. How to absorb the excess liquidity was a big challenge for central bank in 2006. One puzzling phenomenon was the inflation rate at the second half of 2006 remained at a relative low level even when there was excessive liquidity in the financial system. Economists believed that the increasing price was mainly reflected in asset price at that time but not in consumer price. Therefore, low inflation remained. Massive capital was absorbed by real estate market. In 2006, the GDP growth rate was 12.7% and inflation rate was as low as 1.5%.

Because of excellent economic performance and beneficial external environments, the stock market also boomed after several years' glooming. The stock index doubled after rapid growth since 2006. The Shanghai complex stock index rose from 2,000 to 3,000 within 18 months, after that speeded up to 4,000 within 31 working days, eventually to 6,200 high in Oct. 2007.

After the succeeding high-speed growth in five years since 2003, the economic growth suddenly slowed down in the second quarter of 2007. The stock market broke down in the end of Oct. 2007. The Shanghai Stock index rushed down to 2,500 and remained afterwards.

Meanwhile, the inflation rate deteriorated since the fourth quarter of 2006. Initially, the inflation rate was mainly driven by the pork price. Governors and economists believed that, when supply of pork recovered, the pork price and inflation rate would return to normal. However, the reality went the opposite direction. Even the pork price was topped in Aug. 2007 and the economic growth rate remained strong, the inflation rate kept rising puzzlingly. In Feb. 2008, the annualized inflation rate was 8.7%, which was 11 years' new peak. Meanwhile, economic growth began to slowdown.

This situation placed a dilemma before the Chinese authority. But haven't when the authority decided whether to proceed with contractionary or expansionary policy regime, the global financial crisis broke out in the US. The global slowdown swept across the world. There is no escape for any single economy including China. The export was first bearing the brunt of external shock and was free falling from 20% in Oct. 2008 to -2.2% in Nov. 2008. The export growth was 6.8% in the fourth quarter of 2008, which was the worst record in decade. This was an enormous strike on GDP growth, because in 2007, the export to GDP ratio was as high as 36%. After this, the inflation pressure was suddenly gone with a deflation happened in Feb 2009. The real estate price and the stock index also dropped sharply.

The authority reacted immediately. In Sep 2008, the central bank ceased the exchange rate floating and turned to expansionary monetary policy. The stimulate package was launched in Nov 2008, with a massive amount of fiscal injection of 4 trillion Yuan (equivalent to 580 billion dollar, 404 billion Euro or 354 billion Pound Sterling). As a result, the GDP growth in second quarter of 2009 was returned to 7.9%. Investment growth rate in 2009 was 30.5%, which contribute to 8% in GDP growth. The inflation rate returned to positive in Nov 2009.

Although the recovery is successful, but the stimulate packages and the over-expansion of monetary policy also bring severe negative effects later years. The over-capacity problem was further deteriorated and the diminishing efficiency of investment is overwhelming. The asset bubble and inflation problem reappeared.

8.1.4 The Period 2010 and Afterward

In the first quarter of 2010, the GDP growth rate reached 12.1% high, and the inflation rate keep growing. In Jan 2010, central bank raised the reserve requirement rate for the first time, in order to prevent real estate bubble and hyperinflation. Later, the reserve requirement rate was raised five times successively. And the policy rate of deposit and loan were raised twice in 2010. Meanwhile, the domestic credit and broad money supply were declining, In 2010, the GDP growth rate and inflation rate was 10.3% and 3.3%. In the last quarter of 2010, the inflation rose to 4.6%.

Because of changing policy regime of monetary and fiscal policy, the inflation was improved in early 2011. However, because of the influence of international commodity price surge, the inflation rate rose again. In Jun 2011, the authority tightened the monetary policy once again, by raising the reserve requirement rate together with the policy rate of deposit and loan. But the inflation rate was still increasing to the three-year high of 6.5% before declining.

The strong compression of liquidity alleviated the inflation pressure eventually. But the economic growth was also suppressed. In fact, the economic growth rate had been declining since the first quarter of 2010. In the last quarter of 2011, the economic growth rate dropped to 8.9%. More importantly, the growth rate of total investment, real estate investment and manufacturing investment were all declining. The sale amount of housing was decreased by 8%. The new construction of housing was decreased by 18.3%. Due to the deterioration of global economic environment, the export performance was also not satisfactory. Therefore, the authority was worrying about the depression. The monetary policy turned the direction again. The reserve requirement rate was reduced in Nov. 2011.

In 2012, the situation continued to worse off. The declining of real estate investment growth was more than expected. The external environment continued to worse off as well, due to the European debt crisis. And more importantly, the economy may reach a critical point of regime-switching to a new normal with a lower growth rate. The economic performance in the second quarter of 2012 was deteriorating. In May 2012, the government started a new fiscal package of 7 trillion Yuan (equivalent to 1.3 trillion US dollar). Now this time, it wasn't a short run stimulate package, but a project used to promote sustainable growth, by changing the mode of economic growth to a more inclusive way.

Together with the reduction of reserve requirement rate and the policy rate of deposit and loan, the recession was recovered since the third quarter of 2012. But this time, once again, the economic growth was pulling by investment. The economists urged that the sustainable economic growth should be more consumption oriented.

More recently, economic growth has been steady at a more moderate pace. The recent lowering of the growth target reflects the widely held view that trend growth will gradually slow as the economy develops further. Over the longer term, China's potential growth rate is expected to ease as the pace of labor and capital accumulation slows. For the past few years, the difficult policy challenge has been to sustain activity in the face of adverse global conditions while achieving a smooth transition to a more consumer-based, inclusive, and sustainable growth path.

Despite weak and uncertain global circumstances, the economy was growing by 7.75% in 2013. Although first-quarter GDP data were sluggish, the pace of the economy picked up moderately in the second half of the year, as the lagged impact of recent strong growth in total social financing (a broad measure of credit). The infrastructure spending and retail sales showed more resilience than exports and private nonresidential investment. The external demand for China's exports remained subdued.

Inflation rate in 2013 remain moderate around 3%. Nonfood prices, a proxy for core inflation have been fairly stable for many years. Inflation had only been loosely linked to output fluctuations because surplus labor has helped prevent wage-price spirals and agricultural supply shocks have been the dominant driver of price volatility. With little sign of

The GDP growth rate in 2014 was 7.5%, in line with the authorities' target. In 2014, after a weak start, growth picked up in third quarter and the annual target of 7.5% was exceeded. Domestic demand moderated reflecting a welcome reduction in the growth of total social financing, slower investment growth, and a correction in real estate activity. The authorities had taken a number of measures to support real activity, including targeted cuts in required reserve rate, tax relief for SMEs, and accelerated fiscal and infrastructure spending.

In 2014, Nonfood price inflation has remained around 2%. Although headline CPI inflation has been somewhat more bouncy, this reflects volatility in food prices largely related to agricultural supply shocks. PPI, however, have been declining for over two years reflecting excess capacity and weak external demand.

The GDP growth was moderating in 2015, a slowdown that is largely a by-product of moving the economy away from the unsustainable growth path since the global financial crisis. The GDP growth was 7% in the first quarter and recent supply side indicators, such as industrial value added and electricity production showed continued moderation. The demand indicators also pointed to moderation, led by a correction in real estate construction, household consumption and retail sales.

China continued to transition to a more sustainable growth path and reforms have advanced across a wide domain. The GDP growth slowed to 6.7% in 2016 and Inflation rose to 2% in 2016. Important supervisory and regulatory action was being taken against financial sector risks, and corporate debt was growing more slowly, reflecting restructuring initiatives and overcapacity reduction.

Fiscal policy remained expansionary and credit growth remained strong in 2016. Growth momentum declined over the course of the year reflecting recent regulatory measures which have tightened financial conditions and contributed to a declining credit impulse.

The GDP growth moderated from 6.8 percent in 2017 to 6.6 percent in 2018, as a result of necessary financial regulatory reforms and tighter conditions for local government (LG) infrastructure funding. Trade tensions with the U.S. have weakened sentiment and heightened stress in financial markets. The authorities have responded with a wide range of policy measures, including import tariff cuts, tax cuts, monetary easing, and a marginal relaxation of the pace of regulatory strengthening.

The trade conflict with the U.S. escalated since its start in spring 2018, and the outlook for the global economy in 2019 is weaker than previously expected. Two rounds of U.S. tariffs and counter-tariffs were implemented before a 'truce' and negotiations began in December 2018, which broke down in May and led to another round of tariff increases. The conflict goes beyond bilateral trade and extends to structural issues related to China's foreign investment regime, intellectual property (IP) protection, technology transfer policies, industrial policy, cyber security, and, more broadly, the large economic role of the state.

Amid slowing activity, core CPI inflation fell just below 2% in mid-2018, and further to 1.6% in May. Headline CPI inflation rose to 2.7% in May, driven by rising food inflation. Driven by a global decline in commodity prices and weak infrastructure and construction, Industrial Producer Price Index (PPI) inflation fell sharply to below 1% in 2019, renewing pressure on corporate earnings and debt servicing capacity.

In the beginning of 2020, the global economy was hit by COVID 19 pandamic, global growth was -4.9% in 2020. Economic activities contracted and global economy fell into deep recession. However, the Chinese recover from the crisis due to a strong containment effort, and marcoeconomic and financial policies. The economic growth in 2020 was -4.2% and inflation was 2.5%. The growth is still urbalanced in 2021 as the recovery heavily relied on public support while comsumption is legging. Rising financial vulnerabilities pose risks to future outlook.

8.2 Monetary Policy

8.2.1 Financial System

The People's Bank of China (PBC) was officially performing only central banking task since 1984. The commercial banking tasks were redirected to the Big Four commercial banks. In Jan. 1996, the interbank market was established. In Mar. 1998, the reserve requirement system was first built. The bank reserve account and the excess reserve account were merged. All the bank reserves were paid by the unified interest rate. The reserve requirement rate was first set at 8% at that time, 5% lower than before. In Dec. 2003, the reserve and excess reserve again was paid by different interest rate, that is, 1.89% and 1.62%, respectively. In March 2005, the interest rate of excess reserve was adjusted to 0.99% and remains. In 2012, the reserve requirement rate was adjusted to 20% high.

The money market of China includes interbank market, the bond repurchase market and note discount market. The capital market includes bond market and stock market. The interest rate of interbank market is called "Chinese interbank offer rate" (CHIBOR). It is determined by the demand and supply of loans by 12 commercial banks and 15 non-bank institution. The interest rate of bank reserve and the re-borrowing rate set the up- and lower- bound of interbank interest rate. The interest rate in bond-repurchase market, REPOR is determined by the supply and demand of government bond. In Jan 2007, Shanghai interbank offer rate SHIBOR was launched as new baseline interbank rate. SHIBOR is more market oriented. It is calculated using the arithmetic mean of the interbank loan rate reported by 16 major commercial banks at 11:30am each day. SHIBOR is similar to the London interbank offer rate (LIBOR), which aim to become the baseline interest rate of China.

The financial system of China is dominated by banking system. In 2011, the ratio of bank loan to total financing was 75%, while the debt financing and stock financing accounted only for 10.6% and 3.4%, respectively. At the same year, the government bond, financial bond, corporate bond and central bank note accounted for, in total bond issuance, 35.5%, 32.82%, 22.32% and 9.36%, respectively. Recently, there is merely increase in other financing than bank loan.

8.2.2 Monetary Policy Goal

Since 1978, the ultimate goal, midterm goal and the monetary policy tools has experienced several reforms. Chinese national economic policy is determined by the State Council, which sets out the five-year plans containing the government broad long terms economic agenda, including targets for urbanization, industrialization and gradual market liberalization. Recent five-year plans have also provided medium-term targets that lay down the path to achieving the longer-term objectives. While the State Council determines the overall objectives of policy, implementation is the responsibility of both local and central government agencies. Within the context of the five-year plans, the State Council also sets annual goals for macroeconomic outcomes. Targets for inflation and growth in the money supply and in GDP are announced at the annual meeting of the National People's Congress. Thus, the general stance of macroeconomic policy, as summarized by the budgetary stance and the targets for growth in money supply, is set in a coordinated manner in the context of the State Council's longer-term economic objectives.

A range of institutions are responsible for the implementation of macroeconomic policies. Exchange rate policy is implemented by the People's Bank of China (PBC) and the State Administration of Foreign Exchange (SAFE). The managed float exchange rate regime has necessitated regulatory controls over foreign capital flows in order to provide some leverage over domestic money supply. In the absence of capital controls, it would not be possible to control both the exchange rate and domestic money supply.

The PBC seeks to meet the growth and inflation targets set by the State Council through its control of the exchange rate and influence over domestic money supply and credit growth in the economy. To achieve the economic growth target, stable inflation and stable exchange rate at the same time is not an easy task. According to the Mundell's trilemma, this can only be achieved under strictly capital control. Even under the most strict capital control in the world, it is still hard to prevent the impact of Hot money flow. The experience of Chinese economic history has proved the difficulties. The tradeoff between the high speed growth over 7% and the moderate inflation rate under 3% has been always happened. That is the tradeoff of Phillips Curve (aggregate supply) does exist in Chinese case. And the time inconsistency problem of policy making and policy implementation complicates the scenarios. To executing the economic policies in right timing is a universal tough challenge for economist and policy makers.

Over the past decade, GDP growth has exceeded the targets set by the State Council, while consumer price inflation has both overshot and undershot the targets. The targets for inflation in particular are often adjusted annually reflecting the State Council's assessment of what is an acceptable trade-off between growth and inflation in response to the experience of the most recent year. Unlike the inflation targets in most inflation-targeting monetary policy systems, the Chinese target is not a fixed objective but a guide that is adjusted as conditions evolve.

8.2.3 Monetary Policy Instruments

For monetary policy instrument, it means that central bank use some kinds of monetary variables to quantify the policy targets. The traditional monetary instrument usually includes two types: price instrument and quantity instrument, that is, interest rate and money aggregates. Most of developed economies use the interest rate as an instrument, with the relevant monetary policy rule called Taylor rule. Some other economies use the money aggregate, such as M2, as an instrument, with the relevant monetary policy rule called McCallum rule. In China, the PBC officially announced, in the third quarter of 1994, the broad money supply M2 growth rate as the mid-term target of monetary policy. This implies that China uses quantity type of instrument, that is, money aggregate.

Although in each year, the target M2 growth rate was set, in practice, this target had not been exactly followed. On one hand, when inflation rate exceeds certain critical high level, the monetary growth target would be ignored. The priority became the control of inflation rate. So the money supply will be contracted. On the other hand, when GDP growth is below the target, the monetary growth target would be ignored. The priority became the promotion of economic growth. So the money supply will increase.

The other case to deviate from the monetary aggregate target is usually during the time of over-heating or deflation. The central bank would usually change to credit control under these special circumstances. Command policy may be implemented to control the credit of banking system directly.

Due to the development of Fin-tech, various monetary aggregate other than M2, are also used as the references. The use of M2 as the monetary instrument is under severe critics in recent years.

8.2.4 Monetary Policy Tools

The PBC implements domestic monetary policy using a range of tools in order to control domestic money and credit growth. These include benchmark interest rates on loans and deposits, variations in reserve requirement ratios for banks, open market operations and direct influence over bank lending (referred to as 'window guidance'). And more new types of tools are implemented to influence the liquidity and the domestic credit.

(1) Open Market Operation

First, open market operation (OMO) is a traditional monetary policy. The

OMO can be used to change the supply of monetary base in the money market. Through the money creation process in the banking system, the money supply would eventually change as well. The PBC conducts OMO both on money market and foreign exchange market, with the transactions of RMB asset and foreign exchange, respectively. The OMO of foreign exchange was firstly launched in Mar 1994. The OMO of domestic asset was resumed in May 26th, 1998. The OMO developed quickly since 1999. Nowadays, OMO is one of the most frequently used monetary policy tools.

When central bank purchases the securities to other participants (qualified banks and non-bank financial institution) in the money market, it releases the liquidity to the money market. It is called a repurchase-agreement (repos). When central bank sells the securities in the money market, it withdraws the liquidity from the money market. It is called a reverse repurchase-agreement (reverse-repos). The securities used in the repos transaction are central bank notes, which are the short-term debt issued by the central bank.

Prior to the global financial crisis, the PBC issued bonds that, along with adjustments in the RRRs, helped to sterilize foreign exchange inflows. In recent years, with slower foreign exchange inflows, outright bond issuance has been limited, but the PBC has been more active in using repos and reverse repurchase agreements to influence liquidity conditions in the banking sector. These transactions are similar in nature to those used to implement monetary policy in many developed economies. However, in China these operations are currently used only for higher frequency "fine-tuning" of liquidity conditions as the relevant markets are not sufficiently established for this to be the primary tool for monetary policy implementation. Substantial adjustments in the stance of policy at this stage are still likely to require adjustments in benchmark interest rates and/or RRRs.

As the Chinese financial system continues to evolve there is likely to be an increasing reliance on open market operations in the implementation of monetary policy. The government's current five-year plan for financial sector development emphasizes market-based reforms and the recent rapid growth in non-bank components of total social financing (TSF) indicates that the dominance of the regulated banking sector in the Chinese economy will lessen over time. As these proceeds, the effectiveness of monetary policy instruments that act only on financial institutions' regulated banking activities will be diminished; at the same time a deepening of domestic financial markets will improve the potency of market-based policy instruments.

In addition, starting from Jan. 2013, the PBC launched some new tools to aim liquidity management, which is called "short-term liquidity operations" (SLOs). These tools are the complements to the OMOs, which are used when there is occasionally turbulence of liquidity and prevent elevating of financial risk.

(2) Reserve Requirement Ratio

Second, reserve requirement ratio (a.k.a. required reserve rate) is also one of the traditional monetary policies. The reserve requirement ratio (RRR) determines the proportion of deposit liabilities that the PBC requires banks to hold as assets at the central bank. By varying RRRs, the PBC is able to affect the supply of funds available for lending in the economy, which can influence the growth in credit. RRR does not influence the monetary base, but money multiplier, through which money supply is adjusted.

RRR was first invented by the US central banking in the world. It was initially used as deposit insurance and liquidation, and was commonly used in developed economies in 20th century. But with the mature of financial system and money market management, reserve requirement rate are less used in developed economies nowadays. Instead, the developing countries still apply this tool frequently, for not only the deposit safety but also some new purposes, such as the control of the hot money capital flows.

The PBC introduced RRRs in the mid-1980s, although changes to RRRs were initially infrequent: between their establishment in 1984 and 2005, RRRs were adjusted only eight times. Since 2006, the PBC has used RRRs as an active tool of monetary policy. One reason for this has been the pick-up in foreign exchange inflows. Under its managed float exchange rate policy, the PBC has often been required to purchase foreign exchange inflows in order to keep the exchange rate within its daily trading band. These foreign exchange purchases have needed to be sterilized to prevent an expansion of the domestic money supply and an overshoot of the money growth target. Increases in RRRs have played a key role in withdrawing the excess liquidity resulting from foreign exchange purchases from the banking system, as can be seen by the dominance of reserves on the liabilities side of the PBC balance sheet.

At the same time, RRRs have played a role in enhancing the effect of changes in benchmark rates on domestic credit conditions. For example, increases in RRRs in 2011 were associated with a spike in the share of loans made at above benchmark rates, with this effect unwinding somewhat in 2012 when RRRs were eased.

(3) Central bank Re-discount and Central Bank Lending

Third, PBC also uses the re-discount and central bank lending. The re-discount means central bank rediscount the commercial notes of financial institutions, which is also a supplementary tool of adjusting domestic credit. Since 2008, central bank rediscount policy was lean towards the local medium and small financial institutions, agricultural banks and other rural depositary financial institutions. The central bank lending is also used to adjust the monetary base, similar to the purpose of central bank rediscount. And it is also aim to the fund the credit demand of some important industries.

(4) Standing Lending Facility

Various liquidity management tools were introduced after 2008 global financial crisis. In 2013, the "Standing Lending Facility" (SLF) was launched to meet the relatively liquidity needs in short term. The service was provided to commercial banks mainly. The maturity term is 1-3 month. The SLF is provided with collateral of high credit-rating financial assets. The similar tools with different names used in different counties and regions, such as "Discount Window" for U.S Federal Fund Banks, "Marginal Lending Facility" for European central bank, "Operational Standing Facility" for Bank of England, "Operational Standing Facility" for Bank of Japan, "Complementary Lending Facility" for Bank of Canada, "Standing Loan Facility" for Financial Management Bureau of Singapore, "Secured Loans" for Bank of Russia, "Marginal Standing Facility" for Bank of India, "Liquidity Adjustment Loans" for Bank of Korea, and "Collateralized Lending" for Bank of Malaysia.

8.2.5 Other Credit Control Tools

The PBC directly sets benchmark interest rates on Chinese banks' deposits and loans, with the benchmarks differentiated by the term of the deposit or loan. The benchmark rates are a significant determinant of actual deposit and loan rates and influence both the supply of bank deposits and the demand for bank loans. Benchmark rates previously set a ceiling on deposit rates and a floor on loan rates. Although recent reforms have eased these restrictions, benchmark interest rates still strongly influence the rates faced by businesses and households. The PBC seek to promote the interest rate liberalization, which is more reflected in determination of lending rate instead of deposit rate. Many actual lending rates exceed the benchmark, with the spread to benchmark lending rates influenced by a range of factors including the risk profile of borrowers and the general availability of funds in the market.

The transmission of changes in benchmark interest rates to economic activity is influenced by the structure of Chinese banks balance sheets, which are reliant on household deposits while lending is predominately to businesses. Chinese households were net savers and had low leverage until recently. This may reflect limited access to alternative investment opportunities outside of deposits and the purchase of real estate, coupled with a precautionary savings motive. Low benchmark deposit rates have meant that many households have been receiving interest rates that have been below the rate of inflation on their savings. Due to their large pool of savings, Chinese households have had a lower tendency to borrow and the flow of bank lending to businesses exceeds that to households. The banking system appears to be gradually changing as financial institutions, such as trust companies, have emerged offering wealth management products that pay higher interest rates than bank deposits. This may lead to further evolution of how monetary policy is implemented, by raising the importance of instruments affecting market interest rates directly, relative to those based on the PBC's regulatory control over bank interest rates and lending.

The PBC's ability to directly influence the quantity and type of lending is strengthened by its window guidance activities, where it advises banks on how much and to which industries they should be lending. Although formal credit quotas were abolished in 1998, the PBC continues to maintain considerable input into the decisions about the quantity and composition of bank lending. In part, window guidance has a macroeconomic policy objective, such as supporting the fiscal stimulus during the global financial crisis period. They are also designed to reinforce microeconomic industry policy, such as the government's support for the agricultural sector during the early 2000s and, more recently, providing support for the small and medium-sized enterprise sector.

8.2.6 Chinese Monetary Policy Implications

Since the shift to the managed float regime, the currency has appreciated by around 30-35 percent against the US dollar and on a real effective basis. Although a managed float exchange rate regime implies that the domestic money supply is driven by developments in the current account, the use of tight capital controls in China provides the PBC with the capacity to sterilize the effect of balance of payment flows on the domestic money supply. Moreover, given the dominance of the regulated banking sector in Chinas overall financial system, the PBC's control of a range of regulatory and market instruments that influence banks' funding and loan creation has enabled it to assert considerable influence on the amount of money and credit in the economy and therefore macroeconomic outcomes. Like other central banks, the PBC monitors economic and financial conditions continuously to assess the need for adjustments in the stance of policy; however, the PBC does not have a fixed timetable for policy announcements. Many instruments used by the PBC to adjust the overall stance of policy are less market oriented, which is different from the way that monetary policy is implemented in most developed economies, where typically the short-term interest rate is the key policy instrument.

One implication of the breadth of policy instruments employed by the PBC is that it is not possible to summarize changes in the stance of policy by considering only a single instrument. The overall stance of policy is determined by the combination of instrument settings, with the mix of policy instruments at any one time depending on the PBCs assessment of which instruments will be most effective in achieving the desired financial conditions.

8.3 Fiscal Policy

8.3.1 The Institutional Arrangement of Fiscal Policy

Fiscal and other supplementary regulatory policies are implemented by a broad range of central and local government agencies. While the majority of public revenue is collected by the central government, most government expenditure is undertaken at the local level. This is particularly the case for social security, education and infrastructure spending.

Although local governments are typically responsible for undertaking infrastructure projects, the National Development and Reform Commission

(NDRC) plays an important role in the implementation of this aspect of fiscal policy by providing central oversight of major investment projects. The relatively large size of infrastructure and other public investment spending as a share of the Chinese economy has meant this component of fiscal policy has been an important element of macroeconomic management, in addition to its importance in expanding the supply side of the economy. The complete impact of China's fiscal policy is not reflected in the consolidated local and central government budget position, since the government also relies on its ability to influence the investment activities of state-owned enterprises to achieve policy objectives.

8.3.2 Fiscal Policy Financing

An important feature of macroeconomic policy implementation in China is that fiscal and monetary policies are implemented in a highly coordinated way, with the overall direction of policy set by the State Council. This is in contrast to the trend in developed economies, over recent decades, towards greater independence of central banks from fiscal authorities. An example of this coordination in the Chinese system is where the government implements fiscal policy through its influence over the investment activities of state-owned enterprises and local governments, which are supported by the credit policy actions of the PBC that ensure the Chinese banking system provides the necessary funding. This coordination was particularly evident during the global financial crisis, when state-owned banks lent to state-owned enterprises in industries that the government was seeking to stimulate. This episode also demonstrated how policy authorities in China are able to respond, when necessary, to changing circumstances in a timely manner, notwithstanding the institutional structures that underpin the five-year plans and annual targets.

While the State Council is again responsible for the overall direction of policy, much of the responsibility for implementation resides with local governments, which account for a large proportion of government expenditure. Investment by local governments is financed through a combination of central government transfers, local revenues and borrowing. Local governments are subject to restrictions on direct borrowing, which has led to the creation of local government financing vehicles (LGFVs) that raise funds on their behalf. Local governments raise funds though LGFVs to finance public infrastructure projects. As a result, spending by local governments, and the impact of fiscal policy, is not fully reflected in the consolidated local and central government budget position.

8.3.3 Government Budget Balance

The budget balance nevertheless provides a useful guide to the changes in the stance of fiscal policy. For the most of time in 1990s, the fiscal policies are moderating. The budget deficit to GDP ratio is prudent, under 3%, and the public debt to GDP ratio is below 20%. Only during deflation and financial crisis, active fiscal packages were used. There were only twice these type of emergency happened since 1990s. One was the second half of 1998, when Asian financial crisis happened. The other time was during 2008-2009 global financial crisis.

In 1998, state financial department sold 100 billion RMB government bond to commercial banks. At the same time, state own commercial banks were asked to provide another 100 billion RMB of loans. Both were used to finance the public infrastructure construction. The consolidated local and central government budget shows that the general government sector ran a budget deficit in the early 2000s. Then, as economic growth picked up, the budget balance moved from a deficit of around 2.5% of GDP in 2002, to a surplus of around 0.5% in 2007.

In response to the global financial crisis, the central government announced a 4 trillion RMB stimulus package in the Dec. 2008 to be spent over the following two years. This was equivalent to about 6.7% of GDP in each year, although only part of this was reflected in the consolidated budget, with a significant proportion also financed by local governments through LGFVs. And the state own commercial banks were also asked to provide 9.6 trillion. The stimulus package was directed largely at infrastructure projects executed by local governments, with the focus on smaller projects that could be executed quickly in the early stages of implementation. Around 1 trillion RMB of the expenditure was allocated to reconstruction in areas damaged by the Sichuan earthquake of May 2008. At the same time, and reflecting the close coordination between fiscal and monetary policy, the increase in expenditure was accompanied by an expansion of bank lending, particularly to state-owned enterprises and LGFVs. When economic growth recovered in the years following the global financial crisis, the budget deficit correspondingly contracted to 1.1% in 2011.

More recently, economic growth has slowed; and fiscal policy appears to have been moderately expansionary in 2012 and government estimates suggesting that fiscal policy will again be mildly expansionary in 2013. The shift to a moderately expansionary fiscal policy has been evident in the pick-up in growth in infrastructure investment over the second half of 2012. Notably, on this occasion, the authorities have not eased monetary policy settings, reflecting the PBC's assessment that policy needs to remain prudent given concerns over the lingering effects of the crisis period on asset quality in the banking sector.

Borrowings by LGFVs increased significantly during the global financial crisis and led to concerns about the quality of banking sector assets. After a National Audit Office report in 2010 highlighted the size of local government debt, the CBRC has stepped up its monitoring of, and implemented controls on, lending to LGFVs; these have been strengthened further in 2013. Although the risks associated with the quality of lending during the stimulus period of 2009–2010 is a downside risk to the outlook for the economy, policy flexibility is not as constrained as in many of the North Atlantic economies most affected by the crisis.

Chapter 9

The Opening-up of China under Economic Globalization

9.1 China's Opening-up Structure

In December 1978, the Third Plenary Session of the Eleventh Central Committee of the Party was held. The Communist Party of China made a major decision on reform and opening up. On the basis of summing up historical experiences and studying the characteristics of the contemporary world economy, the Central Committee of the Communist Party of China has adopted opening up as a basic national policy, and then proposed that "based on self-reliance, China will actively develop equal and mutually beneficial economic cooperation with other countries in the world, and strive to use world advanced technology and advanced equipment". Later, it was proposed that two types of resources should be used in economic construction, two markets should be opened, and two sets of skills for organizing domestic economic construction and developing foreign economic relations should be learned to create a new situation for external development.

9.1.1 Overview of China's Opening Up

Opening up to the outside world is a basic national policy of China, which means that China's opening up to the outside world is a comprehensive opening up. That is, China should open to the outside world in politics, economy, culture, science and technology, art, sports, and other aspects. Here we mainly study opening up to the outside world in economic field.

(1) The Definition of China's Opening Up

Comrade Deng Xiaoping said that to implement the policy of opening up is to learn to use international funds and technology to help us develop our economy. Therefore, the basic meaning of opening up in the economic field is to vigorously develop and continuously strengthen foreign economic and technological exchanges, actively participate in international exchanges and international competitions, and replace the closed-door self-sufficiency with the internationalization of production and exchange, promote economic transformation, and make China's economic structure transform from a closed economy to an open economy, accelerate modernization, and catch up with developed countries as soon as possible.

(2) The Main Content of China's Opening Up

The content of China's opening to the outside world mainly includes: vigorously developing foreign trade, including trade in goods, services and technology; actively introduce foreign advanced technology equipment and management, especially advanced technologies that are helpful for technological transformation of enterprises, meanwhile developing technology exports; actively, effectively and rationally utilize foreign investment, especially focusing on foreign direct investment, establishing Chinese-foreign joint ventures and wholly foreign-owned enterprises, and working hard to develop China's foreign direct investment; actively carry out foreign contracting projects and international labor service cooperation, and develop various forms of foreign economic and technical assistance and mutually beneficial cooperation; constructing special economic zones and opening coastal cities to promote the opening up of the mainland and the development of the western region. The most important of these are the first three, namely the development of foreign trade, technology introduction, and utilization of foreign capital. The development of foreign trade is the basis for the use of foreign capital and technology introduction, so that it is the basic content of opening up.

(3) Geographical Direction of China's Opening Up

China's opening up policy is to open to all countries and regions. Whether developed or developing countries, countries with economies in transition or capitalist countries, regardless of the size of the country, rich or poor, strong or weak, we are willing to develop economic and trade relations with them on the basis of equality and mutual benefit. China's opening to the outside world is to absorb the advantages and strengths of various countries and regions in the world. The geographic direction of China's opening up should include the following four types of countries and regions.

I Developed capitalist countries

Developed capitalist countries mainly refer to industrialized countries such as North America, Europe, Japan, and Oceania. During the 40 years of reform and opening up, China has imported a large number of advanced technologies and equipment and high-tech achievements from these countries, which has greatly promoted China's economic development. While learning from the advanced management experience accumulated in practice in these countries for hundreds of years, the management level of Chinese enterprises can be improved. Developed countries have high per capita income, large market capacity, and great demand for various commodities, which is conducive to China's expansion of production and exports. They also have a large amount of capital seeking for investment markets, which will help to accelerate the opening process of China using their funds and capital. Besides, the developed countries have a high level of education and obvious advantages in talents. Through the introduction of intelligence and talents from these countries and sending personnel to study, the quality of human resources in China is rapidly improved, and the pace of national development is accelerated.

II Developing countries and regions

The economic rise of developing countries and regions is a major event of the contemporary world economy. A basic policy of China's opening to the outside world is to actively develop economic and trade relations with developing countries and carry out "South-South Cooperation" to change the development pattern of the world economy. There is a lot of room for cooperation between China and developing countries: China needs to import a large amount of materials from developing countries to make up for the shortage of energy and resources; most developing countries and regions have a single economy and a strong dependence on the international market, creating opportunities for China to expand exports. Some developing countries and regions' economic backwardness and shortage of funds have created opportunities for Chinese enterprises to develop foreign direct investment and realize "going global"; the newly industrialized countries have advanced technology and management, and a large amount of capital seeking investment markets, which are the main sources of China's technology introduction and utilization of foreign capital. In short, China actively develops economic cooperation with developing countries, and can use the economic complementarity of both sides to promote the increasingly perfect economic structure.

Ⅲ Countries with economies in transition

The drastic changes in Eastern Europe in 1989 and the disintegration of the Soviet Union in 1991 resulted in great changes in the political and economic structure of the region. There are many favorable conditions for China's opening up and the economic and trade development of the Commonwealth of Independent States as well as Eastern European countries. China, Russia and Central Asian countries are adjacent. Therefore, they have long land borders and enjoy regional advantages in bilateral trade. China and these countries have strong economic complementarities. China's agricultural products, textiles, and light industrial products have extensive demand in these markets, while these countries have rich energy, wood, nuclear power technology, and heavy chemical products, which have strong competitiveness in the Chinese market. Historically, China has had long-term cooperation with these countries. Most of China's early large-scale industrial projects were imported from these countries.

Ⅳ Hong Kong, Macao and Taiwan

Hong Kong, Macao and Taiwan are an integral part of China, but they are also relatively independent customs zones in international economic relations. Therefore, although the trade between the mainland of China and Hong Kong, Macao, Taiwan is a trade activity between regions within a country, it has always been operated and counted according as international trade. China is committed to developing trade and capital movements with this region, which is conducive to the economic development of the Mainland and the upgrading of industrial structure. Direct investment from Hong Kong, Macao and Taiwan has become the main source of foreign investment in the Mainland. Exports to Hong Kong and Macao are the main channels for China to earn foreign exchange. The largest investor and technology in the mainland's technology and information industry are from Taiwan. The Mainland and Hong Kong, Macao and Taiwan regions have special advantages in developing economic exchanges since the geographical location is close and transportation is convenient and efficient. The economic complementarity is very strong. The Mainland needs technology, capital and advanced management, while Hong Kong, Macao and Taiwan need resources, markets and labor from the Mainland. Especially after a closer economic cooperation agreement has been signed between the Mainland, Hong Kong and Macau, the region's economic and trade development has become more rapid.

9.1.2 Implementation Steps of China's Opening-up

In terms of opening-up pattern, China does not adopt the policy of opening up across the country at the same time. Instead, a multi-tiered, roller-coaster and gradual development in depth and breadth are selected. This is determined by China's national conditions, in which China's economic development in the east, the center and the west is quite unbalanced while geographic conditions in these areas are different. Moreover, under a closed and highly centralized pattern during the planned economy period, a synchronized opening policy is less feasible. Therefore, taking a policy from part to whole, from coast to inland and from the east to the west step by step is more agreeable, which proved to lead to a remarkable result.

(1) The Opening Up of China's Coastal Areas to the Outside World

In 1979, China's opening up started including with the eastern coastal areas from the north to the south, include eight provinces and three municipalities, Liaoning, Hebei, Tianjin, Beijing, Shandong, Jiangsu, Shanghai, Zhejiang, Fujian, Guangdong and Hainan directly under the central government. The eastern coastal region enjoys a coastline of 18,000 kilometres with more than 300 ports with a throughput of 300 million tons. It also embraces solid industrial, agricultural and service industries and a large number of high-quality human resources. Therefore, the central government decided on the economic development strategy of "focusing on opening up the coastal areas and gradually opening up to the interior regions" at the early stage of opening up.

I The content and background of economic development strategy in coastal areas

In 1987, the central government formulated the strategy for the economic development of the coastal areas. The specific meaning of the strategy includes: fully exploit the advantages of the coastal areas in terms of the labor resources; step into the world market with leadership, plan and procedures; further participate in international exchange and international competition; promote the effort of industrial restructuring, and vigorously develop the export-oriented economy.

There are internal and external conditions that push the formation of the coastal economic development strategy. The internal conditions refer to that with the opening up of the coastal areas, the contradiction over wining the market and material between the coastal areas and the central and western regions is getting intense. In the long term, not only the economic development of the central and western regions will be restrained, but also the industry and agriculture of the coaster areas will get into trouble due to the raw materials and the market issues. External conditions refer to that the international market is facing a new round of industrial structure adjustment. With the economic development and rising labor costs, the Asian "Dragons", who used to rely on labour-intensive exports to achieve their economic take-off, are in need of industrial reconstruction. They have to transfer the labour-intensive industries to those countries and regions with lower labor cost. Under such conditions, China's coastal economic development strategy was made and implemented.

II Steps to open coastal areas to the outside world

1. Guangdong and Fujian were endowed with special policies

Guangdong and Fujian provinces, adjacent to Hong Kong, Macao and Taiwan, are at the forefront of China's opening to the outside world. That's the reason why the opening policy was first launched in these two provinces. In July 1979, the central government approved special policies and flexible measures for Guangdong and Fujian provinces on foreign economic activities. These policies mainly include granting certain power over developing foreign trade, attracting foreign investment, introducing advanced technology and other aspects. Most of the new revenue from the two provinces is left to the provinces for economic development, so that the regions can seize the opportunity to take the first step in reform and opening up in order to boost their economy as soon as possible.

2. Five Special Economic Zones were established

In May 1980, the State Council approved the establishment of Special Economic Zones in Shenzhen, Zhuhai, Shantou and Xiamen. Later in 1988, the establishment of Hainan Special Economic Zone was approved. The construction of Special Economic Zones is a major measure of opening up in China's coastal areas. Special Economic policies and more flexible policies and measures are adopted in the Special Economic Zones. These policies include that with foreign-invested enterprises occupy a large proportion, a variety of economic components coexist; with market regulation as the main means, make full use of market mechanism; give more preferential treatment to foreign enterprises that invest in the special zones; grant the governments of the special zones with economic management powers equivalent to the provincial level; and give preferential policies and support to the construction of the special zones.

3. Fourteen coastal cities were opened

The special economic zones only include some parts of Guangdong and Fujian provinces while opening up along the coast means opening up in all directions to the whole of China's coastal areas. To this end, the CPC Central Committee and the State Council announced the opening of fourteen coastal port cities in 1984, from the north to the south, including Dalian, Qinhuangdao, Tianjin, Yantai, Qingdao, Lianyungang, Nantong, Shanghai, Ningbo, Wenzhou, Fuzhou, Guangzhou, Zhanjiang and Beihai. To support these port cities, the country gives preference in policies over the autonomy of foreign economic and trade activities, the preferential treatment of enterprises with foreign investment and the technical renovation in old enterprises. Meanwhile, in most of these cities, economic and technological development zones are constructed. By doing so, to give full play of the advantages of the old industrial base, transportation, science and education in these cities, so as to speed up the economic development.

4. Coastal Economic Open Zones were established

If the opening up of coastal cities is about the "spots" of opening the coastal areas, then in February 1985, the central government's decision on establishing coastal open areas is all about "the entire areas". There are three open deltas in the south of the Yangtze river, namely the Pearl River Delta with Guangzhou as its centre; the Yangtze River Delta with Shanghai as it centre, and the southeast Fujian triangle with Xiamen, Zhangzhou and Quanzhou as its centre. These areas enjoy strong processing capacity, vibrant urban and rural economies and high opening degree to the outside world. In the northern part of the Yangtze river, the open zone was extended to two peninsulas on the northern coast, namely the Liaodong peninsula and the Shandong peninsula, together with some counties and cities along the coast, plus with the eastern part of Hebei province, Beijing and Tianjin, constituting circum-Bohai Sea Economic Zone.

5. Opening Shanghai Pudong Development Zone

Shanghai is a largest port city of industry and commerce in China. In April

1990, the State Council decided to open up the Pudong Development Zone, with the policy similar to Shenzhen Special Economic Zone. What makes it different from general economic development zone is that Pudong Development Zone revolves around the third industry. It aims at making Shanghai a centre of international economy, trade, finance, shipping, culture and telecommunications, leading to the economic take-off of the Yangtze River Delta and even the Yangtze river basin as a whole. At present, Shanghai has become the most developed and most widely open region in China.

6. Establishing Tianjin Binhai New Area

Entering the 21st century, China's opening up strategy is gradually shifting north. The 17th national congress of the CPC formally took the construction of Tianjin Binhai New Area as a national opening strategy. In March 2008, the State Council's "Approval about the comprehensive reform experiment of Tianjin Binhai New Area's overall plan" requires that a perfect socialist market economic system should be built firstly in Tianjin Binhai New Area, with the steps to promote the new area to constantly improve the comprehensive strength, innovation ability, service ability and international competitiveness, so as to promote the development of Tianjin, Beijing-Tianjin-Hebei area and the circum-Bohai Sea area. Meanwhile, the new area should take a role to promote the interaction of the east, the centre and the west of China as well as the coordinated development of national economy as a whole.

7. Beijing-Tianjin-Hebei integrated and coordinated development strategy

In NPC and CPPCC held in Beijing in 2014, Prime Minister Li Keqiang put forward the "The Integration of the Beijing-Tianjin-Hebei Region" as a national development strategy in the government work report for the first time. He also pointed out that it is important "to strengthen the economic cooperation between the circum-Bohai Sea area and the Beijing-Tianjin-Hebei region, to differentiate the economic policies, to promote industrial transfer, to develop a big traffic flow in different regions, and to form a new regional economic growth pole". In 2015, the National Development and Reform Commission (NDRC) formulated the "Program outline for coordinated development of the Beijing-Tianjin-Hebei region", which pointed out that promoting coordinated development of the Beijing-Tianjin-Hebei region is a major national strategy. The core of the strategy is to relieve the non-capital functions of Beijing in an orderly way, adjust the economic structure and spatial structure, blaze a new path of intensive development, explore a mode of optimal development in densely populated and economically intensive areas, promote coordinated regional development and form a new growth pole.

8. Xiong'an New Area was established

On April 1, 2017, the CPC central committee and the State Council issued a notice, announcing the establishment of Hebei Xiong'an New Area. This is another new area of national significance after Shenzhen Special Economic Zone and Shanghai Pudong New Area. Located in the hinterland of Beijing, Tianjin and Baoding, Xiong'an New Area is endowed with obvious geographical advantages, with its convenient and smooth transportation, excellent ecological environment and strong carrying capacity of resources and environment, while the degree of development is relatively low and there is ample space for development. The purpose of this new area is, firstly, to relieve the non-capital functions of Beijing and transfer the over-concentrated institutions in Beijing to this new area; secondly, to adjust the industrial structure in Beijing-Tianjin-Hebei region and help it steadily shift to a high-end manufacture and technological innovation industries. For these reasons, Beijing-Tianjin-Hebei region is gradually moving towards the integration of transportation, the integration of environmental protection, the integration of industrial structure and the integration of public services.

Ⅲ Main features of coastal areas' opening up

1. The entry point to international market has gradually shifted from labor-intensive industries to technology-intensive ones

In the early stage of China's reform and opening up, for coastal areas, labor-intensive industries were principal entry point to international market. Based on that, they developed export and processing trade, increased foreign exchange, introduced advanced technology and equipment, promoted domestic economic development and further expanded foreign trade. Since 1990s, the market economy in China's coastal areas developed and improved rapidly. The import and export of high-tech products boomed, the industrial structure of coastal areas underwent great changes, simple and labor-intensive industries began transferring to the central and western regions, technology-intensive industries gradually became the preferential ones in coastal regions, and thus the structure of export products started tilting.

The technology-intensive products in the coastal areas are predominated by computers, aerospace technology and communication electronics. The trade development is mainly based on processing trade. And foreign-funded enterprises occupy an important position in China's high-tech exports.

2. The mode of trade has shifted from "two ends outside, large inflows and outflows" to independent innovation and self-own brands

The so-called "two ends outside" refers to putting the two ends of production and operation, that is, to put raw materials and sales in the international market, importing a large number of domestic raw materials and parts that are in shortage, processing them in coastal areas, and then exporting them to the world market in order to resolve competition between coastal and inland areas for raw materials and market. In the development of "large inflows and outflows" trading methods, coastal areas gradually improved localization, strived to develop the component and raw material industry instead of relying on import, and raised the value-added and export product grades. Entering the 21st century, China's labor cost advantage no longer existed, and this trade pattern had had a certain negative impact on China's foreign trade. For example, there is a large gap between trade statistics and actual returns, serious imbalances in trade with developed countries such as the United States, and slow progress in the optimization of China's export structure. Therefore, the development of China's foreign trade should shift to high-tech products based on independent intellectual property rights. Meanwhile, processing and manufacturing can be placed in countries with lower labor costs or China's western regions. From "two ends outside" to "two ends inland", enterprises in coastal areas can mainly focus on R&D innovation and external sales.

3. Direct investment has become the main methods to utilize foreign capital in coastal areas

There are two basic ways to introduce foreign capital, namely direct investment and indirect investment. In the early days of reform and opening up, China was mainly based on the use of foreign indirect investment. However, by the advantage of their geographical advantages, cheap labor, and a good investment environment, the coastal areas focused on using foreign direct investment to develop Chinese-foreign joint ventures, Chinese-foreign cooperative enterprises and wholly foreign-owned enterprises from the very beginning. The establishment of the above three types of "foreign-invested enterprises" is conducive to enhancing the external competitiveness of export products, improving the level of marketization in coastal areas, and promoting the integration of the region with the world market as soon as possible. On the basis of the local economic development, the coastal areas, in addition to introducing foreign direct investment, has gradually implemented the "going out" strategy, vigorously developing foreign direct investment and building transnational investment enterprises with Chinese characteristics.

(2) The Opening Up of Chinese Inland Cities and Western Regions

I The opening up along the Yangtze River

The middle and lower reaches of the Yangtze River are rich in products, obviously advantageous in human resources, developed in transportation, and have a strong industrial foundation. "Opening along the Yangtze River" is to use the Yangtze River's golden waterways to connect the central and western regions along the Yangtze River with Shanghai ports, so that the central and western regions can pass through the Yangtze River waterways to reach the world. In August 1992, the State Council decided to further open the six cities along the Yangtze River, Chongqing, Yueyang, Wuhan, Huangshi, Jiujiang and Wuhu, approved the establishment of the Yangtze River Three Gorges Economic Development Zone, and implemented relevant policies for coastal open cities and coastal economic open zones. The development of these cities and the establishment of the Yangtze River Three Gorges Economic Development Zone will make the Middle and Lower Yangtze River Open Belt, with Shanghai Pudong as the leader, a solid base on accelerating China's modernization. The coast is like a bow, and the Yangtze River with Pudong as the leader is like an arrow. China's opening to the outside world penetrates the hinterland from the coast through the Yangtze River, and the inland economy is bound to develop to the world's advanced level.

II The opening up of Mainland Chinese cities

Following the opening up of the coastal areas and regions along the Yangtze River, China further opened up a number of inland provincial capitals in August 1992 to implement the policy of opening cities along the coast. These cities are four provincial capital cities along border or coast: Harbin, Changchun, Hohhot, Shijiazhuang; and eleven inland capital cities: Taiyuan, Hefei, Nanchang, Zhengzhou, Changsha, Chengdu, Guiyang, Xi'an, Lanzhou, Xining, and Yinchuan. Economic and technological development zones and national high-tech industrial development zones have also been established in some of the above-mentioned cities, given a series of preferential policies in terms of finance, investment and taxation. At this point, China's all-round opening-up pattern has taken shape.

Ⅲ The Great Western Development and opening up of the western region

Compared with the coastal and central regions, the western region is vast in area and rich in resources, However, the infrastructure is backward, the industrial foundation is weak, the ecological environment is tough, the investment environment is inferior, and various types of talents are in shortage. These problems have left the western region lagging in economic development, utilization of foreign capital, foreign trade and technology introduction in medium and long term. Comrade Deng Xiaoping put forward the concept of "two overall situations" in the early 1990s: one overall situation is that the eastern coastal areas should accelerate the opening up so as to develop faster, so the central and western regions should take care of this overall situation; the other is that in a certain period, it is necessary for the eastern region to devote more efforts to help the central and western regions accelerate their development, so the eastern coastal regions must also take care of this overall situation. At the Fourth Plenary Session of the 15th Central Committee of the CPC in 1999, it was clearly stated that China should implement the strategy of The Great Western Development, and put forward in the outline of the country's tenth five-year plan that we should focus on the exploitation and development of the western economy, make China's western region be promising economically developed regions, turn their resource advantages into economic advantages, work hard to improve the investment environment and prompt the opening up of the western region.

The key points of China's implementation of the Great Western Development strategy include infrastructure construction and improvement of the ecological environment. In terms of infrastructure construction, we must concentrate our efforts on a batch of major projects of strategic significance in fields like Water resources, transportation and communications, such as west-to-east gas transportation, west-to-east electricity power transmission, and Qinghai-Tibet railway. Meanwhile, in the developing of the western region, the protection, conservation, and development of water resources must be given a prominent place, and planning and reasonable allocation must be strengthened to improve the efficiency of water utilization; step by step, we should suit our measures to local conditions to promote the construction of important projects, such as natural forests protection, farmland-to-forests and grass returning, desertification prevention and control and grassland protection, and gradually establish a solid green ecological barrier in western China.

(3) Development of China's Pilot Free Trade Zone

Since 2013, China has approved a total of 18 pilot free trade zones, which have gradually developed into a "geese array" pattern in five batches. The current layout of 18 pilot free trade zones reflects the combination of the overall promotion of coastal openness and the key advancement of central and western China. On September 27, 2013, the State Council approved the establishment of the China (Shanghai) Pilot Free Trade Zone. On April 20, 2015, the State Council decided to expand the implementation scope of the China (Shanghai) Pilot Free Trade Zone and approved the establishment of three free trade zones including Guangdong, Tianjin and Fujian. On March 31, 2017, the State Council approved the establishment of 7 free trade zones including Liaoning, Zhejiang, Henan, Hubei, Chongqing, Sichuan, and Shaanxi. In October 2018, the State Council approved the establishment of the China (Hainan) Pilot Free Trade Zone. In August 2019, the State Council approved the establishment of 6 free trade zones including Shandong, Jiangsu, Guangxi, Hebei, Yunnan, and Heilongjiang.

I Reasons for the establishment of the Pilot Free Trade Zone

Liberalization of trade and investment is the most important feature of today's world economic globalization. Since the reform and opening up, China has joined the global industrial division of labor system. By taking advantage of its comparative advantages, China's foreign trade has grown rapidly, and its overall national strength has been greatly improved. It has become a beneficiary of globalization. After the outbreak of the international financial crisis in 2008, the global economy and its governance mechanism have entered a period of deep adjustment, and China's economic development has entered a new normal. Facing the new situation and new challenges at home and abroad, it is necessary to coordinate the top-level design of the open economy, accelerate the construction of a new open economy system, further remove the institutional barriers, implement a new round of high-level opening to the outside world, promote reform, development, and innovation through openness, cultivate new advantages in participating in and leading international economic cooperation and competition. Therefore, the establishment of the Pilot Free Trade Zone is to give full play to the role of the Pilot Free Trade Zone as a "test field" for institutional innovation, explore the establishment of a new system and mechanism that is compatible with the expansion of the service industry, and follow-up tests are linked with international trade and investment rules. The new system and mechanism of the government will test and build the spirit of the reform of the relationship between the government and the market, explore new ways and accumulate new experiences for comprehensively deepening reform and expanding opening up.

II Strategic positioning of the Pilot Free Trade Zone

Based on the analysis of the original intention of the establishment of the Pilot Free Trade Pilot Zone, the strategic positioning of the Pilot Free Trade Pilot Zone should highlight the functions of "testing the system for the country, building a platform for opening up, and seeking development for the local area".

"Testing the system for the country" is to highlight system innovation, take system innovation as the core task, deepen the reform of the relationship between the government and the market, build a new open economy system, and take the lead in forming an internationalized, market-based, and rule-of-law business environment. The new round of reform and opening up nationwide can replicate the experience that can be promoted, making the Pilot Free Trade Zone a pioneering zone and a "testing ground" for institutional innovation.

"Building a platform for opening up" is to highlight opening to the outside world, give play to the advantages of a new open economic system, form a global-oriented opening up pattern, gather international and domestic high-end elements, and create a group of internal and external opening-up phases to promote each other, a new platform combining "bring in" and "going out" to serve the country's "Belt and Road" construction, "going out" strategy and free trade zone strategy.

"Developing for the local" is to highlight the creation of regional almighty, use the free trade pilot zone to gather domestic and foreign high-end resource elements, improve resource allocation capabilities, create regional functional areas such as international shipping, logistics, trade, and finance, and form various modern production service industry and high-end manufacturing clusters, drive the industrial transformation and upgrading of surrounding areas and promote the coordinated development of regional economies.

Ⅲ Institutional Innovation of the Pilot Free Trade Zone

The core task of the construction of the Pilot Free Trade Zone is the institutional innovation. The exploratory experiments carried out by the Pilot Free Trade Zone in the area of institutional innovation can form a powerful "spillover effect". From the perspective of various free trade parks established by developed countries, free investment, trade, financial freedom, and business rules in line with international practice are the essential characteristics and development trends of free trade parks. Therefore, the main task of institutional innovation is to build the basic institutional framework of the China Pilot Free Trade Zone, which includes the following four aspects.

1. Innovation of foreign investment management system centered on negative list management

The so-called negative list management refers to the government's list of industries, fields, and businesses that are prohibited and restricted from entering. The areas outside the list can be freely entered. That is, "things can be done without prohibition from the law." In areas other than the negative list, a record system is generally implemented without additional review. The implementation of the Negative List of Foreign Investment in the China Pilot Free Trade Zone has transmitted signals such as non-discrimination, marketization, and liberalization to foreign investors, which helps to strengthen the transparency of policies, enhance investor confidence and predictability of investment effects.

Since the establishment of the Shanghai Pilot Free Trade Zone in 2013, the special access measures for the negative list have been reduced from the original 190 to 40 in 2019 (see Figure 9-1).

2. Innovation of trade supervision system focusing on trade facilitation

The goal of promoting the innovation of the trade supervision system is to simplify the customs clearance procedures to the greatest extent and implement a fast customs clearance system while ensuring the safety of the goods. Based on the customs clearance supervision service model of "front-line deregulation" and "second-line safety and efficient management",

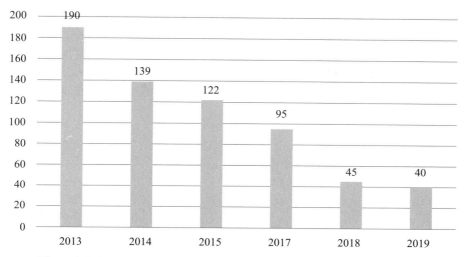

Figure 9-1 The change in negative list of foreign investment from 2013 to 2019
Source: http://www.gov.cn/.

the respective trade pilot zones have carried out a series of reforms and innovations, mainly including: to build a "single window" for international trade; to establish a cross-department comprehensive management service platform for businesses such as trade, transportation, processing, storage, etc.; to implement "entering zone in advance, declaring later"; to carry on "entry and exit in batches, declare in one time"; to simplify and unify record filing list for entry and exit, to inspect and release through intelligent bayonet, etc. Among them, the "single window" is an important and critical basic project to implement trade facilitation reform. It achieves this by establishing a "single" public platform for trade-related information exchange between traders and government agencies, government agencies and government agencies to implement simplification, coordination and efficiency of trade supervision.

3. Financial system innovation aimed at capital account convertibility and opening of the financial services industry

In terms of financial innovation and supervision, the China Pilot Free Trade Zone insists on the advancement of important areas and key links such as FT account business, RMB capital account convertibility, RMB cross-border use, and foreign exchange management reform on the premise of macro prudence and controllable risks. The basic goals of innovation in the financial sector are to serve the real economy, facilitate cross-border investment and trade, promote the convertibility of RMB capital items, improve the financial regulatory system, and serve to deepen financial reform and expand financial openness. From the perspective of building a framework for financial system innovation, the core of financial innovation in the Pilot Free Trade Zone is the innovation of FT accounts, which is to open a small mouth on the convertibility of RMB under capital account in order to obtain replicable and propagable experience.

4. On-event and post-event supervision system innovation with the transformation of government functions as the core

Judging from a series of system innovations made by the China Pilot Free Trade Zone in changing government functions, changing the "priority approval before the event" to "mainly on-and-after event supervision" is one of the most valuable measures to promote replication. In the Pilot Free Trade Zone, six basic comprehensive supervision systems have been established in terms of supervision during and after the event, which has promoted governance systems and capabilities in the social and economic fields, and the modernization of governance systems. These six basic systems include: the national security review system, the antitrust review system, the social credit system, the company's annual report disclosure and business anomaly list system, the information sharing and comprehensive law enforcement system, and the social force participating in the market supervision system.

9.1.3 "Belt and Road" and China's Opening to the Outside World under New Situation

(1) The Background of the "Belt and Road" Initiative

Chinese President Xi Jinping has proposed to build a "Silk Road Economic Belt" and "21st Century Maritime Silk Road" (hereinafter referred to as "Belt and Road") in September 2013. At that time, China's development faced many specific background.

I From the perspective of domestic development, China is entering the stage of "going out" strategic upgrade

At the beginning of the 21st century, China implemented the "going out" strategy, and foreign investment continued to grow rapidly. In 2014, China's foreign investment achieved a historic breakthrough in the "first year of surplus". For the first time, outward foreign direct investment (OFDI) surpassed inward foreign direct investment (IFDI) and China became a net exporter of capital. The «going out» strategic upgrade requires China to transform from quantity to quality, from acquiring resources to allocating resources, from product export to industry export, from a bilateral win-win situation to a trilateral win-win situation, and from a passive rule-participating to an active rule-making.

II From the perspective of regional competition, China needs to hedge the US's "Asia-Pacific rebalancing" strategy

Since Obama came to power in 2009, the United States government has implemented the so-called "Asia-Pacific rebalancing" strategy based on real economic interests, that is, to adjust its power allocation globally and transfer its power in Europe to the Asian region. They are increasing military, diplomatic, and economic pressure in the Asia-Pacific region to limit China's growing influence. The adjustment of the United States' strategy has placed certain external pressures on China, which has made China's surrounding environment more complicated, and made China 's influence in the Asia-Pacific region been challenged.

III From the perspective of international status, China urgently needs to improve the right to change international trade rules

With the gradual decline of the global multilateral trading system led by the WTO, developed economies are actively promoting a new round of negotiations on a free trade agreement. In 2010, the United States led the negotiation of the TPP (Trans-Pacific Partnership Agreement). In 2013, United States and Europe launched the TTIP (Trans-Atlantic Trade and Investment Partnership). In addition to the obvious "exclusive of China" nature, they also focus on the restructuring of economic and trade rules. China's foreign economic and trade negotiations started late, and China has long played the role of receiver and adaptor in terms of rules. We have not yet established the right to change the rules that match our own economic or trade scale.

V From the perspective of key areas, China needs to strengthen energy security and promote the internationalization of RMB

Since entering the 21st century, China's dependence on foreign energy has increased significantly. At the end of 2014, China's dependence on crude oil reached 59.3%, and the dependence on natural gas was 31.6%. Of these, 60% of crude oil imports and transportation needed to pass through the Strait of Malacca. China urgently needed to strengthen energy security. During the year of 2000-2014, China's foreign exchange reserves amounted to an average annual growth rate of 25.2%. In June 2014, China's foreign exchange reserves set a record of up to 39,932 billion dollars. Higher foreign exchange reserves meant higher foreign exchange rate risk, which needs to accelerate the process of RMB internationalization for the use of the RMB tax, international bond and bills markets, and global foreign exchange reserves.

(2) The Value and Layout of the "Belt and Road" Initiative

The "Belt and Road" clarifies the principles, goals and content of the "Three Communities, Three Bodies and Five Directives", and demonstrates the value of dedication to promote peace, prosperity, openness, innovation and a civilized world.

The first is the basic principle of "co-negotiation, co-construction and sharing". Co-negotiation refers to respecting the choice of governance models in other countries, and the pursuit of the greatest common divisor; sharing refers to the pursuit of mutual benefit and win-win, for the benefit of the peoples along the line; Co-construction refers to closely linking the interests, destiny and responsibilities of the countries along the line, focusing on third-party cooperation and building a new global economic governance system.

The second is the cooperative goal of "community of interest, community of responsibility, community of destiny". Building a community of interest is the keynote of the "Belt and Road" initiative. Through in-depth economic cooperation such as interconnected countries and trade and investment facilitation, we will create a new growth pole for the world economy and achieve mutual benefit. Setting up a responsible community is the responsibility of the "Belt and Road" initiative. In order to connect different civilizations with a new cooperation model, we have to promote the harmonious coexistence and try to listen to the voice from different countries and different people, and jointly solve international problems. Establishing a community of destiny is the sublimation of the "Belt and Road" initiative, which will promote the realization of the community of destiny among nations and among regions and Human Destiny Community.

The third is the main content of "policy communication, facility connectivity, unimpeded trade, monetary circulation, and people-to-people communication." The "Belt and Road" not only attaches importance to pragmatic cooperation in key areas such as interconnection, capacity cooperation, trade and investment, but also promotes various forms of humanistic exchanges between countries along the route to achieve common economic and cultural development. Among them, policy communication is an important guarantee, facility connectivity is a priority area, smooth trade is the key content, financial accommodation is an important support and the connection of people's hearts is the social foundation for the construction of the "Belt and Road".

The "5+6+N" strategy has planned overall layout of 5 major trends, 6 economic corridors, and multiple countries and ports, which provides a clear framework for China's leadership and the participation of countries in the "Belt and Road" cooperation.

"The Silk Road Economic Belt" is planned for three major directions, one is from northwest China, northeast through Central Asia, Russia to Europe, and the Baltic Sea; another one is from northwest China through Central Asia, West Asia to the Persian Gulf, and the Mediterranean; the third is from the southwest China Indochina Peninsula to Indian Ocean. The 21st Century Maritime Silk Road has two major directions planned. One is to cross the South China Sea from China's coastal ports, and extend to the Indian Ocean through the Strait of Malacca to Europe; The other is to cross the South China Sea from China's coastal ports to the South Pacific.

The "Belt and Road" runs through the Eurasian and African continents. One is an active East Asian economic circle and the other is a developed European economic circle, including the New Eurasian Continental Bridge, China-Mongolia-Russia, China-Central Asia-West Asia, China-Indochina Peninsula, Pakistan, Bangladesh and Myanmar, which are six international economic cooperation corridors.

"Multi-country" refers to a group of countries with early cooperation and strategic fulcrum. "Multi-port" refers to a number of cooperative ports that ensure the safe and smooth passage of maritime transport corridors. By co-building a number of important ports with countries along the "Belt and Road", it will further prosper maritime cooperation.

(3) The Significance and Role of the "Belt and Road" to China's Economic Development

The "Belt and Road" initiative is in line with China's development requirements for a new pattern of comprehensive opening up and an open economic system, which will help China to explore new levels of opening up. The reasons are as follows.

Ⅰ "Belt and Road" initiative is conducive to the rational use of excess savings

For a long time, China's national savings have continued to grow at a high speed, and the savings rate has always been among the highest in the world. In 2015, China's gross national savings are more than 33 billion RMB and the savings rate is 47.9%, which is higher than the level of the global (26.5%), developed economies 22.5%, G7 countries 20.8%. In the context of ultra-high savings, China's foreign exchange reserves have grown continuously and rapidly, forming excess reserves. China's foreign exchange reserves reached a maximum of 3.9 trillion dollars in 2014 and have gradually declined in the past five years. At present, China's official foreign exchange reserves still exceed 3 trillion dollars, which is 2.4 times that of Japan ,16.3 times that of Germany, 21.1 times that of Britain, and 25.2 times that of the United States.

The "Belt and Road" initiative has a positive effect on reducing China's high savings and savings rate. On the one hand, it is possible to directly broaden the use of foreign exchange reserves and explore diversified foreign exchange utilization measures, such as the establishment of the Silk Road Fund (the proportion of foreign exchange reserves in the first phase of capital funds is 65%), expanding imports from the Belt and Road countries, which could increase the use of foreign exchange reserves efficiency and resolve excessive foreign exchange reserves. On the other hand, it is possible to increase the overseas investment channels of domestic enterprises and the government, which could transform the savings surplus into foreign direct investment. With these schemes, we may solve the new cycle of high savings rate caused by the limited and blind domestic investment channels and overcapacity and excessive trade surplus. The expansion of overseas consumer markets is also conducive to reducing excess savings.

Ⅱ "Belt and Road" initiative will accelerate the process of RMB internationalization

In 2015，IMF formally took the RMB into Special Drawing Rights (SDR)

and RMB has become one of the main international reserve currency since then. However, compared with international mainstream currencies such as the dollar, euro, yen, and pound, the internationalization level of the RMB is still relatively low. From 2014 to 2015, the RMB internationalization index was slightly lower than the pound and the yen, and much lower than the US dollar and the euro. At the end of 2015, the RMB accounted for only 30.9% of the Japanese yen and 1.35% of the dollar in the balance of the international bond and bill markets. At the end of 2016, the proportion of RMB in global foreign exchange reserves was only 1.67% of the dollar, even lower than the Australian dollar and Canadian dollar.

The implementation of the "Belt and Road" and the internationalization of the RMB will promote and coordinate each other. On the one hand, the "Belt and Road" initiative creates opportunities for the internationalization of the RMB. From goods trade to cross-border direct investment, from current accounts to open cooperation under capital, cross-border credit, financial markets, and currency markets, the implementation of the "Belt and Road" has generated realistic and huge demand, and the "Belt and Road" will become the main battlefield for RMB internationalization. On the other hand, the internationalization of RMB provides capital protection for the "Belt and Road". Through international tools or means such as currency swaps, RMB settlement of foreign direct investment, RMB cross-border payment, RMB settlement of cross-border trade, and overseas RMB clearing, the "Belt and Road" has methodically implemented the functions of the RMB as a means of circulation, a means of payment, a value scale and a reserve currency, which promotes the in-depth implementation of the "Belt and Road" in return.

Ⅲ "Belt and Road" initiative is conducive to China's exploration of international economic and trade rules

During the 40 years since "reform and opening up" strategy, China has played different roles in the global open economy. In the first stage, China was "a follower". In 1978, "reform and opening up" strategy became a basic national policy of China. In order to attract foreign investment and participate in the global industrial division of labor, China approved the establishment of special economic zones such as Shenzhen, and carrying out the introduction of international economic rules. The second stage, China became "a participant". In 2001, China officially became a member of the WTO, and began to fully integrate into international multilateral trade rules and systems to achieve "parallel running." At present, China is gradually becoming the "leader" at the third stage. As China becomes the world's second largest economy, the world's largest trading nation, the world's largest foreign investment attracting country, and the world's second largest foreign investment country, Chinese power in the global economic governance system has been significantly improved. At this stage, it will achieve a "leading position" in the global open economic system by exploring full openness and giving play to the leading role of rules.

The "Belt and Road" initiative is an important platform for China to play the role of "a leader" in the leading phase of the open economy. On the one hand, China has continued to promote economic globalization toward greater openness, tolerance, preference, balance, and win-win situation in the context of the weak global economy, imbalanced development, dilemma in governance, fair deficits, and other anti-globalization trends. On the other hand, it is conducive for China to represent the developing countries along the "Belt and Road" in grasping the institutional rights of global economic governance, participating in and leading the formulation of rules. This is not only a requirement of economic globalization, but also a reflection of the power of developing countries.

Ⅳ "Belt and Road" initiative is conducive to China's "going out" trend

The "Belt and Road" initiative helps to form a new pattern of "going out" and "introducing" with equal emphasis on development. On the one hand, the "Belt and Road" initiative has helped many countries to understand deeply China's investment opportunities and prospects, especially helped those countries that have complementary advantages with China to deeply integrate production factors and the market with China. On the other hand, the "Belt and Road" has a vast territory and many countries. Along the route, emerging economies and developing countries are the main players. Most countries have huge demand for Chinese products, technologies and experience. From 2014 to 2016, China's import and export volume with the countries along the route has reached 3.1 trillion dollars, accounting for more than a quarter of China's total foreign trade during the same period. Direct investment in countries along the route was nearly 50 billion dollars, constituting 1/10 or more of China's foreign direct investment in the same period.

The "Belt and Road" initiative also helps to form a new pattern of "both the sea and the land" and "emphasis on the mutual development of the east and the west." The "Belt and Road" includes both the " 21st Century Maritime Silk Road" and the "New Silk Road Economic Belt", which takes into account both land and sea. In particular, the Silk Road Economic Belt realizes land-sea connectivity from China through Central Asia, Russia, West Asia, and South Asia to the Mediterranean, Baltic Sea, and Indian Ocean through the construction of the Eurasian Continental Bridge, opening up the Silk Road that was interrupted in history and allowing Eurasia to return the heart land of human civilization.

V "Belt and Road" initiative is conducive to the full participation of China's major regions.

The "Belt and Road" initiative provides consistent guidance for the major regions in China to promote openness and helps promote China's new era of open economic system from "regional polarized development" to "regional coordinated development" and then to "regional joint development" "change. In the early stage of focusing on the backward development of the central and western regions and the promotion of an open economy in the central and western regions, the "Belt and Road" initiative encourages all regions, provinces, and cities in China to participate, connects the international and domestic markets, and gives full play to the Beijing-Tianjin-Hebei, the Yangtze River Economic Belt, the Guangdong-HongKong-Macao Greater Bay Area and other proactive regions, formulating the two core provinces (Xinjiang and Fujian), targeting 18 provinces, and planning 7 highlands and 15 ports. The "Belt and Road" initiative will make a significant adjustment to China's opening up to the outside world, forming a North-South response, and East-West linkage, and a shared responsibility for China's opening-up economic development.

9.2 China's Foreign Trade Development and Its Strategy

Foreign trade is an important driver of Chinese economy and plays a significant role in economic growth, industrial upgrading, job creation and tax increases. During the past four decades, the pattern of China's foreign trade has undergone fundamental changes. Since the 18th CPC National Congress, Chins has introduced a series of policies and measures to promote the healthy development of foreign trade and vigorously optimize the market layout, domestic regional distribution, commodity structure and trade modes. Chinese government has been making efforts to accelerate the transformation of foreign trade. Create better business environment and help reduce the cost. The 19th CPC National Congress further proposed that China will promote further and deeper opening up the world and the construction of a stronger trade country, marking a new chapter of China's foreign trade.

9.2.1 Development Status and Development Strategy of China's Goods Trade

In the past forty years, China has gradually realized an important transition from poverty to prosperity. The "Chinese speed" of economic development has surprised the world, and China's foreign trade in goods has achieved world-renowned achievements.

(1) Development Status and Main Features of China's Goods Trade

Ⅰ China's foreign trade in goods has reached an unprecedented volume, and the trade surplus has increased year by year

In 1978, China's total imports and exports amounted to USD 20.64 billion; in 2018, China's total imports and exports increased to USD 4.62 trillion, and its total imports and exports increased by 224 times compared with the beginning of reform and opening-up, with an average annual growth rate of 14.1%, far exceeding the world average, and even the world's major economies. At the beginning of the reform and opening-up, China's exports of goods were less than 1% of the world market. In 2018, China became the world's largest country in goods trade, with exports accounting for 12.8% of the world, ranking first in the world; followed by the United States, its imports rank second in the world; China's trade surplus in goods has long ranked first in the world (see Figure 9-2).

Figure 9-2 China's Trade in Goods from 1999 to 2020

Sources: http://www.stats.gov.cn/.

Ⅱ The commodity structure of China's foreign goods trade is constantly optimized

Take China's exports as an example. Before 1980, primary products accounted for a large proportion of China's exports; in the late 1980s, industrial manufactured products gradually replaced primary products and became the main products in China's exports; in the 1990s, China's exports were dominated by light textiles; after a 10-year transition, the structure of export commodities mainly based on mechanical and electrical products was established; after entering the 21st century, scientific and technological progress promoted the birth and development of high-tech products, among which, the proportion of electronic information technology products in China's exports has been increasing. It can be seen that China's export commodity structure has undergone significant changes, gradually shifting from focusing on labor-intensive products to focusing on capital and technology-intensive products (see Table 9-1 and Table 9-2).

Table 9-1 Structure of China's Exports from 2011 to 2020　　Unit: Billion USD

Index	2011	2012	2013	2014	2015	2016	2017	2018	2019	2020
Total value	1898.4	2048.7	2209.0	2342.3	2275.0	2098.2	2263.5	2486.7	2499.5	2590.6
Primary product	100.6	100.6	107.3	112.7	104.0	105.1	117.7	135.0	133.97	115.47
Food and live animals	50.49	52.07	55.73	58.92	58.16	61.05	62.64	65.47	65.0	63.55
Drinks and tobacco	2.28	2.59	2.61	2.88	3.31	3.54	3.47	3.71	3.47	2.48
Inedible ingredients	14.98	14.34	14.57	15.83	13.92	13.08	15.44	18.02	17.22	15.92
Fossil fuels, lubricants and related materials	32.27	31.01	33.79	34.45	27.94	26.84	35.35	46.81	47.12	32.11
Animal and vegetable fats and waxes	0.53	0.54	0.58	0.62	0.64	0.56	0.81	1.07	1.15	1.40
Manufactured goods	1797.8	1948.2	2102.7	2230.0	2171.0	1993.1	2145.8	2351.7	2365.5	2475.2
Chemicals and related products	114.8	113.6	119.7	134.6	129.6	121.9	141.3	167.5	161.8	169.2

Contd.

Index	2011	2012	2013	2014	2015	2016	2017	2018	2019	2020
Finished products by raw materials	319.6	334.2	360.7	400.4	391.3	315.2	368.1	404.8	406.7	434.2
Machinery and transportation equipment	901.8	964.4	1039.3	1070.6	1059.5	984.5	1082.9	1208.1	1195.4	1258.3
Miscellaneous products	459.4	534.7	581.5	622.2	588.2	529.6	547.8	565.8	583.5	584.9
Unsorted other products	2.34	1.42	1.73	2.28	2.38	5.57	5.76	6.17	18.07	28.55

Source: http://www.stats.gov.cn//.

Table 9-2 Structure of China's Imports from 2011 to 2020   Unit: Billion USD

Index	2011	2012	2013	2014	2015	2016	2017	2018	2019	2020
Total value	1743.5	1818.4	1950.0	1959.2	1682.0	1587.4	1841.0	2135.7	2078.4	2055.6
Primary product	604.3	634.9	657.6	647.4	473.0	440.2	577.1	701.7	729.95	677.07
Food and live animals	28.77	35.26	41.70	46.82	50.50	49.14	54.29	64.80	80.74	98.19
Drinks and tobacco	3.68	4.40	4.51	5.22	5.77	6.10	7.03	7.66	7.66	6.21
Inedible ingredients	284.9	269.7	286.1	270.1	210.5	201.9	260.2	272.2	284.94	294.48
Fossil fuels, lubricants and related materials	275.8	313.1	314.9	316.8	198.8	176.3	247.8	349.2	347.23	267.54
Animal and vegetable fats and waxes	11.11	12.53	10.34	8.49	7.48	6.73	7.68	7.78	9.38	10.65
Manufactured goods	1139.2	1183.5	1292.7	1312.9	1208.9	1147.3	1263.9	1434.0	1348.5	1378.5
Chemicals and related products	181.1	179.3	190.3	193.4	171.3	164.0	141.9	223.7	218.73	213.33
Finished products by raw materials	150.3	146.3	148.3	172.4	133.3	121.9	135.1	151.5	140.04	168.28

Contd.

Index	2011	2012	2013	2014	2015	2016	2017	2018	2019	2020
Machinery and transportation equipment	630.6	652.9	710.4	724.5	683.4	657.9	734.9	839.5	786.64	828.59
Miscellaneous products	127.7	136.2	139.0	139.8	134.7	126.0	134.2	143.8	144.21	146.01
Unsorted other products	49.51	68.77	104.7	82.76	86.13	77.45	66.08	75.61	58.83	22.33

Sources: http://www.stats.gov.cn//.

With the continuous deepening of international division of labor, mechanical and electronic products with high added value, high technology and easy realization of economies of scale play an important role in international trade and global industrial division of labor. Mechanical and electrical products are the leading products in China's high-tech products, involving machinery, electronics, automotive, light industry and home appliances. China's exports of mechanical and electrical products have increased more faster than other products from 2001 to 2020 (see Table 9-3), which has made important contributions to the stable and rapid development of the national economy.

Table 9-3 China's Exports of Mechanical and Electrical Products from 2001 to 2020

Years	Export Value (Billion USD)	Growth Rate of Exports (%)	Percentage of Total Exports (%)
2001	118.79	12.8	44.6
2002	157.08	32.23	48.2
2003	227.46	44.81	51.9
2004	323.4	42.18	54.5
2005	426.75	31.96	56
2006	549.42	28.75	56.7
2007	701.11	27.61	57.6
2008	821.73	17.20	57.5
2009	713.11	-13.22	59.3
2010	933.43	30.90	59.2
2011	1085.6	16.30	57.1
2012	1179.4	8.64	57.6

Contd.

Years	Export Value (Billion USD)	Growth Rate of Exports (%)	Percentage of Total Exports (%)
2013	1265.5	7.30	57.3
2014	1312.2	3.69	55.7
2015	1310.72	-0.11	54.2
2016	1209.4	-7.73	53.7
2017	1321.46	9.27	58.4
2018	1460.72	10.54	58.7
2019	1459.02	-0.12	58.3
2020	1541.11	5.63	59.5

Source: http://www.stats.gov.cn//.

III Market coverage of China's foreign trade in goods has been expanded

At the beginning of reform and opening-up, China had only a dozen trading partners, and the scope of the import and export trade market was very limited. Currently, 231 countries and regions have established trade partnerships with China, and their trade markets cover the world. China's main trading partners include both developed countries and regions such as the European Union, the United States and Japan, and developing countries and regions such as ASEAN. After entering the 21st century, while China continues to maintain trades with developed countries in Europe and the United States, its trade relations with emerging markets and developing countries have become more and more consolidated. The more typical are the trades with ASEAN and Africa. The percentage changes from the original 7% and 2% to today's 12.5% and 4%. In 2018, China's largest trading partners were, in order, the European Union, the United States, ASEAN, Japan, South Korea, and Hong Kong (China) (see Figure 9-3). In view of the influence of COVID-19 and Sino-US trade war, ASEAN became the largest trade partner of China in 2020.

The potential for trade cooperation between China and the countries along the "Belt and Road" is continuously being unleashed, and has become a new driving force for China's foreign trade development.

In 1979, China and the United States formally established diplomatic relations, and Sino-US trade relations were normalized. At the end of the

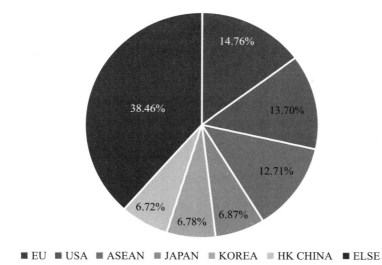

EU   USA   ASEAN   JAPAN   KOREA   HK CHINA   ELSE

Figure 9-3 Trade proportion of China's top six goods trading partners in 2018

Sources: http://www.stats.gov.cn/.

1970s, China's reform and opening-up brought Sino-US trade into a fast track. In 2001, China's accession to the WTO injected strong vitality into China-US trade development. The scale of China-U.S. Trade is huge, and the speed of development has attracted worldwide attention. However, affected by the global financial crisis in 2008, the volume of Sino-US trade in goods decreased by 10.6% in 2009. At the same time, the imbalance in China-US trade in goods has grown significantly. China replaced Japan in 2001 as the largest source of US trade deficit. According to the latest statistics from the Ministry of Commerce, China exported USD 478.4 billion of goods to the United States in 2018, and the trade surplus between China and the United States reached USD323.3 billion, which set a historical record again (see Figure 9-4).

(2) Development Strategy and Master Plan of China's Goods Trade

Foreign trade development strategy refers to the embodiment of a country's or region's economic development strategy in the field of foreign trade, which is a global decision and plan for foreign trade development over a relatively long period of time under the guidance of the country's overall national economic plan. Foreign trade is largely divided into two major parts: trade in goods and trade in services, and trade in goods has long been the major part of China's foreign trade.

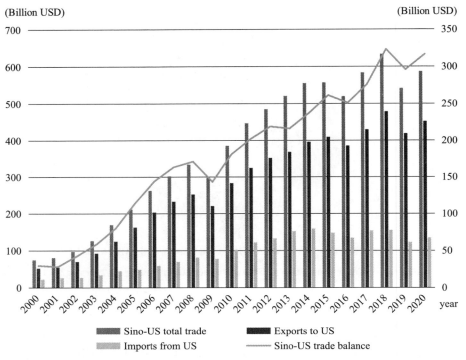

(Billion USD)   (Billion USD)

■ Sino-US total trade   ■ Exports to US
▨ Imports from US   — Sino-US trade balance

Figure 9-4 Imports and Exports of Sino-US Goods Trade and Trade Surplus from 1999 to 2020

Sources: http://www.stats.gov.cn/.

Ⅰ Strategic goals set in 1980

In the early 1980s, the Chinese government formulated a 20-year national economic development plan, that is, from 1981 to 2000, to achieve the goal of quadrupling the gross national product, and the national per capita income should also be quadrupled accordingly. China should enter a well-off society before the next century. In the development goals formulated by various departments, a plan to quadruple in 20 years is also proposed. The overall development strategy of China's goods trade is based on 1981, and it should be increased by 4 times by 2000. The total value of China's import and export of goods in 1981 was 40 billion USD, which should reach 80 billion USD in 1990, and should reach 160 billion USD in 2000. According to this requirement, during this historical period, the average annual growth rate of China's import and export of goods must reach 7.5%, which is much faster than the average annual growth rate of world goods trade at the time of 3% to 4%. In the first 20 years of China's reform and opening up, due to the continuous deepening of the reform of the national economic system and the reform of the foreign trade system, rapid economic development in the coastal areas and vigorous development of an export-oriented economy have promoted the development of China's goods trade into a rapid growth stage. In 1987, the total value of China's import and export of goods trade reached 82.6 billion USD, which was the first doubling in three years; in 1992, it reached 165.6 billion USD, and achieves the strategic goal of quadrupling 8 years in advance.

Ⅱ Adjustment to the development plan of goods trade in 1992

In the first 20-year development plan after the reform and opening up, due to various reasons, such as the speed of opening up to the outside world, the acceleration of the development of coastal areas, and the continuous increase degree in China's market access, the strategic goal of quadrupling the 20-year trade in goods proposed originally was realized 8 years in advance. At that time, when setting the development goals of the goods trade, the domestic price increase factors were not taken into account, and the development goals were calculated based on trade value instead of "trading volume". In addition, practice has proven that the growth rate of foreign trade always exceeds the growth rate of the country's GDP. In formulating the development goals of foreign trade in goods, China formulated them in synchronization with the development of domestic GDP. In 1992, China convened the 14th National Congress of the Communist Party of China, which officially announced that the goal of China's economic system reform was to build a socialist market economy, and proposed a strategic plan for further opening up and accelerating the development of foreign trade. In this way, after the goal of quadrupling the value of foreign trade in goods was achieved in advance in 1992, the goals of China's foreign goods trade development plan were adjusted, and claimed the goal that the total value of China's import and export trade of goods was to reach 400 billion U.S. dollars in 2000. After 8 years of hard work, China's goods trade in 2000 reached 474.3 billion USD, of which 225.1 billion USD was imported trade and 249.2 billion USD was exported.

Ⅲ Formulation and Development Strategy for the import and export of goods in 2001

In December 2001, after 15 years of hard work, China officially joined the World Trade Organization and finally became a member of this global multilateral trading system. China's accession to the WTO has greatly improved its market openness and a wider range of foreign markets. WTO members will give China more general non-discriminatory treatment, which will be more conducive to the rapid development of China's goods trade.

Therefore, China has formulated a new strategy for the development of the import and export of goods in accordance with changes in the domestic and foreign economic environment. Take 500 billion USD of trade volume in 2001 as the base, by 2020, the total value of import and export trade will increase fourfold, that is to reach 200 billion USD, of which imports and exports will each reach 100 billion USD. By then, China will become the world's third and even second largest trading country. In fact, after China's entry into the WTO, as China has been on the track of free trade, China's import and export trade of goods has entered a stage of rapid development. In just 7 years, that is, in 2008, the total value of China's trade in goods reached 251.5 billion USD, of which 14285 billion USD was exported and 1133.3 billion USD was imported. The trade surplus for the year reached 295.5 billion USD, both exceeding the plan to quadruple. China has thus become the world's largest foreign exchange reserve country.

IV New Development Strategy of China's foreign trade in 2016

The 18th National Congress of the Communist Party of China has proposed the 13th five-year plan for China, and 2016 is the starting year. In the "Thirteenth Five-Year Plan" formulated by the country, China proposed a new overall strategy for opening up to the outside world: the implementation of the strategy of "excellent import and excellent export", promoting the transformation of foreign trade into high-quality and excellent prices, and excellent import and excellent export, and accelerating the construction of a strong trade country. China should actively expand imports, optimize the import structure, and import more advanced technology and equipment as well as high-quality consumer goods. China has to actively respond to foreign technical trade barriers, strengthen early warning of trade frictions, and resolve trade frictions and disputes. The formulation and implementation of this strategy is of great practical significance, and will provide a basis for strengthening and improving the macro-adjustment and management of foreign trade, which will help solve a series of deep-level problems that are currently facing the development of foreign trade , break the isolation layer between markets and the boundaries between domestic departments and regions and will help promote professional cooperation and union. At the same time, the strategy will improve the layout of opening to the outside world, further promote cooperation in international capacity and equipment manufacturing, accelerate the optimization and upgrading of foreign trade, and improve foreign trade. The new system has created conditions for the realization of corporate groupization and international operations and has very positive significance for promoting China's reform and opening up in the field of foreign trade.

V Guidance on promoting high-quality development of trade in 2019

Guided by Xi Jinping's socialist ideology with Chinese characteristics in the new era, the formulation of trade should fully implement the spirit of the 19th sessions and the party's second, third and fourth plenary sessions of the 19th sessions, adhere to the new development concept, persist in promoting the development of high quality, and take the structural reform of supply side as the main line to accelerate the transition from institutionalized opening of commodities and factors to institutional openings such as rules, build a higher level of open economic new system, and improve the foreign-related economic and trade laws and rules system. It is of necessity to deepen reform in the field of foreign trade, adhere to market-oriented principles and business rules, strengthen scientific and technological innovation, institutional innovation, model and format innovation, focus on co-construction of the "Belt and Road", vigorously optimize the trade structure, and promote the coordinated development of imports and exports, trade in goods and services, trade and two-way investment, trade and industry, promote the orderly and free flow of international and domestic factors, the efficient allocation of resources, and the deep integration of the market, promote the basic balance of international payments, achieve high-quality trade development, and create the new situation of opening and cooperation, tolerance and preference, and win-win international trade, which makes greater contributions to promoting China's economic and social development and building a community of shared future for mankind. Promoting the high-quality development of trade is a major decision-making plan made by the party's central government in the face of profound changes in the international and domestic situations. It is also an inevitable requirement for striving to advance the cause of socialism with Chinese characteristics in the new era. By 2020, the trade structure should be further optimized, the trade benefits will be significantly improved, and the trade power will be further strengthened. An indicator, policy, statistics and performance evaluation system for high-quality trade development will be established.

9.2.2 Development of China's Trade in Service and the Openness of Service Market

With the rapid development of the world economy and the continuous adjustment of the industrial structure, the service industry has become a key industry for development in various countries in the world, and service trade has become an important way for countries to compete for commanding heights. Since the reform and opening up, China's service industry has developed rapidly. The proportion of the service industry's output in GDP has increased from 31.3% in 1990 to 52.2% in 2018. The contribution of the service industry to China's cumulative GDP growth is 59.7%. The development of the service industry has led to the rapid development of service trade. However, due to the lag of economic development and the imperfection of the market economy, there are many problems in the development of China's service trade. With China's accession to the WTO, the degree of opening up of China's service market has continued to increase, and it has begun to fully interface with the world service market.

(1) Development Status and Characteristics of China's Trade in Service

I China's service trade is developing fast, and it has a big economy but not a strong one

China's total trade in services in 1982 was only $ 4.6 billion. Since 2001, China's trade in services has achieved unprecedented development, rising to approximately 768.6 billion USD in 2018, ranking second in the world, with an average annual growth rate of 14.8% (see Table 9-4). Compared with other countries in the world, China's service trade has developed rapidly, and its service trade accounted for 12.58% of the world's service trade in 2018. However, because of the effect of COVID-19, China's trade in service declined sharply in 2020.

Table 9-4 Development of China's Service Trade from 1999 to 2020

Years	Export Value (Billion USD)	Import Value (Billion USD)	Total Trade (Billion USD)	Share of the World (%)	Trade Balance (Billion USD)
1999	26.25	31.59	57.84	4.03	-5.34
2000	30.43	36.03	66.46	4.37	-5.6
2001	33.33	39.27	72.6	4.76	-5.94
2002	39.75	46.53	86.27	5.28	-6.78
2003	46.76	55.31	102.07	5.38	-8.55
2004	64.91	72.72	137.63	5.98	-7.81
2005	74.4	83.97	158.37	5.96	-9.57

Contd.

Years	Export Value (Billion USD)	Import Value (Billion USD)	Total Trade (Billion USD)	Share of the World (%)	Trade Balance (Billion USD)
2006	92	100.84	192.84	6.43	-8.84
2007	122.21	129.13	251.34	7.01	-6.92
2008	147.11	156.4	303.51	7.54	-9.29
2009	129.48	145.98	275.46	7.65	-16.5
2010	162.17	193.4	355.57	9.07	-31.23
2011	186.01	247.84	433.85	9.84	-61.83
2012	201.58	281.3	482.88	10.64	-79.72
2013	207.01	330.61	537.62	11.11	-123.6
2014	219.14	432.88	652.02	12.55	-213.74
2015	217.4	435.54	652.94	13.16	-218.14
2016	208.4	452.1	660.5	13.13	-243.7
2017	213.06	467.59	680.65	12.54	-254.53
2018	233.57	525.04	758.61	12.58	-291.47
2019	244.36	505.51	749.87	12.20	-261.15
2020	235.21	380.54	615.75	/	-145.33

Source: http://www.stats.gov.cn//.; https://unctad.org/statistics//.

Ⅱ The service trade export structure is mainly traditional labor-intensive

In terms of service product structure, there is still a large gap compared with the United States and Britain and other service trade powers. Therefore it is not yet a real powerhouse in trade in services. Abundant labor resources are China's comparative advantage. Although China's service trade structure has changed significantly in recent years, traditional labor-intensive service products are still the mainstay in service exports. Taking 2020 as an example, transportation, tourism, construction, and other business services are still the main sources of revenue for trade in services, with revenues of 56.65 billion USD, 14.23 billion USD, 12.65 billion USD, and 70.22 billion USD, with four totaling 153.74 billion USD. It accounts for 65.36% of the total revenue from service trade (see Table 9-5). In addition, the COVID-19 led to inevitably a sharp decrease in the revenue of travel services from 40.39 billion USD in 2018 to 14.23 billion USD in 2020.

Table 9-5 China's Service Trade Structure in 2020   Unit: Billion USD

Item	Export Value	Import Value	Total Trade	Trade Balance
Shipment Service	56.64	94.7	151.34	-38.06
Travel Services	14.23	130.5	144.73	-116.27
Construction Services	12.65	8.06	20.71	4.59
Insurance Services	5.38	12.34	17.72	-6.96
Financial Services	4.27	3.31	7.58	0.96
Other Business Services	70.22	50.44	120.66	19.78
Computer and Information Services	38.87	32.96	71.83	5.91
Government Services	2.51	3.56	6.07	-1.05

Source: http://www.stats.gov.cn//.

Ⅲ Trade in services has been in deficit for a long time

From Table 9-4, we can clearly see that China's service trade deficit has been in deficit for 20 consecutive years from 1999 to 2018; the service trade deficit has not changed much in the first 10 years, hovering between billions of dollars; since 2009, China's The trade deficit has increased rapidly, from a deficit of 16.9 billion USD to 291.5 billion USD in 2018, an increase of 17.25 times in 10 years. Among the projects with large deficits are transportation, tourism, insurance, royalties and royalties. In 2018, the tourism service deficit accounted for 81.8% of the total service trade deficit, becoming the most important factor driving the growth of the service trade deficit.

(2) Problems Existing in the Development of China's Service Trade

I The overall level of development of service trade is not high enough and international competitiveness is weak

Since the reform and opening up, although China's trade in services has developed rapidly, the overall level of development has not been high and is not compatible with the development of China's overall national economy. Compared with developed countries, China's service trade accounted for a relatively low share of world service trade. In 2018, China's service exports accounted for only 3.4% of world service trade. In addition, China's trade in services has not been able to keep pace with trade in goods, and the proportion of trade in services in China's foreign trade is relatively low, which will ultimately restrict the further development of China's trade in goods. China has abundant natural resources and primary labor resources, and has certain advantages in resource-intensive and labor-intensive service industries such as international tourism, marine transportation and labor export. The impact of primary factors is getting smaller and smaller, but the dependence on advanced elements such as knowledge, talents, and communication means is growing. Therefore, the lack of high-level resources and talents has become an important obstacle to the development of China's trade in services.

Ⅱ The internal structure of the service industry is unreasonable, and the service industry gap between regions is also widening

From the perspective of the internal structure of the service industry, developed countries are mainly dominated by emerging industries such as information, consulting, technology, and finance, while China's service trade advantage sectors have long concentrated in traditional areas such as shipping and tourism, accounting for more than half of China's total service trade exports. And some basic service industries (such as post and telecommunications, communications) and the rapid development of global service trade in finance, insurance, consulting, patent services and other technology-intensive, knowledge-intensive and capital-intensive emerging service sectors are still in the development stage in China. The competitiveness is not strong, which is incompatible with the requirements of the era of knowledge economy. At the same time, the gap in the development of service industries in the east, middle, and west is also expanding.

Ⅲ Inadequate legislation for trade in services lags behind the development of the service industry and trade in services

The current management system, policies and regulations of China's service trade and service industry are still not perfect and complete. Although *The Foreign Trade Law* has included service trade as an important content, it still has obvious shortcomings compared with the development requirements of international service trade. So far, China does not have a general law on service trade, and existing legislation has failed. There are gaps in the law in a considerable part of the system. Existing regulations are mainly manifested in the rules and internal documents of various functional departments. Not only is the level of legislation low, but also the lack of coordination has affected the uniformity and transparency of China's service trade legislation. In addition, there are many service departments, many of which have no specific regulations, and such sector laws and industry regulations should have corresponding foreign-related economic provisions that are compatible with *The Foreign Trade Law*. *The Foreign Trade Law* also lacks specific detailed provisions against the establishment of foreign countries' barriers to trade in services, the implementation of discriminatory treatment and unfair trade.

IV Statistical analysis information and data are incomplete, lacking a unified standard and caliber

In the second half of the 20th century, international trade in services became a relatively independent field of trade development. Compared to trade in goods and international investment, theoretical research on international trade in services is still a new field. In China, the understanding of international trade in services and the corresponding academic viewpoints have only emerged since the Uruguay Round negotiations in 1986, and have developed with the conclusion of the General Agreement on Trade in Services, and are therefore in their infancy. In addition, due to the intangibility of service trade, it is difficult to carry out uniform and strict supervision through customs and taxation. At present, in addition to the situation reflected in the balance of payments statement, all departments lack a unified statistical caliber. It is urgent to develop a set of statistical indicators system and statistical management methods for service trade around tools to strengthen macro-control and testing of service trade.

(3) Opening of China's Service Trade Market

In the latest stage of China's "re-entering" negotiations, the issue of opening up the service market is unavoidable. Joining the WTO must make a clear commitment on the opening of the service market. We must not only meet the requirements of national economic development to the opening and development in service market, but also reach the request from other major WTO members.

I Principles of China's service market opening up

The opening of the service market is directly related to the long-term and fundamental interests of China's national economic development. Therefore, it is important to grasp the degree of openness to the outside world. The Chinese government insists on taking the overall and long-term interests of China's economic and social development as its core, on the premise that it is conducive to the development of China's service industry and the improvement of people's living standards. The principle stance of joining the WTO, is, to adhere to the status of developing country, gradually to open up in a phased and sectoral manner, to grasp the initiative of openness, and effectively to adopt the quantitative control method allowed by the WTO, thereby reducing the great impact on domestic related service companies from opening of the Chinese service industry. The Chinese government is not simply and passively accepting the requirements of other WTO members, but rather conducting effective communication and negotiation with other WTO members in a rational, structured and well-founded manner. Negotiations on China's service market have become one of the most intense and time-consuming areas in China's accession negotiations.

II China's commitment to open its service market to the outside world

After several rounds of negotiations with the main WTO members, the Chinese government made specific commitments on trade in services, forming a final schedule of specific commitments, which is reflected in Annex 9 to the Protocol of the People's Republic of China on WTO Accession. China committed to gradually remove most of the current restrictions on many service industries on the premise of maintaining the existing market access level of other member service providers engaged in service industry operations, including banking, insurance, securities, telecommunications, tourism, distribution Services, business and computer related services, film and audiovisual services, etc..

III China's management of trade in services

The orderly opening of the service market is inseparable from the good management of service trade. For a long time, China's service trade has been underdeveloped and the service trade management is very imperfect. It has only gradually been on the right track in recent years. "Accelerating the development of modern service industry and increasing the proportion of the tertiary industry in the national economy" is an important goal of China's industrial restructuring. Expanding the opening up of the service industry has become an important part of China's extensive participation in international competition. Along with it, China's service trade system and management system have been continuously improved.

At present, the basic principles of China's management of service trade are mainly reflected in Chapter IV "International Trade in Services" of *The Foreign Trade Law*, which includes the principles of service trade management, competent authorities, the scope of prohibition and restriction of service trade, and the market access directory. And other general requirements. In recent years, China has promulgated some important laws and regulations in the field of trade in services, such as *The Commercial Bank Law, The Insurance Law, The Maritime Law, The Advertising Law, The Civil Aircraft Law, The Registered Accounting Law, The Lawyers Law and the Regulations on the Administration of Foreign Financial Institutions*, which have played a significant role in regulating China's service trade market. Regarding the management of specific sectors in service trade, the state stipulates that specific management agencies should implement the management. For example, the banking industry is managed by China Banking Regulatory Commission (CBRC), the education industry is managed by the Ministry of Education, the tourism industry is managed by the Tourism Bureau, and the transportation industry is managed by the Ministry of Transportation.

After China's joined into the WTO, it has actively and orderly expanded the opening up of the service industry. The government has promulgated new regulations and rules on foreign market access in some important service trade areas. Regarding the export of service trade, the government promotes innovation in the management system, enterprise mechanism, organizational form, and variety of services by expanding opening up; it promotes the introduction of advanced service technologies and standards to drive the overall level of the service industry; it promotes and fosters the comparative advantages of service industry, which enhances international competitiveness and reduces the deficit in trade in services. In addition, the government encourages qualified enterprises to "go out" and develop multinational companies in the service industry, encourages design consultation, foreign engineering and technology contracting, service outsourcing, and labor service cooperation. The relevant departments have also created the necessary conditions for enterprises to develop international markets, expand market share, and improve international competitiveness in areas such as finance, insurance, foreign exchange, finance and taxation, talents, law, information services, and immigration management.

9.2.3 Import and Export of China's Technology Trade

With the rapid development of economy, science and technology, technology trade has become more and more important in world trade. In July 2004, China's implementation of *The Foreign Trade Law* explicitly identified technology trade, trade in goods, and service trade as the three pillars of China's foreign trade, and announced that the country permitted free import and export of technology.

A basic content of China's opening to the outside world is the large-scale introduction of foreign advanced technologies and equipment in order to change the long-term technological backwardness. Science and technology are the primary productive forces. Practice has proved that technology is the "engine" of economic growth and technological progress is the only way to revitalize the economy. China's long-term technology introduction work has divided the introduction into the following five items: first, advanced equipment and components; second, new and high-quality materials; third, new principles, data, and formulas; fourth, new processes and scientific operating procedures; and fifth, advanced management methods.

After over 40 years of reform and opening up, economic construction and the digestion and absorption of imported technologies, China has established a comprehensive scientific research system and production system with a combination of practical industrial and agricultural technologies and cutting-edge technologies. China has a large number of mature industrialization technologies, many of which have been developed, reaching the advanced level in the world. China has abundant technical resources, forming a comprehensive and multi-level technology export capability. China's complete sets of equipment and high-tech products not only have strong supporting capabilities, but also have considerable competitiveness in price, which is very suitable for developing countries. At the same time, the field of technology exports has also expanded from a few specialized fields to multiple specialized fields. China's export of complete sets of equipment and high-tech products involves machinery, shipbuilding, building materials, electronics, chemical, textile, metallurgy, energy, communications and pharmaceutical industries. Although the current proportion of foreign trade exports is still small, with future development of the economy and the improvement of science and technology, China strives to achieve multi-sectoral coordination and cooperation, and form enterprise alliances and groupings, so that China will gradually become a strong exporter of such products.

9.3 China's Introduction of Foreign Investment and Foreign Direct Investment

Since 1979, China has unswervingly expanded its opening to the outside world from the beginning of reforms. From the establishment of special economic zones to the opening of coastal, riverside, border, and inland areas to accession to the World Trade Organization, the establishment of a free trade pilot zone, and implementation of the "The Belt and Road Initiative", from large-scale "introduction" to large-scale "going out", China has used two markets and two resources to continuously improve its level of opening up.

9.3.1 The Policy Evolved from "Bringing in" to "Going out"

At the end of 1970s, international investment is in a stage of rapid development, foreign direct investment and indirect investment become a key driving force for economic globalization. As the world's largest developing country, China confronted with "Double gap" in the savings and foreign exchange. Facing the dual pressures at home and abroad, the biggest difficulty for China to get rid of poverty and modernization is to lag behind in technology and lack of funds. For this reason , the Third Plenary Session of the Eleventh Central Committee of the Communist Party of China in 1978 established open strategy with the introduction of foreign investment and the construction of foreign-related enterprises as the main content. The scale and scope of China's use of foreign capital has been continuously expanded, and the level and quality of foreign capital utilization have been continuously improved. China's use of foreign capital has transformed from making up for insufficient funds to exerting technical effects, and has achieved remarkable results in the use of foreign capital.

The report of the 15th National Congress of the Communist Party of China (1997) established the strategy of "encouraging foreign investment that can take advantage of China's comparative advantage". The report of the 17th National Congress of the CPC (2007) clearly pointed out that the strategy of opening up includes two aspects: "introduction" and "going out": adhere to the basic national policy of opening up, and better combine "introduction" and "going out", expand the field of opening up, optimize the opening structure, improve the quality of opening up, improve the open economic system of internal and external linkages, accomplish open economy system of mutual benefit and win-win, safe and efficient, and form a new advantage of participating in international economic cooperation and competition under the conditions of economic globalization. "Bringing in" refers to the use of foreign capital, which not only solves the problem of capital, but also brings in many technical factors such as technology and management through the absorption of foreign capital. "Going out" refers to economic and technological cooperation with foreign countries through investing in overseas factories, contracting projects and exporting labor services, etc., which is an economic development strategy proposed by the Communist Party of China in the new period and stage.

The Fifth Plenary Session of the Eighteenth Central Committee of the Communist Party of China in 2015 further proposed that: improve the strategic layout of opening up, promote two-way opening up, and promote the orderly flow of domestic and international elements, the efficient allocation of resources, and the deep integration of the market, Improve investment layout, expanding open areas, relax access restrictions, and actively and effectively introduce foreign funds and advanced technologies, support enterprises to expand foreign investment, promote equipment, technology, standards, and services to go global, integrate deeply into the global industrial chain, value chain, and logistics chain, build a batch of overseas production bases for commodities, and cultivate a number of multinational enterprises. The report of the 19th National Congress of the Communist Party of China in 2017 pointed out: Promote the formation of a new pattern of comprehensive opening-up, opening-up brings progress, and closure will inevitably lag behind. The "Belt and Road" initiative once again emphasizes the two-way investment layout that places equal emphasis on "bringing in" and "going out".

The continuous adjustment of China's overseas investment strategy is consistent with the overall trend of China's economic development, and is in line with China's continuous expansion of opening up. When China first proposed the "going out" strategy in 2001, China's economy was in a period of rapid development. The positioning of its overseas investment strategy was to drive exports to support the rapid growth of the domestic economy, and to obtain various types of resources that domestic economic development wants through foreign investment. With the continuous enhancement of China's comprehensive economic strength, companies' multinational operations, investment in overseas infrastructure construction, and RMB internationalization continue to enrich and supplement the connotation of

China's overseas investment strategy, and provide corresponding theoretical guidance for the practice of China's overseas investment strategy.

9.3.2 The Development Process of China's Two-way Investment since Opening-up

During the 40 years since the implementation of the strategy of opening up to the outside world, China's two-way investment has grown rapidly. Since 2003, China's scale of attracting foreign investment and the scale of foreign direct investment have entered a stage of rapid development.

(1) The Phase of Development of China's Introduction of Foreign Capital and Its Main Characteristics

Since the reform and opening up in 1979, China's absorption of foreign investment has undergone a process from quantitative change to qualitative change from a concept breakthrough, scale expansion, and domain expansion to structural upgrading. According to its development characteristics, China's development of foreign investment can be divided into the following four stages.

Ⅰ The initial exploration phase (1979–1991)

From 1979 to 1991, China accumulatively utilized foreign investment of 81.156 billion USD, and actually utilized foreign direct investment of 25.057 billion USD, accounting for 30.88%; cumulative foreign borrowing amounted to 52.562 billion USD, accounting for 64.77%; The scale in foreign investment was very small and foreign borrowing was dominated, foreign direct investment accounted for a small proportion in this phase. As foreign borrowing cannot solve the problems of capital utilization efficiency and technology introduction, China's efficiency in using foreign capital in the early stage of opening up was relatively low. Foreign direct investment in this stage was mainly invested in the fields of energy, transportation, communications, and raw materials industries. Among them, from 1979 to 1984, the source of foreign direct investment was mainly from Hong Kong, Macao and Taiwan; from 1985 to 1991, mainland China began to introduce foreign direct investment from Europe and the United States, but it still mainly absorbed Hong Kong, Macao and Taiwan foreign capital.

Ⅱ The rapid development stage (1992–2001)

From 1992 to 2001, China accumulatively utilized foreign investment of 488.966 billion USD, and actually utilized foreign direct investment of 370.169 billion USD, accounting for 75.7%; cumulative foreign borrowing amounted to 94.596 billion USD, accounting for 19.35%; the scale of China's introduction of foreign investment expanded and the introduction of foreign capital was mainly in the form of foreign direct investment, China's efficiency in using foreign capital has begun to improve. This change was mainly due to Deng Xiaoping's speech in 1992, which greatly stimulated large-scale multinational companies from developed countries to invest in China. During this period, while strengthening key constructions such as agriculture, water conservancy, energy, transportation, communications, and pillar industries, the Chinese government has paid more attention to accelerating the pace of transformation and adjustment of existing enterprises and old industrial bases.

Ⅲ Field expansion phase (2001–2006)

At the end of 2001 , China joined the WTO, and the domestic market was further opened to the outside world. As promised to WTO, the field of China's opening up gradually expanded from manufacturing to services. On the first of April, 2002, new "Foreign Investment Industrial Guidance Catalog" began execution, civilian satellites, the design and manufacture of launch vehicles and the traditionally monopolized telecommunications, railway transportation, and commodity wholesale industries of the state are open to foreign investors, indicating China's determination to reform and open up the high-tech sectors and monopoly industries. In addition, China have gradually eliminated quota management in automobile and other industries and implemented substantial reductions in import tariffs; distribution services, legal services, tourism services, education services, and commercial retail have also gradually opened to the outside world. Through the above-mentioned methods, the scale of China's foreign investment absorption has reached a new height. From the focus on scale to the quality, China's absorption of foreign capital has improved.

Ⅳ Upgrading stage (2007 to present)

The US subprime mortgage crisis broke out in 2007, and the global investment landscape has undergone major changes. Developed countries have been greatly affected, their position in global investment has declined, and the status of emerging economies has gradually increased. After

2009, European and American countries successively launched the "re-industrialization" strategy and introduced a series of policies and measures to encourage the return of manufacturing industries. Some European and American multinational companies withdrew some production capacity from emerging developing economies due to dual economic and political considerations , International industry transfers have shown a reverse flow. Against this background, China's absorption of foreign capital was once faced with the withdrawal of some foreign investors, but its overall development was stable and its global investment position was stable. According to the 2015 World Investment Report data released by the United Nations Conference on Trade and Development (UNCTAD) , China›s foreign investment absorption in 2014 reached 12.85 billion US dollars, surpassing the United States for the first time to become the world›s largest recipient of foreign direct investment.

In recent years, China's labor costs have risen rapidly, but China still has a vast consumer market, good infrastructure construction, lots of skilled labor force, and increasingly sophisticated investment policies. In particular, at present, China's absorption of foreign capital continues to develop steadily on a high level, showing a new trend of accelerating the transfer to the high-end links of the industrial chain, further optimizing the industrial structure, and continuously improving the quality.

(2) Case Study: Why should we use Foreign Capital When we have Excess Funds

Around 1997, many domestic companies in China were hit by foreign investment, and their operations met difficulty. There were strong voices against foreign investment. At that time, many not-so-low department leaders wrote to senior leaders that foreign investment should not be introduced when domestic capital was already surplus. Some newspapers also directly titled "Introducing a Project and Falling Down an Industry", which did cause considerable controversy. The research team led by Professor Jiang Xiaojuan was ordered to investigate this issue and found that this issue requires both theoretical interpretation and practical analysis.

Money is an element, and it is often the carrier of many other elements. At that time, Chinese domestic enterprises were inadequate in terms of technology, human capital, international market channels, management experience, etc., and surplus in money didn't signify competitive advantage. Therefore, we need not only foreign funds, what is more important is a series of elements related to the funds. As a carrier of multiple production factors, the two are not the same. At the same time, strengthening competition can promote reform of state-owned enterprises. Professor Jiang made a series of researches on this, to a certain extent, reversed the mainstream views in academia, and then further affected decision-making and public opinion. Later, it became an important point, that is, when production capacity and capital are surplus, domestic capital cannot replace foreign capital. There are "three important" points on this issue. Firstly, the theoretical background is very important. Globalization is not only for mutual exchange of needed products, but for optimizing the allocation of resources on a larger scale. Secondly, actual research is very important. Research shows why foreign investment is not the same as domestic investment; thirdly, international comparisons are very important. The United States and the United Kingdom are the most abundant in capital, but foreign investment must also be introduced. Therefore, we must understand that funds are the carrier of multiple factors under the conditions of an open economy.

9.3.2 Periodic Development of China's Foreign Investment and Its Main Characteristics

Since the implementation of the strategy of opening up to the outside world, China's outward investment has grown from scratch, with investment scales ranging from small to large.

(1) According to the Scale and Speed of Development, China's Outward Direct Investment Development can be Divided into Four Stages

Ⅰ The initial exploration phase (1982–1991)

From 1982 to 1991, the main body of China's foreign direct investment were mainly large state-owned foreign engineering companies, foreign trade companies, and financial enterprises, and the investment scale was small and private enterprises made very little foreign investment. In 1982, China's net foreign direct investment was 44 million USD. Since 1985, China's net foreign direct investment has increased to a certain extent and manufacturing foreign investment has begun to increase, but the scale is still limited. By 1991, China's foreign direct investment cumulative net investment is 5.368 billion USD.

Ⅱ The initial stage of development (1992–2001)

In 1992, China proposed a new strategy for overseas investment. In 1997, the

15th National Congress of the Communist Party of China proposed "encouraging foreign investment that can make use of China's comparative advantages, and better use of domestic and foreign markets and resources." The strategy has promoted the increase in overseas investment by China's large industrial and commercial enterprises. The quantity and quality of China's foreign direct investment at this stage have improved compared to the previous stage, but the total investment of private enterprises does not occupy the mainstream. As of 2001, China's cumulative net foreign direct investment reached 34.654 billion USD.

Ⅲ The steady development stage (2002–2007)

In 2001, China's accession to the WTO made foreign direct investment usher in a period of steady development, net foreign direct investment increase from 25.18 billion USD to 265.06 billion USD, an increase of 9 times. The "11th Five-Year Plan" outline in 2006 pointed out the continued implementation of the "going global" strategy, supported conditional enterprises' direct foreign investment and transnational operations, emphasized the cooperation and opening up of overseas resources, and proposed for the first time to encourage enterprises to participate in overseas infrastructure construction. As of 2007, China's cumulative net foreign direct investment reached 101.926 billion USD. With China Investment Co., Ltd. established in 2007 as a symbol, China's foreign investment has entered a new stage of development.

Ⅳ The high-speed development stage (2008 to present)

Since 2008, the pace of Chinese enterprises' active participation in international investment cooperation has further accelerated. In 2008, China's foreign direct investment exceeded 50 billion USD for the first time. Mergers and acquisitions have become the main forms of Chinese enterprises' foreign investment, and SMEs have increased significantly as investment entities.

According to the statistics from Commerce Department, in 2017, China's domestic investors accomplished the investment to 6236 non-financial direct investment in the global total of 174 countries and regions, accumulating investment of 120.08 billion USD, down 29.4% compared to the previous year. The irrational foreign investment was effectively contained. Meanwhile, China's foreign investment "along the way" countries developed steadily, Chinese enterprises have new investment in along-the-way 59 countries, reaching a total of 143.6 billion USD, accounting for the total amount of the same period by 12%, compared with the year of 2016 an increase of 3.5

percentage points; Foreign investment mainly flows to leasing and business services, wholesale and retail, manufacturing, and information transmission, software and information technology services; Enterprises have completed 341 M&A projects, distributed in 49 countries and regions worldwide , involving the national economy 18 industries, the actual transaction volume 96.2 billion USD, of which 21.2 billion USD was direct investment.

(2) Case Study: Lenovo Acquires IBM's Global PC Business

In 2005, Lenovo officially announced the completion of the acquisition of IBM Global PC business, the new Lenovo after the acquisition will become the world's third-largest PC maker after Dell and Hewlett with 130 billion USD in annual sales. After the transaction was completed, Lenovo will pay IBM 600 million USD worth of Lenovo shares. IBM owns a 18.9% stake in Lenovo. Lenovo will also assume a net debt of about 500 million USD from IBM.

Lenovo can effectively increase market share and strengthen market control through cross-border mergers and acquisitions. Lenovo merges IBM with its own advantages and uses IBM's brand and sales channels to effectively enter the international market. From 2005 to 2011, Lenovo Group's annual business scale increased 10 times, profits increased 4 times, and global market share expanded 5 times. Lenovo grew from a regional brand to an internationally renowned brand. In the past 5 years, Lenovo Group has completed a series of international layout adjustments through mergers and acquisitions. The global supply chain cost has been reduced to half of its competitors, delivery efficiency has increased to 117%, and cash flow rate has increased by 14%. Tsinghua University's Qin Hezheng believes that Lenovo has not only enlarged its scale and consolidated its global operation capabilities through cross-border mergers and acquisitions, but also demonstrated its excellent cost control advantage in the international arena.

(3) Main Characteristics of the New Pattern of China's Two-way Investment

Ⅰ China has become a net exporter of capital

In 2015, China's net foreign direct investment exceeded China's actual net foreign investment for the first time, with a difference of 10.06 billion USD; from 2016 to 2017, China continued to achieve net capital export under two-way direct investment; in 2018, foreign direct investment declined; China has become the largest investor in developing countries, with investment three times that of the runner-up country. During the "Twelfth Five-Year

Plan" period, the scale of China's use of foreign capital and foreign direct investment was 1.5 times and 2.4 times that of the "11th Five-Year Plan" period. In 2015, China's foreign investment achieved a historic breakthrough of "exceeding the first year". The scale of China's foreign direct investment exceeded that of foreign investment for the first time, and a new pattern of China's two-way investment has taken shape(see Figure 9-5).

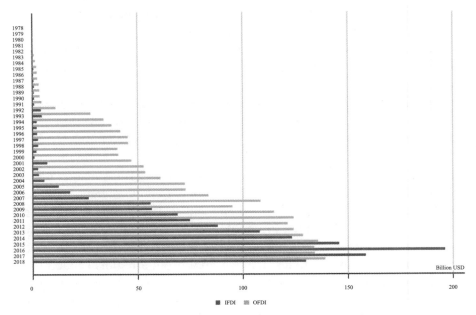

Figure 9-5 China's two-way FDI from 1978 to 2018

Source: https://unctad.org/.

For a long time, China has been a structural country in the international industrial transfer, and has less participation in the international capital market. The rapid growth of China's foreign direct investment reflects the objective needed for Chinese enterprises to go international and participate in international competition. The net amount of foreign investment exceeds the net amount of foreign capital actually used, which means that China can not only complement other countries' foreign trade areas such as commodity trading in the international market, but also participate in international capital investment, Change China's foreign trade change from one-way exchange to two-way exchange.

Ⅱ China's two-way investment promotes the upgrading of China's industrial structure.

In recent years, the structure of China's two-way investment has been further optimized. The proportion of the tertiary industry in the industrial structure of China's actual use of foreign capital increased, and the proportion of the secondary industry in the industrial structure of China's foreign direct investment increased. From the perspective of the industrial sector's distribution of two-way investment, the service industry is becoming a key area for two-way investment. The scale of attracting foreign investment in real estate has fallen sharply, and the scale of attracting foreign investment in the manufacturing industry as a whole has fallen. However, the attraction of foreign investment in high-tech manufacturing has grown rapidly.

Ⅲ Investment subjects and methods are becoming diversified.

The diversification of investment subjects and investment methods has become the main development pattern of China's two-way investment. In recent years, wholly foreign-owned enterprises, Sino-foreign joint ventures, Sino-foreign cooperation and joint-stock enterprises have become the main force in China's use of foreign capital, of which 90% are wholly foreign-owned enterprises and Sino-foreign joint ventures. However, non-state-owned enterprises dominated by limited liability companies, including diversified investment entities such as private, joint-stock, individual, and collective, have become the backbone of China's foreign investment. At the same time, China's foreign investment has formed a diversified pattern of coexistence of multiple investment methods such as merger and acquisition, equity investment, income reinvestment, and debt instrument investment.

9.3.3 Coordinated Development of "Belt and Road" Construction and Two-way Investment in China

The new direction of China's foreign investment, centered on the "Belt and Road", is an important part of China's opening up. With the formation of a new pattern of China's two-way investment, the construction of the "Belt and Road" will lead to a two-way coordinated and balanced development of domestic and foreign investment, which will play an important role in China's economic development and the stability of China's international investment status. Not only is it a great choice for China's open economy development in the new situation, but it will also lead China's new type of open economic development: "introduction" and "going out" two-way interaction to achieve the coordinated development of the "Belt and Road" construction and China's two-way investment.

(1) Take the "Belt and Road" as a Drive to Implement the Coordinated Development of Two-way Investment and Foreign Trade with the "Belt and Road" Initiative

First, investment creates trade. The "Belt and Road" construction will become a model for stimulating corporate investment. State-owned capital will lead private capital to invest in countries along the "Belt and Road", enhancing the development capacity of countries along the line through "Five Links", achieving the development of comprehensive economic and trade relations between China and these countries, and win-win cooperation, and realizing the coordinated development of an open economy. Therefore, the construction of the "Belt and Road" has promoted the economic and trade cooperation between China and the countries along the "Belt and Road", and implemented the coordinated development of two-way investment and foreign trade.

Second, investment promotes trade. Through the continuous operation of the "China-Europe Train" such as Yuxinou and Zhengxinou, it will promote the foreign trade and two-way investment of inland cities such as Chongqing and Zhengzhou, create new highlands for inland opening, and promote the coordinated development of inland and central and western regions' opening to the outside world. Taking Yuxinou as an example, the cost is 1/5 of the air freight, and the transportation time is reduced by 1 month compared with the sea freight, which has great economic value. At present, the "China-Europe Train" has not only regularized and stabilized its outbound journey, realizing full-load transportation, but the no-load rate of its return journey has also been greatly reduced, which is conducive to driving economic and trade development in the areas along the "Belt and Road".

Finally, investment and trade integrate. To establish overseas economic and trade cooperation zones along the "Belt and Road" could realize the mission of key industries and enterprises to go abroad. The Overseas Economic and Trade Cooperation Zone can not only provide a full range of investment services, and relieve the worries of local laws, intellectual property, accounting, finance, infrastructure, and policy risk assessment for "going global" enterprises. Its scale have provided the conditions for key industries and key companies leading SMEs to invest abroad and build an industrial cluster of upstream and downstream affiliated enterprises. Under the principle of "co-negotiation, co-construction and sharing", the overseas economic and trade cooperation zone provides conditions for promoting China's customs clearance cooperation with the countries along the "Belt and Road".

(2) Take the "Belt and Road" as an Opportunity to Realize the Coordinated Development of Countries and Regions

The first is the coordinated development of the "Belt and Road" and the "Free Trade Pilot Zone". Building a convenient, internationalized and legalized business environment could reshape the new advantages of open coastal highlands. The superposition of the "Belt and Road" regions and the Pilot Free Trade Zone pattern has consistently implemented the inland and coastal areas, opened up the flow of people, logistics, and capital, enabling the two-sided investment in the divided domestic markets to achieve coordinated development.

The second is the coordinated development of urban cooperation and internal and external opening. Take key cities like Shanghai and Chongqing as the fulcrum, strengthen the two-way investment between coastal and inland open cities and countries along the "Belt and Road". Economic and trade exchanges and investment cooperation between key cities and fulcrum cities, especially the two-way investment between port cities, economic and trade hub cities along the "Belt and Road" countries and China's coastal and inland open highlands, not only drive import and export trade, but also be conducive to the coordinated development of the "Belt and Road" and the Yangtze River Economic Belt.

Finally it is the coordinated development of regions under the two-way investment strategy. After considering central and regional coordination, it is also necessary to consider the relationship between regions, that is, the coordination of foreign investment between regions. In fact, whether it is introducing foreign capital or foreign investment, the eastern coastal areas must far exceed the central and western regions. This has both historical and geographical reasons. There are differences in industrial development among different regions. In the same region, large cities and small are also different, and they cannot all be the same model.

(3) Using the "Belt and Road" as a Link to Promote the Coordinated Development of Attracting Foreign Investment in Various Regions

First, it is necessary to reasonably guide the flow of funds and promote "group-type" investment introduction in various regions. On the one hand, the eastern coastal areas should direct foreign capital to high-end manufacturing and service industries, and encourage the headquarters of multinational companies to settle down; the central and western regions should mainly introduce applicable technologies to solve local employment and social development, and break through technical and management bottlenecks. On the other hand, the government should promote the implementation of "group-type" investment in different regions, and gradually forming a pattern of mutual benefit between the East and the West. Attracting foreign investment in the eastern, central, and western regions should focus on coordinated development with the regional economy. Based on the different needs of high, middle, and low-end industrial chains, to formulate industrial plans and promote the formation of industrial clusters.

Second, it is important to promote the formation of the headquarters-processing base development model. The development of the headquarters economy is an important way to use foreign investment strategies and policies in the eastern coastal areas. In the field of manufacturing, the Yangtze River Delta, the Pearl River Delta, and the Bohai Rim should target the whole country, take the central region as the hinterland, and explore and promote the feasibility of forming a headquarters-processing base development model in the eastern, central, and western regions. In the field of modern service industry, the eastern, central and western regions should explore the economic development model of the headquarters—sub-headquarters—inland sub-sub-headquarters, forming a support point through the convergence of capital flows, and provide sharing platforms of information, financing, talent, Logistics to service for the central and western regions, and further leverage the headquarters economy in the eastern coastal areas.

Finally, it is to promote the transfer of foreign investment in processing trade to the central and western regions. The key lies in: first, the eastern coastal areas must transfer, and the central and western regions must undertake; second, the foreign capital transferred from the eastern coastal areas must be prevented from migrating to neighboring countries; and third, the low-end manufacturing foreign capital from the eastern coastal areas has been transferred and foreign investment in high-end manufacturing cannot be introduced. "Being empty for birds" in the coastal areas is a question of where the foreign investment in processing trade will go. Some low-efficiency enterprises with no or little pollution, although at the low-end of the industrial chain, should be encouraged to move to the central and western regions, which can produce good employment effects. For some foreign investment in processing trade with more polluted, the government should promote them to accelerate transformation and upgrading, and find suitable locations for transfer.

Chapter 10
Employment and Income Distribution in China

People's welfare and employment is the top priority of Chinese government. This chapter discusses the employment and income distribution in China.

10.1 Employment in China

China's labor force was one of the most important factors accounting for the country's unparalleled economic development over the past decades. Initially benefitting from its ample supply of cheap labor, the country's demography and labor dynamics are now changing with the slowdown of the economic growth.

With about 1.4 billion people in 2020, China's population ranks first in the world. The employment has always been an important issue in Chinese social and economic development. The labor force market in China has experienced dramatic change from "government-planning assignment" to "bilateral selection and independent option". The Chinese government has actively taken various policies and measures to promote sustainable and effective employment creation of the whole society, continuously improving the quality of labor force and employment, and fully satisfying the employment development of workers.

10.1.1 The Historical Evolution, Main Measures and Development Strategies of China's Employment System

(1) The Evolution of China's Employment System

During China's transition from a planned economy to a marker based one, its employment system has experienced changes from planned disposition by the government to bilateral selection between the employer and employee.

From the 1950s to the 1970s, China implemented planned economy and highly nationalization and its employment system maintained rural-urban segmentation and focused on the urban employment system. The employment system carried out in that particular historical situation played an important role at providing sufficient labor force to satisfy the demand of socialist economic construction and industrialization, in the meanwhile, maintaining social stability. However, under the process of China's market economy reforming and opening up to the world, the original employment system was no longer adapted to the new need of the economic development, so the reform of the original employment system got into the stage.

The reform of China's employment system has mainly gone through four stages. In the 1980s, it broke the framework of "government-planning assignment", and under the guidance and the overall consideration of the state, put forward the employment policy of "Combinations of Three Methods", i.e., the combination of employment opportunities provided by the administrative departments of labor, by organizing themselves to start business and by self-employment. Furthermore, with the reform of state-owned enterprises (SOEs), other employment policies have been put forward. From 1983 to 1986, the recruitment and employment mechanism of SOEs was changed, thus the enterprises were entitled to make plans in hiring, training and setting standards to recruit the employees. From 1986 to 1992, permanent-and-fixed worker system in SOEs was abolished. From 1992 up to now, taking the establishment of modern enterprise system as an opportunity, Chinese government implemented the market-oriented employment system reform.

(2) Employment System and Its Main Measures under Different Economic Systems

I Employment system and its main measures under planned economy

Under planned economy, the fundamental way to ease the unemployment problem was to resume and develop national economical production rapidly. Only by raising the level of economic development can create more jobs for the society. At this stage, the government adhered to the economic development route of giving priority to SOEs development and taking private enterprises as auxiliary means of economic development, utilizing available resources in China to resume and develop national production, promoting economic increase, improving the level of economic development, and striving to increase the job opportunity.

The central planners and overall allocations were strictly reinforced in both the process of labor recruitment and labor redistribution. Under government-planning assignment, an overall plan for urban labor force was made by the central government, and the distribution of labor force between regions and labor departments also was decided by the central government, thus achieving a relative balance between labor supply and demand. Employee growth plans made by the authorities was statutory and served as the only means of allocating labor force. The state assigned jobs to population during all working age, including graduates who have completed their studies in higher education, junior and senior school students who are no longer enrolled in higher education, and demobilized soldiers who came from cities or towns. In this period, the only way that labors can get employed was to be assigned to work by the state. Meanwhile, any employer wanted for new workers can only obtain workers through national distribution. Neither the demand side nor the supply side had the freedom to choose. As mentioned previously, this system had a positive effect on accelerating industrialization, expanding employment scale and ensuring social stability. But its disadvantages are obvious. On one hand, because of lacking the freedom of recruiting talents, employers could not allocate labor according to business needs; therefore, business performance was poor. On the other hand, workers had no freedom of choice of jobs, which hit the enthusiasm of workers. The "Iron Rice Bowl" and" One Big Pot" system led to inefficiency. The government became the dual main body of "choosing jobs for the labor force" and "employing workers for enterprises", while trying to meet the needs of both sides, but can't satisfy either side.

The nationwide labor and employment plan focused on urban employment issue. There was a lack of guidance for the employment of rural labor force, and the channel of labor flow in towns and villages was blocked. The government promulgated two important normative documents, i.e. "the interim measures for the rationing of grain in urban areas" and "the household registration regulations of the People's Republic of China". With two normative documents, a strict distinction was made between urban population and agricultural population, and the movement of farmers to cities and towns is strictly restricted. Rural labors attached to the land were isolated from industrialization process, thus a large number of redundant rural labors cannot transfer to non-farm industries in time, which causes great waste and loss. The invisible unemployment rates in both rural and urban area were high.

II Employment system reform and its main measures under the market economy

After the Third Plenary Session of the Eleventh Central Committee, China began to implement the reform and opening up policy. Under such a background, the employment system in China had also undergone radical changes. In the early stage of reform, China practiced household contract responsibility system in rural areas, and it presented great system performance at the beginning of the reform. With income linked to output, commonly known as "an all-round contract", allowed farming households to contract with the collective economic organizations, whereby the means of production still belonged to the collectives and the farming is operated by individual families in the principle "to each according to his work". The system encouraged the productive output of individual farmers while maintaining unified collective operation. Rural labor productivity increased, the rural economy developed, and the standards of living of farmers were improved. The household contract responsibility system has proven well-suited to Chinese agriculture, rural productive forces, and land management, which freed farmers from the land. The rural labor force surplus emerged and gradually transferred to other agricultural departments and township enterprises, as well.

From 1980, by the end of "Movements of Chinese Educated Urban Youth Going and Working in the Countryside", millions of returnees looked for jobs in urban areas. In order to alleviate the employment pressure, the government put forward the employment policy of "Three Combinations". This policy is a breakthrough of the original planned employment system, which marked the establishment of the labor force market. In 1986, China began to reform the labor contract system. The State Council has promulgated a series of regulations to promote the reform of the labor contract system. All these series of regulations emphasized the role of the market power. The establishment of the labor contract system, on the one hand, has gradually weakened the influence of the previous planned employment system, which is equipped with the main characteristics of administrative orders and national plans. In adidition, in reformed employment system, employers and employees become market players. Then how to regulate behaviors of enterprises in the labor market is primary task in order to maintain the healthy and stable development of the market.

In 1994, China promulgated the China Employment Promotion Law (CEPL). CEPL was enacted with three main purposes in mind: to promote employment; create a fair employment environment; and prohibit employment discrimination. CEPL ensures that employees have equal rights to employment and shall not be discriminated against on the basis of their ethnicity, race, gender or religious beliefs. Under the law, employers may not use gender to deny women employment or to raise recruitment standards for them. In China, however, employers are prohibited from causing female workers to engage in work that the law deems to be unsuitable, such as working in mine pits and work with Grade IV physical labor intensity. The CEPL also provides that limitations based on women's marital or childbirth status may not be placed in labor contracts. The CEPL also prohibits discrimination on the basis of physical disability and health conditions. For example, discrimination against workers who are carriers of infectious diseases such as Hepatitis B or HIV is prohibited. Workers who are carriers of infectious disease, however, cannot work in certain types of jobs that are regulated by law until they are confirmed to be non-infectious. Unlike federal and state laws in the U.S., however, the CEPL does not ban employment discrimination based on age. Although the CEPL's provisions render the above noted types of employment discrimination illegal, there are no corresponding statutorily prescribed penalties against employers that engage in discriminatory employment practices. Notably absent from the CEPL also are specific remedies available to aggrieved employees as there would be under the US discrimination laws. Nevertheless, the CEPL permits employees to protect their employment rights by filing lawsuits against employers who have allegedly engaged in unlawful employment discrimination. We will continue to monitor the CEPL, and update you on further developments in the law pertaining to protections, remedies and potential penalties for unlawful discrimination. The CEPL promotes stable employment, and protects the legitimate rights and interests of laborers, thus promoting the healthy development of the labor market, which is of epoch-making significance.

With the increasingly extended reforms of SOEs, large quantities of SOE workers were laid off or went unemployed, living hard lives. In late 1990s around 30 million workers were laid off as a result of SOEs reform. The government attached great importance to the reemployment of laid-off workers and vigorously promoted the reemployment process of laid-off workers with multiple measures. The enterprises which the employees used to belong to would continue to retain its "work relations" with them in a certain period and undertake to ensure them a basic living standard. The central and local governments helped the laid-off workers to be re-employed by introducing policies to expand employment and encourage business venturing. Government launched a series of policy measures which have basically ensured stability among the laid-off workers. Specifically, the government established records of laid-off workers to provide them with job information and guidance; Refocused employment funds to strengthen skills training for them. Labor and social security agencies were set up in various localities; they provided employment information and support to laid-off workers, thus enhanced their ability to reemployment. At the same time, Government encouraged laid-off workers to start their own businesses, and provided favorable locations, startup service and low administrative fees so as to encourage urban workers and rural migrants to start their own businesses that will create jobs. In case of insufficient self-raised funds, Self-employed entrepreneurs can get small amount of guaranteed loans. To those low profit projects, the financial departments also fully discount the interest. The separation of rural employment from urban employment was broken up, and the rural labor are no longer limited to seek employment in their rural places and are beginning to move into the cities and towns for employment. A large number of rural populations began to work in the city. Because of this trend, the government formulated a series of regulations to crack down on such malpractices to ensure that the lawful rights and interests of all rural migrant workers were fully protected.

Ⅲ Employment target and development strategy in the new era

Employment was regarded as the biggest measure to improve people's livelihood in the 19th National Congress of the CPC. China's economic development has entered a new normal, and the new characteristics of China's employment problem have gradually emerged. While the contradiction of total employment tends to be eased, the conflict between frictional and structural employment is more prominent, and the task of improving the quality of employment is urgent. The key to solve the frictional employment lies in perfecting the labor market mechanism and enhancing the matching between the supply and demand of labor.

The key to solve the structural unemployment lies in promoting the skills of workers, enhancing the adaptability of human capital endowment to the transformation of economic development mode and the optimization and upgrading of industrial structure. The key to improve the quality of employment lies in the establishment and improvement of the labor market system and the development of harmonious labor relations. The focus of the government's employment policy has shifted from promoting economic growth and creating jobs to reducing the structural unemployment and promoting employment quality of the labor market and providing basic public employment services.

In the report of the 19th National Congress of the CPC, it is proposed for the first time to eliminate the institutional and constitutive defects that hinder the social mobility of labor and talents, and put forward corresponding measures: first, maintain the horizontal mobility of labor, increase personal and family incomes and increase labor productivity; second, The government should provide policy and surroundings and public service platform to promote the vertical flow of workers, so that workers have the opportunity to realize their self-worth through employment, break the solidification of social identity, and break the intergenerational transmission of poverty; finally, deepen the reform of related fields, and remove the institutional obstacles that hinder the horizontal and vertical flow of workers.

(3) From the Current Reform Measures of the Employment System in China, the Employment System in China is Developing in the Following Aspects

Ⅰ Promote employment equity

Employment equity includes: gender equity, education equity and so on. To ensure employment equity can provide a more equal competition platform for workers, which is also the essential requirement of market economy. In a fair atmosphere of employment competition, every worker can be treated equally, and can find employment opportunities with their own quality, which is conducive to improving the overall quality of the laborer in the competition.

Ⅱ Construct law-based employment system

Amid reform and opening up crusade, China has gradually built a socialist state ruled by law. In the field of employment system, it is an important measure in line with the goal of building a socialist country ruled by law that establishing a complete legal system and forming a perfect employment management system and also an important measure to improve the current situation of China's employment system.

III Establish and improve the social security system

The social security system is the social safety net of the employment system. With related laws and regulations, it ensures citizen's basic life rights, including social assistance, social insurance, social welfare, social preferential treatment, endowment insurance, social medical insurance and social unemployment insurance. China's current individual employment contract-based social security system gradually emerged in the late 1990s and the 2000s. Prior to that, the government provided a welfare system (pension, healthcare, and housing) for urban workers. The new system emerged through a series of specific regulations and provisions in *The Labor Law* in 1994 and *The Labor Contract Law* in 2008. It was not until 2011 that these separate parts were codified into a comprehensive national framework under *The Social Insurance Law*, in which the basic principles of China's social security system are outlined.

IV Establish the public employment service system under the GSP

The public employment service system with various services is established to help the people with difficulties in employment or reemployment. It is led by the labor and employment service institutions affiliated to the administrative department of labor and social security, with the joint development of other departments and social employment service organizations, and integrates multiple functions such as career certificate, career guidance, vocational training, labor dispatch and guidance on entrepreneurship.

V In line with international standards

In today's interlinked world, international flows of goods and capital will inevitably expose China to external economic fluctuations. The globalization brings not only opportunities for China's economy, but also challenges and pressures for economic development and domestic employment. The employment system is constantly impacted by external factors. For example, after the international financial crisis in 2007, China's economic growth and employment have already been hit hard, as seen in the waves of jobless migrant workers in coastal regions returning to their homes in rural areas. The first victims were export oriented firms and industrial sectors in the coastal regions of east China. Then the impact spread to manufacturing, foreign-funded firms and SMEs. The third set of victims is rural migrants and other low-skilled labor. Among manufacturing, exports and foreign-funded enterprises, a large proportion of the workforce are rural migrant workers.

Last, the financial crisis has put downward pressure on the economy and squeezed urban employment growth potential.

In response to uncertain externalities, China's macroeconomic policies must focus on employment and combine counter-shock and counter-cyclical measures under the background of the continuous development of globalization, the continuous emergence of various trade frictions and anti-dumping and other sanctions also greatly affects the development of China's employment. Therefore, we must be based on China's national situation, strengthen the legislation in the employment system, pay close attention to the international economic development situation, and utilize the favorable conditions to improve and maintain the development of China's employment. In addition, we should wholly encourage enterprises to participate in the global economy. It is not only the internal requirement of the development of China's employment system, but also an important weight to strengthen and standardize the export of foreign labor services and ease and improve the pressure of domestic employment.

10.1.2 The Status Quo and Development of China's Population and Its Impact on the Employment Market

(1) The Status Quo of China's Population

Ⅰ The change in age structure

According to the classical demographic transition theory, which shows how population growth is related to the stages of industrial development., China, like the western developed countries has experienced a long transformation from "high birth rate, high death rate and low growth rate" to "high birth rate, low death rate and high growth rate" and then to "low birth rate, low death rate and low growth rate".

From 1950 to the early 1970s, the process of population reproduction in China was in the second stage of population transformation: a sharp decline in population death and a high birth rate. From the early 1970s to the end of the 20th century, the process of population reproduction in China is in the first half of the third stage of population transformation: the slow decline of population death rate and the sharp decline of birth rate. Since the end of the 20th century, China's population reproduction process is in the second half of the third stage of population transformation: the level of population death rate has been very low, and almost stopped declining, while the birth rate has been slowly declining.

The population transformation in western developed countries is the result of spontaneous birth control caused by the change in people's fertility concepts after the high level of economic development, but the population transformation in China is different, which is caused by government policies. Since the 1970s, through the implementation of family planning policy to control population growth, China's total fertility rate for women of child-bearing age has gradually declined, and reached a low level of about 1.5 in 2014, marking China's entry into the ranks of low fertility countries. With the full implementation of the family planning policy, the age structure of the Chinese population is problematic. In 2010, the absolute number of the labor force declined for the first time in a long time, and problems such as the difficulty of recruitment occurred in southeastern coastal areas. The labor force began to shift from unlimited supply to insufficient supply. The Fifth Plenary Session of the 18th Central Committee of the CPC proposed that China should adhere to the basic state policy of family planning and fully implement the policy of one couple having two children. The newly revised family planning law of the PR China stipulates that the policy of "the universal two-child policy" was implemented from January 1, 2016. After the implementation of the twochild policy, the total fertility rate of women is expected to increase from 1.5 to about 2.0.

In the short term, the implementation of the "the universal two-child policy" led to an increase in the number and proportion of the young population, and increased the burden of supporting the working age population; in the medium term, the implementation of the "comprehensive two child" policy led to an increase in the number and proportion of the working age population; in the long term, the implementation of the " the universal two-child policy" will lead to an increase in the number and proportion of the elderly population, the extension of working life and the burden of support for the elderly. For the foreseeable future, implementation of "the universal two-child policy " will have a deep-depth impact on the trend of population size and population age structure in the coming decades.

Ⅱ Changes in the age structure of the population

After the founding of the People's Republic of China, the child dependency ratio of population has been continuously increasing, and in 1966, it reached 74.76%. After 1966, it began to decline slowly in the fluctuation, and reached a historical lowest level of 22.10% in 2011. After 2011, it began to show a slow upward trend, rising to 23.7%. It means that the proportion of the economically active population in this country began to decrease and the social burden will be heavier and heavier, which is obviously not conducive to economic growth. The economically active population is also called the labor force population, including all the employed people who are engaged in social labor and the unemployed people who are looking for work.

Table 10-1 Statistics of total dependency ratio, child dependency ratio and elderly dependency ratio in 2010-2018   **unit:%**

Year	Total Dependency Ratio	Child Dependency Ratio	Elderly Dependency Ratio
2010	34.2	22.3	11.9
2011	34.4	22.1	12.3
2012	34.9	22.2	12.7
2013	35.3	22.2	13.1
2014	36.1	22.5	13.7
2015	37	22.6	14.3
2016	37.9	22.9	15
2017	39.2	23.4	15.9
2018	40.4	23.7	16.8

Source: World Band Database.

In 1950-1965, the number of elderly people in China remained stable, ranging from 24 million to 25 million. However, due to the increasing number of working age population, the dependency ratio of the elderly population has gradually declined slowly. After 1965, the dependency ratio of the elderly began to increase slowly. After China entered the aging society in 2000, the dependency ratio of the elderly began to increase rapidly, and reached the level of 16.8% in 2018.It is predicted that in 2030, the proportion of the population aged over 65 will reach 14% of the total population. In 2040, it will reach 20.9%.China will become the fastest aging country in the world and one of the most serious aging countries in the world.

Ⅲ Population quality

After the founding of the PRC, the education level of the Chinese population has been improved, and the cultural quality of the population has been greatly improved. Nowadays, the overall adult literacy rate in China is at a high level. According to the UNESCO, the overall literacy rate of the adult population over 15 years old in China is 96.4%, and the literacy rate of the population aged 15-24 is close to 100%. With the rapid development of education in China, It has realized the full popularization of compulsory education and basically popularized high school education and the popularization of higher education. According to the data of the fifth and sixth national censuses, the average education level of each age group of China's main working age population can be increased by one year if they are ten years younger. The data of the sixth census also showed that the average age group of 40-44 had about 9 years of education, while the age group of 20-24 had more than 11 years.

The net enrollment rate of primary school increased from 20% in 1949 to 99.95% in 2018; the gross enrollment rate of junior high school increased from 3.1% in 1949 to 100% in 2018; the gross enrollment rate of senior high school increased from 1.1% in 1949 to 88.8% in 2018; the gross enrollment rate of higher education increased from 0.26% in 1949 to 48.1% in 2018. A series of policies have been carried out in China, such as expanding the enrollment of colleges and universities, "constructs all the people to study, the lifelong study society, promotes human's full scale development". And so on, which have expanded the scale of education and training at all levels of academic qualifications, making the education level of the population in China continuously improve.

However, due to the imbalance of education investment between urban and rural areas and between different regions, the development of education between urban and rural areas and between regions is unbalanced. Finally, the education level of laborers between urban and rural areas and between regions is unbalanced, either.

(2) The Status Quo of Employment in China

At the founding of the PRC, the word "employed" was not directly used in China, and the word "social worker" was generally used. The word "employment" appeared only after the reform and opening up, which also reflected the government's attitude towards employment and its related issues. The National Bureau of statistics defined the employment personnel in China as: the employment personnel refer to the personnel who engage in certain social labor and obtain labor remuneration or business income. They include employed staff and workers, re-employed retirees, owners of private enterprises,owners of self-employed individuals, persons employed in private enterprises and self-employed individuals.

Employment has three basic characteristics: first, the qualification of the main body of employment. It means that the employees must be of a certain age and have a certain ability to work. In China, the age of 16 is generally considered the lower limit for the working-age population, while the upper limit is defined as 60 for men and 55 for women. However, retirees who are re-employed beyond the working age are still included in the labor force. Some countries set the upper and lower limits of the working age of the employees according to their own national conditions, but some countries do not. Second, paid. The main body of employment takes obtaining certain reward or income as the premise of offering certain amount of labor. The amount of labor remuneration determines whether workers are willing to work. This relationship is related to the survival and development of employees, and directly affects the distribution of social income. Employment and its system are related to income distribution and social equity. Third, legitimacy. The socio-economic activities of employment must be legal Labor. Illegal labor and socially unacceptable labor do not belong to the scope of employment.

I Employment scale

Since 1949, China's working age population began to increase. From 1950 to 2013, the number increased from 34.11 million to 1005.82 million. After 2013, the number of working age population in China began to decline slowly. In 2017, the number of working age population in China was 998.29 million, 7.53 million less than that in 2013. The "double change" of the quantity and quality of the working age population has brought direct and indirect effects in upgrading and transformation of the industrial structure. And the crux of the issue is whether the laborer's employment structure is rational, whether the labor's disposition is efficient, which influences industrial structure adjustment, as well. According to the data from the National Bureau of statistics, in general, China's labor force is in a steady growth stage. By the end of 2018, the total number of employed people reached 776.4 million, an increase of 93% over 1978, with an average annual growth of 9.61 million; the total number of urban employed people reached 424.62 million, an increase of 346% over 1978, with an average annual growth of 8.45 million. More than 15 million new growing labor force are employed in urban and rural areas every year, including nearly 8 million college graduates, accounting for more than half of the new growing labor force. In addition, there are more than 3 million newly transferred rural labor force.

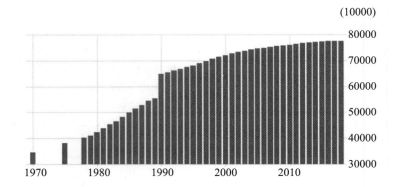

Figure 10-1 China's employed population 1970-2018
Source: World Bank Database.

The labor force participation rate is the "share of the population 16 years and older working or seeking work", which directly affects the actual number of labor engaged in social labor. The influencing factors of labor force participation rate are different in different countries and regions. In general, the higher the wage level is, the higher the labor force participation rate is. The level of education development will also affect the labor force participation rate. The prolonged education will reduce the number of working age population, especially the number of young people participating in labor, thus reducing the labor force participation rate. Social culture is also the main cultural factor affecting the labor force participation rate. In a conservative society, the labor force participation rate of women will be lower. Like most countries in the world, female labor participation in China falls behind male labor participation, but the gender gap in China seems to be less significant than in many other countries. In 2018, female labor participation rate in China stood at 61.3 percent, thus ranging about 13.5 percent above world average. Overall, labor force participation rate in China is higher than the average level in the world. Compared with developed countries, it is also higher than their labor force participation rates. This means that the actual number of people in need of employment is very large.

Ⅱ Age structure of employed population

Age structure of employed population change and development is a key factor affecting employment. Because of the inertia effect of population movement and development, it is feasible to predict the future population

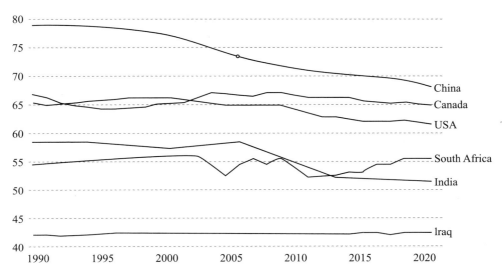

Figure 10-2 Labor force participation rate, total % of total population ages above 15 during 1990-2019
Source: World Bank Data Bank.

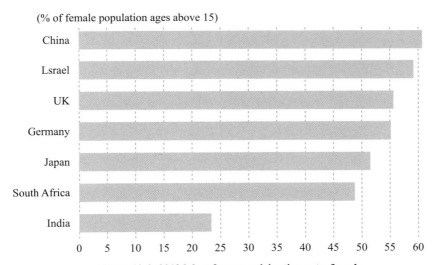

Figure 10-3 2019 labor force participation rate, female
Source: World Bank Data Bank.

change. Population prediction can provide the basic trend of population change, thus providing a certain degree of reference for decision-making.

Based on the data of previous censuses, the implementation of family planning policy and the continuous progress of economy and society are predicted by integrating the parameters of fertility level, death level, and population migration and education transformation. The fertility rate in China declined and remained low for a long time, so as to reduce the employment pressure facing China. However, the decrease of children also represents the decrease of working age population in the future. The decrease of the absolute number of working age population does not necessarily mean the shortage of labor force, which depends on the demand of labor force for China's economic development and the substitution of technology for labor. The decline of the proportion of the working age population will also lead to the increase of the dependency ratio of the population and the increase of the burden of the working age population, which will have a negative impact on the economy.

According to the internal structural change chart of the working age population drawn by the United Nations data, the working age population can be divided into four groups: 15-24, 25-39, 40-54 and 55-64. From 2000 to 2015, the population aged 40-54 and 55-64 in China is on the rise, while the population aged 25-39 is significantly down, while the population aged 15-24 is slightly down. Although the population in the 15-24-year-old group belongs to the working age population, with the development of economy and the popularization of education, the number of years people have received formal education is increasing, and a considerable part of the population in this group will not be employed. Therefore, only considering the other three groups, China's labor age population participating in the labor market has an aging trend. By 2030, 55-64 will account for a quarter of the labor age population.

Ⅲ Employment structure

Occupational structure refers to the proportion of different types of workers in the total, which reflects the level of economic development and changes of social status of a population group. During the early years of the PRC, a crucial political emphasis was attached to agriculture. On the following the implementation of economic growth planning, more importance was attached to industrial labor during the late 1990's and early 2000's. With the ongoing transformation of the Chinese economy towards a more service-oriented industry, employment in the service sector underwent a considerable expansion over the past years and accounted for 46.3 percent of the labor force in China in 2018.

There is the evergrowing demand for qualified personnel in China. In spite of the overall rural labor surplus, the structural labor supply and demand contradiction has begun to become acute and rural labor supply and demand relationship has been shifting from long-term "oversupply" to "overall surplus versus structural shortage". According to the relevant investigation report of the Ministry of labor and social security, the proportion of skilled workers is 32.3%. Among the skilled workers, the proportion of senior skilled workers is 3.9%, of which technicians account for 3.2% and senior technicians for 0.7%. While the demand for senior skilled workers in enterprises are far beyond the supply, i.e., technicians account for 9.6% and senior technicians for 4.5%. Investigation conducted by the Ministry of labor and social security showed in 66 cities in 2018, more than 77% of the unemployed have no technical rank or title. Therefore, reducing the burden of education and prolonging the years of education for young people is the key to improving the employability of the labor force. Entering the new era, with the vigorous development of the new economy represented by "Internet +" and intelligent manufacturing, there has been a wave of entrepreneurship and innovation. It has not only become a new driving force for economic growth, but also created more new jobs and lots of new jobs. According to the survey of the National Bureau of statistics, the contribution rate of the new economy to the total employment increase in 2017 is about 70%.

IV Urban and rural structure of employed population

From the perspective of urban and rural structure, the scale of urban employment has been expanding, from 95 million in 1978 to 425 million in 2017, accounting for 23.7% of the total employment, up to 54.7%. With the modernization and intensification of Chinese agriculture, possibilities to find employment in rural areas have decreased gradually. This in turn led to a massive stream of migrant workers seeking employment in urban areas of China. According to the Chinese government, the number of migrant workers has reached 277.47 million in 2015. In 2014, the number of urban employment exceeded rural employment for the first time. Among migrant workers in 2015, about 55.2 percent were under 40 years old, while 17.9 percent were elder than 50 years old. The female proportion of migrant workers amounted to 33.6 percent in 2015, which was 0.6 percent higher than that in the previous year. At the end of 2017, the total number of migrant workers nationwide reached 287 million, becoming a new force in the modernization drive.

The trend of urbanization level of China's labor population can be described as high in the East and low in the west, and the highest in the eastern coastal areas and Northeast China. This pattern will continue to exist in the next 30 years. Average annual salary in China's urban regions increased to about 74,318 RMB as the end of 2018. A large income gap still existed between coastal and western regions in China. While employees in Beijing had the highest annual salary with around 145,766 RMB on average, Heilongjiang province had displayed the lowest average annual salary with only around 60,780 RMB per year.

V Structure of employment population ownership

China is undergoing a large-scale economic restructuring. The restructuring of ownership has shifted jobs from SOEs to mixed ownership enterprises including collectively owned urban and township enterprises, urban and rural self-employed industrial and commercial households, private enterprises and non-state-controlled joint-stock enterprises, as well as wholly foreign-owned enterprises operating in China. The non-public economy has become the main department of urban employment. The proportion of urban non-public economic employees increased from 0.2% in 1978 to 83.6% in 2018, among which, the number of urban private enterprises and individual employees was 139.52 million and 104.4 million respectively, accounting for 32.1% and 24.0% of urban employees.

VI Unemployment rate in China

The unemployment rate in China has been fairly constant at around 4% over the last few years. This may be partly explained by the fact that due to its socialist heritage, full employment policy historically has played a major role in economic considerations of the Chinese government. Another possible explanation may be found in the index's methodology, which, according to the National Bureau of Statistics, gathers only employment data for urban regions. The debate as to whether to adjust the methodology accordingly in order to create a more accurate statistical image is still ongoing among Chinese politicians and statisticians. A main concern in China's current state of employment lies within the still large regional differences. The unemployment rate in more central and western regions of China was notably higher than in China's eastern parts. Youth unemployment is also apparent in China, but with its own characteristics. Young people with higher education are more likely to have difficulty finding a job, according to the China Household Finance Survey. One reason for this might lie in the enrollment expansion since 1999.

The number of unemployed people in cities and towns shows an increasing trend, and there is a phenomenon of unemployment clustering. The real unemployment rate continues to rise.

The urban registered unemployment rate is stable at about 4.0%, and the urban survey unemployment rate is stable at about 5.0%. China's urban registered unemployment rate does not include at least the hidden unemployed. In fact, according to the estimates of relevant research institutions and World Bank experts, the actual unemployment rate in Chinese cities is about 8%-10%. In China, urbanization has a great impact on employment. According to relevant data, China's annual rural age population of new urban employment is about 9 million. Among them, there are more than 5 million rural labor force entering the city to work, more than 2.5 million policy-based "agricultural to non-agricultural" personnel, and no less than 1 million people entering the cities and towns to go to school. The situation of large number and high proportion of rural population in China will not be reversed, and the situation of rural labor supply exceeding demand will continue for a long time. This determines that for a long time in the future, rural labor will continue to move to cities. The long-term task of Chinese governments at all levels is to solve the employment problem of rural labor and do a good job in the employment service and management of the floating population.

10.1.3 The Relationship Between Employment and Economic Growth

(1) Employment Growth Plays an Important Role in Economic and Social Development

The International Labor Organization, in its global employment agenda, states that "work is central to people's lives". It is not only because many people in the world depend on work to make a living, it is also a means for people to integrate into society, realize their value and bring hope for next generations. This makes work a crucial element in social and political stability.

The 19th National Congress of the CPC pointed out that socialism with Chinese characteristics has entered a new era, and the major social contradictions in China have been transformed into the contradiction between the people's growing needs for a better life and the unbalanced and inadequate development. Employment determines the degree and mode of people's participation in social and economic activities and sharing economic development achievements. Only by fully ensuring social employment and meeting people's most basic survival and development needs, can the masses of working people live and work in peace and contentment, the society can maintain a long-term stable order, and the country can enjoy long-term stability. Full employment concerns the bottom line of society. "Bottom line equity" is to establish the basic point of social equity, define the "boundary" of government responsibility, and determine the guarantee of minimum living. In order to establish the pattern of interest relationship with the bottom line fairness as the core, we must guarantee the fair employment among the members of the society, and make the workers enjoy equal employment opportunities and equal employment treatment on the premise of equal rules.

(2) The Relationship between Employment and Economic Growth

Simon Kuznets believes that the economic growth and social progress of a country can be defined not only as the increasing supply of goods to its own people, but also as the guarantee of full employment[1]. The source of economic growth is the progress of capital, labor and technology, technical status, the amount of labor and capital invested to promote economic growth. At the same time, employment growth depends on the mode of economic growth and economic growth, and on the benign interaction between economic growth and employment growth. The positive interaction between economic growth and employment growth mode has laid a solid foundation for the overall development of society.

From 1978 to 1989, China's annual GDP growth averaged 9%, during this period, the secondary industry and tertiary industry experienced double-digit increases. Fast growth also created substantial job opportunities. The national total employment increased from 401 million to 647 million, the annual average growth of 20 million. The employment elasticity of economic growth was as high as 0.62, which means that when GDP grows by every one percentage point, employment increases by 0.62 percentage points. This is rarely seen in the world economy history. It shows that economic growth between 1978 and 1990 led to grand job creation, giving full play to resource allocation through market mechanisms.

---

[1] Simon Kuznets, *Economic Development, the Family and Income Distribution: Selected Essays*, Cambridge: Cambridge university Press, 1989.

From 1991 to 1995, the annual growth rate of national GDP was 11.56%, and the employment growth rate was 1.21%; from 1996 to 1999, the annual growth rate of national GDP was 8.30%, and the employment growth rate was 0.96%. It can be seen that since 1991, the pulling effect of GDP growth on employment in China has been greatly reduced compared with that in the 1980s. This time, another perspective shows that the employment problem in China is atypical.

China is in the primary stage of socialist construction. To speed up the construction of a modern economic system, China is experiencing an unprecedented large-scale economic restructuring. The impact of economic restructuring on employment growth is extremely profound. Generally speaking, for the traditional industries and unskilled labor, it is mainly the "destruction" of total employment, while for those emerging industries, emerging sectors and skilled labor, it is mainly the "creation" of total employment. However, the proportion of this kind of employment creation is relatively low, and even negative net employment creation occurs, which leads to the rise of the actual number of unemployed. First of all, the adjustment of industrial structure makes the labor force of the primary industry and the secondary industry, especially the unskilled labor force, transfer passively to the tertiary industry. In this way, it is inevitable that the labor force that is not suitable for the employment in the tertiary industry is unemployed. Secondly, the mode of economic growth changes from extensive to intensive, from labor-intensive to capital intensive. On the one hand, labor-intensive industries lose development advantages due to market, capital and technology factors; on the other hand, capital intensive and technology intensive industries fail to show employment advantages and the total employment growth is not rapid. In this way, some people who could not meet the needs of capital intensive and technology intensive industries and were originally engaged in labor-intensive industries will be unemployed. Just as Cobb Douglas production function describes the impact of the transformation of economic growth mode on employment, the transformation of economic growth mode from labor-intensive to capital intensive and technology intensive reduces the number of employees per unit of capital to some extent.

The growth rate of employment keeps pace with the economic growth, and promoting economic growth to drive the growth of employment is also our goal. Theoretically, the actual employment can reflect the local economic development. When the economy and employment growth can develop simultaneously, it shows that the employment elasticity is stable. The direct source of the pattern of "high growth and low employment" is the decrease of employment elasticity coefficient. Therefore, on the premise of maintaining economic growth, improving the employment elasticity coefficient through public policy choice is the choice to get rid of the dilemma of "high growth, low employment".

10.2 China's Income Distribution

Rapid economic growth has been accompanied by rising income level for Chinese households. China's transition from a planned economy to a marker based one has transformed resource allocation. Under dominant public ownership that coexists with other ownership systems, China has also developed a distribution system where distribution according to labor coexists with other forms of income distribution. Over the past seven decades of economic transition, China has transformed from a low-income economy with per capita disposal income less than 200 USD to one with per capita disposal income above 4400 USD. It is an achievement barely seen in human history. China's economic successes have been widely acclaimed and aroused a great deal of concern and research on "China path" and "China model".

10.2.1 The Evolution of China's Income Distribution System

In a planned economy, income distribution is determined only by ownership, industrial and employment structures and labor system. Back then, leftist ideology, planned economic system and egalitarian distribution were the norms of China's political and economic life. Egalitarianism was both necessary and politically correct. In fact, egalitarianism created another form of unfair distribution: the results of work were taken by force from those who worked more to those who worked less or did not work at all.

China is currently in the primary stage of socialist development. In this stage, the ownership structure is the ownership structure of the means of production with the public ownership as the main body and the co-development of various forms of ownership. Production decides distribution, and distribution reacts on production. This determines that China's current distribution system is an income distribution system with distribution according to work as the main body, while diversified modes of distribution coexist, which is conducive to the consolidation and development of the public economy, the protection of workers' interests and the realization of common prosperity.

A brief review of the process of the CPC exploration of the distribution system under the conditions of socialist market economy will not make it difficult to understand the practical and theoretical inevitability of upgrading the "distribution system with distribution according to work as the main body and multiple distribution modes coexisting" to the basic economic system. China's economic reform introduced market mechanism that allows income distribution to be determined by individual enterprises free from government intervention. The advantage of this transition is obvious.

In the Third Plenary Session of the 11th CPC Central Committee, China's government finally set a clear message of a single form of distribution according to work. From the Third Plenary Session of the 11th Central Committee to the 13th National Congress of CPC, the idea of income distribution system reform in China is mainly to break the equalitarianism and rethink the issue of primary distribution in income distribution. On one hand, income gaps have been widening between urban and rural areas, different regions, sectors, occupations and groups of people. On the other side, changes have occurred in the standards, principles and mechanisms of income distribution. This also shows that the starting point of income distribution system reform in this stage is to improve labor productivity. In rural areas, the household contract responsibility system was implemented to break the egalitarian distribution model. It creatively implemented the basic principle of distribution according to work, effectively linked farmers' income with their labor input, so as to better encourage the enthusiasm and creativity of farmers.

In cities, the incentive mechanism of interest distribution was carried out to improve the efficiency of labor production, by the means of reform of the income distribution system in state-owned enterprises. In the Third Plenary Session of the 12th Central Committee of the CPC ,The decision of the Central Committee of the CPC took on the specific measures for the distribution of urban enterprises according to work, including "making the wages and bonuses of the employees of enterprises better linked with the improvement of the economic performance of enterprises", " Within the enterprise, the widening wage gap fully reflects the rewards for diligence, the penalties for demotivation, the rewards for excellence, the penalties for inferiority, and the scores for full performance reflect more work, less work and less gain". In essence, the reform of income distribution system linked to work efficiency not only breaks the pattern of egalitarianism in the planned economy, but also lays a foundation for the market-oriented reform of independent management of enterprises. It is the result of China's transition from a planned economy to a market economy.

From the 13th National Congress of the CPC to the 16th National Congress of the CPC, it is the stage of the in-depth reform of the income distribution system. The 13th National Congress of the CPC clearly pointed out that the income distribution mechanism in the primary stage of socialism must implement the principle of diversified development, i.e., to adhere to the principle of distribution according to work mainly while coexistence of multiple distribution modes, and to prevent excessive income distribution gap on the basis of breaking equalitarianism and improving income level. In the report of the 14th National Congress of the CPC, it was proposed that in the distribution system, further attention should be paid to both efficiency and fairness and it also encouraged to use various means of adjustment, including the market, to not only encourage the advanced, reasonably widen the income gap, but also prevent polarization and gradually achieve common prosperity. Although for the first time the Third Plenary Session of the 14th Central Committee proposed to solve the problem of fairness, the focus of income distribution at this stage is still on efficiency. The nature of the distribution system in which distribution according to work is the main body and multiple modes of distribution coexist, as well as the ways, connections and differences of multiple modes of distribution coexist have not been clearly explained.

In the report of the 15th National Congress of the CPC, it was emphasized to adhere to and improve various distribution methods with distribution according to workload as the main body, allowing some regions and some people to get wealthier first, driving and helping other regions and people, and gradually moving towards common prosperity. On this basis, it puts forward more specific incentive policies for income distribution, explored in detail the income distribution system in which multiple distribution modes coexist, and linked distribution according to work with distribution according to production factors. Compared with the 13th National Congress of the CPC, the 15th National Congress of the CPC has a more scientific and specific policies and arrangement on income distribution. It is required that, on the basis of the system of distribution according to work as the main body and coexistence of multiple distribution modes, various categories of production factors participating in income distribution were clearly stated out, and the necessity and rationality of capital, technology, land, intellectual property rights and other production factors participating in income distribution are affirmed. In particular, technology as a factor of production is included in the framework of income distribution, which is also an affirmation of technology as a factor of production and endogenous power. It can be seen that with the growth of multi ownership economy, in order to adapt to China's basic economic system, the reform of China's income distribution system has been deepened.

From the 16th National Congress of the CPC to the 18th National Congress of the CPC, the income distribution system moved to the perfect stage. Gradually fairness was emphasized and paid more attention to the problem of income distribution gap. With the deepening of economic system reform, China's economy showed the characteristics of sustained and high-speed growth, but the growth rate of residents' disposable income was much lower than the economic growth rate, and the income distribution gap was widening step by step. Therefore, the focus of income distribution system reform in this stage is mainly to emphasize the fairness of distribution, forming a fair oriented income distribution system reform, in order to further slowdown the trend of widening income distribution gap.

The 16th National Congress of the CPC finally established the principle of labor, capital, technology, management and other factors of production participating in the distribution according to their contribution. It is the embodiment and extension of the 15th National Congress of the CPC that factors of production participate in the distribution of income, which is an important breakthrough in the theory of income distribution in the new era. Labor factors and non-labor factors get corresponding reward according to their contributions, which is a positive affirmation of the role of non-labor factors in the process the value and using value of commodity formation, which is conducive to improving the efficiency of optimizing resource allocation, especially the efficiency of optimizing the allocation of scarce resources. However, the participation of non-labor factors in distribution will not affect the status of distribution subject according to work. Although it is clear that the participation of production factors in distribution according to their contribution will make people's income sources present diversified and multi-level characteristics, there are different effects of this distribution system on the income promotion of production factor owners. It resulted in a large range of income promotion for the owners of production factors such as capital, technology, management, etc., while it brings income promotion for farmers, grass-roots workers and other ordinary workers. The increase is relatively small or almost negligible, which to a certain extent continues to expand the income gap between related industries and social groups.

The 16th and 17th National Congress of the CPC especially stressed on that more attention should be paid to fairness in the reallocation field. At the 17th National Congress of the CPC, in addition to the continuous emphasis on adhering to and improving the distribution system with distribution according to work as the main body and multiple distribution modes coexisting, and improving the system of labor, capital, technology, management and other factors of production participating in distribution according to their contributions, it was particularly emphasized that the relationship between efficiency and fairness should be handled well in the primary distribution and redistribution, and that more attention should be paid to fairness in redistribution. This is a major adjustment to "the first distribution pays attention to efficiency, and the second distribution pays attention to fairness". It not only reflects the deepening of the CPC's understanding of the distribution system in the primary stage of socialism, but also reflects the essential requirements of socialism. It is the innovation and development of the socialist distribution system. The 18th National Congress of the CPC further enriched and developed the content of the socialist distribution system, and raised the reform of the income distribution system to the height of " development must be for the people and by the people and its benefit should be shared among the people.". For the first time, it explicitly put forward "two synchronization" and "two improvements"—realizing the synchronization of the growth of resident income and economic development, the growth of labor remuneration and the improvement of labor productivity, increasing the proportion of residents' income in the distribution of national income, and increasing the proportion of labor remuneration in the primary distribution. "Two synchronization" and "two improvements" endow the distribution system of China with the characteristics of dynamic development. It not only has the system stipulation of top-level design, but also has the guidance and operation of policy level, which fully embodies the basic requirements of socialism with Chinese characteristics, that is, sharing development by the people and realizing common prosperity.

The 19th National Congress of the CPC further enriched and developed the socialist distribution system of "distribution accords to work as the main body and multiple distribution modes coexisting". Firstly, it improved the system and mechanism of distribution according to factors to promote a more reasonable and orderly distribution of income; secondly, it encouraged hard work and law-abiding to get rich, expand the middle-income group, increased the income of low-income people, adjusted the high income, ban illegal income, and put income distribution into the track of the rule of law; thirdly, it expanded the channels of property income to increase resident income.

The decision adopted at the 4th Plenary Session of the 19th Central Committee of the CPC put forward the basic economic system of "adhering to distribution according to work as the main body and multiple distribution modes of coexistence", which marks the "four beams and eight pillars". Under the socialist market economy with Chinese characteristics, a distribution system has been mature and completed, and must be maintained for a long time. As an integral part of the basic economic system, the distribution system of China itself is also an institutional system. Each subsystem has unique emphases and individual functions, but they cooperate with each other to form an organic whole with complete functions. The primary distribution system, which combines distribution according to work and distribution according to the contribution of factors, is the decisive force to realize the development achievements shared by the people and the realization of social equity and justice; the national income redistribution system adjusts the distribution relationship between urban and rural areas, regions and groups by means of taxation, social security and transfer payments, so as to promote social equity. Justice is an important corrector to reflect the superiority of socialism and make up for the lack of primary distribution function; the third distribution system is an important development of the distribution system in the decision, the development of public welfare charity with the help of social forces, the realization of targeted relief for special groups, and the important supplement t the primary distribution and redistribution; scientific and reasonable income distribution system is to form a correct incentive It is an important mechanism to encourage and guide, standardize the power boundary of distribution subject and bring distribution into the orbit of rule of law. This three-dimensional distribution system provides a strong institutional guarantee for our country to develop in the road of scientific socialism and achieve the goal of sharing and common prosperity.

10.2.2 China's Income Distribution System Reform

The development and innovation of income distribution theory bring about the reform of income distribution system in every stage of our country. From the perspective of the development of Chinese distribution theory, it mainly focuses on the relationship between government intervention distribution, functional distribution and scale distribution, fairness and efficiency.

(1) Government Intervention in Distribution

Because of the imperfection of both the market economy system and the economic actions in China, it should be recognized that income distribution in China is not the most inequitable in the world but China's income gaps are widening at a staggering pace. It is fair to say that China has transformed from an egalitarian society to a highly unequal society which may even affect the social equity, reduce the economic efficiency, even destroy the stability of the society, and affect the normal operation of the economy. Therefore, it is necessary for the government to intervene in income distribution and control the income gap within an acceptable range. The government's intervention is mainly reflected in the field of primary and redistribution.

Primary distribution occurs in production activities. As the main body of distribution, enterprises include the distribution of GNP among states, enterprises and individuals. It refers to the distribution of factor income. The unified relationship between the owners of production factors and remuneration is the most basic primary distribution relationship. In terms of distribution, the government only readjusts factor income according to the results of the primary distribution. The primary distribution is mainly based on the principle of efficiency and market forces. The government regulates and standardizes through tax lever and laws and regulations. In general, it does not directly interfere with the primary distribution. After the primary distribution forms the "original income", the government redistributes the national income through tax and fiscal expenditure, bank credit and price system, so as to intervene and correct the results of the primary distribution and realize the relative fair distribution, which shows that the main principle of distribution is the principle of "fairness comes first". Realizing the function of redistribution is the key for the government to raise revenue. International experience and China's reality show that to achieve the goal of raising the income level of all people, primary distribution is as important as distribution, and the government needs to perform a series of indispensable functions. In the field of primary distribution, the government should focus on creating a fair, transparent, positive and business-friendly policy environment, so that every participant can enjoy fair opportunities to take part in the production, engage in employment and entrepreneurship, and access to public services. In the field of redistribution, the government adjusts income distribution through public policy channels such as taxation, labor legislation and law enforcement, transfer payments, social security and other basic public services. The government rationally adjusts the order of income distribution, adjusts the result of primary distribution, and protects the rights and interests of vulnerable groups in the labor market through institutional reform and structural adjustment.

(2) Functional Distribution and Scale Distribution

Functional income refers to the income earned from the factors of production by the owners of those factors. According to this definition, functional income can be divided into wages earned by labor, rent from land and interest on capital. Functional income distribution is directly related to the production process. It naturally has theoretical advantages, which helps people understand the efficiency and fairness in economic activities. In 1961, Nicholas Kaldor claimed that the growth rates of real GDP per worker and real capital per worker exhibit no trend and that the gross return on capital, the capital-to-output ratio, and the GDP share of the payments to capital exhibit no trend growth, developing what is nowadays known as Kaldor facts, it is fair to say that Kaldor facts are still in line with the real economy. Since the mid-20th century, economists have focused on the scale distribution of national income, mainly on the micro decision mechanism of individual and different groups' income distribution. scale distribution of income or individual income distribution refers to the final distribution of all kinds of income among people (individuals, families or households). The former is directly related to "production" and more reflects the "fairness" of income distribution; the latter is more related to people's living standards and quality of life and more reflects the "equality" of income distribution.

At the beginning of China's income distribution system reform, it emphasized distribution according to work and opposed equalitarianism, and then emphasized the combination of distribution according to work and distribution according to production factors. Later, it proposed distribution according to the contribution share of factors. It can be seen that the focus of the early and mid-term reform of China's income distribution system lies in the improvement of functional distribution. With the expansion of income gap, large-scale income distribution has been concerned. For example, the 19th National Congress of the CPC proposed to promote hard work and law-abiding, expand the middle-income population, increase the income of low-income people, adjust the high income, ban illegal income, and put income distribution into the orbit of the rule of law. China is at a critical stage of economic restructuring, economic development and improvement of people's livelihood. In this process, economic growth, structural adjustment and improvement of people's livelihood are indispensable. Functional income distribution helps to explore the efficiency and justice in economic growth and structural adjustment, and scale income distribution helps to explore the improvement of people's livelihood in the process of social and economic development, including social security Internal. Redistributive policy helps to create a link between the two and provide a buffer mechanism.

(3) Fairness and Efficiency

Efficiency is an economic concept, but fairness is a very complex and abstract proposition. Political science, economics and sociology have different interpretations of fairness. To define the meaning of fairness correctly is the first step to solve the relationship between them. Marxism holds that any social equity is not abstract, absolute and unchangeable, but concrete, relative and historical, reflecting the existing economic and social relations in a period of time. In the contemporary era, China is establishing the socialist market economy, in which multiple forms of ownership coexist, hence there being many kinds of economic and social relations, so the principle of fairness also contains multiple meanings. First of all, China should meet the principle of fair exchange as the basic rule of market economy; second, China should reflect the fair principle of rights corresponding to socialist human rights; China should also reflect the fair principle of labor corresponding to socialist public ownership and distribution according to work; finally, China should reflect the fair principle of income distribution results. At the beginning of China's reform and opening up, from highly centralized planned economy to market economy, the expansion of income gap is inevitable. In the early stage of economic transformation, it is proposed to oppose equalitarianism and improve economic efficiency. Therefore, strong efficiency takes priority. Then, the reform of China's income system has undergone a series of changes around the "relationship between fairness and efficiency". From the 1993 decision of the CPC Central Committee on Several Issues concerning the construction of the socialist market economy system, "the principle of giving priority to efficiency and giving consideration to fairness" to "striving to achieve the unity of fairness and efficiency on the basis of the development of social productivity".

The relationship between fairness and efficiency is not completely opposite; Yet, they promote each other. The relationship among exchange equity, right equity, labor equity and efficiency is more positive. Fair competition environments, equal social rights and the principle of distribution according to work are conducive to giving full play to the incentive and regulatory role of the system, so as to improve economic efficiency.

The undermentioned characteristics can be concluded in the long-term reform of China's income distribution. First, widening income gaps are not come along with polarization. Although nowadays, the rich became richer, the poor did not become poorer. In another way to say that, low-income groups still get their income increase, although at a slower speed compared with high-income group. This has been verified by the notable reduction of rural poor people over the past decades. Income growth allowed the poor to benefit from economic development despite widening income gaps. This is why China managed to maintain social stability amid increasing income gaps. Second, China's employment priority policy played a pivotal role in reducing income gaps and poverty. Employment is the foundation for people's livelihood and an antidote to poverty. The implementation of employment priority strategy by the Chinese government since the 21st century has undeniably done an feasible work in preventing income gaps from further increasing. In the end, public policies also eased income inequalities to some extent, particularly inclusive social security, poverty relief and support to backward regions and agriculture. These policies have played out well and will play a bigger role in the future as they are improved.

10.2.3 Research on Income Distribution Gap

(1) China's Income Distribution Gap

I Excessive income gap between industries

Most of the highly paid four sectors (financial sector, mineral extraction sector, electric power, heat and water supply and other services sector) are sectors with a significant share of traditional state ownership or significant proportions of the workforce employed in the state sector of economy.

In comparison, labor compensation is relatively low for sectors with a significant share of private economy, while per capita labor compensation is the lowest for wholesale, retail and agriculture with a significant share of individual economy. The income distribution gaps among industries remain high. The continuous high gap of income distribution among industries is an obstacle to the reform of income distribution system in China. The data shows that the wage ratio of the highest and lowest income industries in 1987 is 1.38; while one decade after the reform, the difference between the highest and lowest level of the average income of industries is 1.55 times, and the gap has expanded to 2.99 times by 2002. By 2010, the difference between the highest average wage and the lowest average wage was more than 10 times.

According to relevant statistics of China Statistics Bureau, during 2003-2018, the per capita wage income level of information transmission, computer service, software industry and financial industry was the highest for 13 consecutive years, among which the per capita wage income level of information transmission, computer service and software industry exceeded that of financial industry for three consecutive years since 2018, becoming the industry with the highest per capita wage income level in China. The per capita wage income level of technical services and geological exploration industry is still in the third place, while that of agriculture, forestry, animal husbandry and fishery remains at the lowest level. From 2014 to 2018, the income gap between the industries with the highest per capita wage (information transmission, computer service, software industry and financial industry) and the industries with the lowest per capita wage (agriculture, forestry, animal husbandry and fishery) slightly rose. In 2018, the income gap between them was 4.04 times, 0.5 times larger than the lowest level of 3.54 times in 2014.

II Large income gap between regions

There is a large gap in income distribution among regions in China, which is mainly caused by the large gap in economic development among regions in China. For a long time, China has actively promoted the development of the central and western regions and implemented the strategy of the rise of the central region and the development of the western region. However, there is still a large gap between the economic development level of the eastern coastal areas of China and the central and western regions. Under the joint action of various factors, the per capita income level of the eastern region is far higher than that of the central and western regions. In 1980, the per capita GDP ratio of the eastern and central western regions was 1.8:1.18:1, which expanded to 1.9:1.17:1 in 1990, and further expanded to 2.63:1.26:1 in 2002.This shows that in 1990, the regional gap between the East and the central and western regions increased by 5.9% and 5.6% respectively compared with 1980, and in 2002, it increased by 28.4% and 38.4% respectively compared with 1990. In 2009, the per capita GDP ratio of the eastern, central and western regions was 2:1:0.86.The expansion of per capita GDP gap between regions shows that the level of income gap between regions is also increasing. According to relevant data in 2018 China Statistical Yearbook, in 2017, the per capita disposable income of Chinese residents was 25,973.8 RMB, the highest in Shanghai, reaching 58,988 RMB, and the lowest in Tibet Autonomous Region, only 15,457.3 RMB, the former 3.82 times higher than the latter, and the gap between the two provinces reached 44,000 RMB.

Ⅲ The large income gap between urban and rural residents

Significant income gaps still exist between urban and rural areas. According to NBS data, urban-rural income gaps noticeably increased from 2000 to 2009 with urban and rural household income ratio up from 2.78 times to 3.33 times, reaching the highest level in 2009. Afterwards urban-rural income gaps increased slightly and this process lasted for eight years. The difference dropped to 3 times in 2013 and further decreased in 2019. Although the income gap between urban and rural areas in China has declined since 2009, it is still 1.5 times higher than that in the developed countries in the world, almost 2 times higher than that in the developed countries. And compared with the early stage of reform and opening-up, current urban-rural income gaps are also rather high. If the welfare and material subsidies for urban and rural residents, such as public health care, financial subsidies, pension insurance and unemployment insurance, are taken into account, the urban-rural income gap will be even larger. There are both historical and institutional reasons. In the planned economy, the Chinese government adopted differentiated socio-economic systems and policies between urban and rural areas to finance for industrial development at the expense of farmers' interests. Urban and rural divide was manifested in backward social security and public services in the countryside as compared with cities and slow income growth of farmers as compared with urban residents. After reform and opening-up, urban-rural divide left over from the planned economy persisted, so did the household-registration system that impeded rural labor and population migration. The countryside remained relatively backward in its socio-economic development. In this sense, tremendous urban-rural income gaps resulted from an unfair development strategy. It stemmed from an unfair socioeconomic system and unfair public service policies that led to serious income inequalities.

It can be seen that the gap between urban and rural income distribution in China is still prominent for quite a long time, the appropriate adjustment of the gap between urban and rural income distribution will continue, and this problem will continue to affect the stability, health and sustainable development of China's economy and society.

IV The income gap between social members is too large

Internationally, economists usually use the Gini index to show the distribution of wealth in a country or region. This index is between 0 and 1. The lower the value is, the more evenly the wealth is distributed among the members of the society. Generally, 0.4 is regarded as the "warning line" of income distribution gap in the world.

Upon the founding of the People's Republic of China in 1949, huge income gaps existed in China. According to a study, China's Gini coefficient in 1953 was 0.558. Initially after the new government took over the economy, China's economic landscape, income distribution and income gaps were left over from the old China. In this sense, the huge income gaps are understandable. As the planned economy took shape and especially after the first and second Five-Year Plan periods, household income gaps swiftly narrowed. In 1965, a year before the Cultural Revolution, China's Gini coefficient was about 0.27[1]. The initial stage of rural economic reform is the "best times" of simultaneous income growth and narrowing income gaps with a balance between fairness and efficiency. In the late 1970s and early 1980s, rural economic reform not only led to a rapid increase in farmers' income but reduced income gaps in the countryside as well. According to a household survey, Gini coefficient fluctuated within a range of 0.24-0.26 during 1979-1984. This shows that income inequality was limited and did not change much. However, this period was short-lived. From 1985, income gaps expanded swiftly primarily due to industrial development. China's Gini coefficient has exceeded the warning line of 0.4 in 1994-1998 and 2000-2018, especially in 2000-2017. China's Gini coefficient has reached a dangerous peak of 0.49 in 2001, and was at a high level above

---

[1] Dowling, J.M. and Soo, D. "Income Distribution and Economic Growth in developing Asian Countries", Asia Development Band Economics Staff Paper No.15, 1983.

0.48 for five consecutive years from 2005 to 2010, and created a new peak of 0.491 in 2008. In 2017, the Gini coefficient of the world has exceeded 0.7, exceeding the "danger line" of the Gini coefficient of 0.6 in the world. The serious imbalance of Gini coefficient at home and abroad and the sharp instability of income distribution environment are great challenges for China to reverse the income distribution gap. In 2018, the Engel coefficient of the national residents was 28.4%, meeting the rich standard of 20% to 30% set by the United Nations. Although it was below the "warning line" of income distribution gap, the over average distribution pattern extreme also had a negative impact on the development of China's productivity, and even greatly damaged the improvement of China's social production efficiency. China's Gini coefficient has been at a high level for a long time, which is a major challenge for China to narrow the income distribution gap, and also shows that China's income distribution system reform will be a long-term arduous task.

(2) Causes of Income Distribution Gap

Ⅰ Resource factor utilization structure

The elements of wealth creation include labor, capital, land, technology, management, mineral resources and other resource elements. In terms of primary distribution and value formation, when creating new wealth, it is also the process of distributing new wealth. China is a country with a large population, with frequent labor transfer and high employment pressure. The unlimited supply of labor under China's current dual economic structure constitutes the main reason for the declining share of wage income in national income. The unlimited nature of this supply of labor has kept wages low and made them insensitive to changes in supply and demand in labor market and in labor productivity. As a result, when economic growth is very high and labor productivity is rising rapidly, wages cannot possibly keep up, so the share of wage income in national income falls still lower. Therefore, the key to improve the primary distribution of income among owners of different factors is to change the utilization mode of development factors and balance the utilization structure of capital and labor factors.

Ⅱ The slower urbanization, the greater the income gap between urban and rural areas

According to statistics, the proportion of agricultural added value to GDP decreased from 33.4% in 1982 to 10.6% in 2009, while the proportion of rural population decreased from 78.87% to 46.59%, especially the proportion of employment in the primary industry, only decreased from 68.1% to 38.1%. While the proportion of rural and agricultural wealth production continues to decline rapidly, the transfer of agricultural population and agricultural labor force to urban and non-agricultural areas is too slow, resulting in the relatively less and less agricultural added value being distributed by more and more rural population and labor force. Compared with the distribution of urban and non-agricultural population, the gap is bound to widen. China's unequal income distribution is to a large extent expressed in unequal functional income distribution, that is, as China's economy develops, the share of wage income in national income falls. The unlimited supply of labor under China's current dual economic structure is the major reason for this.

III The lower the proportion of the tertiary industry, the less the distribution of workers

With the increase of wages, social security and other costs, the increasing proportion of capital in the secondary industry is a trend, i.e., the industry generally replaces labor force with capital through technological progress and automation, and promotes more and more capital with less and less labor force. Under such a trend, if the production and employment of the service sector (tertiary industry) does not expand in time accordingly, the labor force will have more surpluses, unemployment will rise, the income distribution between capital and labor becomes even worse, and the income distribution gap is further widened.

IV Relatively fewer small businesses, the larger the income distribution gap

The more small and micro enterprises a country has, the larger the proportion of enterprise size and structure. The higher the level of quantity per thousand people and the higher the labor intensity, the more small and medium-sized investors there are, from the perspective of wealth creation and distribution, the more middle-income people are. As labor is fully utilized, the fewer the unemployed, the smaller the income gap; Conversely, when the number of large enterprises and large enterprises in a country increases, the number of small and micro enterprises and investors will decrease. The number of enterprises per thousand is low, the labor force is underutilized, the middle-income population is shrinking, the number of people impoverished by unemployment is increasing, and the income distribution gap is widening.

(3) The Impact of Income Distribution Gap

The impact of income distribution gap mainly includes the following aspects: first, the widening income gap between urban and rural areas has led to a slow increase in farmers' consumption and a shrinking rural market, which is not conducive to boosting domestic demand and economic growth. The widening income gap among regions has weakened the ability of backward regions to absorb and cultivate talents, made the development of central and western regions more difficult, and affected the formation of a national unified market. Second, the widening of the industrial income gap distorts the concept of employment and causes the waste of human resources, which is not conducive to economic development. Urban and rural residents "spend money" and "dare not spend money" are caused by the current pattern of income distribution. To expand domestic demand, we must effectively increase people's income. Since the reform and opening up, especially in recent years, the contribution rate of final consumption to economic growth has gradually declined, which makes it difficult to effectively boost consumption. The root cause is the declining share of workers' wages. Some believe that the crux to solving the economic imbalance is to raise wages. The reasonable proportion of labor remuneration should be determined according to the contribution rate of human capital to GDP. Excessive will lead to the unfair society of income distribution gap, the sense of unfair growth and people's dissatisfaction, resulting in a sense of relative deprivation and hatred of the rich, leading to crime, affecting social stability, and ultimately resulting in a negative impact on the whole society. The dissatisfaction caused by the excessive income distribution gap keeps accumulating until the negative or deviant behaviors that affect social stability occur. It can be seen from the occupational characteristics that the subject of negative social psychology is some social vulnerable groups and high-risk groups.

(4) Deepening the Reform of Distribution System

The reform of China's income distribution system over the past 40 years has been a process of constant exploration and improvement in respond to the needs of social and economic development. Income distribution system has a direct connection of the interests of the people. Therefore, the reform must follow the path of gradual and orderly reform. The path should remain the maintenance of high-speed growth and the acceleration of urbanization and industrialization so that surplus rural labor can be absorbed as soon as possible.

To solve the problem of high profit in monopoly industry and limit the scope of monopoly, China should improve market access for some monopolized industries, introduce competition mechanisms, narrow the scope of state monopolized industries, and narrow the income gap between monopolized and non-monopolized industries. Let the monopoly law play its due role in industries such as telecommunications and automobiles.

Taxation is a very important policy tool. Tax distribution participates in the redistribution of national income enhance the role of taxation in regulating income distribution. China's current tax system has a limited effect in regulating income distribution. Tax structure, for instance, is tilted in favor of indirect tax such as VAT that contributes to increasing income gaps, while the share of direct tax such as personal income tax that helps narrow income gaps is too small. Moreover, personal income tax is a salary tax imposed on salarymen and cannot regulate the income of people with other income sources. Personal income tax contributed more to narrowing income gaps between urban and rural residents since 2005 but the effect was limited. In 2009, personal income tax only reduced Gini coefficient between urban and rural residents by about one percentage point. It is necessary, therefore, to adjust tax structure by including taxes that help regulate income distribution: among them, property tax and inheritance tax are worth considering. Property tax will increase the share of direct tax and allow the government to conditionally exempt certain indirect taxes and invigorate enterprises. It will also effectively regulate the income of high-income groups.

The government has taken steps to create a minimum income security system covering urban and rural residents since 2003. By the end of 2014, 70.89 million people have benefited from the minimum income security system, including 18.8 million urban residents and 52.09 million rural residents. Minimum income security has some effects in alleviating poverty, raising the income of the poor and reducing income gaps. Through the implementation of a series of preferential policies such as the Two Exemptions One Subsidy Policy in alleviating poverty in rural China, the farmers' income has been increased and their living standards have been improved. China's government have raised the basic pension standards for retirees of enterprises for many times, actively implemented the policy of living and medical treatment for the object of preferential treatment, basically realized the minimum living guarantee for urban residents, vigorously promoted the reemployment of laid-off and unemployed people, improved the minimum wage system, raised the deduction standard of personal income tax and wage expenses, and obtained the basic life for urban low-income people Effective guarantee.

After an average annual high-speed economic growth of more than 9%, China's total economy has changed significantly. However, with the increase of CPI coefficient, the real income of Chinese residents shows a negative trend. The increasing income gap among social members, urban and rural residents, different industries and different regions has made the national income distribution pattern fall into a difficult situation, and the excessive income distribution gap has become a prominent social contradiction. Too large income distribution gap will lead to a series of economic and social problems. Therefore, it is imperative to narrow the income gap and build a harmonious society. The government should strengthen the reform and supervision in many aspects such as the legal system and system, gradually narrow the gap and realize common prosperity. Under the control of the Chinese government and with the joint efforts of the whole society, China will usher in a new future.

Chapter 11

Easing Doing-business Environment

11.1 Doing Business Environment and Index by the World Bank

The business environment is directly related to the economic competitiveness and soft power of a region or city. Building a high-standard business environment is an important support for a nation to accelerate the construction of an international economic, financial, trade, shipping, scientific and technological innovation center, and constantly improve the core competitiveness of a city.

Since the beginning of the 21st century, the world bank has set up a team called "Doing Business to Create a Business Environment Indicator System" and enhance business activity that constrain it. "What gets measured gets done" illustrates aphorism of Doing Business. It provides objective measures of business regulations and their enforcement across 190 economies and selected cities at the subnational and regional level. The indicators and indexes helps governments to increase transparency and accountability and foster an easing and enabling environment for entrepreneurs and small and medium-size enterprises.

Based on an economy's performance, Doing Business benchmarks aspects of business regulation and practice in 11 measured areas covering the life of a business, including starting a business, dealing with construction permits, getting electricity, registering property, getting credit, protecting minority investors, paying taxes, trading cross borders, enforcing contracts, resolving insolvency and labor market regulation. The Doing Business Group reports different themes and indicator index based on different focus of business environment and regulations every year. For example, the reports focus on business life cycle in 2004, intellectual property protection and cross-border trade in 2006, efficiency and quality in 2015, regulatory quality and efficiency in 2016, Equal opportunity for all in 2017, and reforming to create jobs in 2018. The indicators in Doing Business have been incorporated into the evaluation index of many institutions, which has spurred the government to create more supportive business climate to drive inclusive and sustainable economic growth.

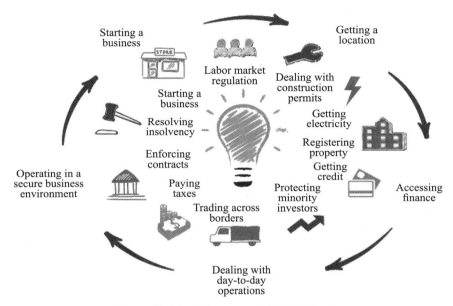

Figure 11-1 What is measured in Doing Business

Source: Doing business database.

Here are the index and features of Doing Business in the 11 measured areas.

① Making it easier to start a business: including starting a business by simplified registration formalities, reducing minimum capital requirements, simplifying post-registration procedures and improving one-stop shop by combining different registrations. ② Making it easier to process construction permits: including the permitting reduced the processing time to issue building certificates, streamlined. ③ Making it easier to get electricity: including facilitated more reliable power supply and transparency of tariff information; improved process for getting an electricity by increasing the stock of material the utility carries, streamlined approval process by setting up a dedicated task force that coordinates the external works without the need for customer interaction; reduced connection costs. ④ Making it easier to register property:

including increased the efficiency and transparency of information to the public, created a Single Window for the issuance of land certificates, reduced taxes or fees of property titles and securing land, decentralized the process of property registering and transfer, and increased administrative efficiency. ⑤ Improving the sharing of credit information: including improved access to credit information, improved regulatory framework for credit reporting, expanded scope of credit information, and guaranteed by law borrowers' right to inspect data. ⑥ Strengthening minority investor protections: including expanded shareholders' role in company management, enhanced access to information in shareholders' actions, and increased disclosure requirements for related-party transactions. ⑦ Making it easier to pay taxes: including facilitated one-stop tax systems, reduced profit tax rate, labor taxes and mandatory contributions, and allowed for more tax-deductible expenses, simplified tax compliance processes, merged or eliminated taxes, and improved tax audit processes. ⑧ Making it easier to trade cross borders: including improved electronic submission and processing of documents for exports and imports, strengthened border infrastructure for exports and imports, and enhanced customs administration and inspections for exports and imports. ⑨ Making it easier to enforce contracts: including introduced or expanded electronic filing system for commercial cases, expanded court automation by introducing electronic service of process, automatic assignment of cases to judges or by publishing judgments, and expanded the alternative dispute resolution framework. ⑩ Making it easier to resolve insolvency: including improved the likelihood of successful reorganization and introduced priority rules of insolvency proceedings, strengthened creditors' rights, and streamlined insolvency procedures. ⑪ Changing the labor legislation: including altered hiring rules and probationary period, changed redundancy rules and costs, reformed legislation of worker protection and social benefits.

Around the world, registering a business takes an average of 20 days and cost 23% of income per capital, compared to 47 days and 76% of income per capital in 2006. The average paid-in minimum capital that entrepreneurs must deposit is 6% of income per capital, compared with 145% of income per capital in 2006. And the global average time to prepare, file and pay taxes has fallen from 324 hours in 2005 to 237 hours in 2017. The ease of doing business score shows an economy's position to the comprehensive reform on the efficiency and quality of the business environment and regulatory practices. The top three economies of the ease of doing business in 2018 are New Zealand, Singapore and Denmark. China ranked 46 in ease of doing business.

READING①: What is the ease of doing business score?

This year the name of the *Doing Business* distance to frontier score has been changed to "ease of doing business score" to better reflect the main idea of the measure—a score indicating an economy's position to the best regulatory practice. Nevertheless, the process for calculating the score remains the same. The score combines measures with different units such as time to start a company or procedures to transfer a property. The score captures the gap between an economy's current performance and a measure of best regulatory practice set in Doing Business 2015 across the entire sample of the same 41 indicators for 10 Doing Business indicator sets used in previous years. For example, according to the Doing Business database, across all economies and over time, the least time needed to start a business is 0.5 days, while in the worst 5% of cases it takes more than 100 days. Half a day is, therefore, considered the best performance, while 100 days is the worst. Higher scores show absolute better ease of doing business (the best score is set at 100), while lower scores show absolute poorer ease of doing business (the worst performance is set at 0). The percentage point scores of an economy on different indicators can be averaged together to obtain an aggregate score.

11.1.2 Three Approuches to Build Doing-business Enviroment for Government

Regardless the background, any economy can improve their business regulation when the will of policy makers is strong. There are three approaches to build doing-business environment for government based on the studies of international cases.

First, Singapore's "big government" and efficient control approach: it highlights the duty and leadership role of the government in attracting and nurturing business, creating an industry-oriented enterprise service mechanism which boots the economic growth. The Singapore Economic Development Board (EDB) carries out meticulous and in-depth strategic discussions on priority industries every three years to attract investment. Once a priority industry is identified, the EDB sets up an industry-oriented professional framework and establishes a "service commissioner" system.

---

① www. doingbusiness.org.

The system provides policy flexibility and a full range of services, which has helped Singapore's electronics, IT, communications technology, bio-tech and healthcare industries to attain rapid growth.

Second, Ireland's "demand-driven" approach: although its geographic location and other natural endowment attributes limit attraction to external investment, the central government maintain the long-term communication with target enterprises and seeks to understand enterprise growth dynamics, and help them find solution for local investment. Industrial Development Agency Ireland (IDA) focus on industrial planning and provides targeted a high-quality solutions as well as high efficient services to help enterprises address the issues faced by investors. Meanwhile, IDA set up a long-term partnership mechanism with local and foreign enterprises to better understand their development plans so that more sub-sectors in the industry chain will gravitate towards Ireland.

Third, Hong Kong's free and open "small government" approach: Hong Kong relies on open market and attracts more investors by leveraging its geographic advantages in Asia Pacific, lowering tax rates and efficient services. Hongkong has been providing free and confidential "one-stop" investment services to various types enterprises in different industries over the past 15 years. Hongkong has successfully attracted overseas enterprises that use Hong Kong as a base for entering Asian markets, as well as Chinese mainland enterprises to go out by using Hong Kong as a platform.

11.1.3 The Performance of Economics in Doing-businecs

Regardless of the geographic endowment of regions and their different governing approaches, all of these government provide all-round convenience, streamlined procedures, and personalized services to enterprises.

The economics of Europe, central Asia and sub-Saharan Africa are the most active areas in reforming their regulatory frameworks in recent years. Both regions captured reforms in almost every topic measured by Doing Business, and the number of reforms represent half of all reforms globally. The lowest share of reformers is OECD high-income group where 16 of 34 economies implemented reforms with 7% of the global count. In the worldwide, the top ten economies showing the most notable improvement in performance of easing of doing business are Afghanistan, Djibouti, China, Azerbaijan, India, Togo, Kenya, Cote d'lvoire, Turkey and Rwanda. And these top ten improvers implemented the most regulatory reforms in the areas of starting a business, getting credit and paying taxes. In 2017 and 2018, almost one-third of reforms were implemented in two areas—starting a business and enforcing contracts (Table 11-1).

Table 11-1 Regions with the highest shares of reformers in 2017/2018

Areas of reform	Number of reforms in 2017/2018	Region(s) with the highest share of reformers
Starting a business	50	East Asia& Pacific
Dealing with construction permits	31	Europe & Central Asia
Getting Electricity	26	East Asia& Pacific
Registering property	28	Sub-Saharan Africa
Getting credit	29	Middle East& North Africa and South Asia
Protecting minority investors	23	Middle East & North Africa
Paying taxes	31	South Asia
Trading across borders	33	Europe & Central Asia
Enforcing contracts	49	Sub-Saharan Africa
Resolving insolvency	14	South Asia

Sources: Doing Business database.

China and India are the two economies with the largest populations, and both governments take careful and impressive reform agendas to improve the business regulatory environment over the recent years. China is the only economy from East Asia and the Pacific to join the Doing Business 2019 list of 10 top improvers. China demonstrates progressive agenda to increase the efficiency of business processes and improve the efficiency of cross-border trade, reducing border and documentary compliance time for both exports and imports.

Variation across areas of regulation, as measured by the ease of doing business ranking, is also frequently observed across all economies, regardless of income level. Among high-income economies, for example, New Zealand ranks 1 for starting a business, but 21 for enforcing contracts. Rwanda, a low-income economy, ranks 2 for registering property and 3 for getting credit, but 88 for trading across borders and 51 for starting a business. China is ranked 6 for enforcing contracts but 28 for starting a business, while Morocco—

classified as a lower-middle-income economy—ranks 25 for paying taxes but 112 for getting credit.

11.2 China Major Urban Cities Doing Business in the New Era

Since 2017, President Xi Jinping has repeatedly mentioned the importance of improving the doing business environment. In the practical departments, optimize the business environment has developed vital strategy in major cities and consider them as the major measures to promote regional sustainable economic growth and competitiveness. Anchored in the current situation which the economy has transferred from a phase of growth to high-quality development, optimizing the economic structure and changing the driving force of growth have become the internal requirements of the construction in modern economic system. China is ranked 31 among 190 economies in the ease of doing business in 2019, improved from 46 in 2018 according to the latest World Bank annual ratings. Ease of Doing Business in China averaged 78.67 from 2008 until 2019, reaching an all time high of 99 in 2012 and a record low of 31 in 2019.

The 40-year development of China's reform is a process of improving China's business environment. In the early stage, China enhanced the legal framework for infrastructure construction and labor market in order to attract foreign direct investment. The government in major cities relied on "hard environment" such as building roads and bridges and enabling water and electricity utility, and fundamental "soft environment" such as providing tax revenue preferential policies and government subsidies. However, there is no concrete measures related with market permission, commercial registration, getting credit and fair competitive environment. Furthermore, there is lack of regulatory policy and protect mechanism on doing business. In 2012, the executive council of the State approved Guangdong province as a comprehensive pilot reformer and put forward the goal of building justified, transparent and efficient business environment. There are three characteristics at the early stage of building doing business environment: firstly the main purpose of doing business construction is to provide efficient service to all kinds entities in the market more than attracting foreign investment. Secondly, the approach to reform aimed to improve "soft environment", including simplified documentation requirements, introducing a unified application for inspections, setting up market regulation and increasing the efficiency of business process. Lastly, the construction of doing business should take legalization approach to uniformed, justified and transparent business environment, encouraging innovation, protecting private property and strengthening investors' expectation.

The reform of doing business stepped into allover promotion stage since 2015. This reform applies to both Beijing and Shanghai. The governments in two cities made starting a business easier by eliminating both the minimum capital requirement and requirement to obtain a capital verification report from an auditing firm. By making paying taxes easier, the government enhance electronic system for filing and paying taxes and adopting new communication channels within its taxpayer service. In addition, the measures make paying taxes less costly in both cities by reducing the social security contribution rate. In 2017, China government put forward the ideas that doing business is productivity. China continued to implement regulatory reforms in starting a business, getting credit and paying taxes. China improved access to credit information by starting a report payment histories from utility companies and providing credit scores to banks and financial institutions in Beijing and Shanghai. In 2018, the government set up the time table of reforming doing business in more major cities. China made starting a business easier by streamlining registration procedures and paying taxes easier by introducing several measures of easing compliance.

Judging from China's changes both in rankings and scores in the top 10 fields, we can see remarkable progress in the fields of getting electricity, starting a business, protecting minority investors, and dealing with construction permits, with the ranking increased by more than 50.

Table 11-2 2018-2019 Ranking and change of China Doing-business environment in Major Areas

Areas	DB2018 China Ranking	DB2019 China Ranking	Changes in Ranking
Getting Electricity	98	14	+84
Starting a Business	93	28	+65
Protecting Minority Investors	119	64	+55
Dealing with Construction Permits	172	121	+51

Source: World Bank database.

As the continuous improvement of easing doing business in China, the development of business environment in major cities presents notable trends. Firstly, targeting at reform to streamline administration and service,

China implemented initiatives to improve the "soft" business environment. The reform of commercial system is the starting point by promoting doing business. Starting a business is the first measure in the measured index by the World Bank, which includes sub-index of simplified registration formalities, reducing the time of procedures, costs and minimum capital requirement. Following those measured indices, China implemented business registration system reform since 2014. Until 2018, there are 106 reforms on licenses separation of administrative approval, which increases the efficiency of business processes and transparency in both starting a business and after getting the license. In addition, China implements innovative administration and service system, expanding "one-stop online + administration and service" system to streamline the interaction between different departments and increase administrative efficiency.

Secondly, promoting financial reform and innovation resolves the financing difficulties of medium and small-size enterprises. Since the launching of doing business in 2013, the government improve access to facilitate financing by the three ways. The government optimizes financing allocation, improves financing services of financial institutions, and develop vigorously direct financing of enterprises. In addition, the government attach importance to policy-based financial allocation and play position role of policy-based financial institutions. Furthermore, the local governments mobilize non-government financial allocation and develop private equity and other venture capital funds.

Thirdly, building "Chinese characteristic" doing business assessment mechanism based on the index of the World Bank is another trend. According to the 2019 report of Doing Business, the rank of doing business in China has moved from 78th in 2017 to 46 in 2018, and remarked as the most 10 reformers economies. Based on the measured index of the World Bank, China builds three dimensions from the aspects of business life cycle, investing attractiveness of cities, and high-quality city development standards to reflect the Chinese characteristic on the process of the reform.

In the context of rising deglobalization and trade protectionism, China has firmly promoted reform and had launched a series of major opening-up measures in 2018, further improving the business environment. First, the overall tariff rate has been reduced to 7.5 percent, involving 1,585 tax items, with an average reduction of about 26 percent. Of these, the tax rate on automobiles has been reduced from 25 to 15 percent, and the tax rate on auto parts has been reduced to 6 percent. Second, China continues to relax market access and encourages market competition. Local governments significantly ease market access for banking, securities and insurance industries, and significantly expand the scope of business. China give national treatment to foreign investors in industries such as business credit reporting, credit rating, bank card clearing, and non-bank payments, and steadily promote the two-way opening of the capital market. Remarkable progress has been made in market access and business expansion for foreign-funded financial institutions, and foreign ownership limits on aircraft and shipbuilding industries have been lifted. Over the past three years, China has shortened the negative list for foreign investment three times, and the restrictive measures against foreign investment have been cut by 57 percent.

Third, China keeps speeding up the development of pilot free trade zones and open up new prospects for reform and opening up at a higher level. The building of a free trade port in Hainan will be explored. The government set up a new area in the China (Shanghai) Pilot Free Trade Zone to encourage and support Shanghai's innovative effort in promoting investment and trade liberalization and facilitation.

According to a World Bank report in 2019, China ranks 46th out of 190 economies in the world in terms of business environment, up by 32 places from the previous year. In ease for starting a business, obtaining electricity, registering assets, and execution of contracts, China ranks 28th, 14th, 27th and 6th, respectively.

11.3 Localized Assessment System of China Doing Business Environment

Prior to evaluating the urban business environment in China, an evaluation system that conforms to the national conditions of the country has to be established. When China put the World Bank's evaluation system into Chinese characteristics, China's vast size has meant that the rate of urbanization and industrial structures differ from region to region. Doing Business report in China 2008 divides China pilot 30 cites into 6 areas based on geographic location and evaluate their performance on doing-business.

Based on the report, China selected 4 major measured indexes to assess: starting a business, registering property, getting credit and enforcing contracts. And the results shows that the first ten cities of easing doing business focus on Southeast and Bohai coastal regions, while the business environment in middle and west regions are relatively poor.

Academy of Greater Bay Area Studies rely on World Bank indicators and released the report of China's Urban Business Environment Index 2018 by making survey of selected 35 cities in China and comparing their strengths and weaknesses when enforcing doing business. The report applies the index into four levels: the first level is city environment of doing business, the second level has six indexes including soft environment (25%), market environment (20%), business cost environment (15%), infrastructure surroundings (15%), ecological environment (15%), and social service environment (10%); the third level has 29 indexes, and the fourth level has 32 indexes. Some are positive index which the higher assess value, the higher the index scores. Based on the report, we find out that the overall business environment in east-coastal areas perform better than others (see Table 11-3).

Table 11-3 Surveyed Cities in Doing Business in China

Southeast Regions	Fuzhou, Guangzhou, Hangzhou, Nanjing, Shanghai
Bo Hai Coastal Regions	Jinan, Shijiazhuang, Beijing, Tianjin
Northeast Regions	Chuangchun, Haierbing, Shenyang
Middle Regions	Changsha, Hefei, Nanchang, Wuhan, Zhengzhou
Southwest Regions	Chendu, Guiyang, Haikou, Kunming, Nanning, Chongqing
Northwest Regions	Huhehaote, Lanzhou, Taiyuan, Xian, Wulumuqi, Xining, Yinchuan

Source: China Doing Business Report 2008.

11.3.1 Indicators and Assessment of China Major Urban Business Environment in 2017-2018

The structure of Doing Business system in China major cities focus on business and entrepreneurs, showing "three themes, three logic, six dimensions". The three themes, based on the current situations in China, refer to innovation-driven strategy, supply-side structural reform and supported real economy development. The three logic relies on streamline administration and institute decentralization, ease the burden on all businesses, and guaranteed administration performance. And the six dimensions focus on easing of starting a business, ease dealing of construction permits, liquidity easing of factors of production, easing of trade, less burden of paying taxes, and performance of administrative act and service.

(1) Easing of Starting a Business

Starting a business is a threshold for starting-up, and the first stage of business life cycle as well. The easing of starting a business is the first and important measured index of World Bank doing business. In China, starting a business includes seven stages: pre-approval of business name, applying business license, applying cachet of a business, producing cachet of a business, applying business invoice, registration of recruitment documents, and registration of social security.

Based on the measured index and evaluating methods, the first three cities of easing to start a business are Hangzhou, Zhoushan (Zhejiang) and Shenzhen. Shanghai listed on eleventh on the list. And the last three cities are Kunming, Changchun and Chongqing. The first ten and last ten cities of easing to start a business are shown on table 11-4.

Table 11-4 The Doing Business Index and Scoring

2018 ranking	2017 ranking	City	Index of DB	2018 ranking	2017 ranking	City	Index of DB
1	3	Shenzhen	0.611	19	19	Dalian	0.318
2	4	Shanghai	0.524	20	17	Nanchang	0.313
3	1	Guangzhou	0.512	21	18	Fuzhou	0.313
4	2	Beijing	0.51	22	27	Nanning	0.312
5	5	Chongqing	0.478	23	24	Hefei	0.303
6	13	Chengdu	0.405	24	16	Changchun	0.301
7	6	Nanjing	0.398	25	26	Shenyang	0.298
8	7	Hangzhou	0.397	26	14	Haikou	0.297
9	20	Changsha	0.391	27	15	Jinan	0.294
10	10	Wuhan	0.388	28	31	Wulumuqi	0.289
11	12	Xi'an	0.377	29	32	Xining	0.271
12	9	Qingdao	0.375	30	34	Yinchuan	0.268

Database: China's Urban Business Environment Index Report 2019.

Table 11-5 The evaluated scoring of easing starting a business in 33 cities

City	Easing of registration	Easing of preparation	Total Score	City	Easing of registration	Easing of preparation	Total Score
Hangzhou	10.29	4.8	15.09	Taiyuan (Shanxi)	4.69	3.6	8.29
Zhoushan (Zhejiang)	9.09	4.8	13.89	Hefei	5.69	3.6	8.29
Shenzhen	7.91	4.8	12.71	Nanning	5.56	3.6	8.29
Guangzhou	9.51	2.8	12.31	Shijiazhuang	6.49	1.6	8.09
Qingdao	7.69	4.6	12.29	Haikou	6.26	1.6	7.86
Nanjing	8.27	3.6	11.87	Beijing	4.69	2.6	7.29
Xiamen	7.74	3.8	11.54	Nanchang	6.49	0.6	7.09
Fuzhou	7.69	3.8	11.49	Kunming	5.82	0.6	6.42
Chengdu	7.63	3.6	11.23	Changchun	5.44	0.8	6.24
Xi'an	6.49	4.6	11.09	Chongqing	4.76	0.6	5.36

(2) Dealing with Construction Permit

Construction permit is the chronic problem against easing doing business in many cities. The problems concern on weigh too complicated approval procedures, various departments involved, and miscellaneous of approval process. All these problems cause inefficiency of construction. Based on the measured index of the World Bank, local governments simplify and decentralizes the construction permit in approval time, approval procedure, and approval costs.

(3) Liquidity Easing of Factor of Production

This indicator focuses on the three aspects: financing environment, cost of labor and cost of using land and electricity. Capital is the blood of any business. Easing of getting credit is the first three most important index of Doing Business measured by the World Bank, especially for medium and small enterprises. China takes measures to improve by optimizing commercial financial allocation and encouraging private financing. In addition, lowering the "five social insurance and one housing fund" is the important measure by relieving the burden of labor costs. Meanwhile, land

and electricity are the necessity to operate and expand for any business. Based on the research data, the higher costs of electricity exert negative influences on a business. As the price of electricity goes up, a firm will switch its production to lower-density electricity ones and causes slowdown of production efficiency.

(4) Easing of Transactions

Improving degree of transactions creates fairer and integrity competitive environment. The index differs from Doing Business Report issued by the World Bank. The index of easing of transactions concerns both domestic and cross-border trade, which measures the differences of easing of trading between cities and further reflects the degree of internalization when doing business with the world. The index focuses on the trading differences among major urban cities in China. To be specific, the index is measured from the five factors: competitive environment, easing of E-commerce, credit system, easing of transportation, and the difference of cross-border trade and service.

(5) Easing the Burden of Paying Taxes

Higher taxes will restrain the economic growth and easing the burden is the driving force to the development of a business. In order to create better doing business environment, China implemented the four aspects to reduce the burden: comprehensively launched "camp to add" pilot policy, cleaned up and standardized governmental funds, canceled government-involved administrative and institutional fees, and dramatically reduced business service fees.

(6) Performance of Administrative Services

In order to strengthen and optimize the business environment, China implemented online one-stop administrative service to complete "cutting procedures, simplifying process, cutting time, and improving efficiency".

11.3.2 Optimize the Doing-business Environment in Shanghai as a Pilot City in China

Based on the global economic development, the State Council has made a momentous decision to optimize the doing business environment, and

Shanghai follows the policy and raise its energy level in urban development. A series of key measures have been implemented to intensify doing-business environment construction and have achieved remarkable effects. Shanghai established the Pilot Free Trade Zone and facilitate systemic innovation on investment, trade and finance. Shanghai have implemented a single window system for cross-border trade, decreased the special administrative measures for foreign investment in the Zone from 190 to 95, and reduced the time for customs clearance by one third.

Shanghai implements a further package of reforms in the administrative examination and the approval system. Local government has canceled over 1800 items concerning adjustment and approval in the past five years, and initiated a pilot reform to separate operating permits and business licenses, which saves the time of starting up a business by more than one third. In addition, Shanghai government accelerated the smart government with "one network" and a "general portal" online system for diverse administrative service. In most cases. Enterprises and citizens "ran at most ONE errand".

In 2018, there are over 80,000 foreign-funded enterprises, over 600 regional headquarters of transnational corporations, and 400 foreign-funded R&D centers in Shanghai. There are averagely more than 1,300 enterprises created every day. According to the Doing Business Report 2019 by the World Bank, the overall ranking of China, 46th on the list, moves up 32 places from the previous year, with up to 55% contribution from Shanghai.

Several reforms implemented by Shanghai were particularly notable, which also contributes the performance that China became the second faster Doing Business reformer around the world. The performance is manifested in the following aspects: ① Starting a business: Shanghai cut the time to start a business from 22 days to only 9 days, significantly reduced the cost of registering a company and limited the complication of procedures, which on par with most OECD high income economics. ② Dealing with construction permits: Shanghai cut the time need to get a permit from 279 days in 2017 to only 169 days in 2018. It also increased the quality of construction professionals. ③ Getting electricity: Shanghai introduced a "three zero" policy-zero visits, zero approvals, and zero costs, which is likely to be emulated around the world. ④ Enforcing contracts: Shanghai continued to be one of the world's leaders in high-quality and efficient solution of commercial disputes. ⑤ Protecting minority investors: Shanghai increased shareholders' rights and their role in major corporate decisions and clarified ownership and control structures.

Optimizing the doing-business environment is a part of China's ongoing reforms and its occurring in the context of opening up to the world . It is also an ongoing and constant systematic project. As China's comprehensive national power continues to increase, an increasing number of cities will join in the competition for international resources, capital and talent. Optimizing the doing-business environment will become a key long-term task for more local governments in China.

11.4 Effect of Business Enviroment on Entrepreneurship in Guangdong, Hong Kong and Macau

The business environment refers to the practices and costs required by companies to comply with policies and regulations in terms of opening, operating, trading, taxation, termination or execution of contracts. Since 2019, the executive meeting of the State Council has repeatedly focused on the topic of the business environment. Through continuous deepening of the reform of streamlining administration, delegating powers, and improving regulation and services, efforts are made to improve and optimize the business environment. The business environment is a systemic environment, which is the general term referring to the various surrounding situations and conditions that accompany the entire process of economic and social activities carried out by market entities. It usually includes the politic environment, market environment, international environment, legal environment, enterprise development environment and social environment. The business environment is the fertile soil that nourishes the development, innovation and entrepreneurship of enterprises, so the quality of the business environment directly affects the quality and speed of national or regional economic development. Thus, the business environment is an irreplaceable productivity. From 2012 to 2019, the global ranking of China's business environment has increased from 91st to 31st, indicating that the series of reform measures China has taken to optimize the business environment, including the reduction of tax and fee, and the deepening of 'decentralization of power and optimization of service and management', have achieved significant results.

Table 11-6 Global ranking of China's business environment (2012-2019)

Index	2012	2013	2014	2015	2016	2017	2018	2019
Ease of doing business	91	96	90	80	78	78	46	31
Starting a business	151	158	128	134	127	93	28	27
Dealing with Construction Permits	181	185	179	175	177	172	121	33
Getting Electricity	114	119	124	92	97	98	14	12
Registering Property	44	48	37	42	42	41	27	28
Getting Credit	70	73	41	78	62	68	73	80
Protecting Minority Investors	100	98	132	118	123	119	64	28
Paying Taxes	122	120	120	127	131	130	114	105
Trading across Borders	68	74	98	94	96	97	65	56
Enforcing Contract	19	19	35	4	5	5	6	5
Resolving Insolvency	82	78	53	53	53	56	61	51

Source: The World Bank.

11.4.1 Accelerate the Construction of the International Science and Technology Innovation Center in the Guangdong-Hong Kong-Macao Greater Bay Area and Explore the Establishment of a Sound International Cooperation Mechanism for Innovation and Entrepreneurship

The *Outline of the Development Plan for the Guangdong-Hong Kong-Macao Greater Bay Area* (February 18, 2018) clearly stated that it is necessary to expand the space of employment and entrepreneurship, support Hong Kong and Macao youth and small and medium-sized enterprises to develop in the Mainland, and include eligible Hong Kong and Macao entrepreneurs into the scope of local business subsidy support, promote the construction of innovation and entrepreneurship bases and platforms in various regions of the Greater Bay Area. Support Hongkong to encourage young people from Hong Kong and Macao to work in Guangdong Province through program such as 'Guangdong-Hong Kong Summer Internship Program'. Support Hong Kong to help Hong Kong youth with Entrepreneurship and employment through the 'Youth Development Fund' in the Greater Bay Area. Support Macao to build a youth innovation and entrepreneurship exchange center between

China and Portuguese-speaking countries. Support government to hold Guangdong-Hong Kong and Guangdong-Macao labor inspection cooperation meetings and law enforcement training courses.

In the State Council's *'Opinions on Promoting the High-quality Development of Innovation and Entrepreneurship and Creating an Upgraded Version of 'Double Innovation'(September 26, 2018)*, the term *'accelerated construction of a highland for innovation and entrepreneurship development'* was also proposed innovatively. The opinion point out that the construction of the Guangdong-Hong Kong-Macao Greater Bay Area International Science and Technology Innovation Center need to be accelerated as well as exploring the establishment and improvement of a new international mechanism for innovation and entrepreneurship cooperation. Innovation is the primary driving force for development and the strategic support for the construction of a modern economic system. At present, China's economy growth has experienced a shifting from a period of rapid growth to a period of high-quality development, which puts forward new and higher requirements for promoting mass entrepreneurship and innovation. In order to further implement the innovation-driven development strategy and further stimulate market vitality and social creativity, there is an urgent need to promote the high-quality development of innovation and entrepreneurship and create an upgraded version for Double Innovation'.

11.4.2 Innovative and Entrepreneurial Talents are the Core Driving Force for the Sustainable Development of the Greater Bay Area

The promulgation of the Outline of the Development Plan for the Guangdong-Hong Kong-Macao Greater Bay Area clearly confirms that the construction of the Greater Bay Area has a very important strategic position in China's future development. The Guangdong- Hong Kong-Macao Greater Bay Area will follow the pace of other three major bay areas in the world and strive to become the fourth world-class Bay Area in the future. The Greater Bay Area will form a model zone for in-depth cooperation between the Mainland and Hong Kong and Macao, and will gradually grow into an international science and technology innovation center with global influence, and promote leap-forward development of national innovation, science and technology, economic strength. As the main body of scientific and technological innovation, high-quality personnel must be the key to achieving the grand goals of the Greater Bay Area.

Among the three major Bay Areas in the world, the San Francisco Bay Area is the world's most important high-tech R & D center and university innovative talent cultivation center, with strong resources and rich development experience. The greater bay area's goal of becoming an international innovation center of science and technology with global influence is consistent with that of the San Francisco Bay Area. Although there is a large gap of in cultural soil, industrial advantages, and education foundation between the development basis of the Greater Bay Area and the San Francisco Bay Area, which has a history of more than 160 years. attaching great importance to technological innovation and talent cultivation is a common feature of the development of the two Bay Areas. Thus, the San Francisco Bay Area provides a valuable learning sample for the cultivation of innovative entrepreneurship talents in the Guangdong, Hong Kong, and Macau Greater Bay Area.

11.5 Entrepreneurial Willingness and Business Environment

The impact of the business environment on the entrepreneurial willingness of young people in Guangdong, Hong Kong, and Macao is of great significance to the practical education of entrepreneurship. In recent years, research on entrepreneurial willingness at home and abroad has mostly focused on the factors affecting the willingness to start a business. In fact, the factor that Youths are most closely connected to and their entrepreneurial willingness are most likely to be affected by is the business environment in their area. This study will focus on the Guangdong, Hong Kong, Macao Greater Bay Area Physical Infrastructure and Government Policies, Financing Environment and Cultural and Social Factors, Entrepreneurship Education and training environment three aspects to explore its impact on entrepreneurial willingness.

The term "business environment" comes from the World Bank Group International Finance Corporation (IFC) 'Doing Business' project survey. Many Chinese scholars translated 'Doing Business' into business environment. In addition to IFC 'Doing Business', there are also some Institutions and scholars specifically define or divide the definition of business environment. For example, The Donor Committee for Enterprise Development (DCED) defines the business environment as: The business environment is a complex fusion of the policies, laws, systems, and rules necessary to govern business activities. Besides, a business environment is a subset of the investment climate, including administrative and enforcement systems that implement government policies, and institutional arrangements that affect the way businesses operate (e.g. government agencies, regulators, some business member organizations such as Women entrepreneurs associations, civil society organizations, trade union organizations, etc.). Business Monitor International (BMI) divides China's domestic business environment indicators into the following areas: transparency, cronyism and corruption, and flexibility of labor market, corporate tax burden, interest rate level, complexity of banking and stock market, business confidence level, Infrastructure and information technology.

The business environment can be divided into micro business environment and macro business environment. The so-called micro business environment refers to various types of participants that are closely connected to the enterprise itself and directly affect the normal operation of the enterprise; the macro business environment is a combination of the population environment, Economic environment, natural resources environment, science and technology environment, political and legal environment, social and cultural environment, etc., which is a important soft powers of a region. The business environment of a region has a direct impact on the success of business development in the region. Also, the government policies Regulations and the regulatory conditions will stimulate or inhibit entrepreneurial entrepreneurship. This chapter will use the concept of a macro business environment to discuss and analyze the impact of the business environment on the entrepreneurial willingness of young people in Guangdong, Hong Kong, and Macao.

11.6 Classification of Elements of the Business Environment

Based on the conclusions of previous studies, this article presents the classification of the elements of the business environment in the form of a table, as shown in Table 2.7 below.

Table 11-7 Classification of elements of the business environment

Representative scholar	Element classification	Elaboration
Wach Krzysztof (2008)	Capital availability and financial support; Local government autonomy initiatives; Entrepreneurial infrastructure; Availability and quality of business-to-business (b2b) services; High-quality talent; Infrastructure such as transportation and telecommunications; Mobility of local communities; Knowledge and technology transfer; Living standards of local communities	The regional business environment plays a vital role in promoting the development of small businesses, confirming that 'capital availability and financial support' and 'entrepreneurial infrastructure' are highly related to the development of small businesses; the other two factors' 'Local community mobility' and 'knowledge and technology transfer' are also highly positively related to companies in growth stages
EL-hadjBah and Lei Fang (2011)	Five areas:Regulatory environment, corruption, crime, infrastructure improvement, financial development	The impact of the first four areas on enterprises can be measured by the tax burden paid by enterprises, which is the corporate loss caused by the business environment. Since this tax burden is uniform for all enterprises in a country, it does not affect capital accumulation.The field of financial development is measured by the execution of corporate contracts
Dan Li, Manuel Portugal Ferreira(2011)	Supervision, political and financial systems in an institutional environment	The supervision system includes the effectiveness of supervision and whether government supervision can cover all aspects; the political system includes the effectiveness of the legal system and the existence of corruption; the financial system includes the development status of the financial system
Benne Eifert & Alan Gelb and Vijaya Ramachandran (2005)	Policies, institutions, infrastructure, human resources, geographical environment, etc. that affect the operating efficiency of different enterprises and industries	The business environment is not necessarily perfect, but it must be good enough in a series of key aspects to stimulate investment and competition, drive industrial growth and self-reinforcement of the industry

Notes: Wach, Krzysztof, 2008, "Impact of the Regional Business Environment on the Development of Small and Medium-sized Enterprises in Southern Poland", Enterprises in the Face of 21st Century Challenges. Development - Management - Entrepreneurship, pp. 397-406; Bah, Ec-hadj M. and Fang Lei, 2011, "Impact of the Business Environment on Output and Productivity in Africa", MPRA Paper No. 32517; Dan Li, Manel Protual Ferreira, 2011, "Internal and External Factors on Firms Transfer Pricing Decisions: Insights from Organization Studies", Global Advantage Working Paper No. 6; Benne Eifert, Alan Gelb and Bijaya Ramachandran, 2005, "Business Environment and Comparative Advantage in Africa: Evidence from the Investment Climate Data", Center for Global Development working paper NO. 56.

The scholars' classification of the elements of the business environment mainly focuses on the political system, legal system, infrastructure and financial system, while emphasizing the importance of the business environment to the development of enterprises and the role of industrial growth. Based on the status quo of the Guangdong, Hong Kong and Macau Greater Bay Area, this article divides its business environment into physical infrastructure, government policies and projects, and financing environments to conduct specific research.

11.7 Business Environment for Youth Entrepreneurship in the Greater Bay Area

The business environment optimization is a new strategy for economic development proposed by the Party Central Committee with Comrade Xi Jinping as the core, and it is also the new goal of the 'decentralization and optimization of service' reform after the 19th CPC National Congress. *Business Environment and Talent Environment*[1] proposed that the business environment problem is essentially a talent environment problem. Talent is the main body of innovation and entrepreneurship, and it is also the main body of business. As a conclusion we should improve the business environment from the perspective of the talent environment to form an environmental advantage to attract talents. "Research on the Development of Hong Kong and Macau Youths in the Guangdong, Hong Kong and Macau Greater Bay Area" (2019)[2] points out that the coordination and guidance of youth development policies need to be strengthen and an internationalized and legalized business environment should be created. It is believed that this will provide better services for promoting the innovation and entrepreneurship of young people in Hong Kong and Macao. To respond to the proposal, local governments have proposed that they should strengthen policy guidance and create a healthy atmosphere for 'double innovation' talent highlands.

---

[1] Ji Yangzhou, "Business Environment and Talent Environment", *China Personnel Science*, 2019(04): 61-66.

[2] Xie Baojian, Hu Jieyi, "Research on the Development of Hong Kong and Macao Youth in the Guangdong-Hong Kong-Macao Greater Bay Area", *Youth Exploration*, 2019 (1): 5-14.

11.7.1 Related Policies of Government Environment for Youth Entrepreneurship in the Greater Bay Area

The government environment is the most important environment for attracting talents of innovation and entrepreneurship. In order to create a good environment for youth innovation and entrepreneurship, the regions of the Guangdong-Hong Kong-Macao Greater Bay Area have introduced the following related policies.

Regarding the simplification of the registration approval process, the *Notice of the Guangdong Provincial People's Government on Printing and Distributing Action Plans for Deepening the Reform of the Commercial System in Guangdong Province* [1] clearly reformed and optimized the process of starting a business, which reduces the overall time to start a business to within 5 working days. Cities in the Guangdong-Hong Kong-Macao Greater Bay Area generally exceed their targets. For example, Guangzhou's pilot reform areas such as Yuexiu, Huangpu, and Nansha district have already achieved their target in advance, using one day to start and settle the business. The Guangzhou Municipal Government Service Center will also achieve the target of completing the entire process in one day before the end of 2019. In Shenzhen, government has launched and pilot operated the "Approval within seconds System" for individual business. And the new system has successfully issued its first business license. Facing the Guangdong-Hong Kong-Macao Greater Bay Area, Shenzhen will fully implement the 'Shenzhen-Hong Kong Stock Easy Register' and 'Shenzhen-Macao Stock Easy Register' commercial services in 2019. Hong Kong and Macau investments can be made locally by "One-stop registration of Shenzhen enterprises". In addition, *Guangdong-Hong Kong-Macao Greater Bay Area Development Planning Outline* [2] also proposed that Hong Kong citizens can access to more than 100 Greater Bay Area government services including business registration, personal tax list inquiry, and social security printing in the "Citizen's Window". The "Smart Counter" integrates ID card authentication, face recognition, paper material scanning and other functions. It can also provide one-on-one video online guidance services when remotely working, and achieve the goal of zero approval, zero media, and zero running.

---

[1] Published by the People's Government of Guangdong Province on July 25, 2018.

[2] Issued and implemented by the CPC Central Committee and the State Council in February 2019.

In terms of regulating the system related to entrepreneurial behavior, the *Implementation Plan for Strengthening the Construction of Innovation and Entrepreneurship Bases for Hong Kong and Macao Youths* mentioned that the construction of the 12355 Hong Kong–Macau youth hotline will be strengthened to provide legal rights protection, immigration and other consulting services. The *Notice on Preferential Policies for Personal Income Tax in the Guangdong-Hong Kong-Macao Greater Bay Area* points out that if the applicant is found to have the behavior of violating laws or regulations and false declarations, he will be disqualified from the preferential policies after being verified, and the financial subsidy funds will be recovered. For the situation of being suspected of crime, the suspects shall be transferred to the judicial organs and be prosecuted for criminal liability according to law.

As an important macro national policy, the government environment related policies play an important bridge role in promoting youth entrepreneurship. Entrepreneurship efficiency raised by the establishment of business-related approvals systems and entrepreneurial legal guarantees provided by relevant systems for regulating entrepreneurial behaviors passes the signal of strong support and encouragement given by the national work of youth entrepreneurship, which provides a reassuring business environment for youth entrepreneurship.

11.7.2 Related Policies of Economic Environment for Youth Entrepreneurs in the Greater Bay Area

The economic environment is a platform and carrier environment of attracting talents for innovation and entrepreneurship, an incentive environment, and a contribution return environment. In order to create an economic environment that is in line with the youth entrepreneurship of the Greater Bay Area in new era, the greater bay regions have issued the following policies to support.

In terms of tax incentives, the *Notice on Implementing the Preferential Policies on Individual Income Taxes in the Guangdong, Hong Kong, Macao Greater Bay Area* mentioned that for overseas high-end talents and people in short supply who work in the Greater Bay Area, the portion of the individual income taxes paid in the nine cities of the Pearl River Delta that exceeds its taxable income calculated at 15% shall be financed by the People's Government of the Pearl River Delta Nine Municipalities, and the subsidy is exempted from personal income tax.[①]

In terms of construction for entrepreneurial bases and exchange and development platforms, the Guangdong, Hong Kong, and Macao Youth Entrepreneurship Incubator created by the Panyu District Government, Hong Kong Haifu International Finance Group, and Lihe Science and Technology Innovation Group has launched a "rooting plan" to absorb the landing of projects in the Greater Bay Area. The team provides industrial and commercial docking services, Hong Kong and Macao residents registration services for free. It will also provide an enterprise-level ERP system, allowing entrepreneurs to focus on market expansion and product development; reduce entrepreneurs' internal management costs through shared service centers; provide one-to-one entrepreneurial guidance, financial support and industrial resource. In addition, the *Implementation Plan for Strengthening the Construction of Innovation and Entrepreneurship Bases for Hong Kong and Macau Youths* mentioned that by 2020, Hong Kong and Macau Youth Innovation and Entrepreneurship Base will be built in three free trade zones in Guangzhou Nansha, Shenzhen Qianhai, and Zhuhai Hengqin; by 2025, each of the 9 cities in the Pearl River Delta will build at least one Hong Kong and Macau youth innovation and entrepreneurship base.At that time, taking Guangdong-Hong Kong-Macao Greater Bay Area (Guangdong) as the lead, the layout of the "1 + 12 + n" incubation platform carrier base will be basically completed.

In terms of financial support, the rules of implementation in *Several Measures on Supporting the Development of Hong Kong and Macau Youth in Qianhai*[②] mentioned that during the period of entrepreneur and employment in Qianhai, the Hong Kong and Macao youths who are identified as high-level professionals in Shenzhen or overseas high-level talents in the 'Peacock Plan' will be given a 1 : 1 matching subsidy based on the city's funding amount, averagely divided in 5 years to issue. In addition, the support for young entrepreneurs in Hong Kong and Macao to start a business, cost of starting a business, cultivating businesses, key projects, incentives of listing, and entrepreneurship exchanges are also included in the detailed rules of the implementation .

In terms of start-up subsidies, the *Implementation Plan for Strengthening*

---

① Issued by the Guangdong Provincial Finance Department on June 17, 2019.
② Notice issued by Guangdong Provincial Government.

*the Construction of Innovation and Entrepreneurship Bases for Hong Kong and Macau Youths*① proposed that young people from Hong Kong and Macau who start their businesses in Guangdong can enjoy the same employment support policies such as entrepreneurship training subsidies, one-time entrepreneurship subsidies, entrepreneurship-driven employment subsidies, rent subsidies, entrepreneurship incubation subsidies, and quality improvement training for start-up business operators. The implementation plan also emphasizes that measures such as actively communicating with Hong Kong and Macao and covering preferential policies and measures such as the Hong Kong and Macao Science and Technology Innovation Fund and Youth Development Fund to Hong Kong and Macao youths who set up businesses in Guangdong are needed.

To sum up, economic environment related policies provide a stable development platform for the convenience of youth entrepreneurship, which is conducive to the exchange and interaction of entrepreneurial talents around the world, and allows for open development. In addition to the tax relief for the first-time entrepreneurs, the funding support and start-up subsidies received by the young entrepreneurs through multi-channel and multi-faceted have further eased the issue of funding pressure for initial business start-ups and provided a safe business environment for young entrepreneurs.

11.7.3 Related Policies on the Service Environment for Youth Entrepreneur in the Greater Bay Area

The service environment is a soft environment that attracts talents for innovation, entrepreneurship and development, as well as an environment that can form a competitive advantage for talents. In order to create a good service environment, the Guangdong-Hong Kong-Macao Greater Bay Area has issued the following related policies.

In terms of investment and financing service, the *Implementation Plan for Strengthening the Construction of Hong Kong and Macau Youth Innovation and Entrepreneurship Bases* proposes the establishment of a multi-level financing support system, the establishment of a perfect angel investment risk compensation system. Besides, the government fund such as the Guangdong Province's innovation and entrepreneurship fund should play the role of

---

① Notice issued by Guangdong Provincial Government.

guiding the introduction of high-quality social capital, then set up a fund of funds (FOF) and sub-funds that support Hong Kong and Macao youth start up a business and cover the entire stage of entrepreneurship. The government should implement a business guarantee loan and discount interest policy, and make the best use of "China Youth Gem" financing platform. In addition, the implementation rules of *Several Measures for Supporting Hongkong-Macao Youth Develop in Qianhai* also mentioned in detail the policies related to funding for risk compensation and financing costs.

In terms of living and housing services, rules in the *Implementation Plan for Strengthening the Construction of Innovation and Entrepreneurship Bases for Hong Kong and Macao Youths* support eligible Hong Kong and Macao youths to rent houses and stay in stations for talents; house-renting subsidies is provided in areas where conditions permit; explore various ways to support Hong Kong and Macau youths who have the ability to purchase a house and meet the requirements for housing purchases to purchase commercial house; include eligible Hong Kong and Macau youths in the innovation and entrepreneurship base into the scope of local public rental housing protection; explore and develop housing with shared property rights, and support Hong Kong and Macao youths who meet the corresponding conditions to purchase houses with shared property rights. In addition, regular transportation subsidies will be provided to Hong Kong and Macao entrepreneurial youths whose public transport expenditures between Guangdong and Hong Kong and Guangdong and Macao exceed the prescribed level. Achieving the goals of unifying the telecommunications rates in the three regions, introducing education, medical and community services in Hong Kong and Macao Institutions to build a community that integrates living, education, medical care, culture and entertainment are also key implementation details in the plan.

The service environment-related policies provide timely and effective investment and financing services for youth entrepreneurship, and solve the long-term problem of investment and financing difficulties that have restricted young entrepreneurs. The implementation of risk compensation, entrepreneurship guarantee loans, and discount policies also encourage more young people to embark on the road of independent innovation and entrepreneurship. In addition, effective and timely living and settle down services are the aspirations of entrepreneurs in the new era. To a certain extent, they can stabilize the flow of talents and provide a settled living environment for young entrepreneurs.

At present, the Greater Bay Area is one of China's most attractive regions for talents, and the business environment has obvious advantages because of solid foundation laid by the complete industrial chain and infrastructure of the Greater Bay Area. To build a world-class bay area and world-class city clusters, it must have a first-class business environment with global competitiveness. Therefore, among the environmental factors that affect entrepreneurial willingness, business environment as an external variable is of high research value.

11.8 Problems and Suggestions

Under the background of the continuous acceleration of economic integration between Hong Kong, Macao and the mainland and the vigorous promotion of the construction of the Guangdong-Hong Kong-Macao Greater Bay Area, the state's encouragement of young people in Hong Kong to 'head north' and study, find employment and start a business is a policy-orientation and general trend. The Xi Jinping's report at 19th CPC National Congress first proposed that the government should support Hong Kong and Macao integrating into the national overall development situation, focus on the construction of the Guangdong-Hong Kong-Macao Greater Bay Area, and comprehensively promote mutually beneficial cooperation between the Mainland and Hong Kong and Macao.

The policies of the Guangdong-Hong Kong-Macao Greater Bay Area have performed well in improving the entrepreneurial system and tax incentives. However, policies in terms of promoting simplification of procedures, financing and loans still need to be continued.

The Global Business Environment Report 2018 states that the ranking of China's business environment has steadily increased, and the main changes are that certain improvements have been made in three aspects of paying taxes, starting a business, and construction permits. The state should continue to optimize and promote the policies of simplification of entrepreneurial procedures, financing and loan preferential. More attention should be paid to the provision of entrepreneurial funds and projects, so that it is easier for young people to turn entrepreneurial enthusiasm into entrepreneurial actions. We recommend that next the government should continue to carry out policies on entrepreneurial financing and loans and pay more attention to the method of better providing materialized funds and project support directly to young people, so that young people in Guangdong, Hong Kong, and Macau can see the tangible benefits brought by these policies and turn their entrepreneurial will into entrepreneurial behavior.

In the future, the Greater Bay Area Government should provides sustainably stable and complete entrepreneurial support and preferential measures for young people in the Greater Bay Area. At the same time, it can also provide entrepreneurs with more preferential policies on taxation and venue leasing, so as to create a good administrative environment.

The local governments in the Greater Bay Area should provide long-term plans to address issues such as medical care, transportation, social security, and house ownership, but they hope that the Greater Bay Area government will give more incentives to start-up companies and preferential policies on site lease in the future. For the reason that entrepreneurship requires a long period and patience to cultivate in both places. Cities in the Greater Bay Area can continue to provide entrepreneurs with support for hardware facilities such as office space by setting up youth entrepreneurship bases in their respective trade zones and providing incubators with land and revenue support in the Greater Bay Area. Governments in the Greater Bay Area should focus on creating a sustainable entrepreneurial environment for governance, providing stable and predictable guarantees for innovative companies; breaking down information barriers, integrating existing information, and providing more convenient and accurate entrepreneurial support services; implement equal treatment to provide a more suitable social environment for entrepreneurship; strengthen cooperation with the Hong Kong and Macao governments and social organizations to attract outstanding entrepreneurial talents and cultivate the next generation of entrepreneurs.

In the future, it can be extended to all cities in the Greater Bay Area, and implement preferential policies for innovation and entrepreneurship on business income tax and personal income tax. Firstly, industry restrictions can be gradually lifted for start-ups, and for the industries that meet the condition of youth entrepreneurship in the Bay Area, a certain percentage of business income tax concessions are granted. Secondly, the current policy of granting personal tax concessions to only qualified overseas high-end talents and talents in short supply may be released, and all young entrepreneurs in the Greater Bay Area are included in the scope of individual tax benefits to achieve youth entrepreneurs in the Greater Bay Area pay individual tax at low standard.

First, establish a one-stop online innovation and entrepreneurship information release platform in the Greater Bay Area, integrate existing information, and open channels for information disclosure. Through the horizontal coordination mechanism, co-ordinate information of internal government approvals and government public service, so as to place the information and process that need to be approved, and government public service information need to apply in various parts of the Bay Area on a unified information disclosure platform to facilitate the Bay Area youth entrepreneurs conduct multiple administrative approvals through hyperlinks on the platform. The platform can organize entrepreneurial support projects launched in various places, and put key information such as relevant application procedures and conditions in specific columns for the Bay Area youths to review. The platform is promoted by the government as the authoritative information publisher, which can list the information about the entrepreneurship competition in the Greater Bay Area into a separate column, where details of the conditions, procedures, time, and support funds for each competition are listed. It will help promoting existing entrepreneurial policies, which facilitate entrepreneurs to accurately understand the policies and apply for entrepreneurial benefits and subsidies in a timely manner. At the same time, it also focus on the diversification of promotional methods and the easy-to-understand promotional content through various channels, including television, video websites, billboards, Symposium, WeChat, Weibo, etc., condensed important entrepreneurial documents into a relaxed, lively and vivid anime videos and brochures and so on.

Second, Guangdong, Hong Kong, Macau and Greater Bay Area universities should provide a more comprehensive and professional service system in talent innovation and entrepreneurship. All universities in the Greater Bay Area should establish a comprehensive and comprehensive "double innovation" education system, take the outstanding universities in other bay areas in the world as benchmark to develop human resources based on the education resources and industrial advantages of the Bay Area, and penetrates the concept of "practical education" into all levels of teaching, scientific research, practice, and student career development, so as to realize the mutual promotion of innovative research and entrepreneurial practice. In schools, it can be started from three levels. The first level is establishing the dual mentor system of corporate mentors and school mentors to guide students' "double innovation" practice. The second level is providing campus support for campus communities and entrepreneurial clubs. The third level is providing career planning services for alumni and entrepreneurial students.

Third, carry out global cooperation to stimulate the energy of innovation and create a good financing environment. Carrying out global cooperation involve injecting capital, intellectual support, talent-driven and innovative projects into the cultivation of innovative talents in universities in the Guangdong, Hong Kong, and Macao Greater Bay Area, and provide unprecedented opportunities for the construction of the Guangdong, Hong Kong, and Macao Greater Bay Area for the training of talents in universities. Universities in the Greater Bay Area should attach high importance to three unions. The first is to jointly develop new technologies with internationally renowned universities, carry out academic exchanges of innovative talents and high-level talent training projects. The second is to strengthen the cooperation between universities in various regions of Guangdong, Hong Kong, and Macao, and exchange information to enhance strengths and avoid weaknesses. The cultivation of innovative talents in various parts of the Bay Area must combine subject characteristics and industrial advantages to form a joint effort to expand the innovation and entrepreneurship space of students in the three regions. The third is to cooperate with well-known domestic and foreign enterprises, financial institutions, venture capital institution, etc., so that the elements of collaborative innovation can be used fully. Through multi-level cooperation across regions, universities, and subjects, universities can expand the breadth and depth of students' participation in innovation and entrepreneurship activities.

Fourth, enhancing entrepreneurship publicity, encouraging entrepreneurship, and improving entrepreneurship among young people in the Greater Bay Area. Increasing entrepreneurial propaganda is to create a relaxed and conducive environment for entrepreneurial behavior and mobilize the public's interest in new enterprises. The Greater Bay Area youth entrepreneurial willingness will be driven by social attitudes. Society must cultivate a cultural atmosphere that respects entrepreneurs. We must respect the behavior of self-employment. No matter they succeed or fail, they should be widely respected by people. Only in this case will the entrepreneurs be encouraged and praised by the public, so as to build a kind of cultural atmosphere that encourages entrepreneurship. Giving entrepreneurs sufficient respect, the attitude of young entrepreneurs will be stubborn, and they will actively participate in the entrepreneurial process. When encouraging entrepreneurship, changes in the quality of life of successful entrepreneurs can also be introduced appropriately to increase attitudes of young entrepreneurs in the Bay Area, because taking the correct way to obtain money, fame, and status is a return on the efforts they have made. This is also a finding that the entrepreneurial willingness are closely related to self-efficacy of this study.

Fifth, government investment providing leverage to optimize the investment environment. The Guangdong, Hong Kong, Macao Greater Bay Area should continue to deepen reform and opening up, improve market integration, regional coordination and other institutional constructions. Funding support is mainly based on commercial funds, private sector investment is the main force, and government investment provide leverage and guidance to the private sector investment. Government should also focus on building a unified, open, competitive and orderly market system, establish fair and transparent market rules, improve the financial market system and price mechanism, and improve the market environment for fair competition.

Sixth, the nine major cities in the Pearl River Delta region of the Greater Bay Area must break through institutional barriers, achieve a high level of industrial factor resources, and improve the level of market integration in the Greater Bay Area. Deepen cooperation between Guangdong, Hong Kong, and Macao, and further optimize the investment and business environment for the nine cities in the Pearl River Delta region, fully docking with rules of international high-standard markets system. The second is to build a Bay Area collaborative innovation system and create a first-class innovation platform. Through institutional innovation, we will break through the bottleneck of the aggregation and flow of innovation elements, and build an open collaborative innovation system across regions and systems.

Seventh, deepen the openness and innovation of Guangdong, Hong Kong, and Macao institutions and mechanisms, and promote talent collaboration. Established a human resources coordination agency in the Guangdong-Hong Kong-Macao Greater Bay Area. Strengthened close coordination and communication between governments, explored and resolved differences in human resources systems and policies between Guangdong, Hong Kong, and Macau; integrated talent policies, innovation, entrepreneurship and service guarantee in Guangdong, Hong Kong, and Macau and other information resources, build a human resources public service big data platform, promptly release market supply and demand reports, urgently needed positions and talent demand directories, provide comprehensive information services for talents in the Guangdong-Hong Kong-Macao Greater Bay Area, and improve the deployment efficiency of human resource market; strengthen Chinese and foreign cooperative education.

Chapter 12

Towards a Sustainable Future: China's Economic Transformation[①]

12.1 Introduction

The Asia-Pacific region, especially the local developing economies, is at a crossroad. The traditional resource-based, export-oriented, manufacturing-driven growth is facing headwinds from sluggish external demand and rising protectionist trade measures. New technologies have increased the likelihood of labour-intensive jobs in the region becoming automated. Meanwhile, many economies have witnessed widening income and opportunity inequalities. Rising environmental risks and climatic disasters add further burdens to the future development agenda.

Now the questions that most developing countries in the region face are: can they achieve economic convergence by following the traditional growth path? How can they balance economic growth with social inclusiveness and environmental sustainability? This chapter addresses these questions by using China as an example.

12.2 China's Unprecedented Economic Development since the Late 1970s

Structural changes are happening all over the Asia-Pacific region, but the case of

① This chapter is based on *China's Economic Transformation: Impacts on Asia and the Pacific* from Economic and Social Commission for Asia and the Pacific, United Nations. Available from www.unescap.org/resources/chinas-economic-transformation-impacts-asia-and-pacific.

China stands out for its pace and scale. In the past four decades, China has achieved immense economic development at an unprecedented speed. Since 1980, the growth of the economy, at an average annual rate of 9.6 per cent, has outperformed the growth of major economies in the Group of Seven (G7) (Figure 12-1). China's economy is now the second largest in the world[1], contributing more than 30 per cent of world economic growth from 2012 to 2016[2].

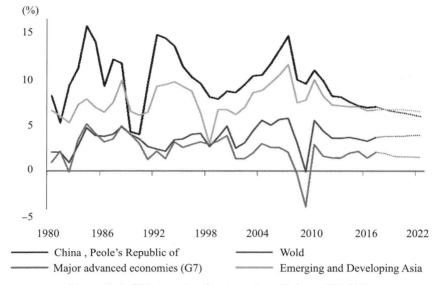

Figure 12-1 GDP growth estimates and predictions, 1980-2022

Note: Real GDP growth rates from 1980 to 2016 are estimates. Figures for 2017 to 2022 are predictions by IMF.

Source: International Monetary Fund (IMF) Data Mapper. Available from www.imf.org/external/datamapper (accessed 18 January 2018).

China's economic growth was driven by export-oriented industrialization. With market-friendly policies, low costs of production factors (such as capital, raw materials, and labour), productivity growth and access to technology, China very quickly became 'the world's factory'. The International Monetary Fund (IMF) estimated that net exports and investment, which is linked to building capacity in tradable sectors, accounted for more than 60 per cent of China's growth from 2001 to 2008, much higher than the G7 and the rest of Asia[3].

---

[1] China overtook Japan and become the world's second largest economy in 2010.

[2] Jun W., "The World economy is recovering stably with China's contribution", http://stats.gov.cn/tjsj/sjjd/201801/t20180119_1575621.html, 2018.

[3] Kai G. and P. N'Diaye, "Is China's export-oriented growth sustainable?", http://imf.org/external/pubs/ft/wp/2009/wp09172.pdf, 2009.

With rapid industrialization, the Chinese economy transformed from a predominantly agricultural one to an industrial powerhouse. The output and employment shares of agriculture trended down, while the shares of industry, especially manufacturing, rose rapidly. This was associated with an increase in labour productivity, which led to higher wages, saving, investment, capital stock growth, and a substantial decline in poverty (Figure 12-2).

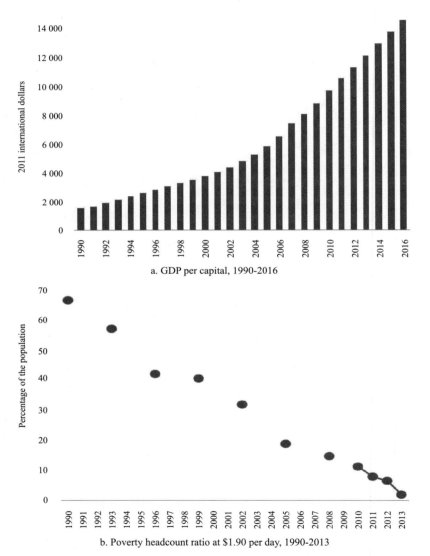

a. GDP per capital, 1990-2016

b. Poverty headcount ratio at $1.90 per day, 1990-2013

Figure 12-2 China's economic growth and poverty reduction in purchasing power parity

Note: Values for GDP per capita and the poverty headcount are measured in constant 2011 international dollars.

Source: World Bank Data, data. worldbank.org (accessed 7 March 2018).

In 2016, China's GDP per capita reached 14,399 USD (purchasing power parity, constant 2011 international dollars), having grown more than nine-fold since 1990. From 1981 to 2012, nearly 800 million people were lifted out of poverty (based on the international poverty line of 1.90 USD per person per day, purchasing power parity, constant 2011 international dollars), contributing more than 70 per cent of the global reduction in poverty[①]. Meanwhile, illiteracy, child mortality and maternal mortality rates have decreased sharply[②].

12.3 Traditional Growth Pattern Poses Constraints for China's Future Growth

The growth of the Chinese economy has been slowing down in recent years. External demand, which was a major driver of China's manufacturing production, has remained sluggish since the global financial and economic crisis in 2008. As China approaches the technological frontier, productivity growth is slowing. With that said, the improvement of incomes has supported a rise in consumption, which has become the major demand-side contributor to global economic growth since 2014.

China is now entering a new phase of structural transformation, from a resource-, investment- and export-driven economy to a more balanced economy driven by consumption and services. Recent data signals that this process is already happening: the output and employment shares of industry (the secondary sector) are declining, and the shares of services (the tertiary sector) are steadily rising (Figure 12-3a). At the same time China is facing emerging challenges internationally and domestically, which are reinforcing the economic restructuring.

Internationally, the global market is likely to remain sluggish. Despite new investments in technologies, the world has not yet found a strong engine to boost economic growth. Meanwhile, the growth rate of the world population is declining. If labour productivity remains unchanged, then the slower growth of

① Xinhua, "China contributes to over 70 percent of global poverty reduction", http://news. xinhuanet.com/english/2016-12/27/c_135936773.htm, 2016.
② China, Ministry of Foreign Affairs, "China's National Plan on Implementation of the 2030 Agenda for Sustainable Development", http://www.fmprc.gov.cn/mfa_eng/zxxx_662805/ W020161014332600482185.pdf, 2016.

the population, an increasing dependency ratio and later a shrinking working population are expected to restrain world economic growth. Therefore, China can no longer rely on external demand as it did in past decades.

In addition, there are evident signs of increasing trade protectionism, which could lead to retaliatory measures and possibly broader trade tensions. Monetary policy normalization in major economies may also spur capital outflows from emerging markets like China, and therefore lead to financial volatility.

Domestically, China is facing macroeconomic constraints. Government-led stimulus has boosted China's economic growth over recent years, but has also been accompanied by excessive credit growth that has led to a sharp increase in debt. Since the 2008 international economic and financial crisis, China has seen an increasing credit gap, defined as the deviation of the credit-to-GDP ratio from its historic trend. It rose from nearly 0 per cent at end 2008 to a peak of 29 per cent in early 2016—well above the 10 per cent threshold for a maximum countercyclical buffer as suggested by the Bank for International Settlements. As a result, China's debt stands at a historic high. The total domestic non-financial sector debt, including household, corporate and government debt, surged from below 180 per cent of GDP in 2012 to more than 240 per cent in 2016, and is predicted to reach nearly 300 per cent by 2022.

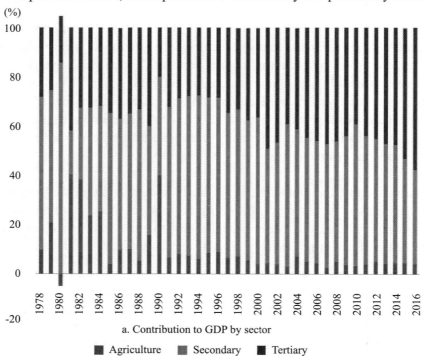

a. Contribution to GDP by sector

■ Agriculture   ■ Secondary   ■ Tertiary

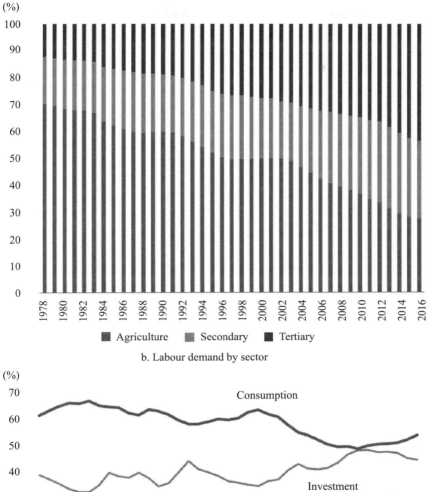

b. Labour demand by sector

c. Composition of GDP by expenditure

Figure 12-3 Economic development and structural changes in China's economy

Note: Secondary sector includes: mining industry; manufacturing; production and supply of power, heat, gas and water; and construction. Tertiary sector refers to services.

Source: China, National Statistics Bureau, data.stats.gov.cn (accessed 18 January 2018 and 5 April 2018).

China's current credit and debt trajectory is not sustainable and entails risks to its medium-term macroeconomic stability for several reasons. First, data suggests that investment efficiency is deteriorating, pointing to growing resource misallocation. Second, international experience suggests that such rapid credit growth and debt build-up is often associated with financial crisis and/or growth slowdown. Third, the surge of credit and debt is linked with growing complexity in the balance sheets of Chinese banks, which could aggravate the banking sector's vulnerability[1].

The demographic dividend, which supported labour intensive manufacturing production in China, is diminishing. China's population is rapidly ageing and is projected to be among the highest old-age dependency ratios globally by 2050. The share of population aged 65 and above has climbed up rapidly as reflected in the potential support ratio (Figure 12-4). Rapid ageing is set to

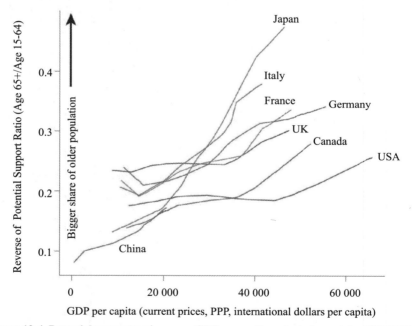

Figure 12-4 Potential support ratio versus GDP per capita, selected countries 1980-2020

Note: Data for GDP per capita 1980-2016 are estimates, 2017-2020 are projections by IMF; data for the potential support ratio 1980-2015 are estimates, 2016-2020 are projections by DESA.

Sources: IMF DataMapper, www.imf.org/external/datamapper (accessed 16 March 2018); Department of Economic and Social Affairs (DESA), World Population Prospects 2017, esa.un.org/unpd/wpp/ (accessed 19 January 2018).

---

[1] S. Chen and J. Kang, "Credit booms: Is China different?", http://imf.org/en/Publications/WP/Issues/2018/01/05/Credit-Booms-Is-China-Different-45537, 2018.

constrain economic growth and could subtract 0.5 to 1 percentage point from annual GDP growth over the next three decades in China[①]. The demographic shift will also likely keep downward pressure on real interest rates and asset returns. This will have an unfavourable impact on long-term economic growth, as seen in the recent economic performance of Japan.

Low costs of production factors were a major contributor to China's trade competitiveness. However, Made in China will not be so cheap in the future. Labour costs have risen rapidly in the past decade. Wages for migrant workers, for example, increased by 14.4 per cent annually from 2008 to 2012, double the growth rate from 2001 to 2007. Land costs are also surging. Before 2007, the price of land for industrial purposes was around $70 per square meter. The price had almost doubled as of the end 2017.

Massive inputs of low-cost production factors have boosted the Chinese economy, but in an inefficient manner. The cheap prices have reduced investors' incentives to optimize resource allocation and China's investment return is much lower than its peer countries. In recent years, five units of capital input were required for one unit of marginal production of GDP. When Japan and the Republic of Korea were at a similar development level, three units of capital were required for one unit of marginal production of GDP.

Technology could help to improve China's economic efficiency, and China's industrial development strategy has focused on catching up with technological advancements. When China started the strategy, it was far from the technological frontier and was able to catch up quickly by importing and learning from existing technologies. However, China is now experiencing diminished room for further catch-up and a reduced late-mover advantage (Figure 12-5). Japan and the Republic of Korea had similar experiences.

China is also concerned about rising inequality. Along with rapid economic growth, income disparities have widened both within and between urban and rural areas. China's income Gini coefficient increased from 27.2 in 1983 to 46.5 in 2016 (Figure 12-6). Furthermore, inequality goes beyond income and is reflected in people's access to public services and other opportunities. For example, children in rural areas are less likely to receive pre-school education than their urban peers, and a person born in Shanghai is expected to live 12 years longer than one born in Tibet (UNDP and State Council DRC, 2016).

---

① IMF, "Regional Economic Outlook: Asia and Pacific, May", http://imf.org/en/Publications/REO/APAC/Issues/2017/04/28/areo0517, 2017.

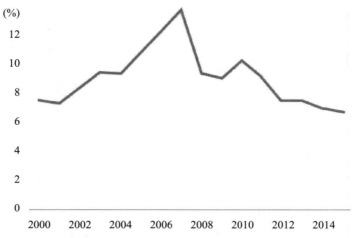

Figure 12-5 China's productivity growth slows in recent years

Source: OECD iLibrary, www.oecd-ilibrary.org/employment/data/oecd-productivity-statistics_pdtvy-data-en (accessed 16 March 2018).

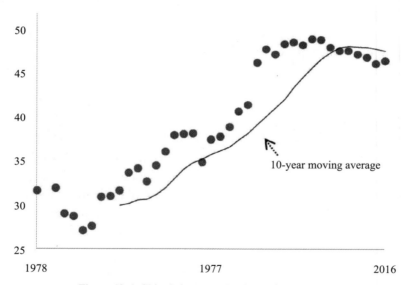

Figure 12-6 China's income Gini coefficient, 1978-2016

Sources: Gini coefficient data 1978-2002: Branko Milanovic (2016) All the Ginis (ALG) dataset; Gini coefficient for 2003-2016: China, National Bureau of Statistics, 2017.

China's economy is increasingly impacted by environmental degradation and climate change risks. In the past, China's growth was based on the rapid development of energy-intensive and high-pollution industries. Without sufficient and effective measures to internalize the externalities of pollution, there was an increasing volume of pollutants and damage to the ecological environment (Figure 12-7).

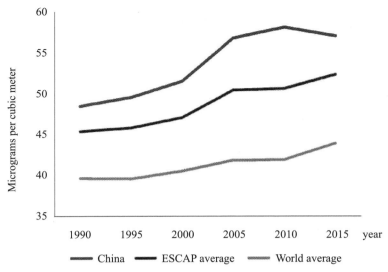

Figure 12-7 Air pollution (PM 2.5 exposure) in China, ESCAP member countries and the world
Source: ESCAP data, data. unescap. org/escap_stat/#data/ (accessed 20 February 2019).

For example, out of the 20 cities worldwide suffering from highest intensity of PM2.5 (fine particulate matter, a major air pollutant), four are in Hebei Province next to the capital city, Beijing[1]. China's temperature is estimated to have increased at a faster rate than the world average since the early 1900s, which has already led to a higher sea level rise and is predicted to cause more rainfall[2]. This threatens China's economic performance. In 2016, the direct economic loss due to floods was 1.5 times as much as in 2000[3].

12.4 The Current Growth Pattern may Lead to Medium-term Challenges

Internal and external challenges have significant implications for China's

---

[1] World Health Organization (WHO), WHO Global Urban Ambient Air Pollution database (update 2016). Available from www.who.int/phe/health_topics/outdoorair/databases/cities/en/.

[2] CMA, "*The Third Climate Change National Assessment Report* shows that China is warming at a faster speed than the global average", http://cma.gov.cn/2011xzt/2015 zt/20151127/2015112705/201511/t20151127_298446.html, 2015.

[3] MEP, "Launch of 2016 China Environment Report", http://www.mep.gov.cn/gkml/hbb/qt/201706/t201, 2017.

economic growth prospects. If China fails to address or ignores those challenges but follows the traditional resource-based, export- and investment-led growth strategy, they are highly likely to face constrained future economic performance. In detail, from the supply side, although capital inputs remain the major driver of the economy, its growth is expected to slow quickly due to population ageing. Empirical results confirm a negative correlation between savings and the old-age dependency ratio[1]. A smaller size of the working-age population will drag down labour's contribution to growth[2]. With China reaching the technological frontier, there is less room for technological progress, which could limit productivity growth.

Despite weaker economic performance, China's current growth path is expected to continue restructuring towards a consumption- and service-led economy, but in a passive manner. Increasing demand for consumption goods and services due to increases in household income, ageing population, and continuing urbanization supports such structural changes. Focusing on the demand side, consumption is predicted to account for more than two thirds of the GDP in 2030 (over 50 per cent in 2016) whereas investment could contribute more than 30 per cent. In terms of sectoral composition, the value added of the service sector as a share of GDP is expected to grow considerably from 49 per cent in 2015 to 66 per cent in 2030. Meanwhile, the agricultural sector's share of GDP is expected to shrink further from 9.5 per cent in 2015 to 3 per cent in 2030. Due to slower investment growth and assuming no major improvement of external demand, the secondary industry's share of GDP is predicted to drop from 41.6 per cent in 2015 to approximately 30 per cent in 2030.

However, such rebalancing does not entail improvement in response to the medium- to long-term challenges. Economic efficiency is likely to worsen. In 2025-2030 the average growth of labour productivity could be 2 per cent less than in 2010-2015. The efficiency of investment is predicted to decline further such that 20 per cent more capital inputs are needed by 2030 to generate the same amount of output as in 2015. Without technological progress, productivity growth is likely to slow further.

Moreover, China could face intensified social tensions and environmental

---

[1] Grigoli, F., A. Herman and K. Schmidt-Hebbel, "World Saving", http://www.imf.org/external/pubs/ft/wp/2014/wp14204.pdf, 2017.

[2] China loosened its one child policy recently, but its impact on the working population through 2030 is limited.

risks. Although both urban and rural residents could receive higher income, companies tend to favour skilled labour over unskilled labour to move up the value chain. Consequently, China is predicted to see rising inequality within and between urban and rural areas. In addition, without measures to tackle environmental and climate risks, total energy consumption and carbon dioxide emissions could grow by 40 per cent and 30 per cent respectively by 2030, relative to 2015 levels. This not only indicates that China might face increasing environment-and climate-related constraints and economic losses, but also that China is highly unlikely to peak its carbon emissions by 2030, as set in its nationally determined contribution (NDC) to the Paris Agreement on climate change.

As China's economy matures, it seems inevitable that growth will slow down. This is in line with the development trajectories of Japan and South Korea. In the post-war period Japan's economy grew rapidly, averaging annual growth of 10 per cent from 1955 to 1970, and around 5 per cent in the 1970s and 1980s[1]. Likewise, the economy of South Korea grew at an average annual rate of more than 9 per cent from the early 1960s to 1980 and slowed in the 2000s after many years of fluctuations[2]. Despite the economic slowdown, the quality of economic growth and the potential for China's future growth are important matters.

12.5 China is Putting More Weight on the Quality of Economic Growth

China's policymakers are well aware of the constraints of the existing growth model and its unsustainable consequences. The Government of China has exhibited strong political will to promote a holistic structural reform of the economy. "Innovative, coordinated, green, open and shared development" have been set as the key characteristics for China's future development[3]. Many policies and measures have been rolled out to address the challenges.

① Harari, D., "Japan's Economy: From the Lost Decade to Abenomics", http://researchbriefings. files.parliament.uk/documents/SN06629/SN06629.pdf, 2013.
② World Bank Data, data. worldbank. org/ (accessed 20 April 2018).
③ China, National Development and Reform Commission, "The 13th Five-Year Plan for Economic and Social Development of the People's Republic of China (2016-2020)", http://en.ndrc.gov.cn/ newsrelease/201612/P020161207645765233498.pdf, 2015.

First, to improve the macroeconomic environment, the Government of China has started to take important initial steps to facilitate the economy's deleveraging. Guidelines were issued to broaden the range of tools that firms could use to restructure their debt. The Central Bank tightened macro-prudential measures for the real estate sector, and also extended the coverage of its Macro-Prudential Assessment to off-balance sheet activity for the first time by including wealth management products[1]. Consequently, China's credit growth is slowing, and its credit gap has been narrowing since 2016.

Second, the Government is pursuing supply-side reforms, including stabilizing labour supply (by lifting the one-child limit and delaying the retirement age) and enhancing the efficiency of resource allocation (with greater resource mobility, price liberalization and tax incentives). Technology and innovation are fundamental drivers in achieving supply-side reforms. The Government has established objectives for China to become an "innovative nation" by 2020, an "international innovation leader" by 2030 and a 'world powerhouse of scientific and technological innovation' by 2050. China is moving aggressively towards advanced manufacturing and the digital economy, with the support of government initiatives such as "Made in China 2025" and "Internet +".

Third, actions are underway to improve the inclusiveness of economic growth. The Government has established objectives for eliminating absolute poverty by 2020, to deliver a "moderately prosperous society". At the end 2016, there were still more than 40 million people living below the national poverty line (equivalent to around $2.40 per day). The Government increased fiscal transfers to enhance social protection while deploying more funds for financing rural infrastructure, agricultural subsidies and discounted loans. Health-care insurance, for example, has expanded massively since the early 2000s to cover more than 95 per cent of the population in the past few years[2].

Last but not least, the Government has taken serious steps to curb pollution while speeding up the transition to clean energy. China has been the global leader in electric vehicle sales since 2015 and is aiming for annual sales of 7 million by 2025. It aims to get 20 per cent of its energy from renewables by 2030; in 2016 alone, it had installed 35 GW of new solar generation, equal to

---

[1] IMF, "Regional Economic Outlook: Asia and Pacific, May", http://imf.org/en/Publications/REO/APAC/Issues/2017/04/28/areo0517, 2017.

[2] Hu, A., "China: Health Care for All", http://social-protection.org/gimi/RessourcePDF.action?ressource.ressourceId=54138, 2016.

Germany's total capacity. China is also proactively using market mechanisms to align private sector incentives with reduced energy consumption and carbon intensity. In late 2017, a carbon emissions trading system was launched in the country.

Holistic structural reforms are important for the Chinese economy. The innovation-driven inclusive and sustainable growth path would help China sustain relatively higher rates of economic growth and achieve a greater level of welfare, even as the labour force shrinks and capital accumulation slows. Under this scenario technological advancement (including measures to invest in human capital and new technologies) and enhanced production factor mobility (including removal of barriers to allow the free flow of factors and integration of the domestic market) are predicted to support growing labour productivity and investment efficiency. Consequently, total factor productivity (TFP) would overtake capital formation to become the major driver of economic growth.

Accelerated urbanization, a rising "middle-class" population, and increasing government transfers to optimize social protection systems would strengthen domestic demand for goods and especially services. In 2030, consumption would be the leading demand-side contributor to GDP (over 70 per cent); and services would become the major sector of the economy, accounting for 70 per cent of GDP (in current prices), very close to the current level in advanced economies.

Moreover, in this scenario China's social and environmental tensions are expected to ease. Income inequalities between urban and rural areas are predicted to narrow, and improved marginal productivity of agricultural labour would improve rural-urban income disparities. China's total energy consumption and carbon emissions could peak in 2025, five years ahead of the timeline for the Paris Agreement, with a quick decline in energy and carbon intensity.

12.6 Further Restructuring Measures to Achieve Longer-term Sustainability

These recent policies and measures show that China is putting more weight on the quality of economic growth, rather than the quantity. The momentum should be maintained. Further actions are needed to deepen the structural reforms to raise the longer-term sustainability of economic growth, as the model simulation suggests.

In order to further harness innovation to drive economic growth, the government should continue creating an enabling environment and institutions by reducing red tape and decentralizing administrative responsibilities. More public and private funding could be attracted and invested in R&D. Market opening policies should be maintained. Manufacturers should accelerate industrial upgrading and move Chinese products up global value chains. The domestic market should be further integrated to facilitate free mobility of production factors, in line with the government's mandate to enhance the market's "determinant" role in resource allocation. Laws and regulations should be improved to ease market entry and exit procedures for enterprises. Measures to increase access, coverage and quality of education and health-care systems should be strengthened to accelerate human capital accumulation.

Further measures should be taken to promote well-rounded human development and share the gains from development with the whole population. The pace of urbanization could be better managed, with measures to facilitate the process of rural migrants becoming urban residents. Basic public and social services across the country should be strengthened to ensure equality of opportunities. Hukou (household registration) reform and improved access to social services (including health, pension and education), particularly in less-developed inland provinces, are needed to ensure an adequate safety net for all. The Government is advised to increase fiscal transfers to enhance social protection and public service provision, which could be supported by increasing state-owned enterprises' dividend payments into the budget. Tax breaks could also be introduced to reduce financial burdens on low- and middle-income households.

To further internalize the externalities of environmental and climate risks, the Government should continue and accelerate price reforms of energy products, setting emission standards for high pollution industries, and optimizing emissions trading mechanisms. Adding environment-related indicators to local government official's performance evaluation systems is critical to change the mindset from the GDP quantity to quality and hold government officials accountable for environmental mandates and the quality of economic growth. The carbon tax could be another powerful tool[①].

Policies to enhance technology and innovation, social inclusiveness and environmental sustainability can uncover and reinforce synergies. Investment in energy or green technologies could not only potentially improve energy efficiency, but also reduce energy and carbon intensity. Increasing government expenditure on social protection systems (such as education and health care) could improve equality of opportunities and meanwhile accumulate human capital to support an innovation-driven economy. Measures to curb carbon emissions could ease the environmental risks, reduce pollution-induced health risks (and benefit human capital accumulation) and lower the occurrence of extreme weather which disproportionately threatens impoverished people.

Moreover, consideration and implementation of several policies to achieve a holistic economic restructuring is more beneficial to the country because some policies may bring undesirable consequences which could be offset by other policies. For instance, technology advancement is the key to improving efficiency and productivity. However, it tends to favour capital over labour which can lead to a declining labour share in national income, suggesting a worsening income distribution and increasing income inequality[②]. However, the increasing inequality could be eased if the Government enhances the provision of social services to ensure income gains are widely shared. Similarly, as income increases, consumers shift their diet from crop- to livestock-based products. However, production of livestock-based food requires greater resource use and could cause more environmental damage[③], which needs corresponding environmental protection policies. Therefore, it is particularly important to implement policies to enhance innovation, inclusiveness and sustainability simultaneously. Different policies should reinforce each other to augment the desired policy outcomes.

It should be noted that the policies to support China's economic transition come at a sizable financial cost. Poverty elimination, for example, entails substantial investment into such areas as basic education, vocational

---

① Please see detailed discussion about carbon tax in *Economic and Social Survey of Asia and the Pacific 2018*.

② DESA, "The Impact of the Technological Revolution on Labour Markets and Income Distribution", http://un.org/development/desa/dpad/wp-content/uploads/sites/4, 2017.

③ World Bank, "China Economic Update", June, http://worldbank.org/content/dam/Worldbank/document/EAP/China/China_Economic_Update_June2014.pdf, 2014.

training, health-care services, housing for poor people, and building major infrastructure facilities (such as railways, roads, energy generation and hydraulic projects). In 2017, the central and local governments allocated more than 140 billion Chinese yuan (RMB) (approximately 21.5 billion USD) from the budget for poverty elimination funds, 40 per cent higher than the amount in 2016[1].

The way financial resources are generated or mobilized could have positive or negative impacts on China's macroeconomic environment. China's local governments have relied on their arms-length investment vehicles for project financing, which contributed to the quick surge of government debt (direct and contingent liabilities). This could potentially generate financial volatility. Financing in a responsible manner will be critical for China's economic restructuring. Idle funding should be better utilized. For example, according to China's National Audit Office, by March 2017, more than RMB 1.9 billion (approximately 300 million USD) ear-marked for poverty reduction has remained idled for more than one year[2]. More public expenditure could be allocated and the private sector and civil society could be encouraged to participate in financing structural reforms, for example, through public-private partnerships.

Policies to support China's transition to an innovative, inclusive and sustainable economy should be implemented sooner rather than later. Some policies could take years or decades to show impacts. The loosening of the one child policy, for example, could take two decades to contribute to the labour supply[3]. Education and vocational training will require students or employees to invest time to accomplish them before yielding productivity improvements. Moreover, some challenges could incur larger costs if they are dealt with at a later time. For example, air pollution has adverse impacts on human health. Empirical analyses show close, quantitative relationships between exposure to high air pollutant concentrations and increased mortality or morbidity over time[4]. This could translate into increasing health-

---

① DSC, "Fiscal Policy Options to Speed up Poverty Elimination", http://drc.gov.cn/
   xscg/20170726/182-473-2894061.htm, 2017

② NAO, "Notice 2017/6. Audit Results on 158 Counties in Poverty", http://audit.gov.cn/n5/n25/
   c97001/content.html, 2017.

③ Zeng, Y. and Hesketh, T., "The effects of China's universal two-child policy", The
   Lancet, 388(10054), 2016: 1930-1938.

④ WHO, "Ambient (Outdoor) Air Quality and Health", http://who.int/mediacentre/factsheets/
   fs313/en/, 2016.

care expenditure and direct economic losses. More importantly, delaying some polices could have irreversible consequences, such as surpassing thresholds in the potential of climate change to threaten human societies and natural systems. Therefore, to achieve long-term economic and development sustainability, China should continue to implement the existing reforms and strengthen measures that are consistent with the innovative.

China is at a crossroads of economic restructuring. Measures to enhance innovation, improve the efficiency of resource allocation, reduce income inequalities, increase equality of access to public and social services and internalise environmental costs will strengthen the sustainability of the economy and build longer-term economic resilience.

Chapter 13

Global Economic Governance

13.1 International Trade Governance

13.1.1 Context of Globalization and Democratization

Before learning international trade governance, its background and related condition should be introduced. This section provides a succinct analysis of some of the challenges faced in building a more balanced globalization. It is divided into three parts: (1) conditions of global inequalities and the problems it caused; (2) asymmetries of the international economic system and the international schemes and national policies needed to overcome them; (3) influences of globalization and society development on democratization.

(1) Global Inequities

In many studies related to global economic order, we could find that most of them emphasize the widespread increase of global inequalities and its uneven distribution of opportunities for different countries. Thus, "virtuous" and "vicious" circles have been put in place in the world over the past decades, resulting in major "winners" but also in a large set of "losers". Several factors may be at work here, particularly the differential effects of major international shocks on different economies, and agglomeration forces, which tend to concentrate economic activity in certain locations. As we have seen, the two major crises of the late twentieth century generated a sharp increase in international inequalities [1]. Given the large number of developing countries that remain commodity-dependent, we must add to this list the strong downward trend of commodity prices that characterized the quarter century or so since 1980, which was, in fact, one of the major determinants of the "lost decade" [2].

(2) The Asymmetries of the Global Economic Order

These asymmetries are of three kinds[3] and the international schemes and national policies[4].

The first asymmetry is associated with the macroeconomic vulnerability of developing countries to external shocks, which has tended to increase with the tighter integration of the world economy. Importantly, the nature of this vulnerability has been changing in recent decades. Although the transmission of external shocks through trade remains important - as made evident by both sharp commodity price volatility over the past few decades and the collapse of world trade and trade finance during the most recent global economic crisis—financial shocks have come to play a more prominent role, revisiting patterns that have been observed in the past in many developing countries, especially during the world financial boom-bust cycle of the 1920s and 1930s. As for these problems, since the 1990s, "self-insurance" in the form of accumulation of large amounts of foreign exchange reserves has become a broad-based pattern in the developing world. During the recent global economic crisis, greater room was provided for counter-cyclical macroeconomic policies, though in quite a diverse way[5].

---

[1] Jose Antonio Ocampo, *Making Global Trade Governance Work for Development: Perspectives and Priorities from Developing Countries*, Chapter 1, "Globalization, Development and Democracy", Part I. Published in the United States of America by Cambridge University Press, New York (2011).

[2] Ocampo, J., & Parra-Lancourt, M. (2010). "The Terms of Trade for Commodities Since the Mid-19th Century", *Journal of Iberian and Latin American Economic History*, 28(1), 11-43.

[3] Jose Antonio Ocampo and Juan Martin, "Globalization and Development: A Latin American and Caribbean Perspective", Published in September 2003.

[4] Jose Antonio Ocampo, *Making Global Trade Governance Work for Development: Perspectives and Priorities from Developing Countries*, Part I, Chapter 1, "Globalization, Development and Democracy", "World Economic Asymmetries", Published in the United States of America by Cambridge University Press, New York (2011).

[5] Jose Antonio Ocampo, *The Global Economic Crisis in Latin America: Impacts and Responses*, Chapter 2, "How well has Latin America Fared During the Global Financial Crisis", Part I. 2012 by Routledge, Editor: Michael A. Cohen.

Ocampo thinks[1], in financial area, what international financial institutions should do is to compensate for the pro-cyclical impact of financial markets, smoothing financial boom and bust at its source through adequate regulation, and providing a large degree of freedom for countries to adopt counter-cyclical macroeconomic policies. In addition, making resources accessible for those countries that are limited to enter private international capital market is also necessary by establishment of multilateral development banks or bilateral financing.

The second asymmetry is derived from the high concentration of technical progress in developed countries. The diffusion of technical progress from source countries to the rest of the world remains 'relatively slow and uneven', affirming Prebisch's[2] classical predicament. This concentration reflects the costs of entry into more dynamic technological activities, including the obstacles that developing countries face in technologically mature sectors, where opportunities for them may be largely confined to attracting multinational that control the technology, global production and distribution networks. For many developing countries, opportunities are further limited to the low-skilled part of the value-added chain (assembly operations). In turn, technology transfer is subject to the payment of innovation rents, which have been rising due to the generalization and strengthening of intellectual property (IP) rights, particularly through the incorporation of IP standards and enforcing requirements into the World Trade Organization (WTO) and bilateral trade agreements.

For this asymmetry, multilateral trade system should play an important role in avoiding erecting obstacles to transfers through protection or subsidies, as well as accelerating developing countries' access to technology and ensuring their increasing participation in the development of society nowadays.

The third asymmetry is associated with the contrast between the high mobility of capital and the restrictions on the international movement of labour, particularly of unskilled Labour. This also remains, as noticed, an area where international cooperation is generally absent, as reflected in the fact that it has been ignored in most international economic agreements; in the WTO, for example, though it is included as one of the modes of service

---

[1] Jose Antonio Ocampo, *The Global Economic Oisis in Latin America: Impacts and Responses*, Routledge, 2012.

[2] Prebisch, Raúl, "Crecimiento, desequilibrio y disparidades: interpretación del proceso de desarrollo económico", En: Estudio económico de América Latina, 1949-E/CN.12/164/Rev.1-1950-P.3-89,1950.

provision, its development has been essentially circumscribed to skilled labour.

To overcome this problem, one of the most essential methods is to pay more attention to labor migration by establishing a globally agreed framework for migration policies and protecting labor rights of migration strictly.

(3) Globalization and democracy[①]

"Social dimensions of globalization" is provided by Ocampo when talking about the globalization process. Despite the biases of the current global economic agenda, the current phase of globalization is a multidimensional phenomenon that has also included the gradual spread of common principles and international declarations and agreements on human rights, and in the UN Development Agenda that has emerged out of declarations and plans of action from the sequence of United Nations Conferences and Summits, including in particular the Millennium Declaration (United Nations 2000) and the associated Millennium Development Goals, which constitute a subset of that broader UN Agenda. As Ocampo mentioned, these principles and international social objectives are considered as "social dimensions of globalization". These processes are also rooted in the long historical struggle by international civil society for human rights, social equity, gender equality, protection of the environment and, more recently, globalization of solidarity and the "right to be different" (cultural diversity), which indeed represents one of the most positive aspects of globalization.

13.1.2 Roles of United Nations

(1) Role in World Trade Governance: Norm-setting

UN organizations, such as UNCTAD, the Second Committee of the United Nations General Assembly, and the UN Economic and Social Council plays important and particular roles in different areas of norm-setting. The trade and development policies these organizations made are considered as national, regional and global policies and measures through translation by countries in need, helping them govern economic events in advanced ways.

---

① Jose Antonio Ocampo, *Making Global Trade Governance Work for Development: Perspectives and Priorities from Developing Countries*, Part I, Chapter 1, "Globalization, development and democracy" "Globalization and democracy", Published in the United States of America by Cambridge University Press, New York, 2011.

These rules are recognized as an essential part of international soft-law, despite these rules lack the force of legal contracts. As Lakshmi Puri says, within the UN system, UNCTAD has played the leading role in such efforts[①].

In the history of UNCTAD Conferences, each period owned different topics and corresponding resolutions. In 1964, the first UNCTAD Conference was held. One of the topics is permission of countries to dispose their natural resources without any limits. Participants in Conference paid attention to positive effects of international trade in economic development. In addition, mutually advantageous effects based on the most favored nation (MFN) treatment should be the mainstreaming of international trade development. More importantly, one non-reciprocal policy was made for promoting the development of developing countries: developed countries should provide both tariff and non-tariff preferences in trade to developing countries, and cooperation with developing countries should be the correct way for developed countries' expectation of expansion of trade. And another special right of developing countries is to protect their infant industries, in order to guarantee development of their countries' basic industries, related to their economies safety of countries. In year 1968 the second UNCTAD Conference made a new policy in tariff called tariff preferences for accelerating developing countries' industrialization. The next conference in 1972 was marked by the adoption of the Charter of Rights and Duties of States, which could lead developing countries to regulate a New International Economic Order in new period of development, to develop more equal and well-organized world trade. In the 1980s, UNCTAD Conferences made a great change in treatment on the relationship between trade and development. Developed countries should pursue adjustment of their economic structure for being productive and more dependent on high technology production, and forgo the protective measures of those sunset industries. Another significant statement provided in the conferences was for export-oriented developing countries to attach importance to endogenous agricultural, industrial and technological revolutions.

(2) Role in World Trade Governance: Research and Analysis

In Puri's view, UNCTAD and other UN organizations have acted as think

---

① Lakshmi Puri, *Making Global Trade Governance Work for Development: Perspectives and Priorities from Developing Countries*, Part I, Chapter 2, "Trade, development and the UN Millennium Development Goals: the United Nations in the Governance of World Trade" "The UN's role in the World Trade Governance: Norm-setting", Published in the United States of America by Cambridge University Press, New York, 2011.

tanks on world trade governance through their empirical and normative research and analysis of trade and development issues[1]. They have made a strong intellectual case for eschewing purely mercantilist and pro-big business approaches to global trade liberalization and regulation or deregulation. They have taken developing countries' special needs, interests and capacities into consideration, especially for least developed countries and other more disadvantaged nations likes SIDS (small island developing countries) and LLDCs (landlocked developing countries). They have tried to keep a specific focus on public interest and public goods issues as well. Their analysis has presented matters from the developing country perspective and has tended to be independent and innovative. They have often identified alternatives that go beyond conventional wisdom and prevailing, sometimes misguided, orthodoxy, particularly which was put forward under the so-called Washington Consensus and Bretton Woods institutions, including structural adjustment programs.

And here are some examples of its value. UNCTAD's research and analysis reoriented the discourse in the negotiations on trade in services in the run-up to the WTO's General Agreement on Trade in Services (GATS) towards a more development-friendly direction while contributing to breaking the North-South negotiating impasse. Its studies made seminal contributions by advancing the idea of modes of delivery (later to be adopted in GATS as the four modes of supply of services), the positive list approach to making commitments, the separation of market access and national treatment commitments, and the Telecommunications Annex. Further, UNCTAD's studies on Trade Related Intellectual Property Rights (TRIPs) and Trade Related Investment Measures (TRIMs) sought to promote greater balance between the rights and freedoms of Intellectual Property Rights (IPR) holders and foreign investors on one hand, and, on the other, the rights and duties of governments to take certain measures to curb these rights for public interest.

13.1.3 Improvement of WTO Governance Fairness

(1) Current Status of WTO Reform

In this part, we introduce the two cornerstone principles of WTO decision-

---

[1] Lakshmi Puri, *Making Global Trade Governance Work for Development: Perspectives and Priorities from Developing Countries*, Part I, Chapter 2, "Trade, development and the UN Millennium Development Goals: the United Nations in the Governance of World Trade" "The UN's Research and Analytical Role", Published in the United States of America by Cambridge University Press, New York, 2011.

making, consensus and the single undertaking, and some existing proposals for reform, namely voting and variable geometry of rights and obligations.

The consensus principle is the first cornerstone principle of WTO decision-making we would introduce. It is a symbolic turning point of multilateral trading system, making the GATT/WTO different from the trading forum before (e.g. Bretton Woods System). What should be emphasized is that, consensus doesn't mean unanimity. In actual GATT/WTO practice, consensus is assumed when no party present at the meeting when a decision is taken overtly objects to the decision, rather than that all the parties must agree. In addition, the GATT and the WTO would prescribe voting for particular circumstances when consensus could not be reached, each requiring specified majority thresholds ranging from unanimity to a two-thirds majority. This condition happened much less frequently in the GATT era, apart from sanctioning new accessions and waivers.

Some of its flaws have emerged in the history of applying this principle. Lacking efficient process and capacity of handling crisis are the most criticized weakness of the consensus principle. For example, the GATT membership concluded eight trade rounds over fifty years, but was not immune to episodic crises.[1] With the changing situation of trade (from bipolar system and a less complex agenda to multipolarity system and a much more complex agenda), more and more people pay attention to the balance between efficiency and consensus. Another controversial shortage should be mentioned here is the equal veto status to block decision. Actually, in today's multipolar trading system, blocking is best orchestrated by coalitions, rather than Members acting in their own right[2]. This unequal power became the main resistance for developing countries to block decisions of interest to the rich and powerful by coming at high political cost, which is called "shadow of power"[3]. Critics therefore argue that the consensus arrangements of the GATT/WTO mask a system of "managed hypocrisy": it produces a false sense of equal participation, erodes procedural transparency and accountability, and leads to frequent frustration among

---

[1] Wilkinson, R., 2006, *The WTO: Crisis and the Governance of Global Trade*, London: Routledge.

[2] Cottier, T., 2009, "A Two-Tier Approach to WTO Decision Making", NCCR Working Paper 2009/06.

[3] Steinberg, R., 2002, "In the Shadow of Law or Power? Consensus-Based Bargaining and Outcomes in the GATT/WTO", *International Organization*, 56 (2): 339-374.

parties excluded from small group negotiations[1].

Although consensus-based bargaining may be a slower and more complex process, it is more sustainable and fairer in the long term[2]. During the process of searching consensus, members involved could build convergences in their position, and make compromises for the interests of WTO as a whole. What's more, countries could learn more through arguing and deliberation under this system.

For solving the problem of efficiency in decision-making process, critics propose a voting system in the WTO, which could be used as a supplementary instrument of decision-making within rounds and in between rounds, or for conducting the WTO's regular business, instead of replace consensus principle[3]. There are two voting system: simple majority voting, which would be unacceptable to major developed countries since developing countries constitute more than two-thirds of the WTO's membership, particular the USA and the EU; the other one is the weighted voting, providing an approximately fair balance of rights and powers among industrialized, emerging and developing countries[4]. A related but more nuanced arrangement proposes a "two-tier" approach in the WTO, with different model of decision-making for the organization's primary and secondary rules[5]. In this scenario, Ismail and Vickers argues that the WTO's "primary" could continue to operate under the consensus principle, or even "consensus-minus" as happens in the Dispute Settlement Body (DSB), or

① Steinberg, R., 2002, "In the Shadow of Law or Power? Consensus-Based Bargaining and Outcomes in the GATT/WTO", *International Organization*, 56 (2): 339-74; Cottier, T. and Elsig, M., 2009, "Reforming the WTO: the Decision-Making Triangle Re-Assessed". Paper presented at the World Trade Forum, World Trade Institute, University of Bern; Low, P., 2009, "WTO Decision-Making for the Future", background paper prepared for the Inaugural Conference of Thinking Ahead on International Trade (TAIT), Geneva.

② Faizel Ismail and Brendan Vickers, *Making Global Trade Governance Work for Development: Perspectives and Priorities from Developing Countries*, Part IV, Chapter 16, "Towards Fair and Inclusive Decision-making in WTO Negotiation" "Current Proposals for Reform", Published in the United States of America by Cambridge University Press, New York, 2011.

③ Cottier, T. and Takenoshita, S., 2008, "Decision-making and the Balance of Powers in WTO Negotiations: Towards Supplementary Weighted Voting", in Griller, S. (ed.), *At the Crossroads: The World Trading System and the Doha Round.* Austria: Springer-Verlag Wein.

④ Cottier, T. and Takenoshita, S., 2008, "Decision-making and the Balance of Powers in WTO Negotiations: Towards Supplementary Weighted Voting", in Griller, S. (ed.), *At the Crossroads: The World Trading System and the Doha Round.* Austria: Springer-Verlag Wein.

⑤ Cottier, T. 2009, "A Two-Tier Approach to WTO Decision Making", NCCR Working Paper 2009/06 (March).

weighted voting with a particular quorum required[1]. By contrast, there may be greater flexibility (including variable geometry of rights and obligations) for the WTO's "secondary rules", such as those related to implementation of a Member's agreed schedules for liberalization and plurilateral agreements. To conclude, weighted voting could increasing developing countries' shares and power in decision-making process, making the possibility of even inciting developed countries' position in WTO.

The second cornerstone of the trading system is the principle of the single undertaking. Established at the beginning of Uruguay Round in 1986, the single undertaking introduced the procedural notion that "nothing is agreed until everything is agreed" in order to maximize cross-linkages and trade-off possibilities within a "grand bargain" package deal[2]. With the establishment of the WTO in 1995, this principle claims all the WTO's founding Members fully take on obligations. Though there are some problems attributes to the single undertaking, it does establish basis for single system rather than a two-tier system. Ismail and Vickers[3] argues that a round of negotiations based on the principle of single undertaking could still conceivably offer the possibility of trade-offs and an exchange of concessions that recognizes the various capabilities of the different stakeholders and results in a fair and balanced outcome allowing all the players to make gains.

Variable geometry has been proposed to be an alternative to the single undertaking. To enhance efficiency of negotiating process, "variable geometry" and "less-than-full-consensus" decision-making has been proposed to substitute the principle of single undertaking[4].

① Faizel Ismail and Brendan Vickers, *Making Global Trade Governance Work for Development: Perspectives and Priorities from Developing Countries*, Part IV, Chapter 16, "Towards Fair and Inclusive Decision-making in WTO Negotiation" "Current Proposals for Reform", Published in the United States of America by Cambridge University Press, New York, 2011.
② Faizel Ismail and Brendan Vickers, *Making Global Trade Gorernance Work for Development: perspectires* and prioritres from developing countries, Part IV, Chapter 16, "Towand Fair and Indusive Decision-making in WTO Negotiation", Cambridge Vniversity Pless, New York, 2011.
③ Faizel Ismail and Brendan Vickers, *Making Global Trade Gorernance Work for Development: perspectires* and prioritres from developing countries, Part IV, Chapter 16, "Towand Fair and Indusive Decision-making in WTO Negotiation", Cambridge Vniversity Pless, New York, 2011.
④ Warwick Commission, 2007, *The Multilateral Trade Regime: Which Way Forward?*, Coventry: University of Warwick; Cottier, T. and Elsig, M. 2009, "Reforming the WTO: The Decision-Making Triangle Re-Assessed", Paper presented at the World Trade Forum, World Trade Institute, University of Bern, 2009, 25-26 September.

According to Low[1], a two-speed system has obvious attractions for those don't support existing decision-making system: (1) advancing a progressive and responsive WTO agenda; (2) blunting the diversion of liberalization initiatives to RTAs; (3) allowing for more efficient differentiation in the levels of rights and obligations among a community of highly diverse economies; (4) and serving as a mechanism for promoting greater efficiency at lower cost in WTO negotiations.

(2) Proposals for a More Reasonable Decision-making System

According to Ismail and Vickevs[2], there are two issues at stake for modern global trade governance in the situation that developing countries occupy over 75% of the WTO's membership. One is for the WTO to clarify the higher level or overall objectives of the organization since the increasing pressures and demands from diverse countries or organizations. The WTO lacks clarity for its main goals and objectives, which are often confused with its main function of trade opening and rules creation. Another challenge for the WTO is how to ensure all the members could participate in the decision-making process equally, especially for the developing countries. Three proposals for a more reasonable decision-making system would be proposed below.

I Strengthen the consensus principle

For this proposal, Ismail and Vickers emphasizes that the challenge for the WTO is to improve the functioning of the consensus principle by reducing its weakness and building on its strengths[3]. WTO members need to put the Sutherland Report's recommendation into practice as for the first measure to reinforce the consensus principle. To reduce the number of blocking decisions by some countries, the Sutherland Report mentioned that countries blocking decisions for their national vital interests through writing declaration should

---

① Low, 2009, Low, P. "WTO Decision-Making for the Future", backgroumd paper prepared for the Inaugural Conference of Thinking Ahead on International Trade (TAIT), Geneva, 2009, 17-18 September.

② Faizel Ismail and Brendan Vickers, *Making Global Trade Governance Work for Development: Perspectives and Priorities from Developing Countries*, Part IV, Chapter 16, "Towards fair and inclusive decision-making in WTO negotiation", Published in the United States of America by Cambridge University Press, New York, 2011.

③ Faizel Ismail and Brendan Vickers, *Making Global Trade Governance Work for Development: Perspectives and Priorities from Developing Countries*, Part IV, Chapter 16, "Towards Fair and Inclusive Decision-making in WTO Negotiation", Published in the United States of America by Cambridge University Press, New York, 2011.

take corresponding responsibilities, which could offset the negative effects of blocking decisions by some dominant countries using reasons irrelevant to trade issues. In a real condition of trade issues, the process of building consensus would be much more complex and challenging than a simple majority or weighted voting system. And then this form of decision making could show its strengths in sustainable and efficient development in the long term.

Ⅱ Resolve the problems of informal small group negotiations

The demand of increasing developing countries' influence on decision-making processes has emerged when informal processes of decision-making has trumped more genuine and inclusive multilateral processes.

Green Room is one of the typical informal small group negotiations. World Trade Organization (WTO) Green Room meetings are small gatherings of representatives from up to 30 member countries, invited by the Director-General. They are designed to provide the basis for a consensus on critical negotiating issues that can be brought to the WTO membership as a whole.

Before discussing the methods to solve these problems, principal supplier approach adopted by the USA and the EU in GATT period should be mentioned. As a matter of fact, principal supplier was proposed as a tool by developed countries to control the tariff cuts privilege. The main players insisted on this method of negotiation, which included the main economic powers only and thus marginalized the developing countries from the negotiations of tariff. It could be explained that a country could only be asked to make tariff cuts on a particular product by the principal supplier of that product to the country. In other words, for any particular product the importing country negotiated its tariff rate with principal supplier and not with all suppliers of the same product. Developing countries were seldom principal suppliers of any product at that time, which meant a discrimination of tariff cuts to developing countries. Even this rule was modified later to allow developing countries to negotiate collectively in requesting concessions, its effect of locking developing countries out of tariff-cutting negotiations could not be ignored.

However, the shortages of informal small group negotiations could be classified into two aspects. One is that such small informal groups result in isolation to those were not be invited to attend, raising more problems on decision-making in the later negotiations. And the efficiency of these informal small groups is deadly low. Without any improvements to be more democratic, democratic and multilateral for this approach, it could not survive nowadays. One of the significant part for this approach is to balance every Members' interests, particularly ensuring developing countries' involve in every stage of the negotiating process. Undoubtedly, the coalitions of developing countries play a positive role in decision-making process and building joint negotiating positions and convergence among the memberships. Before speaking in negotiations, they need to discuss with each other to reach consensus on a topic, which depends on their internal negotiation's mechanism concerning representation and accountability[1]. According to Narlikar[2], the proposal for this approach is for the formalization of coalitions or specific issue-based platforms as the bargaining principals in a two-step negotiation process. The first step would involve the constitution of coalitions, including developed countries and developing countries. And formal recognition of these collective entities as principals could potentially empower even small developing countries by elevating them into the role of principal suppliers as members of coalitions. To reinforce coalition unity and permit greater flexibility to negotiate concessions, there should be a restriction on side-deals. These methods improve the perceptions of fairness of the multilateral trading system. Simultaneously, the efficiency of deliver a result is enhanced.

13.1.4 Proposals for WTO Governance Reform

(1) Role of the Proposed Council for Trade and Development

The primary objective of the new Trade and Development Council would be to establish a development agenda for the WTO and promote development interests in the multilateral trading system. Its role could include: promoting a development agenda and implementation of trade-related development assistance policies; monitoring regulatory development relevant to developing countries; and establishing and supervising subcommittees to address specific development issues.

---

[1] Faizel Ismail and Brendan Vickers, *Making Global Trade Governance Work for Development: Perspectives and Priorities from Developing Countries*, Part IV, Chapter 16, "Towards Fair and Inclusive Decision-making in WTO Negotiation", Published in the United States of America by Cambridge University Press, New York, 2011.

[2] Nalikar, A. and Jones, K. 2009. *The Doha Blues: Institutional Crisis and Reform in the WTO,* Oxford University Press.

For the first duty of the proposed Trade and Development Council, how to promote more effective development measures and policies by setting corresponding agendas would be the critical point. Before making agendas, the ability to identify problems in the trading system by Council should be guaranteed. And then, accordingly, the agenda should be negotiated by Members at conferences to develop a more supportive development system, allowing relevant rules' modification when necessary. In addition, cooperation with relevant international organizations such as the United Nations Committee on Trade and Development (UNCTD) and the United Nations Industrial Development Organization (UNIDO), could be beneficial to make the agenda-setting more effective and consistent. Another method to supervise is Trade-Related Development Assistance Report (TDAR), which is established for developed country Members and participating developing country Members to file a compulsory report regularly. This report could be an examination of Members' activities by the Council. Enforceability of developed country commitments to assist developing countries is weak. As Lee says[1], few developing countries have the economic or political leverage to force compliance by developed countries. Moreover, many of the provisions are non-binding. Thus, the Council's work would help developing countries create further pressure for progress in this respect.

For monitoring section, it could be divided into three parts. Compliance with WTO provisions on development assistance, including SDT provisions (provisions for special and differential treatment in favour of developing countries), would be the first part of monitoring by Council. And the second portion would be the aforementioned Trade-Related Development Assistance Report. It could also monitor the commitments of developed countries to developing countries. In Lee's opinion, the Council should publish an annual report on compliance with these development assistance provisions and provide monitoring of any systematic compliance failure.

Last but not least, the Council should pay attention to some long-term issues of trade and development, such as technological transfer among developed and developing countries. Establishing standing or ad hoc committees to resolve these issues would be one of the best choice. Aid for Trade is such a good example to help developing countries, and particularly least developed

---

① Yong-Shik Lee, *Making Global Trade Governance Work for Development: Perspectives and Priorities from Developing Countries*, Part III, Chapter 16, "Reclaiming Development in WTO Governance" "Implementation of Development Policies and Assistance", Published in the United States of America by Cambridge University Press, New York, 2011.

countries, trade. Many developing countries face a range of supply-side and trade-related infrastructure obstacles which constrains their ability to engage in international trade. The WTO-led Aid for Trade initiative encourages developing country governments and donors to recognize the role that trade can play in development. In particular, the initiative seeks to mobilize resources to address the trade-related constrains identified by developing and least-developed countries. Also, greater assistance to developing countries involved in costly and time-consuming trade disputes should be taken into consideration.

(2) Reform Proposals

There are several proposals for trade governance provided by Lee[1].

For the demanding to facilitate developing countries' economic development in the areas that affect economic development such as tariff bindings, subsidies, anti-dumping, trade-related intellectual property rights and trade related investment measures, a separate agreement providing a coherent standard to determine which developing country Members benefit from certain SDT and set out underlying principles should be established. This agreement may be termed "The Agreement on Development Facilitation". The regulatory ambiguity caused by absence of a definition for developing country Members and the asymmetry of SDT and implemented developing country Members (the same level of SDT to developing country Members with widely different stages of development and economic needs) also need some methods through reaching this agreement. The Agreement on Development Facilitation should provide a definition for what constitutes a developing country Members, as well as differentiate SDT for developing country Members, with the treatment depending on the Member's state of development and economic needs, so as to enhance the clarity and rationality of the system.

Another proposal is an adjustment relevant to tariff bindings. While tariff commitments in the form of bindings stipulated in the Schedule of Concessions play an important role in ensuring the stability of the international trading system, it also impede trade protection to facilitate their

---

[1] Yong-Shik Lee, *Making Global Trade Governance Work for Development: Perspectives and Priorities from developing Countries*, Part III, Chapter 16, "Reclaiming Development in WTO Governance" "Implementation of Development Policies and Assistance", Published in the United States of America by Cambridge University Press, New York, 2011.

industries at early stages of development (infant industries). Fundamental economic restructuring seldom takes place in the absence of governmental intervention[1]. There is no doubt that the rationality of the need to protect infant industries in developing countries, when developing countries with limited negotiating power are often compelled to make concessions beyond the levels that would be detrimental to their industries, due to demands by developed countries with more powerful economies. The adjustment would allow developing countries to increase their tariff rates without limited by scheduled commitments unilaterally when necessary. And some procedural safeguards should be published accordingly to minimize the possibility of abuse, including a formal investigation and hearing requirement, notices to other interested members, consultations, and a maximum duration for its application. Also, the maximum applicable rate of the Development-Facilitation Tariff should also be systematically differentiated according to the development stage of a developing country, as determined by the level of its per capita income[2].

Some may argue that the implementation of a Development-Facilitation Tariff in the world trading system will undermine the import concessions made by developing countries and disrupt the balance of concessions achieved through trade negotiations. However, the influence of it would be rather limited on world trading system since most world trades happen within developed countries, which means that would not be influenced by Development-Facilitation Tariff. Therefore, it would be fair to allow developing countries whose industries condition are satisfactory to using import restriction for meeting their development needs.

The third one for industrial promotion is the use of government subsidies. South Korea is a successful exemplar in utilizing government subsidization to develop. The WTO Agreement on Subsidies and Countervailing Measures (SCM) protects international trade from influence by some irrational subsidies. Countervailing duties (CVDs), also known as anti-subsidy duties, are trade import duties imposed under WTO rules to neutralize the negative effects of subsidies, and also an applicable remedy where subsidization

---

① Rodrik, D., 2004, "Industrial Policy for the Twenty-First Century", Paper prepared for UNIDO,. www.hks.harvard.edu/fs/drodrik/Research%20papers/UNIDOSep.pdf.

② Yong-Shik Lee, *Making Global Trade Governance Work for Development: Perspectives and Priorities from developing Countries*, Part III, Chapter 16, "Reclaiming Development in WTO Governance" "Implementation of Development Policies and Assistance", Published in the United States of America by Cambridge University Press, New York, 2011.

causes or threatens material injury to an established domestic industry or materially retards the establishment of a domestic industry (GATT Article 6.6). For the infant industries in developing countries, they need government support like subsidies to improve their marketing competitiveness both in the foreign and domestic market. The SCM Agreement offers certain SDT to these developing countries, i.e. LDC Members of the WTO are not prohibited from applying export subsidies (Article 27.2 (a))[①], and other developing countries are permitted to apply export subsidies for a period of eight years from the date of entry into force of the WTO Agreement in 1995, which has already expired (Article 27.2 (b)). These prohibited or otherwise actionable subsidies should be allowed for developing countries if they demonstrate a need for such subsidies with a concrete development plan. Such a subsidy specially authorized to facilitate development could be call a "Development-Facilitation Subsidy"[②]. Undoubtedly, according to Lee, the maximum applicable Development-Facilitation Subsidy rate should be differentiated in accordance with the per capita income level of developing countries, the same as the Development-Facilitation Tariff. Potential problems may emerge that if developing countries' blind application would result in cutthroat competitions.

To support developing countries, the proposed Agreement on Development Facilitation could also include provisions that allow for the suspension of developing country commitments under the Trade-Related Investment Measures (TRIMs) and TRIPs Agreements[③].

The inherent complexity and arbitrariness in the determination of dumping would be the essential problem of anti-dumping measures, causing abuse of it. Moreover, inexpensive products are the subject of anti-dumping measures, posing great impediments to developing countries, whose major competitiveness of their products is based on low prices, attributing to low labour costs. The scope for such arbitrariness in the current anti-dumping

---

① This preference ceases to apply to any of these LDC Members when it reaches USD1000 GNP per capita, see SCM Agreement, Annex 7.

② Yong-Shik Lee, *Making Global Trade Governance Work for Development: Perspectives and Priorities from developing Countries*, Part III, Chapter 16, "Reclaiming Development in WTO Governance" "Implementation of Development Policies and Assistance", Published in the United States of America by Cambridge University Press, New York, 2011.

③ Yong-Shik Lee, *Making Global Trade Governance Work for Development: Perspectives and Priorities from developing Countries*, Part III, Chapter 16, "Reclaiming Development in WTO Governance" "Implementation of Development Policies and Assistance", Published in the United States of America by Cambridge University Press, New York, 2011.

rules and its significant adverse effect on trade prompted the inclusion of anti-dumping rules as a topic for the Doha Round negotiations, with a possibility for rule modification. As a result, the suspension of the application of the WTO's anti-dumping provisions to developing countries would be reasonable and beneficial to their development.

The Agreement on Trade-Related Investment Measures (TRIMs) are rules that are applicable to the domestic regulations a country applies to foreign investors, often as part of an industrial policy. The agreement, concluded in 1994, was negotiated under the WTO's predecessor, the General Agreement on Tariffs and Trade (GATT), and came into force in 1995. The agreement was agreed upon by all members of the World Trade Organization. Trade-Related Investment Measures is one of the four principal legal agreements of the WTO trade treaty. FDI may provide developing countries with resources necessary that they lack. Government could set some rules to lead FDI to contribute to their development objectives more when accepting FDI. The multilateral control conducted on TRIMs should be removed since whether a developing country considers the adoption or abandon, both should be done by bilaterally or unilaterally, even without any treaty obligations or mandatory trade rules.

The Agreement on Trade-Related Aspects of Intellectual Property Rights (TRIPs) establishes mandatory standards for protection of various IPRs, including copyrights, trademarks, geographical indications, industrial designs and so on. However, the inclusion of the TRIPs Agreement within international trade regime is not good news for developing countries. In Lee's opinion, there are two major reasons. First, the TRIPs Agreement imposes requirements to establish a regulatory regime to protect IPRs within all WTO Member States, even those where economic and social developments do not yet embrace the concept of IPRs and whose judicial systems have not yet developed sufficiently to recognize and enforce IPRs[1]. Second, the imposition of an IPR regime that is too stringent may prematurely set economic and legal barriers to acquiring advanced technology for development (e.g. TRIPs requires long duration for IPR protection) and thus impede the development prospects of developing countries. Importantly, the huge technological gap between developed and developing countries could not be diminished. From the perspective of the developed countries before, it is unfair for the developing countries to face a much more rigid regime today. However, preservation of developing countries' access to

---

[1] Chang, H., 2002, *Kicking Away the Ladder: Development Strategy in Historical Perspective,* London: Anthem Press.

advanced technology is not equal to hurt their IPRs, but change another way to demonstrate the detrimental impact of violation of their IPR. Also, the TRIPs Agreement should be suspended to those conditions are not ready for establishment of it.

13.2 International Financial Governance

13.2.1 Causes of the Global Financial Crisis

An examination of the causes of the Global Financial Crisis (GFC) is an inextricable part of any study of global financial governance financial governance. Explanations of the GFC have been offered in a fragmented or unified way in a number of works. What this section adds is a new look at the connection between financial innovation, deregulation and free capital flows. For such reconceptualization to be possible, first the most widely discussed causes of the GFC must be considered.

Arguably, "conventional" causes may be divided into two categories. First, causes relating to more general policies and the wider characteristics of the financial system in the past decade, which influenced financial institutions' behavior, regardless of whether they were developed by the institutions themselves (macro-causes). Second, those that originated from within financial institutions and credit rating agencies, due to misaligned incentives (micro-causes).

(1) Macro-cause

Particular emphasis will be given to five macro-causes that overlap to some extent: first, relaxed monetary policies and trade imbalances which helped to build the conditions that led to the global financial meltdown by fueling massive asset bubbles and reinforcing irrational exuberance; second, well meaning government policies with disastrous end results which either promoted universal housing, as happened in the US, or pursued mono-dimensional approaches to development by placing excessive reliance on one or two industries, as happened in Ireland with real estate developers and the growth of the banking sector and in Spain with the constructions industry; third, economic doctrine and regulatory failure, including the absence of institutional capacity to deal with cross-border financial crises; four, flawed use of financial innovation; five, the possible behavioral causes of the crisis.

(2) Micro-causes

I will also highlight three micro-causes of the crisis which focus on the problem of the perverse incentives: first, traders' and bank executives' compensation structures; second, the impact of the originate-to-distribute model on bank credit controls and loan underwriting standards; third, the shortcomings of credit ratings.

Following this analysis, I shall argue that the common theme that bound together most of the above factors to bring about the GFC was the financial revolution. The term financial revolution is used here to describe three phenomena: first, financial innovation, which was the result of two developments: (a) imaginative users of finance in the past thirty years, starting with Michael Milken's junk bonds and ending with the production of highly complex financial instruments and techniques, and (b) advancements in mathematical finance (regardless of the accuracy of the models its developed), which were partly made possible by breakthroughs in computing capacity brought about by technology improvements; second, technological breakthroughs, which created the ability to shift around the globe massive amounts of money within seconds due to the ITC (International trade center) progress from the late 1980s onwards; third, liberalization, which led to free cross-border capital flows due to the nearly universal abolition of national account restrictions in the 1990s and deregulation which allowed free access to foreign financial markets and banking systems for the first time since the first globalization period.

The interplay between innovative finance, technology and open markets led to the linking of previously disparate and independent parts of the global financial markets into a homogeneous, interconnected and interdependent system. Moreover, it exacerbated old problems like the "too-big-to-fail" problem, which became one of the fundamental causes of the GFC, since Large Complex Institutions (LCFIs) took excessive leverage to manufacture a series of systemically important tail risks in an undercapitalized financial system.

13.2.2 Functions of Financial System

As is known to all, financial markets are an efficient means to assign market resources to the most productive and competitive place. According to

Schumpeter's theory of "creative destruction", innovative entrepreneurship leads to gales of "creative destruction" as innovations cause old inventories, ideas, technologies, skills and equipment to become obsolete. The financial system plays a critical role in the functioning of modern economies and their development through the performance of five functions[1]: production of ex ante information about possible investments; monitoring of investments and implementation of corporate governance; management of risk, including risk diversification through trading; mobilization and pooling of savings, which widen access to finance; and facilitation of economic exchange (transactions).

Financial system development is an issue of great importance for the achievement of economic growth, and the link between financial sector development and two of the most important challenges of the modern world: economic growth and poverty eradication would be analyzed.

The first vital function of financial system we will talk about is its mobilization and pooling of savings. Before learning about how it works for mobilization, we need to understand the requirements of mobilizing savings. One is to lower transaction cost caused by the process of collecting capital from individuals. The other is to overcome the information asymmetries concerning building savers' confidence and making them put more savings into investment. Apparently, without the financial system, mobilization of capital would be much less efficient. In this way, financial system development could lower the cost of transaction that promoting specialization and innovation, namely it could encourage productivity and economic development gains.

But how do financial intermediaries convince savers of the soundness of the proposed investments? One of the most necessary measures they would put into action is to establish strong reputations. Another thing for enhancing savers' confidence is regulation. Thus, banking regulation need to create sound and safe environment of investment by setting some institutions, making investment's atmosphere more stable and ordered.

Similarly, securities markets may not be able to release their full potential in the absence of some mandatory legal regimes protecting minority shareholder rights. As a result, legal institutions enforcing mandatory disclosure rules

---

[1] Emilios Avgouleas, *Governance of Global Financial Markets,* Cambridge University Press, New York, 2012, pp. 24-25.

and market abuse prohibitions in securities regulation and strong minority protection mechanisms or remedies in company law could help create a wholesome development environment.

Information production is an necessary function of financial system to help capital flow towards the most profitable and suitable place. In a normal condition, investor would not choose a firm without enough reliable information as investment objective. However, most individual investors could not be afforded the costs of assessment of firms, managers and market conditions. In other words, the capital or other resource would be much less efficiently working in markets when investors could not acquire enough information, especially for those entrepreneurs fail to convey their firms' ideas, technological breakthroughs or other strengths to investors.

Hence financial intermediaries play an important role in alleviating individuals' expenditure in information acquisition, helping savers making more reasonable decisions and improving efficiency of capital market allocation greatly. At the same time, savers will pay more attention to firms' R&D department to evaluate their development potential and prospects that means a powerful drive-force of technological innovation.

As we mentioned before, fewer informational asymmetries and lower transaction costs promote the emergence of financial contracts, markets and intermediaries, enabling transfer, hedging and pooling of risk with implications for resource allocation and growth. Innovative financial instruments/techniques (e.g derivatives, securitization) are well-known means to manage and mitigate risk. Avgouleas argues that financial systems manage risk through three techniques[1]: cross-sectional risk diversification; inter-temporal risk sharing; and provision of liquidity to contain liquidity risk. The financial system provides risk diversification service to affect long-term economic development through rearranging resource assignment and changing savings condition. Risk mitigation and management induce an investment shift towards projects with higher expected returns from low-return projects. Financial system's benefit to technological innovation could embody in augmenting diversified portfolio of innovative projects to mitigate risk. It follows that financial systems which enhance risk diversification can accelerate technological change and economic growth.

---

[1] Emilios Avgouleas, *Governance of Global Financial Markets,* Cambridge University Press, New York, 2012.

Liquidity, a market condition that reflects the cost and speed with which market actors can convert financial instruments into purchasing power at agreed prices, is influenced by information asymmetries and transaction costs. That is the demand of emergence of financial markets and financial institutions, reducing the liquidity risk and increasing liquidity in markets. So what is the effect of liquidity on economic development concretely? In real-life market, investors tend to abnegate projects with higher return that need long-term investment. Insecurity produced by losing control of their assets in long period is the major reason for this phenomenon. While financial system could increase liquidity by the maturity transformation (financial institutions match borrowers and depositors to different periods of funding. For example, borrowers who want to obtain short-term liquidity can also borrow money from long-term investors), more investment is likely to be directed to the higher return projects.

Another function of financial system may be ignored easily concerning corporate governance. Without transparency of corporate operation from financial system, shareholders even could not monitor management's operation, which generating opportunities for managers to make profit for themselves rather than the firm. Especially for the small shareholders, the informational asymmetries are much more serious, since costs of surveillance and acquisition of operation information is exorbitant. Avgouleas suggests[1] that this phenomenon could be impute to free-rider problem. Every investor relies on others to undertake the costly process of monitoring managers, so there is too little monitoring. Under this condition, the voting mechanism and decision-making system will not work effectively. In many countries, legal regimes do not provide adequate protection for small shareholders' rights. For instance, the board of directors may not represent the interests of some small shareholders, since some board of directors may be acted by management, which fosters corruption. Under certain conditions, financial system would become good agents of strong corporate governance. Shareholders and creditors could supervise management and firm effectively and cheaply, inducing managers' work to pursue the maximum of firm's profit. This will be improving the efficiency with which firms allocate resources and make savers more willing to finance production and innovation.

The last function of the financial system we are going to analyze is its

---

[1] Emilios Avgouleas, *Governance of Global Financial Markets,* Cambridge University Press, New York, 2012.

positive effect on poverty reduction. Access to finance would be one of the most important section of this topic. Normally, access to finance is taken to mean access to certain institutions; or access to functions (services) that they provide, such as payments services, savings or loans and credits or use of certain financial products such as credit cards, mortgage and insurance products[1]. And the impact on poverty alleviation at the micro-level caused by availability of financial services could be divided into two types. A developed financial system could raise the income of the poor and make income distribution more equal, which is the direct impact. The indirect impact embodies by stimulating overall economic growth. According to Clarke, Xu and Zou[2], inequality decreases as finance develops and the more concentrated income tends to be in a national economy the higher the country's level of poverty. Thus, availability of finance becomes an necessary factor in alleviating poverty by making income inequality smaller. Moreover, the countries with more developed financial intermediaries experience faster declines in poverty and income equality.

Specifically, Avgouleas argues that availability of finance has special importance for poor households and smaller firms in a number of other ways[3]. For poor household, availability of credit can reinforce their productive assets by building their confidence and enabling them to invest in advanced technologies (e.g. new and better seeds and farming equipment for farmers) or invest in education and health care to pursue higher return in the future. The proportion of low-risk and low-return investment projects would drop as poor household commence their investment in higher-risk and higher-return projects. Also, the availability of insurance help them improving their ability to withstand risks attributing to a sudden illness or a bad harvest. For smaller firms, developed financial services not only support their expansions or even foundations, but generate self-and wage-employment to increase incomes. For all of these reasons, we could easily conclude that availability of finance would become a good agent of economic and social change that improves governance structures decreasing some of the causes of poverty. In

---

① Anne-Marie Chidzero, Karen Ellis and Anjali Kumar, "Indicators of Access to Finance, Through Household Level Surveys, Comparisons of Data from Six Countries", Paper presented in the World Bank conference: "Access to Finance: Building Inclusive Financial Systems", 30 May 2006, p.1.

② George Clarke, Lixin Colin Xu and heng-fu Zou, "Finance and Income Inequality, Test of Alternative Theories", World Bank Policy Research Working Paper 2984, 2003.

③ Emilios Avgouleas, *Governance of Global Financial Markets,* Cambridge University Press, New York, 2012.

the long run, sustainable financial sector development would also be a good agent of the Millennium Development Goals (MDGs).

13.2.3 Evolution of International Financial Governance

In this section, we will discuss the evolution of International financial governance, which will be divided from historical timeline. In Avgouleas's opinion, it could be broadly divided into three phases:[1] (1) The Bretton Woods Phase 1947-97, which also includes the post-Bretton Woods period (from 1972 onwards) when the world moved towards floating exchange rates as the fixed system became unsustainable. (2) The post-Asian Crisis period 1998-2008, which saw the evolution of loose global financial governance structures into a tighter regulatory framework, called New International Financial Architecture (NIFA). (3) The post-2008 period, when national and international policies responding to the causes and consequences of the global financial crisis monopolize the international regulatory reform agenda.

Next, we will discuss International financial governance in these three phases in depth.

The first phase should be named the Bretton Woods and post-Bretton Woods phase, considered as the first attempt to construct a comprehensive and universally binding governance framework for the international economic system and economic relations. The Bretton Woods Treaty's structure was not drawn by the two architects (the US economist and the first managing director of the IMF Henry Dexter White, the most celebrated British economist of the twentieth century John Maynard Keynes) from the beginning without any divergence. Finally, the main policy direction of the Bretton Woods Treaty's structure is following:[2] (1) Formal structures based on international treaties, which allowed for the establishment of international

---

[1] Emilios Avgouleas, *Governance of Global Financial Markets*, Cambridge University Press, New York, 2012, pp.157-8.

[2] The literature on the Bretton Woods agreement, discussion preceding the conference and its impact on the development of global finance in the post-World WarIIyears is vast. Two very useful works are Jacqueline Best, *The Limits of Transparency and the History of International Finance* (Ithaca, NY: Cornell University Press, 2005) and Barry Eichengreen, *Globalizing Capital: A History of the International Monetary System* (Princeton University Press, 2nd edn, 2008). For a concise overview, see Richard N. Gardner, "The Bretton Woods-GATT System after Sixty-five Years: A Balance Sheet of Success and Failure", 2008, *Columbia Journal of Transnational Law*, 26.

institutions with strong powers and capacity in terms of management of international monetary relations and facilitation of post-World War II reconstruction (and subsequent development) efforts; (2) restriction on capital flows, a policy that relied on closed financial markets, which retained a largely domestic focus, at least, until the development of the eurodollar market in the mid-1960s; and (3) open markets for trade and investment.

These principles played an irreplaceable role in promoting development of the Western world, until the Eastern countries, who have withdrawn from the arrangements for many decades, re-engaged in the 1980s. As Avgouleas's description, the web of economic interactions/relationships among closed national systems was based on and managed through two interlinked international organizations:[1] the IMF and the World Bank. Another international body that was part of the original framework, the International Trade Organization (ITO), being responsible to foster liberalization of trade and investment flows. Furthermore, the newly built UN and its Economic and Social Council (EcoSoc) were assigned with responsibility to conduct the overall political co-ordination of economic affairs, even though they never live up to people's initial expectations. In this period, there were a number of various levels of economic crises, destroying the system of fixed exchange rates envisaged in the Bretton Woods framework before the World War I. Hence a great deal of obloquy and doubts attacked the unfettered international capital flows. And the IMF and the World Bank worked for the co-ordination of national financial markets and served as the main approach for capital flows either in the form of foreign exchanges loans or development finance. Subsequently, we will introduce some important international organizations established in this period.

In 1944, the United Nations-sponsored financial conference was held in Bretton Woods. In the same year, the International Monetary Fund Agreement was signed at the meeting. The main designers of the International Monetary Fund are John Maynard Keynes, a member of the Fabian Society, and Harry Dexter White, US Deputy Treasury Secretary. The terms of the agreement were implemented a year later. And in 1946, the International Monetary Fund (IMF) was formally established as part of the reconstruction plan after the end of World War II and officially opened in 1947. Its role is to monitor currency exchange rates and trade among countries, provide technical and

---

① Emilios Avgouleas, *Governance of Global Financial Markets*, Cambridge University Press, New York, 2012, p.160.

financial assistance to ensure that the global financial system is functioning properly. It is headquartered in Washington, DC. The "Special Drawing Rights" we often hear was created by the organization in 1969.

Transnational Regulatory Network (TRN) is one of the most necessary part of international financial governance system. There is a tentative definition of TRNs:[1]they are informal multilateral forums that bring together representatives from national regulatory agencies or departments to facilitate multilateral cooperation on issues of mutual interest within the authority of the participants. This definition distinguishes TRNs from formal treaty-based international organizations, such as the WTO, IMF, World Bank, and European Union, as well as from regulatory forums intended to facilitate the development and implementation of binding international law instruments, such as the multiple networks of national regulators that assist the European Union in its regulation of financial services. It also excludes purely bilateral arrangements, such as mutual recognition and cooperation agreements between the U.S. Securities and Exchange Commission (SEC) and individual foreign securities regulators, and high-level networks of heads of state or government or cabinet-level officials, such as the G-7 or the British Commonwealth. Finally, while this definition does not exclude networks in which nongovernmental actors participate in an advisory capacity, it assumes that government participants retain the authority to approve and implement the resulting regulatory decisions or standards.

Another organization would be introduced here is the World Bank/International Bank for Reconstruction and Development (IBRD). After the World War Ⅱ , the demand of investment in reconstruction was urgent definitely from the countries severely damaged. IBRD was assigned with this responsibility to co-ordinate and provide financial support for post-World War Ⅱ reconstruction and development. Its main objectives were:[2] (1) to assist in the reconstruction and development of member countries by facilitating capital investment for productive purposes, including the restoration of economies destroyed or disrupted by war, the reconversion of productive facilities to peacetime needs and the encouragement of the development of productive facilities and resources in less developed countries. (2) To promote private foreign investment by means of guarantees or participation in loans and other investments made by private investors and when private

---

[1] Verdier, PierreHugues. "Transnational Regulatory Networks and Their Limits", *Social Science Electronic Publishing*, 2009.

[2] IBRD Articles of Agreement, Art. I—unchanged since 1944.

capital is not available and provide loans on reasonable terms.

The IBRD's difference from mainstream banks was that its shareholders were governments and its principal objective was not profit maximization. The World Bank's purpose was to help European countries and Japan rebuild after World War II. In addition, it should assist the economic development of African, Asian and Latin American countries. At the outset, World Bank loans were concentrated on large-scale infrastructure such as highways, airports and power plants. After the "graduation" of Japan and Western European countries (to a certain level of per capita income), the World Bank is fully concentrated in developing countries. Since the early 1990s, the World Bank has also begun lending to Eastern European countries and the former Soviet Union countries.

The emergence of a number of multilateral development bodies between 1960s and mid-1990s was countless, including:[①] (1) UN development initiatives such as the United Nations Development Programme (UNDP) and the United Nations Conference on Trade and Development (UNCTAD). (2) Regional development banks, modeled on the IBRD, such as the African Development Bank (AfDB), the Asian Development Bank (ADB), the Inter-American Development Bank (IADB), and (in the 1990s), the European Bank for Reconstruction and Development (EBRD).[②] (3) A range of other multilateral financial institutions, such as the European Investment Bank (EIB), the International Fund for Agricultural Development (IFAD), the Islamic Development Bank (IsDB), the Nordic Development Fund, and Nordic Investment Bank (NIB) and the OPEC Fund for International Development. (4) National development agencies and aid agencies, such as Australian Agency for International Development (AusAID), the Canadian International Development Agency (CIDA), the Japan International Cooperation Agency (JICA), the UK Department for International Development (DFID) and the US Agency for International Development (USAID). Most of these institutions have played an important role in the development of the global development agenda and have culminated in many aspects by endorsing the UN Millennium Development Goals. In addition to providing low credit, aid donations, project management expertise and technical assistance, regional banks and development organizations are also active in the area of legal reform. And the World Bank in the first decade of

---

① Emilios Avgouleas, *Governance of Global Financial Markets,* Cambridge University Press, New York, 2012, p.181.

② A detailed description of the activities of the EBRD can be found at www.ebrd.com/.

this century and the European Bank for Reconstruction and Development in the 1990s would be exemplars.

Moving to the next phase of International financial governance, we will introduce the overview of Intermediate phase: a "New International Financial Architecture", from 1998 to 2008. First of all, we need to know that any pre-1998 governance structures innovation was no more than an incremental evolution of the Bretton Woods framework, which was disable to adopt the changes of the times (developing wave of financial innovation, liberalization and market integration), proved by the Asian Crisis in 1997. Without any prediction or forward-looking management as improvement for the International financial governance, similar crises were inevitable. Beyond all doubt, there was a strong need for new governance structures with more developed warning system and more stringent regulatory system to prevent and manage crises better after the Asian Crisis. On the one hand, the establishment of a New International Financial Architecture (NIFA) is to restore international confidence in financial governance, and on the other hand, to compensate for the shortcomings of the first phase. The governance/monitoring/regulatory areas that required strengthening were, according to Camdessus, the then head of the IMF:[1] (1) surveillance of national economic policies, which should be facilitated by fuller disclosure of all relevant economic and financial data; (2) regional surveillance in order to encourage countries in the same region to discipline each other in order to prevent contagion; (3) revamped prudential regulation and supervision leading to (resilient) financial sector reform; (4) more effective structures for debt workouts, both at the national level and international level; (5) capital account liberalization to increase the orderliness of and access to international capital markets; (6) world-wide promotion of good governance and reduction of corruption; and (7) strengthening International financial institutions (IFIs), both in terms of resources, authority and legitimacy, by broadening representation.

However, the places including compulsory monitoring mechanisms, supervisory capacity and a binding framework for the management of cross-border crises that really need reform were still not solved. The Financial Stability Forum (FSF) was the only newly established body, while NIFA arrangements strengthened the function and role of already existing standard-setting bodies.

---

[1] M. Camdessus, "The Role of the IMF: Past, Present and Future", IMF Speech 98/4, Remarks at the Annual Meeting of the Bretton Woods Committee, Washington DC, 13 February 1998; M. Camdessus, "Reflections on the Crisis in Asia", IMF Speech 98/3, Address to the Extraordinary Ministerial Meeting of the Group of 24, Caracas, Venezuela, 7 February 1998.

In general, according to Avgouleas, the NIFA system had four levels, compromising both new IFIs and existing ones:[1] (1) inter-governmental (state-to-state contact) groups, mainly combinations of G-7/G-8-10;[2] (2) international standard-setting bodies, largely of a technocratic nature; (3) implementation of standards-in principle a domestic process but in practice developing countries received technical assistance through a variety of international, regional and bilateral sources, which also in some cases lobbied for or "coerced" implementation (e.g. through the IMF conditionality); and (4) monitoring implementation of standards, through the IMF/World Bank Financial Sector Assessment Program.

These four levels of NIFA were the most significant improvements, namely the soft law system acquired harder edges. The analysis of the previous studies by Avgouleas showed six general characteristics of standard-setting under NIFA:[3] (1) The emergence of an international consensus on the key elements of a sound financial and regulatory system, at least within the G-10 countries. (2) The foundation of principles and practices by international groupings of technocratic authorities with relevant expertise and experience, such as the Basel Committee on Banking Supervision (BCBS), International Organization of Securities Commissions (IOSCO), International Accounting Standards Board (IASB) and International Association of Insurance Supervisors (IAIS), where the influence of industry is of critical value. (3) Market discipline, which for the first time becomes an explicit pillar of supervisory practice, probably as a result and natural extension of Washington Consensus policies. (4) Liberalization of access to national markets used as an incentive for the adoption of sound supervisory systems, better corporate governance and other key elements of a robust financial system. (5) Promotion of supervisory independence. (6) No formal supra-national supervisory or regulatory body being created with standing in international law meaning that, as a result, ultimate responsibility for policy implementation and supervision rested with national authorities.

---

[1] Emilios Avgouleas, *Governance of Global Financial Markets,* Cambridge University Press, New York, 2012, p.187.

[2] For an overview of the development of the "G" groups and their impact on the evolution of international financial regulation see Lawrence G. Baxter, "Internationalization of Law: The 'Complex' Case of Bank Regulation", in William Van Caenegem and Mary E. Hisock (eds.), *The International of Law: Legislating, Decision-making, Practice, and Education*, Cheltenham: Edward Elgar, 2010.

[3] Emilios Avgouleas, *Governance of Global Financial Markets,* Cambridge University Press, New York, 2012, p.188.

The third phase of International financial governance is the emerging architecture (the post-2008 period). There are various reform proposals emerging as the serious result of the Asian financial crisis. In Avgouleas's opinion, the reform initiatives were two-fold:[①] (1) reform of supervisory structures to facilitate regulatory co-operation and crisis management; and (2) replacement and enhancement of international standards to radically improve the quality of international financial regulation.

This new architecture is based on three changes or reforms. One is the emergence of the G-20.[②] The second one is FSF's successor the Financial Stability Board (FSB), whose main mission is the co-ordination of the standard-setting process and oversight of the standard-setting TRNs.[③] And the reformed IMF.[④] Another important role designed for the joint regulatory bodies is called "supervisory colleges", taking the responsibilities to provide co-ordination and conduct the supervision of large systemically important cross-border financial institutions.

Nevertheless, there was no radical reform of this system, omitting the regulatory and supervision problems. Moreover, reforms paid no attention to mutually promoting relationship between financial development and economic growth. Although the economic crisis is still very likely to occur in the future, these reforms are also a contribution to the thorough reform later.

13.2.4 A Evolutionary Model for Global Financial Governance

As mentioned above, the previous reforms paid no attention to these shortcomings: (1) the cross-border supervision of very big financial

---

① Emilios Avgouleas, *Governance of Global Financial Markets,* Cambridge University Press, New York, 2012, p.204.

② Claudia Schmucker and Katharina Gnath, "From the G8 to the G20: Reforming the Global Economic Governance System", Garnet Working Paper No.73/09, 2010, www.garneteu,org/fileadmin/documents/working_papers/7310.pdf.

③ Douglas W. Arner and Michael W. Taylor, "The Global Credit Crisis and the Financial Stability Board: Hardening the Soft Law of International Financial Regulation?", *University of New South Wales Law Journal*, 488, 2009.

④ For an overview for the emerging architecture see Mario Giovanoli and Diego Devos (eds.), *International Monetary and Financial Law; The Global Crisis* (Oxford University Press, 2010) and Giovanoli, "The Reform of the International Financial Architecture after the Global Crisis", *New York University Journal of International Law and Politics*, 42, 2009: 81.

institutions; (2) the management of emerging risks due to unpredictable combination/correlation of forces unleashed or shaped by financial innovation with other market and real economy forces; and (3) resolution of cross-border financial groups.

In this section, the corresponding proposals by Avgouleas for an evolutionary model for governance of global financial markets will be provided that would support effectively and further recent reforms protecting the ideal of open global markets and enhancing their legitimacy[①]. As he says, the legitimacy of the proposed structure rests on three arguments. First, the abstract concept of distributive justice in the international context. These should be considered of equal importance to other core human values (such as the protection of human rights) that all democratic societies tend to adhere to. Second, the proposed formal supranational structure would better defend the global systemic public interest than national/regional regulators and existing Transnational Regulatory Networks (TRNs). Thirdly, the new structure will contain a clear set of share values (in the form of general principles and sub-principles of governance), which will not only ensure its coherence, but will also provide greater recognition of the added value of public goods on a global scale (financial stability) : economic development and its impact on poverty eradication.

The four pillars of the proposed global governance structure supported by the same number of global administrative agencies constitute an ideal model for global financial governance: (1) Macro-prudential. The global systemic risk (macro-prudential) supervisor would monitor both macro-economic developments and the state of the global financial system, seen as encompassing national, regional and international financial systems and the shadow banking sector, should comprise a revamped IMF. Assigning this duty, by means of an international treaty, to a revamped IMF makes good sense, given also the IMF's monitoring role with respect to national balance of payments and sovereign indebtedness. in fact, the entanglement of financial sector stability and solvency with sovereign indebtedness and vice versa means that only a revamped IMF could effectively discharge the duties of global macro-prudential supervisor. (2) Micro-prudential. The micro-prudential supervisor will be able to directly supervise the Global Systemically Important Financial Institutions (G-SIFIs), which solves the

---

① Emilios Avgouleas, *Governance of Global Financial Markets*, Chapter 8, "An Evolutionary Model for Global Financial Governance", Part III, Cambridge University Press, New York, 2012.

problem of financial institutions "too big to fail" considered to be one of the cores of rebuilding the global financial governance framework, including banks or other financial institutions, such as insurance companies with large cross-border assets or debt bases. Its scope of powers and responsibilities will gradually extend to the global financial derivatives and securities markets to solve the management problems of block trades. And this role should be played by the restructured and expanded the Financial Stability Board. The Bank of International Settlements (BIS), in addition to its research "division", will be merged with the FSB. And it will basically operate from the existing BIS institutions in Basel, ensuring neutrality. (3) Financial policy, regulation, and knowledge supervisor. The third pillar should be composed of the Organization for Economic Co-operation and Development (OECD) and the research "division" of the BIS that are responsible for the prediction, monitoring, evaluation and management of emerging risks through financial innovation. In the view of Avgouleas, this new institution can be called the Global Financial Policy, Regulation and Knowledge Organization, and become the guiding ideology of international financial governance. (4) A global resolution authority. This pillar should comprise a newly built Global Resolution Authority which should deal with the resolution of big cross-border financial groups on the basis of a single resolution and insolvency model, aiming to allow bank shareholders and creditors to 'self-rescue' when the bank goes bankrupt, rather than accepting government bailouts as they did in the last European debt crisis. In addition, a single settlement agency can help insolvent banks to orderly bankrupt and keep the healthy part of the banking industry alive.

A new international treaty proposed by Avgouleas to support the following reforms can be concluded[1]: (1) Build the infrastructure to properly understand the emerging risks arising from financial innovation and financial regulation through a transparent process that leverages TRN's expertise and valuable private sector inputs. International institutions providing such valuable public services for global markets should be based on the capacity of the OECD and BIS research divisions. (2) Give the fund the role of global systemic risk/macro-prudential supervisors and provide them with the tools to correctly and timely identify risks arising from the shadow banking sector. (3) Establish a global structure of G-SIFSs micro-prudential regulation with a cross-border asset or liability base to limit its scope for regulatory arbitrage

---

[1] Emilios Avgouleas, *Governance of Global Financial Markets,* Chapter 8, "An Evolutionary Model for Global Financial Governance", Part Ⅲ, Cambridge University Press, New York, 2012.

and to provide appropriate and consistent regulation globally. This is the most sensitive issue of the proposed reforms and is bound to meet with the highest degree of opposition, especially political opposition. Therefore, the key of national regulators should represent the global authority, and the important decisions about G-SIFIs (for example by PCA measures or resolution)[①] will be discussed with key national regulators after making, and only agree with the proposed to simultaneously can make macro-prudential regulators and global solutions authorized institutions. (4) Establish global solution institutions to provide effective, credible and fair cross-border solutions for financial institutions, especially financial groups. (5) The establishment of a set of principles and the principle of secondary and to support the proposed management system operation, the management system will be at its highest point to maintain financial stability, but also will provide enough space for the regulatory standard, and without prejudice to the stability of the financial situation has the potential to promote economic growth and poverty eradication, it is an important part of the UN's Millennium Development Goals.

13.2.5 TFAs, Functions and Power in Global Finance

Contemporary multinational financial institutions include a variety of for-profit financial organizations that conduct business operations and institutional settings on an international scale. Among them, the dominant ones are multinational commercial banks, which are commonly referred to as Transnational Banks. In addition, they include various non-bank financial institutions such as multinational investment banks, mutual funds, arbitrage funds, pension funds, and insurance. the company.

The role of multinational financial institutions in international investment is mainly reflected in three aspects: (1) international direct investment through the establishment of branches overseas; (2) international indirect investment through international securities trading; and (3) multinational corporation financial investment.

The form taken by TFAs and the type of task it performs are determined by certain functions closely related to financial activities. For example, TFAs in the securities market may perform certain clearing and settlement

---

① PCA (Principal Components Analysis) Principal component analysis aims to use the idea of dimensionality reduction to transform multiple indicators into a few comprehensive indicators.

functions that allow the actual traded securities to be exchanged from one participant to another, but these functions may have nothing to do with insurance, which has completely different requirements. A TFA that targets professionals such as accountants or financial planners is likely to put more effort into training and certification than one that focuses on lobbying public authorities.

In views of McKeen-Edwards and Porter,[1] overall there are two main ways that functionality is brought into our analysis of TFAs. One is functional differentiation. This refers to the tendency of societies to become more and more differentiated by function over time, leading to the classification of global financial governance and the proliferation of increasingly specialized TFA, further challenging the unified financial dominant model.[2], functional differentiation is a way of managing complexity. Unique code emerges to manage specific different systems, which develop a degree of autonomy and incommensurable code with other systems. The second way is that form follows function, which we call organizational functionality. Actually, it was an insight of the international functionalism pioneered by David Mitrany in 1943[3]. The organization of TFAs is largely determined by the tasks they undertake. This also challenges the unified dominance model because people believe that the need to perform tasks in a specific way may limit the uniform exercise of power. These tasks may vary depending on the industry sector (such as banking, securities, or insurance) or the tasks they participate in or other characteristics of members, and their primary purpose is to influence public authorities, expand markets, or enhance the capabilities of TFA members.

We should also recognize that members and leaders of TFAs can pass or exercise power through multiple arrangements of people and things, most of which are beyond their full control. TFAs are an important mechanism for organizing networks and delivering actions, and their successes and failures respectively increase or weaken financial actors. TFAs not only participate in

---

① Heather McKeen-Edwards and Tony Porter, *Transnational Financial Associations and the Governance of Global Finance,* Chapter 1, Simultaneously published in the USA and Canada by Routledge, 2013.

② Luhmann, Niklas, *The Differentiation of Society*, New York Chichester, West Sussex: Columbia University Press, 1982.

③ Ashworth, Lucian M., and David Long, *New Perspectives on Inter national Function Alism,* London: Macmillon Press, 1999; Mitrany, D. A War-time Submission, 1941, *A F unctional Theory of Politics,* P. Taylor. London, LSE/Martin Robertson, 1975.

local power struggles, but also participate in the larger global financial power generation compared to other aspects of the contemporary world.

13.3 Multilateralism and Regionalism in Global Economic Governance

In this chapter, we will first classify the global economic governance into three major sectors, and then discuss the problems and solutions of economic governance from the perspectives of multilateralism and regionalism respectively.

13.3.1 Issue Areas and Methods

Global economic governance is our focus, covering different kinds of global economic issues including movement of goods, capital, humans, information and any combination thereof. In this chapter, we will choose three major sectors to be the objects of analysis, namely global monetary/financial affairs, international investment and international trade which are selected based on the traditional classification of international economic law, namely international monetary/financial law, international trade law and international investment law.

Actually, one of the most significant characteristics among these three sectors is the difference in the method of governance. The Bretton Woods system as a multilateral system and informal policy coordination through the club-model mechanism (G7, G8 and G20), are noticeable features of the governance of global monetary/financial affairs. And for the governance of international trade, their rules and policies are provided by a multilateral institution (the GATT and the WTO). However, the rules for governance of international investment are not created by any multilateral agreements. Instead, they come from bilateral agreements (bilateral investment treaties (BITs) and investment chapters of FTAs).

Another striking characteristic in these three sectors is the regional governance mechanism, which has come to play a greater role. Europe and Asia are the typical place with more burgeoning regional governance organizations in international monetary/financial governance. In international trade, an increasing number of bilateral and regional FTAs are being concluded, while Doha negotiation has been almost stalled for quite some time. BITs, investment chapters of FTAs and investor-state arbitration based on them are always the major governance mechanism, and their number has kept rising during the past two decades.

According to Nakagawa,[1] the recent surge of regionalism has made the task of governing the global economy more complicated and burdensome than before, since it has added to the methods of governance and the resulting burden of coordination among the different methods of governance. So in the following sections, we will this issue in these three sectors.

13.3.2 Solutions to Problems in Global Monetary/Financial Governance

The first multilateral global monetary governance mechanism we will analyse is the post-World War II system, namely the Bretton Woods system. Basically, the international monetary system was different from the system that architects of Bretton Woods system had anticipated. The transition period from war to peace was much longer than they predicted. Full convertibility of the major developed countries was not achieved until the end of 1958, though the IMF started its operation in 1947.

In Nakagawa's view, three interconnected problems emerged:[2] adjustment, liquidity and confidence, as the system evolved into a fixed exchange rate gold dollar standard. First of all, under Bretton Woods, the fear of unemployment delayed the deflationary adjustment needed by deficit countries, and short-term capital controls largely undermined the automatic mechanism of balance of payments adjustment. And the liquidity problem with the Bretton Woods system was that the various sources of liquidity were not sufficient to finance the growth of output and trade. By the late 1950s, the world currency had insufficient gold reserves, the international monetary fund had insufficient unconditional rights of drawing rights, and the supply

---

[1] Junji Nakagawa, *Multilateralism and Regionalism in Global Economic Governance.* Chapter 1, "An Introduction", First published 2011 by Routledge, Simultaneously published in the USA and the Canada.

[2] Junji Nakagawa, *Multilateralism and Regionalism in Global Economic Governance.* "The Postwar System for Global Monetary/Financial Governance", Chapter 1, "An Introduction", First published 2011 by Routledge, Simultaneously published in the USA and the Canada.

of dollars depended on the us balance of payments, again linked to the vagaries of government policy and confidence issues. As for the confidence issue, it involves portfolio shifts between the dollar and gold. As the rest of the world's monetary authorities hold more outstanding dollar debt relative to the gold reserves of the us currency, investors have less confidence in the dollar because all dollar holders are less likely to be able to convert their dollars into gold at a fixed price.

The Bretton Woods system became unstable until it collapsed with the termination of the convertibility of the dollar in August 1971. Through two years of realignment, the dollar par value was finally abandoned and the dollar become a floating currency, convertible into other currencies through the foreign exchange market. For this reason, the regulatory functions of the IMF have undergone substantial changes. In order to ensure the implementation of the fixed exchange rate system, it was responsible for monitoring the exchange rate system of each member country, and now it can truly supervise the financial and macroeconomic policies of member states. The IMF's target of providing short-term lending has also become developing countries that need to make up for the deficits, especially emerging market countries and former socialist countries that have been hit by the economic crisis. As well as the World Bank, most of the lending was absorbed into developing countries member through Marshall Plan, which was totally different from the drafters' original envision. After the shift to a floating exchange system, the mid- to long-term lending could be provided for more and more emerging market countries and former socialist countries, helping them reconstruct their economy. Definitely, the shift to a floating exchange system as financial liberalization, promoted the development of global financial markets, but it also increased the price instability and adverse events in the market and the spread and influence of the world, in other words, it binds the countries in the world market to the same rope, increasing the risk that needs to be faced. In order to tackle these problems, developed countries invented a number of new mechanisms for global monetary/ financial governance, which can be sorted into three groups according to Nakagawa's understanding of their areas of operation:[1] coordination of macroeconomic policy, crisis management and regulation of private financial institutions.

---

[1] Junji Nakagawa, *Multilateralism and Regionalism in Global Economic Governance,* "The Shift to a Floating Exchange System", Chapter 1, "An Introduction", First published 2011 by Routledge, Simultaneously published in the USA and the Canada.

Under the floating exchange rate system, the supply and demand of a currency are equated in the foreign exchange market. This does not guarantee an appropriate balance of payments. In addition, under the floating exchange rates, capital flows may be severely distorted due to inappropriate differences in interest rates and speculative activities in the foreign exchange market. This has led to the need to coordinate national monetary policies among national monetary authorities, especially the central bank, which goes beyond the IMF's mandate. Therefore, developed countries have designed an informal forum for monetary policy coordination or monetary governance of the club-model.

The first attempt at club-model macroeconomic policy coordination was the G7 summit meeting held in Paris in 1975. The G7 summit meeting has since been held regularly to discuss macroeconomic policy coordination and occasional issues of common political interest. And there were two club-model schemes launched for monetary policy by club-model coordination. One is the Plaza Accord in 1985, which was made by G5 (France, West Germany, Japan and the US and the UK), to jointly intervene in the foreign exchange market to induce the dollar to depreciate in an orderly manner against the major currencies in order to address the huge U.S. trade deficit. On 22 February 1987, the Louvre Accord was agreed by G6 (Canada, France, West Germany, Japan, the UK and the US), calling a halt to the constant depreciation of dollar caused by the Plaza Accord. The IMF has expanded its role in investigating member countries' monetary and macroeconomic policies, adding conditions to emergency loans for countries suffering from debt crises and/or monetary/financial crises. So the main targets of aid are the newly industrialized countries and least developed countries in the 1980s, as well as the former socialist countries since the late 1980s.The world bank has developed its regulatory functions through its Structural Adjustment Lending (SAL), which was established in March 1986 to help low-income developing countries overcome balance-of-payments difficulties resulting from economic restructuring. Therefore, we can clearly see that the G-7 and the IMF/World Bank have a division of labor in monitoring national monetary and macroeconomic policies. The former's monitoring targets are monetary and macroeconomic policies of developed countries, while the latter's targets are monetary and macroeconomic policies of developing countries and countries in transition.

For crisis management, the first institution for crisis management we will analyse is the Paris Club. The Paris Club is an international informal organization founded in 1956 by sovereign creditors to prevent a default of their lending to Argentina. It is currently composed of the 22 richest countries in the world, providing debt arrangements for debtor countries and creditor countries, such as debt restructuring, debt relief, and even debt cancellation. It had since been held sporadically to tackle sovereign debt default problems (in 1996 Indonesia), 1976 (Zaire) and 1981 (Poland). The Paris Club arranged $2.3 billion in debt for seven African countries under the Toronto terms, which was proposed at the G-7 summit in Toronto, Canada in June 1988 to implement macroeconomic and economic adjustment plans, with the main purpose of helping to reduce debts of low-income countries. The debt relief program proposed by the meeting has three main points: debt relief for one-third of debtor countries, rescheduling of debts at preferential interest rates, and extension of debt maturity. Since then the Paris Club has been the principal forum for dealing with sovereign debts with sovereign creditors.

The G20 is an international economic cooperation forum. It was established on September 25, 1999 by the finance minister of the G8 in Berlin, Germany. The first G20 summit was held in Washington, which is an informal dialogue. Mechanism consisting of the former G8 and the remaining 12 major economies (China, Argentina, Australia, Brazil, Canada, France, Germany, India, Indonesia, Italy, Japan, Korea, Mexico, Saudi Arabia, South Africa, Turkey, United Kingdom, the United States, Russia, and the European Union), aiming to promote open and constructive discussions and research on substantive issues between industrialized and emerging market countries in order to seek cooperation and promote international financial stability and sustained economic growth. One of important purposes for G20's establishment is the financial liberalization that enable more developing countries and former socialist countries to finance their development/transition from private creditors in addition to multilateral and sovereign creditors and this required enhanced coordination of bailout processes among the different categories of sovereign debts.

The 2008 Lehman crisis added something new to the structure and function of this club-mode mechanism. The G20 faces an issue of overlapping functions. As Nakagawa mentioned,[1] the G20 covers monetary and macroeconomic policy coordination, crisis management, global financial regulation, combating transnational money laundering and terrorist financing

---

[1] Junji Nakagawa, *Multilateralism and Regionalism in Global Economic Governance*, "Institutional Framework for Crisis Management", Chapter 1, "An Introduction", First published 2011 by Routledge, Simultaneously published in the USA and the Canada.

and transparency and information exchange on tax matters. For resolving this problem, the Financial Stability Board (FSB) was one of the coordinating mechanisms introduced by G20, formerly known as the Financial Stability Forum (FSF). It is tasked with developing and implementing regulatory policies and other policies that promote financial stability to address financial vulnerabilities. Membership of the FSF brought together:[1] (1) national authorities responsible for financial stability in significant international financial centers, namely treasuries, central banks, and supervisory agencies; (2) sector-specific international groupings of regulators and supervisors engaged in developing standards and codes of good practice; international financial institutions charged with surveillance of domestic and international financial systems and monitoring and fostering implementation of standard; and (3) committees of central bank experts concerned with market infrastructure and functioning.

Compared with the FSB's predecessor, Nakagawa points out several differences.[2] It is equipped with an enlarged membership to cover G20 members and an enhanced institutional structure, owning an FSB Plenary, a steering committee and three standing committees-for vulnerability assessment, supervisory and regulatory cooperation and standards implementation. Also, a Cross-Border Crisis Management Working Group was established by the FSB to supplant the predecessor's function.

The last groups of mechanisms for global monetary governance is the regulation of private financial institutions. Although the global financial market achieved record growth in the 1980s and 1990s, the collapse of financial institutions has increased, which has seriously damaged the financial markets of various countries. This has stimulated financial regulatory authorities in various countries to strengthen domestic financial regulation and international coordination.

Focusing on banking supervision, international coordination is consistent with the Basel Accord established by the Banking Supervision and Oversight Committee (Basel Committee) in 1988. The Basel Accord includes the capital component, the risk weight of the calculated assets, the indicator standard ratio (8%) and the transition period (by the end of 1992). After

---

① FSB, "History" Online, https://www.fsb.org/history-of-the-fsb/.

② Junji Nakagawa, *Multilateralism and Regionalism in Global Economic Governance.* "Institutional Framework for Crisis Management", Chapter 1, "An Introduction", First published 2011 by Routledge, Simultaneously published in the USA and the Canada.

several revisions, the Basel Accord was replaced by Basel Ⅱ in 2004. The basic principle of Basel Ⅱ is that banks are under the supervision of the main responsibility of risk management under the supervision of domestic banks. Basel Ⅱ also expands risk coverage to increase the computational risk weight of operational risk.

The Basel Committee on Banking Supervision, composed of 27 national banking regulators and senior representatives of the Central Bank, announced on September 12, 2010 that representatives of the parties reached an agreement on the content of Basel Ⅲ. As a new capital rule for the global banking industry, Basel Ⅲ will become a major financial reform measure after the financial crisis, and its results will be submitted to the G20 Seoul Summit in November 2010 for a final vote.

Under the agreement, commercial banks must raise capital ratios to strengthen their ability to withstand financial risks. The management meeting of the Basel Committee on Banking Supervision adopted a reform plan to strengthen the capital requirements of the banking system, namely Basel Ⅲ. The core content is to raise the minimum capital supervision standard for the global banking industry.

Although the Basel Accord is not a statutory clause, it actually plays a very important role as a standard, providing security for international banking activities in more than 100 countries, including non-Basel Member States.

As a whole, the regionalism monetary system becomes one of essential mechanisms for international finance governance. Some regionalism monetary mechanisms would be introduced here. The Asian Development Bank was conceived in the early 1960s as a financial institution that would be Asian in character and foster economic growth and cooperation in one of the poorest regions in the world. The ADB[1] is committed to achieving a prosperous, inclusive, resilient, and sustainable Asia and the Pacific, while sustaining its efforts to eradicate extreme poverty. It assists its members and partners by providing loans, technical assistance, grants, and equity investments to promote social and economic development. In terms of membership composition, it is composed of 68 members, 49 of which are from the Asia and Pacific region. Another regionalism monetary mechanism

---

[1] ADB, "Who we are" Online, https://www.adb.org/about/main.

is the European bank for reconstruction and development (EBRD),① created to help build a new post-cold war era in central and eastern Europe. Since then, it has played a historic role in fostering change in the region and beyond, acquiring unique expertise and investing more than 130 billion euros in a total of more than 5,200 projects, committed to further progress in 'market-oriented economies and promoting private and entrepreneurial innovation'. This has been the guiding principle of the EBRD since its inception in the early 1990s. Despite the new challenges and the welcome of new countries, this will continue to be the mission of the EBRD for years to come. The Inter-American Development Bank (IDB), a cooperative development bank founded in 1959 to accelerate the economic and social development of its Latin American and Caribbean member countries, is also a typical regionalism financial mechanism. It is owned by a total of 47 member countries, including the United States and some European nations. The IDB assists Latin American and Caribbean countries in formulating development policies and provides financing and technical assistance to achieve environmentally sustainable economic growth, increase competitiveness, enhance social equity, fight poverty, modernize the state, and foster free trade and regional integration.② There is a growing desire in all regions to establish regional economic organizations. While the region has global institutions to promote this, regional organizations are more focused on discussing the issues and policies of the region or of a relatively small number of member states. There is scope for further cooperation in strengthening markets and institutions in order to accelerate integration and stability in the region and to deepen common preferences in policy objectives, including currency and exchange rate issues.

13.3.3 Solutions to Problems in Global Trade Governance

The relationship between multilateralism and regionalism in global trade governance is really special, for their fungibility and complementarity. From the GATT to the WTO, global trade governance experienced substantive transformation of both structure and functions. In Nakagawa's opinion, it can be summed up in two aspects: one is the universalization of the WTO. The WTO is a virtually universal organization for trade liberalization, which originally started with 128 members and it had 164 members as of July 2016, with 23 countries on the list of observers who are conducting

---

① EBRD, "History of the EBRD", https://www.ebrd.com/who-we-are/history-of-the-ebrd.html.

② IDB, https://www.investopedia.com/terms/i/idb.asp.

accession negotiation. Another is the success of the judicialized dispute settlement mechanism. Establishment of a panel and the adoption of the reports of the panel and the Appellate Body were practically automated with the introduction of the negative consensus formula. The establishment of the Appellate Body enhanced confidence in the quality of reports provided through the dispute settlement procedure. Since 1995, 590 disputes have been brought to the WTO and over 350 rulings have been issued.

However, the WTO, which seems to have made great achievements, actually faces the problem of inefficient decision-making due to these improvements. Due to the increasing membership and the reform of the decision-making mechanism, the decision-making process is no longer as efficient as before. Countries with different opinions try to solve the existing differences by raising questions and communicating and negotiating. Finally, the document is submitted to all members for approval. This "concentric circle" approach applies to every item on the negotiating agenda, and the grouping of members varies from project to project. At the same time, it makes it very difficult for members to reach a joint agreement in negotiations, which makes it very difficult for WTO members to achieve a package deal. The improvements of the WTO dispute settlement mechanism have also increased the difficulty of reaching consensus in the Doha round of negotiations, because members of the WTO, whether developed or developing, know that the outcome of the negotiations will be implemented through dispute settlement mechanisms, so they are always loath to bear any legal obligations that may bring losses in the future.

As these problems caused by the improvements of the WTO, many countries are seeking for further trade liberalization through bilateral or regional channels. Regional trade agreements (RTAs) are a key fixture in international trade relations. Over the years RTAs have not only increased in number but also in depth and complexity. WTO members and the Secretariat work to gather information and foster discussions on RTAs to enhance transparency and to increase understanding of their impact on the wider multilateral trading system. The following figure shows all RTAs notified to the GATT/WTO (1948-2019), including inactive RTAs, by year of entry into force. It shows that the number of bilateral and regional FTAs has been steadily increasing in recent years.

Actually, there is disagreement about the impact of RTA on global trade liberalization. While regional trade arrangements are intended to benefit signatories, the expected benefits may be reduced if resource allocations and

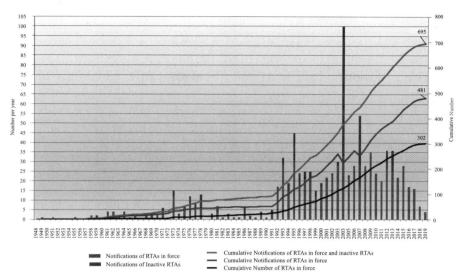

Figure 13-1 Evolution of Regional Trade Agreements in the world, 1948-2019

Note: Notifications of RTAs: goods, services & accessions to an RTA are counted separ ately. The cumulative lines show the numeber of RTAs/notifications that were in fonce for a given year The notifications of RTAs in force are shown by year of entry into force and the notificatios of inactive RTAs are shown by inactive year.

Source: WTO, www.wto.org/english/tratop_e/region_e/region_e.htm#facts.

trade and investment transfers are not minimized. In addition, the increase in regional trade agreements has created a phenomenon of overlapping members. When traders have difficulty meeting multiple sets of trade rules, this may hinder trade flows. In addition, as the scope of regional trade agreements expands to include policy areas that are not multilaterally regulated, the risk of inconsistencies between different agreements may increase. Most old regional trade arrangements include only tariff liberalization and related rules such as trade protection, standards and rules of origin. Regional trade agreements increasingly include service liberalization and commitments in service rules, investment, competition, intellectual property, e-commerce, environment and labor, which can lead to regulatory confusion and implementation problems.

According to the information from WTO online, many WTO members continue to be involved in negotiations to create new RTAs. Like the agreements in force, most new negotiations are bilateral. However, a recent development has been negotiations among several WTO members. This includes negotiations in: (1) The Asia-Pacific Region for a Comprehensive and Progressive Trans-Pacific Partnership (CPTPP) Agreement, between 11 parties; (2) Asia between Association of Southeast Asian Nations (ASEAN) members and six other WTO members with which ASEAN has agreements in force (the Regional Comprehensive Partnership Agreement); (3) Latin America to form the Pacific Alliance between Chile, Colombia, Mexico and Peru; and (4) Africa with the Tripartite Agreement between parties to the Common Market for Eastern and Southern Africa (COMESA), the East African Community (EAC) and the Southern African Development Community (SADC) and the African Continental Free Trade Agreement (AfCFTA).

Such plurilateral agreements, once in force, have the potential to reduce the spaghetti bowl of RTAs especially if they supersede existing bilateral agreements and develop common rules (such as for rules of origin) to be applied by all parties to the agreement.

On December 18, 2006, the WTO board of governors adopted the Decision on the Transparency Mechanism for Regional Trade Agreements[1] to guide the WTO committee's review of Regional Trade Agreements concluded among WTO members. Increased transparency is required for WTO members to review relevant regional trade agreements.

Under the transparency mechanism, the WTO Regional Trade Agreement Committee will review RTAs in accordance with Article XXIV of the GATT and Article V of the GATS. At the same time, the Trade and Development Commission will review RTAs in accordance with the terms of the license (trade arrangements between developing countries). This indicates that the way in which the WTO treats regional trade agreements has shifted from coordination to management. Under this mechanism, the obligations that members of regional trade agreements need to perform are mainly early notification obligations, notification obligations, compliance with transparency procedures obligations, and follow-up notification and reporting obligations.

The Mechanism also stipulates issues such as the institutions responsible for implementation and technical support to developing countries. Specifically, it includes the following aspects: (1) parties to regional trade agreements should notify the WTO in a timely manner; (2) the notification obligation of the contracting party is more specific and specific; (3) refined the review

---

[1] Transparency Mechanism for RTAs, WTO online, https://www.wto.org/english/tratop_e/region_ e/trans_mecha_e.htm.

obligations of WTO members and set a procedure for improving the transparency of the review; (4) provision of notification and reporting after the change or revision of the contents of the regional trade agreement and before the end of the implementation period.

The mechanism enables the WTO and its members to keep abreast of developments in regional trade agreements, and parties to new regional trade agreements will be subject to more rigorous and transparent and effective reviews. Although it greatly facilitates the consideration of the agreement by other WTO members, the preparation of the report requires additional information from the parties to the agreement, which makes it more difficult for the parties to coordinate the relationship between multilateral trade negotiations and regional and bilateral trade negotiations.

13.3.4 Solutions to Problems in Global Investment Governance

In terms of international investment governance, there are many obstacles in the development of multilateral governance institutions or institutions. An agreement by the Organization for Economic Cooperation and Development to draft and organize negotiations, the Multilateral Investment Agreement, is one example of this. The main objective of the agreement is to remove barriers and distortions in international investment and promote optimal allocation of economic resources to promote economic growth, employment and improve living standards. The initial framework includes investment protection, investment liberalization and dispute resolution. However, due to the opposition and resistance of developing countries to the general protection rules for foreign investment, it finally failed in 1998.

Compared with the development of multilateralism governance, bilateral investment or regional international investment governance has been fully developed, especially in developing countries. They are more inclined to attract foreign investment in this way, according to the *World Investment Report 2019*[①]published by the UNCTAD, International investment policymaking is in a dynamic phase, with far-reaching implications. In 2018, countries signed 40 international investment agreements (IIAs). For at least 24 existing treaties, terminations entered into effect. The impact on the global IIA regime of novel features in new agreements, including

---

① *World Investment Report 2019*, UNCTAD online, https://unctad.org/en/PublicationsLibrary/wir2019_en.pdf.

some mega-regional treaties with key investor countries, will be significant. Many countries are also developing new model treaties and guiding principles to shape future treaty making. As the surge in investor–State dispute settlement (ISDS) cases continues, with at least 71 new arbitration initiated in 2018, the total ISDS case count may reach one thousand by the end of 2019. About 70 per cent of the publicly available arbitral decisions in 2018 were rendered in favour of the investor, either on jurisdiction or on the merits, namely, the global investment governance has been developed as a regime for the protection of investors' interests against the exercise of host states' sovereignty, where investors are from developed countries and host states are developing countries. In Borchard's views,[1] this one-way traffic characteristic of global investment governance can be explained by its historical origin, which originated in the case law and diplomatic practice of Europe and the USA in the late nineteenth and early twentieth century to protect their investors' interests in Latin America.

The surge in international investment agreements and investor-state arbitration cases in recent years reflects the systemic evolution of global investment governance from a rapid expansion of IIAs at a bilateral level to a more integrated and elaborate approach. Nakagawa proposed that there are some indications that the prospects for international investment agreements are being consolidated in the following areas:[2] (1) efforts to create regional, notably South-South, investment areas; (2) the competence shift within the EU, which is likely to lead an increasing number of IIAs by the EU; and (3) efforts by numerous countries to reassess their international investment policies (Russian Federation in 2001, France in 2006 and Colombia, Mexico, Austria and Germany in 2008) to better align them with development considerations.

In recent years, in the international investment governance, how to achieve coherence between them has become a focus because of the emergence of many international investment agreements. In addition, the development trend of bilateral agreements and regional agreements has also received more attention.

---

[1] Borchard, Edwin M., "Some Lessons from the Civil Law", *University of Peensy Ivania Law Review*, 64, 1915: 570.

[2] Junji Nakagawa, *Multilateralism and Regionalism in Global Economic Governance*, "Changing Landscape of Global Investment Governance", Chapter 1, "An Introduction". First published 2011 by Routledge, Simultaneously published in the USA and the Canada.

Anthony VanDuzer argued that Asia-Pacific Economic Cooperation (APEC) could play a role in governing and rationalizing international investment agreements and addressing the challenges of coherence.[1] A growing number of international investment agreements concluded in the form of uncoordinated, lead to the scope of international investment agreements is becoming more and more diversified and complicated, for each country at least two levels of policy coherence put forward severe challenges: coherence between domestic policy and international obligations and the coherence between different international obligations. He explored the possibility of APEC addressing these challenges by establishing a more coordinated international investment regime. As a broad group of developed and developing countries with the overall goal of promoting sustainable economic growth through trade and investment liberalization in the Asia-Pacific region, he said, APEC is in a good position to develop consistent investment rules among its members. However, at the APEC summit meeting in December 2008, the failure to adopt a model investment chapter for FTAs indicates that the diversity of APEC members is a major obstacle to fulfilling this role.

Markus Burgstaller, a leading individual in public international law in the UK, is also interested in resolving this problem.[2] Nevertheless, he deals with the possibility of securing coherence among IIAs by vertically allocating competences for IIAs within the framework of European regional integration. With the entry into force of the Treaty of Lisbon at the end of 2009, the EU will have full authority to conclude a comprehensive investment treaty with third countries. This will strengthen the Committee's negotiating capacity to promote and protect foreign direct investment. This will also lead to an increase in efficiency, as the EU and third countries will protect investments in 28 member states at the same time. However, even as the Treaty of Lisbon enters into force, continued fragmentation of competences between the union and its member states due to the limitation of the EU's competence concerning foreign direct investment, including portfolio investment, may lead to confusion within the EU and the third states. Compared with the international trade governance, one of

---

① J. Anthony VanDuzer, Rationalizing International Investment Obligations, "The Role of APEC", Chapter 8, First published 2011 by Routledge, Simultaneously published in the USA and the Canada.

② Markus Burgstaller, Vertical Allocation of Competences for EU Investment Treaties, "The Union's Foreign Direct Investment Competence under the Treaty of Lisbon", Chapter 9, First published 2011 by Routledge, Simultaneously published in the USA and the Canada.

significant difference is that less general exception provision to preserve the regulatory autonomy of the state for the sake of public goods was set in the international investment governance. Daniel Kalderimis asserts that this reflects the different philosophical basis of the GATT/WTO regime of "embedded liberalism" as opposed to the "laissez-faire liberalism" of most BITs.[①] He suggests that the absence has contributed to inconsistent and unpersuasive reasoning. As arbitral tribunals should not be forced to create a new law in this area, he suggests that BITs should expressly refer to public goods so that host states may pursue their legitimate policy objectives such as sustainable development and protection of internationally recognized human rights.

As for the analysis of the development of both bilateral investment treaty and regional investment treaty, Chunbao Liu analyses and compares the role of BITs and FTAs in China's investment policy[②]. Through comparative study and analysis, he argues that, older generations of China's BITs tend to be supplanted by investment rules in FTAs instead of revised BITs, namely, FTAs will receive more attention in China's investment policy in the future. He also asserts that international investment rules have been evolving towards becoming more investor-friendly in both China's BITs and FTAs, which can be explained by domestic regulatory reform and the protection of China's outward investment.

To conclude, we have introduced international economic governance by three sectors in the perspectives of multilateralism and regionalism. Even if there are great different of these governance in three sectors as a result of their different development path and different roles they need to play in international economy, noticeably, the surge of regionalism is their common characteristic of the development over these years. The improvement and development of regional economic governance is of course important, but today, when multilateral economic governance is facing many impediments, how to achieve a subtle balance between the two will be an inevitable problem.

---

① Daniel R. Kalderimis, *Investment Treaties and Public Goods*, "The Absence of General Exception Provisions in Investment Treaties", Chapter 10, First published 2011 by Routledge, Simultaneously published in the USA and the Canada.
② Chunbao Liu, *China's International Investment Treaty Policy*, "Overview of China's participation in IIAs", Chapter 11, First published 2011 by Routledge, Simultaneously published in the USA and the Canada.

13.4 The Reform of International Economic Governance

13.4.1 A Redesign of Banking Regulation

After the financial crisis of 2008, Basel II collapsed, and a series of problems have led to the exploration of new ways of governance. After a few years, global banking management has undergone fundamental changes.

In the process of pursuing change around the world, there are two types of governance programs that are constantly being refined and shaped. According to Mika Viljanen,[①] on the global level, the newly founded Financial Stability Board (FSB) oversaw and overhaul of the Basel Accord. In the reforms, global banking regulators attempted to fix the Basel Accord shortcomings unearthed by the crisis. The Basel II 5[②] and Basel III [③] reforms yanked up capital requirements, improved capital quality, enhanced risk coverage and attempted to mend many of the failed risk technologies. At the same time, a series of local regulatory projects were launched outside the framework of the Basel Accord. The United States enacted the Dodd-Frank Wall Street Reform and Consumer Protection Act and the Volcker rule. The EU Commission issued a proposal non-Basel based banking reform package in January 2014, while Germany had already implemented its own set of reforms with Trennbankengesetz that was the US legislation after the Great Crisis of the 1930s, strictly dividing investment banking and commercial banking to ensure that commercial banks avoid the risks of the securities industry. The United Kingdom put together the *Financial Services (Banking Reform) Act in* 2013. Among all these initiatives, the first to be impacted is the rules governing the structure of the banking group, or the activities allowed within the banking group, usually at the same time. In particular, the

---

① Mika Viljanen, *Staying Global and Neoliberal or Going Somewhere Else? Banking Regulation after the Crisis*, "Local and Global Reactions: Diverging Paths", Chapter 5, First published 2016 by Routledge.
② Basel Committee on Banking Supervision, Revisions to the Basel II Market Risk Framework. July 2009 (Bank for International Settlement 2009); Basel Committee on Banking Supervision, Enhancements to the Basel II Framework. July 2009 (Bank for International Settlements 2009).
③ Basel Committee on Banking Supervision, Basel III: A Global Regulatory Framework for More Resilient Banks and Banking Systems. December 2010 (Bank for International Settlements 2010); Basel Committee on Banking Supervision, Basel III: International Framework for Liquidity Risk Measurement, Standards and Monitoring, December 2010 (Bank for International Settlement 2010).

goal of these programs is trade.

The global and local responses are in stark contrast. The core Basel regulatory strategy still pursues a neoliberal agenda that does not regulate if risks (such as current liquidity risks) are captured and properly capitalized. On the contrary, local government initiatives obviously go back to the past paternalistic, interventionist, and obviously non-neoliberal banking regulatory model by imposing business model restrictions. In sum, the two set of reform initiatives seem to diverge radically from each other.

Now, let us focus on the global responses. The New Basel Accord, also known as Basel II, has been implemented globally in 2007 after nearly a decade of revision and implementation, but it was during this year that the subprime crisis broke out and this subprime crisis that swept the world was truly Tested the Basel Capital Accord. Obviously, it has inherent problems such as procyclical effects, lack of effective measurement and supervision of complex risks of non-normal distribution, inherent limitations of risk measurement models, and difficulties in supporting data availability, but we cannot adopt the US umbrella regulation model. The shortcomings and shortcomings caused the subprime crisis to be attributed to the Basel Capital Accord.

In fact, the Basel Accord has also been revised and improved in the crisis. After revision, the Basel Accord has become more perfect, and the regulatory requirements for the banking industry have also been significantly improved. For example, in order to enhance the resilience of banks' unanticipated losses, banks are required to increase buffer capital and strictly supervise capital deduction projects to increase capital scale. And quality; in order to prevent the emergence of a liquidity crisis similar to Bear Stearns Cos, set up liquidity coverage regulatory indicators; to prevent 'too big to fail' systemic risk, assess large scale from asset size, interdependence and substitutability Capital needs of complex banks.

As mentioned above, since the Basel Committee issued and revised a series of regulatory rules in 2007, on September 12, 2010, the Basel Committee on Banking Supervision, composed of 27 national banking regulators and senior representatives of the Central Bank, the content of Agreement Ⅲ was agreed, and the global banking industry officially entered the era of Basel Ⅲ.

The Basel Ⅲ framework is a central element of the Basel Committee's response to the global financial crisis. It addresses a number of shortcomings in the pre-crisis regulatory framework and provides a foundation for a resilient banking system that will help avoid the build-up of systemic vulnerabilities. The framework will allow the banking system to support the real economy through the economic cycle.

The initial phase of Basel III reforms focused on strengthening the following components of the regulatory framework:[①] (1) improving the quality of bank regulatory capital by placing a greater focus on going-concern loss-absorbing capital in the form of Common Equity Tier 1 (CET1) capital; (2) increasing the level of capital requirements to ensure that banks are sufficiently resilient to withstand losses in times of stress; (3) enhancing risk capture by revising areas of the risk-weighted capital framework that proved to be acutely miscalibrated, including the global standards for market risk, counterparty credit risk and securitization; (4) adding macro-prudential elements to the regulatory framework, by: (i) introducing capital buffers that are built up in good times and can be drawn down in times of stress to limit procyclicality; (ii) establishing a large exposures regime that mitigates systemic risks arising from interlinkages across financial institutions and concentrated exposures; and (iii) putting in place a capital buffer to address the externalities created by systemically important banks; (5) specifying a minimum leverage ratio requirement to constrain excess leverage in the banking system and complement the risk-weighted capital requirements; and (6) introducing an international framework for mitigating excessive liquidity risk and maturity transformation, through the Liquidity Coverage Ratio and Net Stable Funding Ratio.

The Committee's now finalized Basel III reforms complement these improvements to the global regulatory framework. The revisions seek to restore credibility in the calculation of risk-weighted assets (RWAs) and improve the comparability of banks' capital ratios by: (1) enhancing the robustness and risk sensitivity of the standardized approaches for credit risk, credit valuation adjustment (CVA) risk and operational risk; (2) constraining the use of the internal model approaches, by placing limits on certain inputs used to calculate capital requirements under the internal ratings-based (IRB) approach for credit risk and by removing the use of the internal model approaches for CVA risk and for operational risk; (3) introducing a leverage ratio buffer to further limit the leverage of global systemically important banks (G-SIBs); and (4) Replacing the existing Basel II output floor with a

---

① High-level summary of Basel III reforms, Basel III, https://www.bis.org/bcbs/basel3.htm.

more robust risk-sensitive floor based on the Committee's revised Basel III standardized approaches.

13.4.2 Consequences of International Financial Reform

The crisis has led to major changes in regulatory standards, stricter regulatory practices, and institutional restructuring of financial regulation. However, in Alexander's view, the shortcomings still exist.[①] Basel III continues to allow global banking groups to use risk-weighted internal models to calculate credit, market and liquidity risk. These risk models rely on historical data and risk parameters based on individual banks' exposures rather than the entire Systemic risk of the financial system. Basel III still essentially relies on risk-weighted models that proved to be unreliable before the crisis because they were too focused on risk management at the individual company level, even though it consists of higher core Tier One and Tier One capital requirements,[②] liquidity requirements and a leverage ratio.[③] After the reform, the overall objective of the G20 and the FSB was set to reconstruct financial regulation along macro-prudential lines. The requirements of this objective could be concluded as two aspects. One is to stricter capital and liquidity requirements for individual institutions. And then to monitor risk exposures across the financial system is requested, including the transfer of credit risk to off-balance sheet entities and the general level of risk across the financial system. In addition, systemically important financial institutions will be subject to more stringent prudential regulatory requirements, including higher capital requirements and more review of their cross-border operations. To regulate the systemic risks and related risks across the financial system

---

① Kern Alexander, *The Reform of International Economic Governance*, "Consequences of Global Financial Governance Reform", Chapter 2. Part II, First published 2016 by Routledge.

② Tier One capital is the core measure of a bank's financial strength from a regulator's point of view. It is composed of core capital,[1] which consists primarily of common stock and disclosed reserves (or retained earnings),[2] but may also include non-redeemable non-cumulative preferred stock. The Basel Committee also observed that banks have used innovative instruments over the years to generate Tier One capital; these are subject to stringent conditions and are limited to a maximum of 15% of total Tier One capital. This part of the Tier One capital will be phased out during the implementation of Basel III.

③ A leverage ratio is any one of several financial measurements that look at how much capital comes in the form of debt (loans) or assesses the ability of a company to meet its financial obligations. The leverage ratio category is important because companies rely on a mixture of equity and debt to finance their operations, and knowing the amount of debt held by a company is useful in evaluating whether it can pay its debts off as they come due.

is the objective of the wide scope of macro-prudential regulation. According to Alexander[1], it will require a broader definition of prudential supervision to include both *ex ante* supervisory powers, such as licensing, authorization and compliance with regulatory standards, and *ex post* crisis management measures, such as recovery and resolution plans, deposit insurance and lender of last resort. The broad area of recovery and resolution will necessarily involve authorities in restructuring and disposing of banking assets and using taxpayer funds to bail out and provide temporary support for ailing financial institutions[2].

Once the macro-prudential regulation was fully executed, the role for host country authorities would be strengthened to regulate the cross-border financial groups' risk-taking compliant with the host country's macro-prudential objectives. Most host countries will be able to achieve macro-prudential goals using traditional macroeconomic policy instruments—exchange rates, interest rates and fiscal policies—and through the application of micro-prudential regulatory tools, such as the use of counter-cyclical capital requirements[3], loan-to-value ratios[4], and debt-to-income ratios[5]. In addition, according to the FSB/G20 proposals, countries early interventions are expected for bank or financial company's business practices, to take swift corrective action to comply with regulatory requirements, and if necessary

---

[1] Kern Alexander, *The Reform of International Economic Governance*, "Consequences of Global Financial Governance Reform", Chapter 2. Part Ⅱ, First published 2016 by Routledge.

[2] Indeed, the FSB has stated in its Key Attributes of Effective Resolution Regimes for Financial Institutions that: '[t]o improve a firm's resolvability, supervisory authorities or resolution authorities should have powers to require, when necessary, the adoption of appropriate measures, such as changes to a firm's business practices, structure or organization... To enable the continued operations of systemically important functions, authorities should evaluate whether to require that these functions be segregated in legally and operationally independent entities that shielded from group problems' FSB Key Attribute 10.5, www.financialstabilityboard.org/2014/10/r_141015/.

[3] The counter-cyclical capital buffer is intended to protect the banking sector against losses that could be caused by cyclical systemic risks. Counter-cyclical capital buffer requirement requires banks to add capital at times when credit is growing rapidly so that the buffer can be reduced when the financial cycle turns.

[4] Loan-to-value (LTV) ratio is an assessment of lending risk that financial institutions and other lenders examine before approving a mortgage. Typically, assessments with high LTV ratios are higher risk and, therefore, if the mortgage is approved, the loan costs the borrower more. Additionally, a loan with a high LTV ratio may require the borrower to purchase mortgage insurance to offset the risk to the lender.

[5] A debt-to-income, or DTI, ratio is derived by dividing your monthly debt payments by your monthly gross income. The ratio is expressed as a percentage, and lenders use it to determine how well you manage monthly debts—and if you can afford to repay a loan.

by requiring change of organization structure, for example, in a separate place for cross-border bank of local business capitalization subsidiary or independent legal entity, so that large systemically important institutions of the local business can be forced to restructure and/or recapitalize by local authorities. In sum, Alexander thinks that the local authority owning tools at its disposal to intervene in bank management (i.e., restrict dividends), restructure creditor claims or use taxpayer funds to recapitalize a systemically important institution or facilitate the transfer of assets to a private purchaser in a bank insolvency is one of key elements of any bank resolution regime.

13.4.3 Introduction to the WTO Law Reform

Faced with the uncertainty of the global economy, the WTO is presented with some interrelated and urgent needs. One of the challenges is to elaborate and clarify existing legal discipline applicable to Membership. Some agreements of the WTO require further clarification, while others require modification. Taking into account the unusually complex negotiations during the Uruguay Round, it is understandable to adopt such a position, but what is not foreseen is that the WTO negotiating department has experienced a widespread stalemate. In addition, the number of members is increasing (now close to universal), the situation related to technological and managerial change is constantly changing, and the need for legal reform has become a reality. Despite some progress in multilateral negotiations, it still faces considerable challenges. Even though it meets some difficulties, it's also a good opportunity for Members to seek for modification and enhance this regulatory system serving their interests. As a matter of fact, an institution such as the WTO with relatively elaborate set of disciplines and compliance mechanisms is especially attractive to Members for this purpose.

Two interrelated areas of WTO law will be analyzed in this section. One is institutional area that is in the creation of the new dispute settlement system at the WTO through the conclusion of the Dispute Settlement Understanding (DSU)[1]. In particular, the role that the Appellate Body has developed for itself. Despite the expectations of the negotiating parties and the implementation of the "constitutional" review, the WTO Appellate

---

[1] Understanding on Rules and Procedures Governing the Settlement of Disputes (15 April 1994) LT/UR/A-2/DS/U/1, http://docsonline.wto.org.

Body still placed itself at the heart of WTO law and provoked strong criticism for judicial activism and expansion of its remit[1]. In the words of one current Appellate Body member, they "shared a nearly missionary belief in the importance of the task entrusted to them"[2]. The Appellate Body has subsequently sought to maintain its legitimacy, acting as a "strategic quasi-judicial actor"[3] through decisions of particular "constitutional" importance[4]. Among the notable innovations, Van Den Bossche has identified Rule 4 of the Working Procedures, which sets out a mechanism for the "exchange of views" between all members before finalizing a report, as a key way to resolve the dangers of inconsistency and reduced authority that the three member divisions may otherwise have caused[5]. More broadly, these Working Procedures help to ensure that the Appellate Body's procedures are of a judicial nature, rather than the more informal dispute settlement practices before the WTO.[6] It is not necessarily that the Appellate Body have interpreted the DSU or ADA incorrectly but rather that the expectation of how they would interpret the text has not been borne out by practice.

The development of an independent judicial identity on the part of the Appellate Body has had a lasting impact on the way in which it interprets the covered agreements, as has the US' expectation of how it was to perform. In the Messenger's opinion, the specific provision made for the standard of review in the area of anti-dumping investigations is of interest. The

---

[1] For example, John Greenwald, "WTO Dispute Settlement: An Exercise in Trade Legislation?", *Journal of International Economic Law,* 2003, 113; Clause E. Barfield, *Free Trade, Sovereignty, Democracy: The Future of the World Trade Organization,* American Enterprise Institute, 2001; and from a Resolution of the US House of Representatives, "the WTO dispute settlement process is not working and has been guided by politics rather than by legal principles" (H Res 441, 17 November 2003) in response to the *US - Steel* dispute (DS252).

[2] Peter Van Den Bossche (n 20) 63-64. Also, Peter Van Den Bossche, "Most, If not All, Members Appointed in November 1995 Shared a Nearly Missionary Belief in the Importance of the Task Entrusted Them".

[3] James McCall Smith, "WTO Dispute Settlement: The Politics of Appellate Body Rulings", *World Trade Review* 65, 79, 2003. See also Ingo Venzke, *How Interpretation Makes International Law: On Semantic Change and Normative Twists,* OUP 2014, 188-195.

[4] Deborah Z Cass, "The Constitutionalization of International Trade Law: Judicial Norm Generation as the Engine of Constitutional Development in International Trade", *European Journal of International Law,* 2001, 39.

[5] Vanden Bossche, Peter, *The Law and Poling of the World Trade Organization: Text, Cases and Materials*, Cambridge University Press, 2008.

[6] Robert E. Hudec, "The New Dispute Settlement System of the WTO: An Overview of the First Three Years", *Minnesota Journal of Global Trade,* 1991, 1.

second area is related to substantive problems, one is the interpretation of Article 17.6 Anti-Dumping Agreement (ADA) and its role in the "zeroing" debate[1]. In 2004 and 2007, the EU filed a lawsuit against the United States for the United States to use the "zeroing" method when calculating the anti-dumping tax rate. A country has the right to impose anti-dumping duties on foreign products that enter its market at prices lower than the normal value of the product on the foreign market. Zeroing is a calculation device used by the United States to establish this anti-dumping duty. WTO rulings have confirmed that this method increases, often substantially, the exporter's margin of dumping and thus the amount of anti-dumping duty that the exporter has to pay. Subsequently, countries such as Brazil, China, Ecuador, Japan, South Korea, Mexico, Thailand and Vietnam also filed similar lawsuits[2]. While the provision, providing a different standard of review for panels in assessing the compliance of anti-dumping determinations than in other areas of WTO law, has been interpreted in a surprising way, contrary to the US administrative law principle upon which it was based (that of "Chevron deference"). Chevron deference is a doctrine of judicial deference that compels federal courts, in reviewing a federal government agency's action, to defer to the agency's construction of a statute that Congress directed the agency to administer. The original, two-step Chevron process was first outlined in the 1984 U.S. Supreme Court opinion for Chevron U.S.A., Inc. v. Natural Resources Defense Council, Inc.

In the Messenger's view, instances of reform or legal change that do not produce expected outcomes can help us to find explanations for how the legal framework at the WTO has developed in the way that is has. The objective here is not to criticize the Appellate Body's institutional development or interpretative method, but rather to identify the disjoint between expectations and outcomes. These failures indicate that there are difficulties in designing a system or set of rules to serve their own interests. Nonetheless, we can learn from these experiences and pay attention to the key role of institutional identity and interest in shaping the subsequent application of rules, although it is important to note that identity is variable and ever more in the increasingly multipolar world economy.

---

① Agreement on Implementation of art VI of the General Agreement on Tariffs and Trade 1994, 15 April 1994, LT/UR/A-1A/3, http://docsonline.wto.org.

② Anti-dumping: What is Zeroing? — guide, EUbusiness online, www.eubusiness.com/topics/trade/zeroing/.

13.4.4 Introduction to Investment Law Reform

For about half a century, the promotion and protection of investment have been the primary conditions on which the international investment law system and the international investment agreement (IIA) have been based. Concluding these agreements, states have offered investors safeguards such as fair and equitable treatment, full protection and security, protection in case of expropriation, most-favoured-nation treatment, and guarantees of free capital transfers, in tandem with the possibility of recourse to investor-State arbitration. To strengthen investment protection, countries are beginning to put their policy space and capacity into action, including measures to protect the public interest in crisis situations. The limits of the system are clear after Argentina's arbitration over measures taken by South American countries to resolve their 2001 economic and financial crisis. This, combined with the experience of the industrialized countries themselves in investor and national/regional arbitration, seems to have created an urgent need for reform in the North American Free Trade Agreement (NAFTA). International investment law has been reformed for the past decade. Reforms are often the result of criticism of systems that threaten or threaten the existence of international investment protection regimes. Part of the criticism is also due to the recent economic crisis, which in Europe, the recent global recession, has been linked to arbitration cases involving Argentina's economic and financial crisis and debt restructuring. While it is difficult to determine the extent to which these specific factors encourage the drafting of special provisions, there is no doubt that new exceptions to EU treaties relating to measures taken in the event of economic crisis and prudential measures, subject to investment agreements, allow room for interpretation of investment courts and allow more freedom for the host economy in dealing with such cases. In this sense, new substantive standards and accompanying exceptions introduce a balanced measure and will be welcomed. Similarly, provisions aimed at improving the functioning of investor-State arbitration systems, including those of States that may deviate from measures taken within the scope of the Treaty, are new sensitive to the protection of the public interest and indirectly refer to the capacity of States to deal with crisis situations. As cases related to Argentina's debt restructuring and the recent financial crisis have yet to be decided, there are still signs of how the court will deal with new issues, including how to deal with new treaty provisions and investment policies in the near future.

Titi gives her opinion on the substantive standards.[1] Under the new investment policy, the EU seeks to achieve a "better balance" between the rights of state management and investment protection and the design of a "clearer and better standard".[2] These two objectives go hand in hand, and the Commission is of the view that investment protection must be clearly defined without leaving room for "interpretative ambiguity", which is a particularly important issue, as it is a question of "State's right to regulate for public policy objectives".[3] In this regard, the relevance of measures affecting the financial sector and dealing with the economic crisis is clearly obvious, and the European Commission stresses that the principles are the right of States to pursue legitimate public policy objectives as enshrined in EU FTAs will apply to the investment protection provisions of the new EU agreements.[4]

According to these Statements, the draft EU-Canada Comprehensive Economic and Trade Agreement (CETA) includes an exception[5] to basic security interests and prudential measures.[6] Unlike the Canada's Model BIT[7], the CETA prudently provides that nothing in this Agreement shall prevent the parties 'from adopting or maintaining reasonable measures for prudential reasons', such as protecting investors and depositors, maintaining the safety, integrity or integrity of financial institutions, or in order to ensure "the integrity and stability of Party's financial system".[8] The same agreement also includes exceptions related to safeguards, where, in exceptional circumstances, capital flows may "cause or threaten serious difficulties in the operation of the economic and monetary union of the European Union",[9] with the exception of balance-of-payments problems in which "Canada or the member States of the European Union that are not members of the European Monetary Union experiences serious balance-of-payments or

---

① Catharine Titi, *The Reform of International Economic Governance*, "EU-Led Reform", Chapter 14, Part Ⅳ, First published 2016 by Routledge.

② European Commission (n 69) 3; European Commission (n 67) Introduction and text accompanying Question 5.

③ European Commission (n 69) 6. See also European Parliament resolution of 9 October 2013 on the EU-China negotiations for a bilateral investment agreement, 2013/2674 (RSP) para 41.

④ European Commission (n 69) 7.

⑤ Art X.05: National Security, Chapter on Exceptions, CETA, version of 26 September 2014.

⑥ Art 15.1: Prudential Carve-out, Financial Services Chapter, CETA, version of 26 September 2014. See also art 20: Investment Disputes in Financial Services and Annex XX of the same Financial Services Chapter.

⑦ Art 18(2) of Canada's Model BIT (version of 2012).

⑧ Art 15.1, Financial Services Chapter, CETA, version of 26 September 2014.

⑨ Art X.03: Temporary Safeguard Measures with regard to Capital Movements, Exceptions Chapter, CETA, version of 26 September 2014.

external financial difficulties".[①]

In seeking, among others, to achieve a "balance" between investment protection and the host economy, the European Commission stressed the importance of drafting treaty standards in a "detailed and precise manner".[②] In this regard, the new EU approach, in particular the two most important standards of investment law, namely fair and equitable treatment and expropriation.[③] Although the specific new reference to fair and equitable treatment has little direct or clear impact on the financial system,[④] and the drafting of expropriation criteria may introduce an important new element in this regard, at least for European agreements. Like US and the Canadian BITs before it, the CETA embraced the theory of police power and pointed out that "except in the rare circumstance where the impact of the measure or series of measures is so severe in light of its purpose that it appears manifestly excessive, non-discriminatory measures of a Party that are designed and applied to protect legitimate public welfare objectives, such as health, safety and the environment, do not constitute indirect expropriation". It is clear that the above-mentioned provisions appear to introduce an element of proportionality, although the draft agreement corresponds to the provisions of article 1 of Protocol One of the European Convention on Human Rights. The annex on Indirect Expropriation further makes it clear that, although the economic impact of measures is one of the factors taken into account when determining whether there has been an indirect expropriation "the sole fact that a measure or series of measures of a Party has an adverse effect on the economic value of an investment does not establish that an indirect expropriation has occurred". The Committee explained that it wanted to ensure that investors were not reduced by regulations promulgated by public policy objectives and that investors should therefore not be 'compensated'. Although measures taken during the financial crisis were not directly cited in the Annex on indirect expropriation, the view was expressed that such measures that adversely affected investors might fall within the scope of such a provision.

---

① Art X.04: Restrictions in Case of Balance of Payments and External Financial Difficulties, Exceptions Chapter, CETA, version of 26 September 2014.

② European Commission (n 69) 7.

③ See also Titi, "Investment Law and the European Union" (n 60).

④ See art X.9: Treatment of Investors and of Covered Investments of CETA's Investment Chapter, version of 26 September 2014.

Like US and Canadian BITs before it,[①] the CETA embraces the police powers doctrine and states that 'except in the rare circumstance where the impact of the measure or series of measures is so severe in light of its purpose that it appears manifestly excessive, non-discriminatory measures of a Party that are designed and applied to protect legitimate public welfare objectives, such as health, safety and the environment, do not constitute indirect expropriations'.[②] Significantly, an element of proportionality seems to have been introduced in the aforecited provision, although the draft agreement falls short of incorporating a provision equivalent to that of article 1 of Protocol One of the European Convention on Human Rights.[③] The Annex on Indirect Expropriation makes further explicit that, although the economic impact of a measure is one of the factors to be taken into account when determining whether there has been an indirect expropriation 'the sole fact that a measure or series of measures of a Party has an adverse effect on the economic value of an investment does not establish that an indirect expropriation has occurred'.[④] The Commission has explained that it wants to ensure that investors shall not be compensated "just because their profits have been reduced through the effects of regulations enacted for a public policy objective".[⑤] Although measures taken in times of financial crises are not directly cited in CETA's Annex on Indirect Expropriation, it is argued that such measures adversely affecting investors could fall under the scope of such a clause.

---

① See the US and Canadian Model BITs' respective annexes on Expropriation.

② Annex X.11: Expropriation, para 3, of CETA's Investment Chapter, version of 26 September 2014.

③ During a 'Right to regulate' roundtable organized by the Dutch Ministry of Economic Affairs, Agriculture and Innovation on 13 July 2012, the majority of participants favoured the incorporation of an ECHR-like provision on expropriation in future EU investment treaties. Such a provision also existed in Norway's Draft Model BIT of 2007.

④ Annex X.11: Expropriation, para 2, of CETA's Investment Chapter, version of 26 September 2014.

⑤ European Commission (n 69) 8; European Commission, 'Investment protection does not give multinationals unlimited rights to challenge any legislation', Brussels, 20 December 2013, trade.ec.europa.eu/doclib/press/index.cfm?id=1008.